THE RISE PROGRESS, AND PRESENT CONDITION of BANKING IN INDIA,

BY

CHAS. NORTHCOTE COOKE, ESQ.,

DEPUTY SECRETARY AND TREASURER,

BANK OF BENGAL,

AUTHOR OF A POPULAR TREATISE ON BOOK-KEEPING•

Amongst all Commercial Professions, that of Banker already holds thte first rank, and every *day increases* its importance -OPERATIONS DE BANQUE, *page* vi.

ISBN: 978-93-5128-451-2(HB)

First Published in 1863
Indian Reprint in 2017

Published by

Kalpaz Publications
C-30, Satyawati Nagar,
Delhi – 110052
E-mail: kalpaz@hotmail.com
Website: kalpazpublications.com
Ph.: +91-9212142040

PREFACE.

In submitting this work to the Banking and Commercial Community of India, I desire to claim for it no other merit than that of being the *first* of its kind in this Country. I could have wished to have made it more complete than it is, but the refusal, in some quarters, to give me the most trifling information, has foiled my best endeavors. Though too late to be remedied, I shall still be happy to receive any suggestions, as they may be useful in the event of the work ever reaching to a second edition. I am sensible of its manifold imperfections: but, with this acknowledgment, and, with the assurance that it has been put forth simply to supply a want, I trust to disarm severe criticism. Some useful hints have been afforded me about Ceylon, by a well-penned and unpretending little brochure by Mr. H. D. Andree, Accountant of the Chartered Mercantile Bank at Colombo, to whom I am under obligations for his courtesy in forwarding it to me. In writing the history of some of the Banks, I have availed myself freely of the information to be found in the *Banker's Magazine*, when my own notes have proved insufficient for the purpose. The articles about the Union Bank of Calcutta, the Benares Bank, the North-Western Bank, and the London and Eastern Banking Corporation have been carried, it may be supposed, to too great lengths; but I have been anxious to place on record, as fully as possible, the dangerous and unprincipled course of action which engulphed these several Institutions. I have to thank Mr. A. L. Agabeg for permitting me to insert his Tables of value of 4 per cent paper, and to acknowledge the ready attention my requests have met with from the Secretaries to the Banks of Bombay and Madras, Mr. W. S. Fitzwilliam, and Mr. R. Campbell of the Chartered Mercantile Bank, Mr. D. B. Clinker of the Commercial Bank, Mr. M. MacIver of the Central Bank of Western India, Mr. Pietsch of the Comptoir D'Escompte (who kindly sent me the necessary French documents from which I made my translations), Mr. Wilkinson of the People's Bank, and, though last, not least, my worthy senior, Mr. G. Dickson.

CHAS. NORTHCOTE COOKE.

CALCUTTA,
No. 2, *Royd Street*,
28*th May* 1863.

ERRATA.

Page 12, line 4, for "periods of *our* history" *read* "periods of history."

Page 296, lines 21 and 22, for "Royal and British Bank in Scotland" *read* "Royal British Bank."

THE

RISE, PROGRESS, AND PRESENT CONDITION

OF

BANKING IN INDIA.

The Origin of Banking.

In the most remote ages of the world, when Arcadian simplicity recognized no other wants than those of being clothed and fed, the standards of value,—in all countries which were essentially pastoral,—were cattle, the skins of animals, and the produce of the soil, things which acquired a certain exchangeable worth, and, ultimately, led the way to a more extensive interchange of commodities.

As population extended, and the wants of men increased, a division of employments began to manifest itself in the habits of the people, till, their ingenuity being taxed to the utmost, some of them found that, by devoting their energies to the prosecution of some particular trade, they might not only fabricate enough to exchange for other commodities, of which they stood in need, but would have more than abundant to minister to their own consumption. The surplus then began to accumulate, and hence the commencement of barter and a more expeditious method of interchange. This system of barter, and the want of a medium wherewith to circulate the commodities to be distributed, rose step by step, until it led to the introduction of money as the measure and standard of value of things, and, finally, terminated in the establishment of Banks.

It cannot be stated, with certainty, when coin was introduced; for there appears to be no authentic record to which we can turn for satisfactory information, unless we except the pages of Holy Writ, and some of the leading works on Grecian and Roman History, where references are made, occasionally, to the exchanging of money, to the places selected as depositories of the precious metals, and to the use to be made thereof, under certain conditions and restrictions. In the earliest periods, when coined money was not in existence, and when a more expeditious and less expensive mode of interchange had not been introduced, the precious metals passed by weight. Gilbart, in his *History and Principles of Banking*, remarks:—"It is probable that the merchants would require that the precious metals they received should be of a certain degree of fineness. We read of Abraham weighing unto Ephron 400 shekels of silver, *current money with the merchant*, a phrase which implies that the money current with the merchant was different from that in ordinary use."*

Prior to the Captivity, or about 600 years anterior to the advent of the Messiah, the Jews, who were more of an

* Gilbart's "History and Principles of Banking," p. 2.

agricultural than a commercial people, do not appear to have had any coined or stamped money among them. Ezra, in recording the return from captivity, and the free offerings of the people towards setting up the house of the Lord, makes mention of certain drams of gold and pounds of silver, which, there is reason to believe, were delivered by weight. But the first intimation we have of coined money amongst the Jews, is when Antiochus Sidetes, king of Syria, granted to Simon Maccabæus the privilege of coining money, about 140 years before our Saviour's advent. Up to that time, the ancient Hebrews transacted their business by weight of metal, and not by stamped coin. Metals, after the division of labor began to take place, were exchanged for other commodities, which the owner of the metals required but had not, and, as they are less perishable than any thing else, and can be divided in the most minute portions, a preference was early given to them as a medium of barter. The baser metals participated with the purer ones in being the instrument of commerce.

"Different metals have been made use of by different nations for this purpose. Iron was the common instrument of commerce among the ancient Spartans, copper among the ancient Romans, and gold and silver among all rich and commercial nations. Those metals seem originally to have been made use of for this purpose in rude bars, without any stamp or coinage. Thus we are told by Pliny, *(Plin. Hist. lib.* 33, *cap.* 3*)*, upon the authority of Timæus, an ancient historian, that till the time of Servius Tullius, the Romans had no coined money, but made use of unstamped bars of copper, to purchase whatever they had occasion for. These rude bars, therefore, performed at that time the function of money."*

Where there was no fixed standard, frauds and impositions would, undoubtedly, creep into the exchanges, and, as the constant weighing of metal would entail considerable trouble, means were taken to establish a coinage of uniform and proper value. In Rome, coined money was first introduced 580 years B. C. Whether its introduction was contemporaneous in Greece, does not appear. It could not, however, have been long subsequent, for, in the description of the fine imposed upon Miltiades by his ungrateful countrymen, 490 years B. C., some describe it as *fifty talents* (about £10,000 sterling), others as *fifty thousand crowns,* which would convey the idea that there was, at that period, a regular coinage.

As money became more plentiful, and the early custom of bartering commodities no longer prevailed, people began to look about for some safe place where they might deposit their wealth, and thus secure it against the strong hand of unlimited power, and the depredations of lawless men. Mitford, in his *History of Greece,* speaking of the temples of Greece, asserts that they frequently answered the purposes of depositories for the precious metals, the general reverence and respect of the people for these places of worship imparting a greater security than could be found to exist elsewhere. The priesthood turned the charge to good account, and lent out, at a high rate of interest, the gold and silver deposited with them. In the Abbé Barthélemy's *Travels of Anacharsis in Greece,* mention is made of the manner in which the Greeks employ their money :—" The greater part of the Athenians employ their money in trade. They receive

* Adam Smith's "Wealth of Nations," lib. i. cap. iv.

an interest for the use of it. The lender has his security, either on the merchandise or goods of the borrower, and the interest thus lent may rise as high as 30 per cent. Commerce increases the circulation of wealth, and this circumstance has given birth to the occupation of Bankers, which facilitates it still more."*

It will be seen, from the above extract, that at Athens the interest of money was excessive, a circumstanee which, although generally the consequence of the insecurity of property, is not always so; for not longer ago than twenty-five years, interest at the rate of 24 and 30 per cent was openly taken in Calcutta by natives, and by not a few Europeans.

There seems some doubt as to the description of coin used in the early ages. It was probably unstamped, and similar to that in use, till a very late period, in the Upper Provinces of British India. These were small thick lumps of copper and brass, of about the diameter of a shilling, perfectly free from any marks or stamps, and cut round, square, and octagonal. In China also, and Cochin China, at the present day, small pieces of copper, of the size of a shilling, and as thin as a French centime, and silver coins, of all sizes, with a hole in the middle, are used as a part of the circulation of the country, and we know that some of the earliest coinage of the Jews consisted of rings, or circular pieces of the precious metals, with the whole of the inner part cut out. In the history of Joseph, and, in several other parts of the Old Testament, where the word *money* is used, we are to understand it to mean the *shekel*, which was a denomination of money and of weight of about 9 grs. 57 troy, and of the value of 2*s.* 3*d.* In the prophecy of *Zechariah*, who exercised

* Abbé Barthélemy's "Travels of Anacharsis in Greece."

the prophetical office about 510 years B. C., we read:—"They *weighed* for my price thirty pieces of silver," by which are, no doubt, meant shekels of the value of half-a-crown, or three shillings.

In the impressions handed down to us of a medal struck by the Emperor Titus, after the destruction of Jerusalem, we have conclusive evidence of the progress which had been made in the art of stamping coins, and can readily understand that the occupation of the money-changers, whom our Saviour twice drove from the station they had taken in the courts of the temple, was, at a certain rate of profit, to give less pieces of money for greater, or greater for less, to accommodate such as came to the solemn feasts, or other worship at Jerusalem. People who have resided many years in India, and have had frequent opportunities of noticing the remarkable correspondence between many of the customs of the Jews and of the natives of this country, can probably better realize the idea than those who have never left Europe. We have the *Shroffs* and *Podars* exercising a separate vocation. The inferiors of the class generally sit in booths in the large thoroughfares, or most frequented places, where they exchange silver for copper, or copper for silver, at a small profit. The superiors almost exclusively confine themselves to the purchase and sale of foreign coins, the value of which fluctuates with the supply, and, not unfrequently, yields them a handsome profit. Comparing Oriental customs, it is quite probable that the business of money-changing was carried on by the Jews as a separate trade, and that they must have employed the funds deposited with them, in order to have earned the interest which they allowed to the depositors. St. Matthew, in his version of the parable of the unprofitable servant,* makes use of the same Greek word as St. Luke,† though the translators have rendered the one "Exchangers" and the other "Bank." In the former, the Septuagint has it Τοις Τραπεζέταις, which Schleusner renders α Τρᾶπεζα, *Mensa, Abacus ad quem Mensarius sedens nummus numerat et computat;* in the latter, we have it Την Τρᾶπεζαν, which is precisely the same word, *viz.* "the table." It would appear, however, that the *usury,* spoken of in the passages, was not a gain made by oppressing the poor, and taking advantage of their necessities, but a fair and adequate profit on money lent for commercial purposes. The names given to the Bankers in the early ages were derived from the metals, coins, and tables in use.

"At Rome, the Bankers were called *Argentarii, Mensarii, Numularii,* or *Colybistæ.* The Banking-houses or Banks were called *Tabernæ, Argentariæ,* or *Mensæ Numulariæ.* The mode of transacting business was somewhat similar to that which is in use in modern times. The Bankers, too, were money-changers. They also lent money on interest, and allowed a lower rate of interest on money deposited in their hands."‡

The science of Banking, as it at present exists, has descended to us from Italy, from whence we derive our knowledge of Book-keeping by double entry. In the Florentine Republic, it was customary for the Bankers and Merchants to conduct their money transactions, and write their Bills of Exchange upon benches in the market-place, and other public thoroughfares,§ and, when a Merchant or

* Matthew xxv. 27. † Luke xix. 23.

‡ Gilbart's "History and Principles of Banking," p. 6.

§ The same practice we have shown to be observed by the Shroffs and Podars in this country, with exception to the benches, the seats of the natives being more primitive.

Banker lost his credit, and was unable to pay his debts, his bench was broken. To this circumstance may be traced the term *Bankrupt* in use in our language, which is derived from two Italian words, *Banco, rotto,** broken bench. From the first of these two Italian words, the terms *Bank* and *Banker* are derived.

Various causes led to the establishment of public Banks, or Banks of a corporate character. Some were founded for the purpose of facilitating Commerce, others to serve the Government. The most ancient Bank was that of Venice. It is supposed to have been established in 1157, to have arisen from the necessities of the State, and to have served almost as a model to every similar Bank in subsequent ages. In the year 1401, a public Bank was established at Barcelona, in Spain. The Bank of Genoa was established in 1407. It was called the Chamber of St. George. The Bank of Amsterdam was founded in the year 1609. This Bank was the model on which were formed most of the European Banks now in existence.† It owed its origin to the great quantity of cleft and foreign coin introduced from all parts of Europe, which reduced the value of the currency about 9 per cent below that of good money, fresh from the mint. In order to remedy the inconveniences resulting from the melting down and carrying away the money, the Bank was established under the guarantee of the City. It received every description of coin, at its real intrinsic value, merely deducting the expenses of coinage and management, and then allowed the remainder to the depositor. The Bank of Hamburgh was founded in 1619, upon the plan of that of Amsterdam.

---

* *Rotto* is evidently a corruption of the Latin verb *Rumpo*, to break.

† Gilbart's "History and Principles of Banking," pp. 8—10.

Private Banking, which was exclusively in the hands of the Jews at the time of the conquest, passed, after a succession of years, into the hands of the Lombards, or Italian merchants, about the thirteenth century, and from them to the goldsmiths, who, being probably the most wealthy subjects of the realm, became the depositaries of the nobility and landed gentry.

The unscrupulous measures which Charles I. resorted to, in order to supply himself with money in his necessities, and the general insecurity of property shortly before the breaking out of the republican spirit in England, led to a more general employment of these people as the depositaries of money, their reputed wealth being supposed to place them above corruption, and to afford them the means of greater security. It was natural enough, therefore, that the goldsmiths should become the Bankers of those who had money for which they had no immediate use.* The necessities of the King and Government, during the times of Charles I., the Commonwealth, and Charles II., no doubt made the trade in money a very profitable one to the private Bankers, who lent out, at a high rate of interest, the money they received, on personal credit, to those who were needy, by which, after paying the depositors a very handsome interest, they were enabled to realize a considerable profit. There seems to have been a general resort to them, for we find a complaint, at the time, that "the trade of Bankers being only in London, doth very much drain the ready money from all other parts of the kingdom."

"The antiquity of some of the private Banks in London will surprise a person unacquainted with their

* Gilbart's "History and Principles of Banking," p. 22.

history. *Child and Co.*, of Temple Bar,* have existed as Bankers since 1663; *Stone, Martins, and Stone*, continue a business commenced by Sir Thomas Gresham, the founder of the Royal Exchange; and *Hoares and Co.*, of Fleet Street, can trace their origin a dozen years prior to the commencement of the Bank of England in 1694,† which was about the period when *Snow and Co.*, of the Strand, were first established."‡ "The business of Banking remained entirely in the hands of the new-fashioned Bankers until the establishment of the Bank of England in the year 1694."§ In 1695 the Bank of Scotland, a joint-stock Bank, was established in Scotland, and incorporated by Royal Charter, and the under-mentioned Banks in succeeding years. The first Bank established in America was at South Carolina, in 1702, about seventy-three years prior to the war of independence, and about ten years after the first issue of paper money by the Government; the *Royal* Bank of Scotland (incorporated) in 1727; the British Linen Company (incorporated) in 1746; Sir William Forbes, Hunter, and Co. in 1763; the Perth Banking Company in 1766; the Aberdeen Bank in 1767; and several private and joint-stock Banks, ten or fifteen years afterwards.

The Bank of Ireland was established in 1783. It would occupy too much space, and too greatly extend the limits of this work, to insert a list of all the different Banks that sprung into existence subsequent to the establishment of the Bank of England; suffice it to say,

* It is not certain, but extremely probable, that the founder of this house was Sir Josiah Child, who published a work, about the time, entitled "A New Discourse on Trade."

† "Banker's Mag.," Oct. 1845, p. 39. ‡ "Banker's Clerk," p. 9.

§ "History and Principles of Banking," p. 25.

the trade in Banking was gradually enlarged by the formation of private partnerships in different parts of the country. As will be seen from the previous statement, the number of private Banks in existence anterior to the American war was but small, but, on the termination thereof, they rapidly increased, particularly after passing of the Act, on the 3rd May 1797, of the 37 Geo. III. C. 43, better known as *The Bank Restriction Act,* which arose out of an order of Council in February 1797, directing the Bank of England to suspend cash payments, it having been apprehended, that, in consequence of ill-founded exaggerated alarms, there might be a want of a sufficient supply of cash to answer the exigencies of the public service.

Its Antiquity in India.

THE knowledge of Banking in India was long anterior to the settlement of the English in this part of the globe, though the system under which it was carried on was widely different from that which European skill and science have introduced.

From time immemorial, the Banker has always been an important member of Indian society. Formerly, in all divisions and sub-divisions of that society, he had his type and representative, discharging functions of indispensable necessity to the well-being of the community. The Empire had its Banker, the Soubah had its Banker, the Zillah had its Banker, and the Village had its Banker. Each in his sphere exercised an engrossing influence; each, in addition to his financial, was charged with a large proportion of social and political responsibilities. The traditions of the Hindoo, and the records of the Mahomedan periods of our history, endow the higher classes of Bankers with the character and powers of Ministers of State. No royal or imperial Council was complete in its members without the Banker. The principal source of the revenue was the land tax, which, according to practice, was paid in kind. The royal or imperial exchequer could not well accommodate the rather bulky forms in which the revenue was collected from the people, and the magnitude of the royal or imperial transactions, as well as the peculiar character of some of them, necessitated the employment of metallic and paper currencies. Standing armies had early become a part of Indian institutions, and mercenaries seldom stipulate for remuneration with necessaries, or with luxuries, in kind. A pervading and a properly organized agency was therefore constantly necessary to convert the proceeds of the taxes into a useful form, and to make the public resources readily available to the demands of the State. Hence the institutional character and political influence of Indian Banking. The general state of society also precluded the independent accumulation of capital in many hands, and the ruler and the provincial governors were often personally the least trustworthy men in the country. None therefore but the possessors of political influence ventured to deal with them. Last of all, *caste* came to the aid of these causes, and consolidated the system into an institution. The son of the Banker could only be a Banker, and he whose father transacted the emperor's or the soubadar's monetary business had, according to the first Indian notion of rights, an indefeasible title to succeed to that business. The action of British laws, and forms of civil government, have, in some measure, destroyed the universality of the institution and the nature of its form, but it nevertheless retains its vitality, though under much alteration. The Banking Corporations and Government Agencies at the Presidencies, that have succeeded the hereditary establishments of the *Dosses* and *Setts* of imperial times, are devoid of the political influence which the latter exercised. The functions of the Zillah Banker have been divided between, and appropriated by, the revenue collector and the independent capitalist. The Village Banker, like most other of our village dignitaries, still maintains his character and position, and may be promptly recognized in the Village Mahajun. The diffusion of capital, and the conversion of taxes in kind into money-taxes, have closed up some and opened other channels of Banking business, and at present, though an extensive system of Banking is carried on, it bears a less peculiar character than before, and is largely mixed up with the funding and general commercial business of the country.

The occupation is not gone. It has only shaken off the trammels with which tradition and conventional forms formerly bound it. The Bankers of the present day may be divided into three classes: the City Shroffs, the Zillah Bankers, and the Village Mahajuns. The first are chiefly engaged in exchange operations, in dealing with the public stock, and making advances on securities to commercial establishments. They possess extensive credit throughout the country, and comprise some of the most honored names in Indian society. The second are the depositaries of the monied wealth of the landed families or their creditors, and have a close connection with the internal trade of the country, in which they are often found engaged directly on their own account. The character and functions of the third are well known. In the North-Western Provinces, the Village Mahajuns are, owing to the impoverished condition of the agricultural classes, and to the severity of the operation of the revenue laws upon them, a thriving, in fact the only thriving class. In Bengal, every man, with a little spare cash, is a Village Mahajun. Of these several classes, the one, which is most directly useful to the community, is the class of Zillah Bankers. Their close connection with the landed interest, and the assistance they afford towards the exportation of the superfluous produce of the interior districts of the country, give a peculiar value to their services. They form efficient props to the fortunes of the landed families which connect themselves with them, and have frequently rendered important aid to the Government. Of this Lalla Joteepersaud is an instance. During the mutiny in 1857-58 he came forward most liberally and nobly to assist the authorities. The urgency of the periodical calls for the public revenue from landed proprietors, and the serious consequences of default in the payment of the assessment, render the assistance of the Bankers of the last importance. Their agents also are to be found in most produce marts, making advances to dealers, and their operations extend in some cases, we believe, to the bonding of produce. By all these means, they afford much assistance to the agricultural interests of the country. The vast improvement that has taken place in Scottish agriculture, owing to the peculiar system of Banking prevailing north of the Tweed, makes us almost wish that a class of large farmers may replace the yeomanry of this country, and that a similar correspondence may grow up between them and the Zillah Bankers.

The character and extent of Indian Banking have been frequently cited in refutation of the unjust calumnies with which the opponents of Indian political reform have aspersed this nation. There can be no surer proof of the soundness of a people's moral condition, and of their habitual regard to truth in the transactions of life, than the prevalence of so much credit as is necessary to the existence of such a system of Banking. The native Bankers themselves are patterns of commercial morality. The dishonoring of a *hoondee* is an event of rare occurrence with them. They transact business with each other, and with their constituents, with a total disregard of those forms which English commercial men deem essentially requisite, and, without the aid of which, indeed, an English house of business would scarcely be secure. One peculiar feature of native Banks has always struck us as peculiarly gratifying. The business is usually carried on by gomashtas, or clerks holding a confidential position in the firm. They are often poor men, and yet are never called upon to furnish security. Their remuneration is not high, and they have often the entire disposal of the capital of a *Cootee;* yet it rarely happens that a firm loses any thing by their dishonesty.*

The fact that Europeans are not the originators of Banking in this country, need not strike us with surprise, for, both from internal evidence, which the successes of the British arms in the Punjab further extended and opened out, we know that civilization and the arts

* The case of the Gomashta of Pemabhoy Hemchund is exceptional, and affords no ground for condemning the whole tribe.

distinguished the *East* for a very considerable period before the *West* had begun to emerge from ignorance and barbarism. "When the Dorian conquerors drove a large portion of the Greeks into exile, the fugitives acquired new settlements in *Asia* (Minor), and established their own national Bank."* Of all the nations of antiquity, none were more persevering in the work of colonization than the Greeks. At a very early date they traded with, and colonized, the shores of the Black Sea, and from thence carried their commodities, probably by way of Persia and the Caspian Sea, far into Asia. The progress also of Alexander the Great, through the Punjab, may have contributed to extend the knowledge which the Greeks possessed, and it is not improbable that, long before England had ranked in the scale of nations, India had adopted a system of Banking which may have originated that now in use with the *Shroffs* or native Bankers. In looking at Asia in this light, we are justified in assuming something from her former position. Asia surpasses all other divisions of the Globe in the antiquity of its population. Here were transacted events of the utmost importance. Here the human race first made their appearance: it was the theatre of their earliest achievements: the grand centre from which population, science, and all the arts of civilized life, have gradually diffused themselves over the other regions of the world. Another means by which Banking might have been introduced into India was through the Jews, many of whom settled in Asia, on the dispersion of the tribes, after the destruction of Jerusalem, A. D. 70. This proscribed people, who are celebrated for their acuteness in monetary dealings, may have

* Mitford's "Greece," vol. i., p. 193.

contributed, in some measure, to the dissemination of Banking as observed by the aborigines of this country. Whoever is conversant with Scripture history, and has given his attention to the customs of this country, cannot fail to notice a very close resemblance between the practices of the Jews and the natives of India. But although the *Shroffs* have, for ages past, been considered the Bankers of the country, there has not always been a general recourse to them; for, whether under apprehension of the exactions of the zemindars, or from some other cause, which we may advert to elsewhere, a very large class of people resorted to the practice, common throughout all Asia, of hoarding up their money, or melting down the gold and silver into ornaments for themselves, their wives and children, and thereby allowing it to lie unproductive. Great astonishment has been expressed, both in England and India, at the constant and continued drain of silver from Europe, without any satisfactory explanation or elucidation of its disappearance; but this wholesale hoarding will afford some clue to the withdrawal from circulation of such vast sums. Still, the profits of the *Shroffs*, or Indian Bankers, were considerable, and some thirty years back they constituted by far the richest class of the people of Bengal and Hindoostan, and the countries appertaining to the Presidencies of Madras and Bombay. The most wealthy are to be found settled in Calcutta, Dacca, Patna, Benares, Mirzapore, and Bombay, but the class are to be found located over India, wherever business exists. Before the establishment of the Bank of Bengal, the European system of Banking had been introduced by the great Agency Houses of Calcutta, the failure of which, for enormous sums, is well known to the Indian public. They were not merely merchants and agents, but they united with that business Banking in all its branches, and were known as the merchant princes of India. They were agents for the whole civil and military service. They were agents for the planters and merchants settled in the Upper Provinces. They were Bankers receiving deposits, Bankers making advances for the produce of the interior, and Bankers issuing paper money. As will be shown under the head of the local Banking Institutions, the defunct Agency and Banking firms had a note circulation which was extremely beneficial to them in carrying on their diversified operations as ship-owners, house-owners, farmers, manufacturers, and money-lenders. After the establishment of the Bank of Bengal, but more especially, after the passing of the Act in 1813, which partially removed the restrictions placed upon Europeans settling in India, great inducement was given to extend the Banking principle, and there successively started into existence several private Banks in connection with Agency Houses. A great commercial crisis occurred in 1829-30, and upon the *débris* of the Calcutta Agency Houses* successively arose the Union Bank of Calcutta, and all the different joint-stock associations now known under the name of *Mofussil Banks.* The abrogation of the East India Company's trade and monopoly, in 1832, gave these last a greater impetus, which the failure of the Agency Houses and the peculiar position of the two services helped to maintain, and, until lately, they were to be found distributed over a large tract of country, and resting on an extensive

* Alexander and Co., Colvin and Co., Fergusson and Co., Mackintosh and Co., Palmer and Co., and Cruttenden and Co.

proprietary interest. But things have now altered. The transfer of the Company's Government to the Crown having led to the introduction of a Government currency, and extended powers to the Bank of Bengal, which is planting its agencies over the country, it is not too much to expect, that there will be, sooner or later, a complete absorption of all the Up-country Banks.

The Monetary System of India.

MONEY being, as Adam Smith well defines it, the great wheel of circulation, the great and universal instrument of commerce, it will not be out of place here to review the system which obtains in India; and, as the object of this work is to furnish data which may be depended on, and serve as a guide, no scruple will be felt in introducing such information as may be collected from unquestionable sources. It is by the intervention of money that goods of all kinds are bought and sold, and, in the progress of industry, commercial nations have found it convenient to coin several different metals into money—gold for large payments, silver for purchases of moderate value, and copper, or some other coarse metal, for those of smaller consideration.

The standard currency of Continental India, observes a very perspicuous writer, consists of silver in coins, generally of the value of about two shillings, on which are invariably impressed, in Persian characters, and in the Persian language, the name of the reigning Mogul, the year of his reign in which they were struck, and the name of the place where they were coined. This is the well-known rupee—a word of Hindoo origin, meaning silver. There are copper coins (counters of course) representing one sixty-fourth part of the rupee, or the quarter of the sixteen parts into which the rupee of account is divided. In native transactions the smallest change is represented by shells, called cowries, of which eighty go to the smallest copper coin, and, consequently, no less than 5,120 to the rupee. The use of so minute a denomination of money is an index of the poverty of the people, and of the low price of wages and necessaries of life among them. In England, a farthing, equal in value to more than fifty cowries, is hardly of any use as money. The shells thus used are a species of cyprea, imported in cargoes, as an article of trade, from the Maldive and Laccadive islands, and are the same as are used in some parts of Africa for the same purpose.

Silver coins, and most probably silver money, were first introduced by the Mahomedan conquerors. Gold, as far as they had coins at all, was the money of the Hindoos; and, in the southern parts of India, rude coins of this metal, from the value of a six-pence up to seven-shillings, known to Europeans by the name of pagodas and gold fanams, are still in circulation.

Since the fall of the Mogul Empire, and very probably also before it, every petty Prince coined his own money, and fixed his own standard. Dr. Kelly has given a list of above eighty different kinds of rupee, varying in the quantity of pure silver they contain, and varying also in sterling value, from 1*s.* 2*d.* up to 2*s.* 2*d.*, but, on an average, their worth is somewhat under 2*s.* Until the year 1836, the British Government had no less than five mints,—three in the Bengal, and one in each of the other

Presidencies, at each of which rupees of different values were coined,—to perplex their subjects and puzzle themselves. The whole of the rupees, now coined in the British territory, are reduced to one value, nearly two shillings sterling each—a very great improvement.

Paper-money, whether in bills or notes, forms a very small proportion of the Indian circulation. Bills of exchange have been known to the Hindoos from very remote periods. They are known to Europeans, under the name of hoondee, a corruption of the Indian word Hindwi, or Hindoo—a word which is Persian, and, therefore, evidently given to them by the Mahomedan conquerors. In every large town of India are to be found native Bankers, or Shroffs, who deal in bills of exchange, and who have correspondents, not only in all the great towns of Hindoostan itself, whether British, tributary, or independent, but even in Cashmere, and some parts of Persia. The hoondee, or bill, it may be observed, is drawn out in a written character, peculiar to the class of bankers, and illegible to any one else. Very generally the Indian Bankers distrust the conveyance by the European letter post, and have *estaffettes*, or special couriers, of their own, which seldom fail in conveying information long in advance of the Government mails.

The business of Banking, among the Indians, is chiefly confined to the issuing and discounting of bills of exchange, money-lending, and money-changing, or the exchanging of one description of coins for another. The receiving of deposits can hardly be said to be part of their business; and the issuing of notes, payable to bearer, or paper-money, has always been unknown to the Indians; and, until lately, these two forms of Banking existed, even under our own Government, but to a very limited extent,—hardly affecting the general conclusion, that the whole money of India was in silver coin; and that, with a single exception, *viz.* that of the treasury of the British Government and the Bank of Bengal, there was no place of absolute safe deposit for money. India, in fact, may be said to have been exactly in the same state that Great Britain would be in, if the whole circulation of the latter were in half-crown pieces, and that there were no place of deposit for money but the public stocks, and the coffers of individual merchants and speculators, exercising, on their own responsibility, in this respect, the functions of Bankers.

Among the Mahomedans, as is well known, all interest is deemed to be usury, and therefore illegal—a law, however, which, if not more honored by them in the breach than the observance, is more frequently broken than observed. With the Hindoos, on the contrary, the profit on money lent, or interest, is not only legal, but the amount which can be exacted may, in general terms, be described as unlimited. British subjects were formerly limited, by law, to an interest of 12 per cent; but the total repeal of the usury laws, by recognizing the right of the free trader to make the most of his money, has removed, not a bit too soon, from the British Code, an absurdity worthy of the dark ages, and not to be justified by the circumstances under which Moses prohibited the lending of money on usury. The rate of interest in India, between native and native, is variable, but always enormous; a great part of the amount, however, consisting, not in the profit of the capital lent, but in the risk of lending to a needy borrower, in a country where the administration of justice is not quite so perfect as it is in England. But we trust that charge will soon no longer be made. The establishment of a High Court, with extensive appellate powers; an increase to the number of judges, chosen from among the able legal men of England; the association with them of some of the finest specimens of the old Company's civil servants,—will, we earnestly hope, wipe out a stigma on the administration of justice in India, which, we lament to say, was too well merited.

Of the class of small Bankers, the best account we have seen is that in Hamilton's *Hindostan*, and which we believe is taken from the manuscript statistical account of Bengal, by the late Dr. Francis Buchanan Hamilton. "Podars, or money-changers," says Mr. Hamilton, "are a very numerous class, but many of them having no shop, sit in the open market, with heaps of cowries placed before them. In the more rural quarters, the money-changer goes to market with a bag of cowries on his head; or, if a rich man, with a loaded ox, which, if strong, may carry to the value of an hundred and fifty rupees. All the early part of the market he sells cowries for silver to the people who wish to purchase goods, and, in the evening, the various hucksters bring back their cowries, and change them for silver. In the morning, the money-changer usually gives 5,760 cowries for a rupee, and, in the evening, he gives a rupee for 5,920 cowries, which is a profit of one thirty-sixth part on every good mint rupee, besides a fluctuating barter, or exchange, on all others. It is also customary with the money-changers to advance cowries to all servants who have monthly wages; and, at the end of the month, when the wages become due, they return the loan in silver, for all this class, if trusted, anticipate their income. To these improvident persons the money-changer gives only seventy puns of cowries for his rupee, so that he realizes four seventy-fourths per month for the use of the money; but occasionally loses his principal."*

The discount charged may here be taken at about 3 per cent on each operation. If the market be held, therefore, once a week, this gross profit on the capital is repeated fifty-two times every year; and if it be a twice a week market, as is more probable, one hundred and four times. What Sir James Stewart said of government payments, in his time, is still applicable, it would appear, to the ordinary disbursements of the great bulk of the people. "The money paid by the laborers of the ground," observes he, "is, at present, interrupted in its course at every change of hands, until, by the repeated *shroffage* (discount), it comes at last reduced, as I may say, to a shadow into the Company's treasury."†

The passage above quoted from Dr. Hamilton gives a very correct account of the system which is followed by the money-lenders in this country, and which we may ourselves notice among our own servants, if we pay any attention thereto. The aptitude of the natives of this country for accounts is a very noticeable feature in their character, and, probably, in the correct and expeditious calculation of interest, there are no people that can compete with them. Usury prevails here to a greater extent almost than in any other country. The great fortunes which used to be so suddenly and so easily acquired in Bengal, and the other British settlements in the East Indies, may satisfy us, that, as the wages of labor were very low, so the profits of stock were very high in these

---

* Hamilton's "Hindostan," vol. i., p. 40.

† "Sketch of the Commercial Resources and Monetary and Mercantile System of British India," pp. 44—48.

ruined countries. The interest of money is proportionably so. In Bengal, money is frequently lent to the farmers (ryots) at 40, 50, and 60 per cent, and the succeeding crop is mortgaged for the payment. As the profits which can afford such an interest must eat up almost the whole rent of the landlord, so such enormous usury must, in its turn, eat up the greater part of those profits.*

. We shall give examples from different parts of India of the rates of interest usually exacted by the Indian money-lenders—the great mass of the borrowers being, of course, the occupants of the soil, because they constitute the great majority of the people. The late Sir Thomas Munro, who had better opportunities of judging, and a mind and acquirements better fitting him to judge of such matters, than perhaps any other European sojourner in India, gives the following official description of transactions of this nature, in a country subject to his own authority, more extensive than the kingdom of Scotland, and containing two millions of people. "Almost every ryot," says he, "has an account with a bazar-man (money-lender) and a balance against him. This account often runs through two or three generations, and is rarely paid off entirely. It usually originates in a small advance by the bazar-man, who probably gives seventy or eighty rupees, and takes a bond for an hundred, with interest at two and a half per centum monthly. The ryot, in return, makes payment in grain, cotton, or other articles, which are usually valued against him, and he receives, occasionally, from a bazar-man, small sums for the discharge of his *kists* (instalments of tax). After going on in this way, for a number of years, the ryot finds, that though he is continually paying, he is only

* Adam Smith's "Wealth of Nations," lib. i., cap. ix.

getting deeper into debt."* The medium interest here exacted is not 30 but 40 per cent; while the Banker in receiving payment of it turns merchant, and in that character exacts a further interest. Both the borrower and the State are plundered by this most miserable system.

The great mass of the people of Bengal, says Mr. Tytler,—the peasants and tradesmen, (who are also cultivators of the land, and whose gains can only increase with the wealth of the peasantry),—are unable to purchase European articles of commerce. They live from day to day, and nine-tenths of them are forced to borrow their daily food, and corn to sow their lands, from the mahajuns (Banker merchants). On the grain supplied for their family consumption, the mahajuns charge the peasant 50 per cent, on that furnished for seed 100 per cent. Besides this, by false accounts, and by taking an inhuman advantage of the situation of the ryots, they often keep them in balance.† The rate of interest in India is very

* "Report of Sir Thomas Munro": 1807.—"Selection of Papers from Records of the India House," vol. i., p. 237.

† "Considerations on the Present Political State of India:" London, 1815. The vituperation of the Indian Bankers, by Mr. Tytler and others, is not justifiable. The Indian Bankers are just what the nature of their position makes them, and neither better nor worse than what any other class of men would be under similar circumstances. The celebrated political economist, Sir James Stewart, in the project of an Indian Bank, which he published sixty-five years ago, gives a juster verdict:—"In this view," says he, "the Bank will be a check upon every one who may have it in his power to oppress the laborer, or the manufacturer; because the profits of the Bank will depend much upon the credit of the inhabitants, and upon the preservation of their property...... What a new phenomenon in Bengal, a *Shroff* Director of a Bank, from a blood-sucker is become the protector of the laboring man! Interest does all. He sucks the blood because it is his interest so to do: he gives his protection from the same motive. By directing the interest of individuals to a proper object, good government is established."—"The Principles of Money, applied to the present state of the Coin of Bengal," &c &c. 1772, p. 81.—"Sketch of the Commercial Resources," &c., p. 48.

high between native and native. Except in special cases, it is much more excessive than among the European community. Twenty and thirty per cent are very ordinary rates; and we could mention cases where 5 and 6 per cent per month, or 60 and 74 per cent per annum, has been, and is still exacted. There is, doubtless, very gross usury in many of these transactions; but, on the other hand, the cases are not numerous where the lender, when he has once parted with his principal, sees any clear way to its easy and punctual recovery. That the necessities of the people are taken advantage of by the lenders, is a fact made apparent to every one, but it is questionable whether any legislative enactments would tend to remedy the evil, or to lessen it. Time was when an opinion prevailed that usury was a system of iniquity, repugnant to the feelings, and little better than extortion. We have got the better of such antiquated notions. It has been found from experience, that free trade in money prevents more evils than it causes, because a high rate of interest—which is nothing more than insurance to cover the risk—added to legitimate earnings, prevents dishonest speculations, and thus contributes to the general good. Those who are compelled to borrow are generally improvident, and, as the lender runs a great risk in lending his money, it seems but fair that he should exact a rate calculated to cover his risk.

There is as much a trade in money as in other commodities, and Governments have no more right to limit the rate at which a person should lend his money than they have to limit the rate at which a merchant shall dispose of his goods. When the usury laws were removed, in 1854, from the Statute Book, our legislators merely acted up to the spirit of the age, which was opposed to the absurdity, condemned their retention as an unmitigated nuisance, and staked its opinion that the rate of interest should be free and unfettered. Many people must borrow, and none will lend without such a consideration for the use of their money as is suitable. The high rate of interest among all Mahomedan nations is accounted for by M. Montesquieu, not from their poverty, but partly from this, and partly from the difficulty of recovering the money. The interest which the borrower can afford to pay is in proportion to the clear profit only, and must be something more than sufficient to compensate the occasional losses to which lending, even with tolerable prudence, is exposed. Were it not, mere charity or friendship could be the only motives for lending.

We have, elsewhere, quoted from the author of the *Sketch of the Commercial Resources of British India* some very valuable remarks on the Indian currency. It must be borne in mind, however, that, since the time he wrote (1835-36) very many and important changes have taken place, both in the banking and monetary system of India. In asserting that the standard currency consists of silver coins, we agree with him, for, although there always has been, and still are, gold coins in circulation, their amount is so insignificant as not to interfere in the least with the silver currency, *i. e.* the rupee, which, for all purposes, is the integer of account. Previous to September 1835, there was a considerable variety of rupees current in India: for example, the Sicca, the Sonaut, the Furruckabad, &c. These classes of coins, in consequence of variations in weight and "touch," (*i. e.* fineness,) were of different values; and, to ascertain the true worth of a mixed parcel of rupees, was a most complex question. The *current rupee* was an imaginary coin, founded upon an arbitration of the different values of the actual currencies. In 1835 a systematic effort was made, by the East India Company, to place the monetary legislation of the country upon a sounder footing. They issued a new silver coin, called a *Company's* rupee, which was declared to be the only standard coin throughout the British possessions. The new coin contains 180 troy grains of silver, of 91·66 fine, or equal to 165 grains of pure silver, and its intrinsic sterling value is 1*s.* 10¼*d.* The old *Sicca* rupee, which was of a higher value, is occasionally used as the measure of payments, in the same way as the superseded *guinea* is sometimes employed in England; but the *Company's* rupee is at present the general integer of account, and measure of price, and will continue so until it yield to a long proposed *decimal* coinage, or the cumbrous English measure of account, the £, *S* and *D.*

The old *Sonaut* rupee was of the same standard value of the present *Company's* rupee. It principally circulated in the Upper Provinces, while the *Sicca* rupee, although it might be met with in different places in India, was more confined to Bengal and the Lower Provinces. The relative value of the British Indian money with the English may be thus stated:—One gold mohur,* 16 rupees = £1-12*s.* One rupee = 16 annas = 2 shillings. One anna = 4 pysa = 1½ pence. One pysa = 3 pies = 1½ farthings. One pie † = ½ farthing. These relations are arbitrary, for it must be borne in mind that the relative value of the money of the two countries frequently varies, being dependent, in a great measure, on the state of trade. Thus a rupee is

* This is the *Sicca* gold mohur. There is also a *Company's* gold mohur, value *fifteen* rupees, and equivalent to £1-10*s.*

† The *pie* is almost an imaginary coin, for, although it is in existence, yet its circulation is very limited.

sometimes worth 2*s.* 2*d.*, and sometimes only worth 1*s.* 10½*d.*, but 2*s.* may be considered its *par* value. Its *intrinsic* value, however, is 1*s.* 10½*d.* In France, where money is reckoned by *francs* and *cents*, it has been determined, by actual experiment, and analysis of the metals, that one pound sterling is equal to 25 francs 20 cents, or 25 : 20. The *par*, therefore, between England and France, is said to be 25 : 20. With this country a different course is adopted. Having ascertained that the *Company's rupee* is intrinsically equal to 1*s.* 10½*d* of English money, the *par* with England is said to be 1*s.* 10½*d.* If, therefore, the course of exchange becomes such that *more* than 25 : 20 is quoted as the value of *one pound*, or less than 22½*d.*, as the value of *Company's rupee*, then it is plain that, in both cases, to the extent of the difference, is the exchange *against* (or unfavorable to) France and India, and *in favor* of England. The Indian monetary notation differs from the English in one or two material particulars. In estimating large sums, they speak, in England, of millions, half millions, and so on. The people of Bengal have a quantity called a *lac*, which they employ for this purpose. A *lac of rupees* is 100,000 rupees, pointed and written 1,00,000, and estimating the exchange roughly at 2*s.* per rupee, it follows that a *lac* is equivalent to about £10,000 sterling. A *crore of rupees* is 100 lacs, pointed and written 1,00,00,000; a *crore*, therefore, corresponds to about £1,000,000 sterling. A *puddo of rupees* is 100 crores. In mental calculations of exchange, where nicety in fractional parts is not absolutely necessary, it will be quite sufficient to take off from the Indian money the right-hand 0, in order to reduce it to English money. Thus: 1,00,00/0 with the 0 cut off becomes £ Stg. 10,000. In like manner, with English money, add to the last 0 another, and the amount becomes Indian.

The adulteration of the coinage is a matter of very common occurrence in India, and is effected in various ways. The natives bore holes in the rim of the rupee, and in place of the silver dust which they extract, they pour in lead. The milled edge of the *Company's rupee* renders this artifice more easy of detection than in the old *Sicca* and *Sonaut* rupee, but still it is frequently practised. In the native independent States, where they have the means, and the power of coining their own money, the currency is frequently depreciated by an unusual mixture of alloy. The following is a case in point, and will form an excellent commentary on the preceding remarks:—

"The zemindars of Goormutkal and Narienpet,* as feudatories of the Nizam Government, have the privilege of coining money at their own mints, necessarily upon the express condition that it shall not be of less value than the current coin of the realm.

They have just started into depreciating the currency by an unprecedented mixture of alloy, by one-eighth more than has yet been tolerated, and agents from these zemindars are now employed in purchasing up the superior coinage of the country, called Kalee sicca, the price of which has risen in the market, in consequence, from 1½ to 3 per cent premium, to re-coin it with the amount of alloy before stated, not relatively to the value of the Kalee sicca, but to that of an inferior specie called Shuhur Chulpee, current by authority in the city and its neighborhood, but which neither passes in the country, nor is received in the Resident's treasury.

---

* See "Prinsep's Tables," p. 25.

The effect of such a depreciation will extend to the whole transactions of the country. The exchange now obtaining with foreign countries will be enhanced, and, with the increased price of grain, all sorts of merchandise and labor will become dearer; whilst, to the Nizam's Government, the same revenues will, as before, be continued to be paid, though calculated to exchange for less than before; its servants and departments will equally suffer, without the Government deriving any advantage from the diminution, in point of fact, of their salaries. If the activity of these mints be considerable, it may occasion an entire drainage of the Kalee sicca, and, by arresting the payments into the Resident's treasury, and the transactions with the districts, lead to the arrangements, which must come at last, for the better regulating the Nizam's affairs.

The extent of mischief likely to accrue from the circulation of a depreciated currency is understood by the sahookars, and it is to be hoped their exposition may sufficiently impress the minister with a sense of his danger, to arouse him to the exertion of annihilating those mints. The right, whatever may be the title or the prescription of the zemindars, is absolutely forfeited by their forgeries. The question would rather be as to what, besides their mints, they had forfeited to the Government by their flagitious conduct?

It is further understood amongst the sahookars that the Resident, who has recently addressed a second note to the Nizam's minister regarding the payment of the debt to the Company, will insist upon receiving an immediate payment of a considerable portion of that debt. This has had no influence in changing the premium on the Kalee sicca, for, as the Government of the Nizam has no credit with capitalists, it is assumed that the debt will be paid out of the hoards of His Highness and his minister, which, consisting of the better sort of coin, will keep down the premium upon that coin by bringing a larger amount of the currency into circulation; but as a full and overflowing treasury will arrest for a considerable time the issuing of his treasury bills on his Government, hoondees have made a sudden start in regard to their exchange; they have risen on Calcutta to 29 per cent from 24, not gradually, but suddenly, and in the same proportion on other foreign markets.

It would be too laborious to seek out precise data. It is sufficient for notice, that mints exist in the Nizam's dominions, which, seemingly under the sanction of the Government, issue a base coinage, and that the current coin of the country is bought openly in the market, for the express purpose of being re-coined into money of less value.

The Kalee sicca, being a currency of greater value than that which passes within the city, has necessarily a fluctuating value in the market. I do not know what its standard value may be relatively to the Shuhur Chulpee, but I have known it to be at a premium as low as 4 annas per cent, and, at one time, during the war with the Peishwa, when there was a great demand for money at the Residency, as high as 4 per cent. Bills on Calcutta had risen at the same time to 32 per cent. If these may be considered as maximum rates, rather as extraordinary rates, then have the exchanges and premiums at the present time undergone an unusual fluctuation, and may be accounted for as arising out of the facts I have stated. The maximum price of pure silver that has ever obtained here, has been 18½ per cent. It is not sold by the tola. A hundred rupees weight is given in exchange for 118½ rupees. It has now risen beyond all former prices, and sells at 20½ per cent."* No one who carefully considers the subject can doubt that the privilege accorded to these zemindars is unwise and mischievous, and calculated, unless stopped at once, to be productive of much misery in the Nizam's dominions.

In collecting the public revenue there must always be much inconvenience from a metallic currency, and it has long been felt that a very expensive instrument of commerce should be replaced by one less costly, and certainly more convenient. That *desideratum* has now been attained, by the introduction of a Government paper currency, of sufficient magnitude and expansion to meet every possible objection in regard to the notes being made a legal tender in payment of revenue, and for all ordinary purposes, at the most extreme limits of British rule in India. But we are not prepared to admit that the substitution of a Government paper currency, in lieu of that of the leading Bank of India, is a move in the right direction—in fact, we doubt whether it is not a grave mistake. Theoretical financial schemes are all very well, but dealing as we have to do, in India, with a people extremely open to distrust, and susceptible of the most extraordinary panics, it is a question how far our rulers have acted wisely in initiating the measure, and whether it may not be fraught with ultimate danger to the country. There are not wanting writers who maintain that, in theory, no valid objection can be taken against this method of issue: that the security of the State ought to be the best guarantee for the intrinsic value of the notes: that no larger pledge can be given

* "Englishman," 19th July 1849.

for payment than the bond of the whole nation: and that Bankers should not be allowed to usurp a function which is essentially national. This is all very well; but what security can be held out that the Government notes shall not pass from Currency into Debt—shall not change their nature, and instead of being an instrument of exchange, and nothing more, shall not become mere bonds and obligations, vouchers for sums which the Government owe, but unconvertible, and unrealizable, except at a depreciated value? An unscrupulous Financial Member might find plenty of reasons for applying the funds received for notes to some part of the public service, and in the event of a panic, and so serious depreciation in the value of the Government stocks, held as a reserve, as to render them unconvertible except at an enormous sacrifice—which happened during the mutiny of 1857—what would be the position of the Government? This is a difficulty of no ordinary calibre. No form of Government can dissipate the danger, consequently direct and discretionary issue of a paper currency ought never to be entrusted to the State.

There is no misunderstanding that pecuniary profit has been the sole object in view; but surely this could have been secured without substituting a Government issue for that of a Bank which had enjoyed the privilege for a period of upwards of fifty years. Besides, it is questionable whether the benefit, derived by the State, is commensurate with the risk incurred of having, at a future period, the notes showered in under the influence of some extraordinary panic. The State notes are issued against bullion, and securities of the several loans, for which purpose the Government has come into the market as a large purchaser. What has been the consequence? At the time we write, nearly the total absorption of the five and a half per cent stock, which has been driven to a premium of twelve and a half per cent, so far benefitting the holders. But it is useless speculating. Time will develop either the wisdom or the folly of the measure.

The question however with which we have more immediately to do is the following:—Is the amount of paper put forth by the Government sufficient to meet the wants of the country? We believe it is. The note circulation of the Bank of Bengal was totally insignificant, and far below the requirements of so extensive an empire. That this was the fault of the Bank we cannot allow, for when the question of an increased circulation was brought before the Government some years back, it was treated with the utmost neglect, though it was clearly demonstrated that an augmented issue was calculated to increase the industry, and thereby add to the prosperity of the country.

The ponderous metallic currency of India, so less portable than that of Europe, has long been a serious objection in carrying on commercial and other business. The expense of conveying treasure about the country was no insignificant item in the public accounts, and although that item has been considerably reduced of late, by the introduction of steam on our rivers, and railways inland, yet it was only within a limited space that these auxiliaries could be brought to bear; consequently, it could never offer the same advantages as a convertible paper currency, acceptable to the people because suited to their character, habits, and necessities. We do not advocate an over-issue, which, by raising prices, and stimulating speculation, might lead to overtrading, and thereby prove injurious to the country; but an issue within proper limits, and such as the circulation could easily absorb and employ.

Under proper safeguards, there ought to be no real difficulty in making the Government currency acceptable to the people of India. A paper currency, although not a sound one, is of very general use in Russia, where it forms the ordinary money, not only in the most civilized parts of the empire, but even among the rudest of its tribes—parties not only ignorant of the Russian language, but even of the arts of reading and writing. For the last thirty years or more a paper currency has been extensively used in Java, among seven millions of people, not one man out of a hundred of whom understands the writing or the language in which the notes are printed. And the experience of India itself, as far as it has gone, is to the same effect. Among the natives of the towns of Calcutta and Madras, paper money is even preferred to metallic, and, in so far as the first of these places is concerned, the Bank of Bengal notes issued in it had a circulation, which extended to Benares,* five hundred and sixty miles above Calcutta. In fact, they were more or less known among a population of some forty millions of people.†

Still the issues of the Bank of Bengal were quite insignificant as regards the magnitude of the country. It is a very curious fact, well deserving of record in the history of paper credit, that a Bank, possessing the sole paper currency of a country so extensive as this, for many years above all suspicion of unsoundness, and not even visited by rumors prejudicial to credit, should never have been able to extend its circulation much beyond a million

* The notes, it is true, were subject to a discount of about 4 per cent.

† "Sketch of the Commercial Resources and Monetary and Mercantile System of British India," p. 61.

and a half sterling. It might be thought that so large a population, carrying on so active and extensive a commerce as that of Bengal, would require, for the mere convenience of trade, a far larger paper currency. The total circulation of England, by the latest returns, was twenty-four millions sterling,* with about nine millions more for Scotland and Ireland. This, it must be recollected, is under a restrictive system. It could therefore not have been thought an extravagant supposition that Bengal might keep ten millions in perpetual circulation. Yet we find that the sole issuers of an undoubted currency could not average more than a little over a tenth of that amount. The difference might, no doubt, in a great measure, be attributed to the different habits of the people, and the mode in which their commerce is conducted. But the convenience and security of paper in a country like this, where gang-robberies are committed in the centre of the capital, leads to the belief that there must be some other causes. The ignorance of the rural population is one. They are distrustful, but it is also doubtful whether the class of bank-notes chiefly in circulation was suitable to their dealings. The Bank of Bengal did not encourage an issue of small notes. There were not enough to be had for the use of the metropolis, and the lowest denomination was ten rupees, which is also the lowest denomination of the Government notes, the Secretary of State having adhered strictly to the descriptions in use by the Bank of Bengal. In many European countries notes circulate of about one rupee value, and we have even seen them as low as four annas. We do not say that such a circulation would be desirable here, and we believe that wherever it has been

* "Banking Almanac," September 1862.

issued, it was rather to satisfy a State necessity than a popular want.

We have already stated that we are not prepared, in the present ignorant state of the rural population, to advocate an over-issue of small notes, but we certainly think they might be put forth of smaller denomination than ten rupees, with great benefit to the Government and advantage to the country. In China, where there is a population as dense and as ignorant as that of India, paper money has been used for ages. In some of the large and populous districts, where banking is carried on, notes of very small amount are in circulation. No inconvenience is found to result, and though there may, at times, be an over-issue and consequent depreciation, it has not, in the long run, been found to work injuriously. The advocates of a purely metallic currency are invariably alarmists on the subject of an issue of small notes. The currency of a country, say they, is liable to constant fluctuations, and the natural and ordinary effect of the circulation of small notes is to cause the specie to leave the channels of circulation, and settle in the vaults of a Bank, or otherwise to be hoarded. This we admit, where the issue is *excessive;* but such we do not advocate. All we maintain is, that the present issue of notes of small amount is far below the requirements of the country, and that it might be extended without endangering the currency. The Government has made *ten* rupees the lowest sum, for which a note shall be issued. Mr. Wilson's limit was one-half this amount—five rupees. On scientific grounds, as a question of monetary principle, we have no hesitation in saying that Mr. Wilson was right. The prejudice against small notes is a disgrace to the state of monetary science. The very object of a paper currency is to substitute a cheap and portable for a heavy and costly instrument. The feeling against notes of small denomination is absurd, and ought to have been put to shame long ago by the example of Scotland.

It may be urged that the plan was tried in America, and failed. Why? Because there was an over-issue. All the petty Banks in the several States of the Union, issued their one, two, three, four, and five dollars notes, and the amount in circulation was so large, that they became at last a public nuisance, and received the appellation of *shin-plasters.* Here, it will be seen, that the evil was engendered by permitting every petty Bank to issue notes, and by want of the intelligence and prudence with which banking is now conducted. This could not be the case now, provided sufficient judgment and discrimination be used in not forcing an undue amount of notes into circulation, and thus fostering that rash spirit of speculation which always manifests itself when there is an abundance of money, and which also leads to incalculable mischief.

Bearing in mind that this book is intended principally for reference, it may not be unacceptable to our readers, nor unsuitable, as a conclusion to this part, to extract from Prinsep's "Useful Tables" in the *Journal of the Asiatic Society* some remarks on the "British Indian Monetary System" as established by Regulation VII. of 1833:—

"Silver is the legally constituted medium of exchange in all money transactions throughout the British Indian possessions. Gold coin is a legal tender, at a fixed value of 16 rupees for the gold-mohur of Calcutta, and 15 rupees for the gold rupee of Madras and Bombay; but it is not demandable in payment, and is left to find its current value in the market. Copper coin is only a legal tender at the established rate of 64 *pysa* to the rupee, on payments falling short of one rupee."

Since going to press, it has been discovered that, not only are Prinsep's Tables copyright, but that it would be hardly possible—if indeed fair—to alter the text so freely as would be requisite, for, accurate and reliable as the tables were at the time they were published, they have ceased to be so from modifications in Mint charges and practices. It has been thought better, therefore, to give afresh so much of the information as is desired, and, in doing so, the best thanks and acknowledgments are due to Dr. Shekleton, the present Assay Master of the Calcutta Mint, for the valuable assistance which he has, with the utmost courtesy and readiness, afforded, enabling accurate data to be furnished on points of great commercial interest and importance.

THE RUPEE* is the unit or standard measure of value throughout India; and, as a perfect assimilation in weight and fineness has been effected, the value of this unit of currency is precisely the same in the three Presidencies of Bengal, Madras, and Bombay. Although the *Moorshedabadee* or *Sicca rupee* is still to be met with all over the country, it ceased to be the legal currency in May 1836, and is disused, except in the valuation of some few articles. The relation, however, of one coin to the other is reduced to great simpilicity; one† Furruckabad and one Company's rupee being equal to 15 annas Sicca precisely. The conversion may be made by adding $\frac{1}{15}$th of the amount of the Siccas to the amount, and the result will be Company's; and, deduct $\frac{1}{16}$th of the amount from the Company's, and the result will be

* This term is derived from *rupya*, which signifies *silver piece*.

† By Regulation VII. 1833, there are four kinds of Furruckabad rupees.

Siccas. The *Furruckabad* rupee, like the Sicca, though no longer the legal currency, is to be found in great abundance in the North-Western Provinces. The weight and value is that of the new or Company's rupee. In the great marts up-country, they are put up in bags containing 1,000 and 500 rupees each, certified by a slip attached to the bags. The uniformity of the coinage causes the local currencies to be exchanged at certain rates of batta or discount, but as these rates must greatly depend on the demand and supply in the different parts of the interior where they circulate, it is impossible to give any fixed sum. At Mirzapore, for instance, the discount on Furruckabad rupees is from 8 to 12 annas per cent; at Patna this coin is altogether unknown *as a currency*, though the transactions, which are very extensive between Mirzapore and Patna, are adjusted in the Furruckabad, or as it is termed the Mirzapore currency.

Small shells, called couries, were formerly made use of for fractional payments of a pice, but their value was always subject to considerable fluctuation. They are now almost entirely superseded by the copper currency, though still to be found passing amongst the lower order of natives, whose transactions are, in most instances, below the value of a pice. They are reckoned as follows :—

4 Couries make	 1	Gunda.
20 Gundas „	 1	Pun.
4 Puns	 1	Anna.
4 Annas.	.... ¼	of a Rupee.

Gold Coins.

The Calcutta, Madras, and Bombay Mints are alone privileged to coin gold. Since 1841* only the Company's

* Financial Notification, 13th January 1841.

gold-mohur has been coined. This mohur weighs $\frac{16}{15}$ths of a rupee, and is of the same proportion—15 to 1—as the gold-mohurs of Madras and Bombay, which pass current for 15 rupees. The weights and purity of these coins are fixed by Act XVII. of 1835, as follows :—

Pure Gold.	*Alloy.*	*Weight in Grains.*	*Weight in Tolas.*	*Legal Value.*
165	15	180	1,000	15 Rupees.

Although authority was granted by the above Resolution of 1841 to coin double, half, and quarter gold-mohurs of proportionate weight to the above, none have yet been coined. The following table, exhibiting the scheme of the British Indian monetary system, will be useful :—

Gold-Mohurs.	*Rupee.*	*Anna.*	*Pysa.*	*Pie.*
Calcutta, Madras and Bombay, 1	15	240	960	2,880
	1	16	64	192
		1	4	12
			1	3

By the Notification, 13th January 1841, the other gold coins, *viz.* the five rupee, ten rupee, and thirty rupee, or double gold-mohur pieces, are declared to be of the same standard as the gold-mohur or fifteen rupee piece and of proportionate weight, and shall bear the same device in conformity with Act No. XVII. of 1835.

Under the old Hindoo system, which succumbed to the Mussulman, the unit of currency was gold; and from the quantity of coins still extant in different parts of the country, it appears to have been a legal tender;

for, even after the Mohammedan power became established, this system of currency continued to be issued by a number of petty rajahs and the rulers of Tributary States. The issues were large in the South of India, but on this side, in the States of Rajpootana, Malwa, and Bundleound, both anterior and subsequent to the time of AKBAR, the Emperor of Delhi, many of the gold-mohurs bore the several impress of the Delhi, Bhopal,* Jeypoor, Joudpore, and Kota† coins, easily recognized by their respective symbols.

Although not actually the standard of value, gold was, prior to 1835, a legal tender in the British territories in India. By Act XVII. of that year, however, the Government of India notified, that "thenceforward" no gold coin should be a legal tender of payment in any of the "territories of the East India Company," and accordingly gold so ceased to be a legal tender from the passing of the Act. The measure appears to have resulted from what is now admitted to have been a groundless apprehension on the part of the Government, that findings of gold in Australia would considerably depreciate the value of the metal.

In 1841 the Government issued a Proclamation that officers in charge of public treasuries were authorized freely to receive the gold coins issued from the Government Mints at the different Presidencies in conformity with Act XVII. of 1835, at the rates, until further orders, respectively denoted by the denomination of the pieces, until they shall have passed the limits of lightness allowed for wear laid down in the annexed table, when they will only be receivable as bullion, and be subject to a deduction of one per cent for seignorage.

* A rude figure resembling a coat of mail.

† A triple bow, or knot—inscription in Nagree.

	THE PIECE FOR			
	30 Rs.	15 Rs.	10 Rs.	5 Rs.
Standard Weight	360 grs.	180 grs.	120 grs.	60 grs.
Limit for Wearage...	3 „	1½ „	1 „	½ „
Minimum Weight	357	178½	119	59½

Consequently gold coins continued thus to be received in liquidation of public demands up to 22nd December 1852, when a Notification was put forth, cancelling some portion of the Proclamation of 13th January 1841, and intimating that "on and after 1st January 1853, no gold coin will be received on account of payments due, or to be made to Government in any public treasury within the territories of the East India Company, but that it would be received for coinage."

The effect of these Notifications was to cause great dissatisfaction to those who were engaged in the trade that was gradually increasing between Australia and India. The putting gold out of circulation in 1835 was considered impolitic, as a measure whereby the Government shut themselves out from the advantage they might have gained by introducing, as a permanent legal tender, that metal which, sooner or later, it is to be hoped, will displace, as a standard in all India, the cumbrous silver coinage now current, which, as in England, would then become a subsidiary circulation only.

Silver Coins.

The old Sicca rupee is extinct. The new Sicca rupee, received only in payment of revenue, is almost absorbed. The weight, fineness, and relative value of the Company's rupee, now in circulation, are as noted below, and are declared by the Financial Notification of the 2nd September 1835 to be the same as the Furruckabad, Sonat, Madras, and Bombay rupees, the Notifications of 11th November 1840 and 13th January 1841 merely altering the device.

Pure grains. Silver.	*Alloy. Troy grains.*	*Weight in Troy grains.*	*Weight in Tolas.*
165	15	180	1

This coin has a straight milling. There are minor coins of proportionate weight to each of the above. Eight-anna pieces *(ut'hunnee)*, four-anna pieces *(sookee, or chou-unnee)*, and two-anna pieces *(do-unnee)*. The standard quality of the metal is eleven-twelfths of pure silver to one-twelfth of alloy. All silver money of the new standard (with a straight milling or a plain edge) is considered by law as of full weight until it has lost by wear, or otherwise, 3·85 pie in Rupee, or two per cent. Coins of the old standard, with the oblique milling, have been out of circulation since May 1836. The limit of weight of the Government and Company's rupee is 180 grains, minimum weight 176·$\frac{3}{5}$ or ·6. Rupees that are of light weight are received by Government officers as bullion, the payer making good the deficiency from standard weight.

The issue of the new "Government" rupee, with its auxiliaries in silver and copper, which bear entirely a new device, will commence about November 1862, and no new divisions of either metal are contemplated.* For converting the rupee into the ordinary divisions of *annas* and *pie*, and vice versâ, the following table from Prinsep's

* For the new Currency Act XIII. of 1862, see Appendix.

work, page 10, will be found very convenient and of constant application in monetary calculations :—

For reducing Annas *and* Pie *into* decimal *parts of a* Rupee.

1 anna = 0·0625.

Annas.	0	1	2	3	4	5	6	7	8	9	10	11 pie.
0	·0000	·0052	·0104	·0156	·0208	·0260	·0312	·0365	·0417	·0469	·0521	·0573
1	·0625	·0677	·0729	·0781	·0833	·0885	·0937	·0990	·1042	·1094	·1146	·1198
2	·1250	·1302	·1354	·1406	·1458	1510	·1562	·1615	·1667	·1719	·1771	·1823
3	·1875	·1927	·1979	·2031	·2083	·2135	·2187	·2240	·2292	·2344	·2396	·2448
4	·2500	.2552	·2604	·2656	·2708	·2760	·2812	·2864	·2917	·2969	·3021	·3073
5	·3125	.3177	·3229	·3281	·3333	·3385	·3437	·3489	·3542	·3594	·3646	·3698
6	·3750	.3802	·3854	·3906	·3958	·4010	·4062	·4115	·4167	·4219	·4271	·4323
7	·4375	·4427	·4479	·4531	·4583	·4635	·4687	·4740	·4792	·4844	·4896	·4948
8	·5000	·5052	·5104	·5156	·5208	·5260	·5312	·5365	·5417	·5469	·5521	·5573
9	·5625	·5677	·5729	·5781	·5833	·5885	·5937	·5990	·6042	·6094	·6146	·6198
10	·6250	·6302	·6354	·6406	·6458	·6510	·6562	·6615	·6667	·6719	·6771	·6823
11	·6875	·69 7	·6979	·7031	·7083	·7135	·7187	·7240	.7292	·7344	·7396	·7448
12	·7500	·755 2	·7004	·7656	·7708	·7760	·7812	·7865	·7917.	·7969	·8021	·8073
13	·8125	·8177	·8230	·8281	·8333	·8385	·8437	·8490	·8542	·8594	·8646	8698
14	·8750	8802	·8854	·8906	·8958	·9010	·9062	·9115	·9167	·9219	·9270	·9323
15	·9375	·9427	·9479	·9532	·9583	·9635	·9687	·9740	·9787	·9844	·9896	·9948

Prinsep says :—

"The several varieties of coin, produced by modifications of weight, standard, or die, from time to time, in the Calcutta and subordinate Mints of the Bengal Presidency, from their all bearing the same legend and date, are not easily recognized, but by an experienced money-changer. As, however, different Regulations regarding deficiency of weight, &c., apply to the coins of the old and new standard, it is convenient to point out a mode of discriminating them.

1. The *old standard Sicca rupee* of 1793—1818 has an oblique milling.

2. The *new standard Sicca rupee of* 1818—1832 has a straight milling.

3. The *new Sicca rupee* has a plain edge, without milling, and a dotted rim on the face.

The distinctions of the oblique and straight milling apply also to the old and new gold-mohur. Of the up-country or Furruckabad coins :—

4. The *old standard Furruckabad rupee* (or 45th Sun Lucknow rupee of Regulation XLV. 1803) has an oblique milling.

5. The *Benares rupee*, coined 1806—1819, has also an oblique milling.

6. The *new standard Furruckabad rupee*, coined at the Furruckabad Mint, 1819—24, and at the Benares Mint, 1819—30, and at the Saugor Mint, has an upright milling.

7. The *Furruckabad rupee*, coined under the new Regulation at the Calcutta Mint, has a plain edge, and a *plain* rim on the face.

The coins struck before 1793, at the old Mints of Patna, Moorshedabad, and Dacca, the Benares rupee anterior to 1806, and the coins of all the native independent States, are known by their having no milling. The Company's coin, up the country, is thus generally called '*kuldar*' (milled, or made by machinery), in contradistinction to the unmilled or native coins, which are fashioned and stamped with the hammer and anvil.

The *Madras rupee* has a dotted rim on the face, and an indented cord-milling : that coined in Calcutta has an upright milled edge." *

Since 1839, Hyderabad rupees are assayed annually to adjust the rates of payments to troops, and since annexation, Nagpore, Lucknow, and Punjab rupees have also been specially assayed, as well as Suddhora rupees from Rohilcund, for the same purpose. 120 Hyderabad and Nagpore rupees were considered equivalent to 100 Bombay or Company's rupees. The old Lucknow used to be estimated at 101 for 100 Furruckabad rupees.

The following assays, giving the average weight and value of these coins in detail, are the latest; and, being from tables recently forwarded to Government, will be valuable to local Banks :—

			Grs.		Intrinsic.	
100	Hyderabad	Rs. wt.	174·375	= Co.'s Rs.	76·619	To obtain the net value, deduct 2 per cent. seignorage, 1 per cent. melting charge, and a melting loss of ¼ per cent. pre-melting, being compulsory for all descriptions of bullion or coin previous to receipt for coinage.
,,	Nagpore	,, wt.	165·937	= Co.'s Rs.	85·065	
,,	Oude (old)	,, wt.	171·887	= Co.'s Rs.	100·942	
,,	Ditto (new)	,, wt.	171·562	= Co.'s Rs.	100·296	
,,	Punjab(new)	,, wt.	171·900	= Co.'s Rs.	99·406	
,,	Ditto (old)	,, wt.	171·180	= Co.'s Rs.	94·125	
,,	Suddhora	,, wt.	162·187	= Co.'s Rs.	69·968	

* Prinsep's "Tables," 1834, pp. 2 & 3. The Madras rupee, of 1845, has the Company's arms.

The par of exchange with other countries may be estimated from the intrinsic and mint produce of their coins.

With regard to dollars there is a great difference in weight, but not in fineness. The Spanish dollar still retains the old weight of 417·65 grains, the American dollar, since 1837, weighing only 412·5 grains. The Calcutta assays of the present day accord with the standard fixed by those Governments 4 wo., whereas Mr. Prinsep, by the cupellation process, valued them at 5 wo.

The corrected tables would stand thus—

Spain.

100 Dollars	= 232·028 tolas, = 227·807 Co.'s rupees, = 213·570 Sicca rupees,	Deducting at 2 per cent.	=223·251 Co's. rs.* =209·310 Sicca rs.

American since 1837.
Weight of dollar 412·5 grains at 4 wo.

100 Dollars	= 229·166 tolas, = 225·000 Co's. rupees, = 210·938 Sicca rupees,	Deducting at 2 per cent.	= 220·500 Co's. rs.* = 206·720 Sicca rs.

The dollars of Spain, Mexico, Peru, Bolivia, with chopped dollars of the same value, are all current in the Straits of Malacca and China, but the Manilla dollar only weighs 402 grains at 20 wo. = 203·030 Company's rupees or Sicca rupees 190·340.

Copper Coins.

The weight and value of the copper coins now in circulation are as follows:—

The Half-anna piece..............	*Troy grains*	200	... *value*	6	*pie of account.*
The Quarter-anna piece	*ditto*	100	... *do.*	3	*ditto.*
The Half-pice piece	*ditto*	50	... *do.*	1½	*ditto.*
The Pie of account	*ditto*	33⅓	... *do.*	1	*ditto.*

* There is also a pre-melting charge of 1 per mille.

The *one-pie* piece, equal to the *twelfth* of an anna, did not take in the country, because it did not correspond with the system of pecuniary transactions and of accounts which prevails. The division of a pice into *three* parts is entirely of English origin, and has never been cordially adopted by the natives, to whom it was an anomalous and useless coin, being more than five couries and less than ten.

Prinsep remarks :—

"By Regulation XXV. of 1817, Section 5, copper pice, struck at the Benares Mint, weighing 98¼ grains, which were intended at first (*vide* Regulation VII. 1814) for circulation in the province of Benares only, and were distinguished with a trident or *tirsool*, the symbol of SIVA, are made current throughout the Bengal Provinces at par with the Calcutta and Furruckabad pice.

The new double pysa or half-anna piece has on one side merely the words 'half anna' in English and Bengalee : on the reverse, the same in Persian and Nagree. The *pie* or third of a *pysa* has in the same manner merely the name 'one *pie*,' which makes it liable to be confounded with the 'one *paee* sicca,' and on this account perhaps it has not found ready currency. The natives reckon only 64 *paee* to the rupee, while English accounts divide the anna into 12 pie ; to distinguish them, this latter (hitherto an imaginary coin) was called the *pie of account*."*

The pice of 1845 have the arms of the East India Company, and so have all the pice struck in England and recently imported, and delivered into the vaults of the Bank of Bengal.

Prinsep observes further with respect to Native Copper Coins :—

"Our information regarding the copper coin in circulation throughout Central India is very limited, but it is well known that as much perplexity exists in the varieties of pyse, and in the greater range of their value, as in the coins of the more precious metals ; so that

* Prinsep's "Tables," 1834, p. 6.

every town and village almost has its separate currency, and its established *nirkh*, or rate of exchange with the rupee, to the great inconvenience of the traveller and of the poorer classes. In weight they vary from 280 grains (the Jypoory, &c.) to 34 grains (the Mewary) : the former passing at about 35, the latter at 378, pyse for a rupee. From the small advantage of melting up copper money, it happens that much of the circulation in this metal is of very great antiquity ; and not only many ancient Hindu coins are met with, but Bactrian and Roman copper coins are also frequently procurable at fairs and in the neighborhood of old towns in Upper India.

The pysa was in some cases adopted as the unit for determining the larger weights of the bazars, as the Gorruckpoory pysa, of which 530 were held equal to a pusseree (five seers) at Ghazeepoor, and generally throughout the Benares province. 2,881 '*Chulun*' of Futtehgurh in like manner were assumed as the weight of a maund in that district. The Delhi pysa, coined till 1818, was 12 mashes or 1 tola in weight.

Most of the native pyse contain more copper in proportion to their value than the present Company's coin, which was however originally one tola in weight, and was gradually reduced to 100 grains (as shown in the table) ; it is at present in fact a Government token, worth intrinsically less than its nominal value.

Within the ceded territories the native coins still predominate, but the Company's pyse is now gradually spreading to westward, and the Saugor Mint* has for several years been employed in converting the native copper money into Benares or *Tirsoolee*† pyse of 100 grains weight, and 64 to the rupee. At Bombay, the old pyse have been brought up by Government, for the purpose of removing them entirely from circulation, aud substituting the new coin. The Bengal Government have also recently adopted a measure tending to withdraw the *Tirsoolee* pyse from circulation, in consequence of their becoming much depreciated in public estimation from a large admixture of spurious coin, and other causes ; the Calcutta Mint being ordered

---

* The Saugor Mint was abolished in 1836. It was the last of the three subordinate ones that were dispensed with.

† "Tirsoolee" pice, so called from having impresed on it a *trident*, the symbol of SIVA, the God of destruction. Most of the old copper pice, to be found about Benares and the districts contiguous thereto, bear this symbol.

to grant 64 new pyse for 72 tirsoolees, for any amount not under 20 rupees in value brought for exchange."*

CHINA.

As we shall have occasion to notice at length the present currency of this country, with which we are becoming better acquainted every day, and with which our commercial and banking relations are extending, it will not be amiss to state the value of the *tael* of the Sycee and Dollar silver current with them.

One Tael = 580 Troy Grains.

100 tael of Sycee silver @ 16 Br.‡	= 322·222 tolas in weight = (120 oz. 16 dwts. 16 grs. @ 14 Br.†		
	= 345·656 C.	Deducting @ 2 per cent.	338·743 C. rs.
	= 324·053 S.		317·572 C. rs.
100 tael of dollar at 4 Wo.	= 316·364 C. rupees,	Deducting @ 2 per cent.	310·037 C. rs.
	= 296·591 S. rupees,		300·660 S. rs.

The present exact process of assay enables a value to be assigned to Dollar silver and Sycee, higher by one *dwt.* than that formerly given.

The Chinese have no regular coinage, but since the establishment of foreign trade, the introduction of the Spanish or Pillar dollar, and the American or Eagle dollar, has, to a certain, though a very limited extent, supplied the want of a regular coinage. For some time a spurious coinage of dollars was carried on and connived at by the provincial treasurers, but the coins fell so far below the standard, that the manufacture came to be disallowed, though it is supposed to be still surreptitiously carried on. In the south of Canton it is believed there is a large establishment where dollars are manufactured of all grades of value; some alloyed with lead, some made of base metal, and coated over with silver, and others deteriorated by cutting out pieces of

* English standard. † "Prinsep's Tables," 1834, p. 8. ‡ Indian standard.

silver, and filling their places with lead, disguised by repeated stamps, a method frequently pursued with genuine Spanish dollars.

Although not quite relevant to the subject of Indian coin, still, as Chinese silver forms so considerable a portion of the bullion importation of Calcutta, we may be permitted to insert a brief account of the Chinese system, extracted from the *Anglo-Chinese Calendar*, not doubting that the particulars will be found both interesting and important.

"Sycee silver, in Chinese *Wan-yin*, is the only approach to a silver currency among the Chinese. In it the Government taxes and duties, and the salaries of officers, are paid; and it is also current among merchants in general. This silver is refined and cast into ingots, (by the Chinese called Shoes,*) which are stamped with the mark of the office that issues them, the names of the banker and workmen, and the date of their issue. The ingots vary in weight, but are most commonly of ten *taels* each. The silver is divided into classes, according to its fineness and freedom from alloy: the kinds most current at Canton are the following:

1*st.* *Kwan-heang*, the Hoppo's duties, or the silver which is forwarded to the imperial treasury at Peking. This is of 97 to 99 touch. On all the imperial duties, a certain percentage is levied for the purpose of turning them into Sycee of this high standard, and of conveying them to Peking without any loss in the full amount.

2*nd.* *Fan-koo* or *Fan-foo*,—the treasurer's receipts, or that in which the land-tax is paid. This is also of a high standard, but inferior to that of the Hoppo's duties, and being intended for use in the province, not for conveyance to Peking, no percentage is levied on the taxes for it.

3*rd.* *Yuenpaou*, or *Une-po*, literally "chief in value."—This kind is usually imported from Soochow, in large pieces of 50 *taels* each. It does not appear to belong to any particular Government tax.

4. *Yen* or *Eem-heang*, "salt duties."—It is difficult to account for these being of so low a standard, the salt trade being entirely a Government monopoly. This class is superior only to

---

* By the natives of India, *khooree*, or hoofs.

5th. *Mut-tae*, or *Wuh-tae*, the name of which signifying "uncleansed or unpurified," designates it as the worst of all. It is seldom used, except for the purpose of plating, or rather washing, baser metals."*

Cash is the only native coin in general use, but it is greatly debased with iron dust and sand. It is metal formed from a composition of copper, zinc, and nickel. We have, elsewhere, referred to the peculiarity of the Chinese coin with a hole in the centre. The coins of Ancient Greece presented the same peculiarity, and they were hung as ornaments round the heads of women and young girls. Paper money, or, in other words, a Government note circulation, was formerly issued by the Government, but grew out of use about two centuries back. Promissory notes, however, circulate with the same facility as in Europe, because the Chinese people see the real value of the expedient and keep it up amongst themselves, depending only on the personal credit of the parties exercising it. This, of course, occasions a want of uniformity. In the province of Fuh-chow, paper money is now nearly the sole circulating medium: of course there is over-issue and consequent depreciation. The notes are longer but narrower than ours. They are printed both from copper-plates and wooden blocks, and represent Cash, Dollars, or Sycee, and vary considerably in valuation. The notes are seldom below par. They pass current with all parties, and are readily cashed by any of the class of bankers. The Canton Banks do not materially differ from similar European establishments. They receive deposits,issue paper money,and will draw bills on demand or after a certain number of days' notice. They also advance money on loan, at a daily interest of about half

* "Anglo-Chinese Calendar."

per cent, for periods of not less than three days. In every large town are *yin tien*, or "money shops," the inferior class of which are establishments of money-changers and shroffs—the more respectable private Banks. The Banking establishments are numerous, and the bankers wealthy. By co-operation they regulate the market, and determine the relative prices of notes, bullion, and dollars. The interest they exact on loans is high. There are some imaginary moneys, of which a knowledge may be useful. They are as follows:—

		Approximate sterling value. *d.*
10 Cash (li)	= 1 Candaneus ("fun")	¾
10 Candaneus	= 1 Mace ("tseen")	7½
10 Mace	= 1 tael ("leang")	75

The *Cash*, however, are not imaginary, but, as we have shown, a *bonâ-fide* coin with a hole in the centre, through which they are strung like beads in various numbers. This coin is found current in *Lassa* in the south of Thibet, a little to the north of Nepal. The silver current in Nepal is in lumps stamped, and procured from China. The Chinese custom of paying and receiving by weight is observed here as well as in Thibet. The English rupee, however, circulates freely through Western Thibet.

BURMAH.

Like the Chinese, the Burmese have no metallic currency, making all their payments by weight in the precious metals. Of course where the British Government is firmly planted, the rupee calculates freely, but amongst themselves there is altogether a distinct and independent system. In Burmah *Proper*, the King has a coin (rupee) of his own, equivalent in value, it is believed, to the Company's rupee, which, now to a certain extent, supersedes the lumps and dumps of silver previously used in exchanges. In *British* Burmah the Government notes pass current for all purposes of trade. The Burmese make use of decimal divisions on estimating the value or purity of gold and silver.

The import trade in European manufactured goods is very limited. The funds for the purchase of timber and produce are principally supplied by shipments of specie, consequently money is of great value. The recent establishment of a Branch of the Bank of Bengal has been attended with the most satisfactory results. Bank notes have taken, on the whole, very well, though they are not *there* a legal tender. Interest, which was ruling very high, has been reduced from 2 and 3 per cent per *mensem*, to 14 and 12 per cent per *annum*. When the rice and timber seasons commence, prices steadily advance, and money becomes in brisk demand.

The following particulars may be useful:—

Vis, *tikal*, and *moo* are business terms used in transactions and accounts: their sub-divisions and multiples are—

1 *pe* or *be*.
2 = 1 *moo*.
2½ = 1 *mat*.
5 = 2 = 1 *hkwe*.
10 = 4 = 2 = 1 *kyat* or *tikal*.
1000 = 400 = 200 = 100 = 1 *peiktha* or *vissom*.

100 *tikals* are precisely equal to 140 *tolas*.

The names of the metals, and the numerals and assay terms used, are subjoined:—

Numerals.		*Metals.*	*Assay terms.*
1. *Ta.*	6. *Khyouk.*	*Shwe*, gold. (*Shwenee*, red or	*Det*, better or above.
2. *Nheet.*	7. *Khwon.*	*pure gold.*)	*Mee*, differing + or −
3. *Thoun.*	8. *Sheet.*	*Ngwe*, silver.	*Meedet*, better in assay.
4. *Le.*	9. *Ko.*	*Ge* or *khe*, lead or alloy.	*Mee shyouk*, worse do.
5. *Nga.*	10. *Tshay.*	*Nee*, copper—*Byoo*, tin.	*Ma*, adulterated.

Thirty-five tolas, or 20 to 30 tikals, is about the weight of the lumps of silver which pass current as coin. Their quality and appearance have invested them with a variety of names. Prinsep states them to be:—

" *Bans** signifies 'pure' or 'touch,' and is the purest obtainable of the Burmese process of refinage.

Kharoobat (shelly or spiral circled) is applied to a silver cake, with marks upon its surface, produced by the crystallization of the lead scoria in the process of refinement: it is supposed to denote a particular fineness, which by Burmese law ought to be ten-ninths *yowetnee* in value, *i. e.* 9 tikals of *kharoobat* pass for 10 of *yowetnee* silver; or it should contain 19¼ *ban* and ¾ copper.*

Yowetnee (red leafed) flower, or star, silver, is so named from the starry appearance of the melted litharge on its surface. *Yowet* is a corruption of *rowek* (leaf), and the word is sometimes written by Europeans *rowanee*, *rouni*, *roughanee*, &c. *Yowetnee* is the Government standard of Ava, and contains by law 85 *ban* and 15 alloy per cent.

Dain, the most common form of bullion met with in circulation, is so called from an assessment levied during the late king's reign upon villages and houses: *dain* signifying a stage, or distance of two miles. These cakes also weigh from 20 to 30 tikals each. Their prescribed legal quality is 10 per cent better than *yowetnee*, which puts this species of silver on a par with *kharoobat*.

There is an adulterated *dain* silver, similar in quality to *yowetnee*, but in reality much worse (42½ dwts. wo.), lately introduced and extensively circulated: it is made by admixture of lead, and is called *madain*.

The following will serve as examples of the mode of valuing bullion:

Dain, ko-moo-det, is dain 9 per cent better. (*See* explanation above).

——, *nga-moo-det*.........5 per cent. better.

Yowetnee,.........standard. (85 touch).

————, *kyat-ge, or ta-tshay-ge*, 1 tikal or tenth of alloy (meaning $\frac{1}{10}$th weight of alloy added to standard).

————, *kyouk-tshay nga-kyat-ge*, 6 tens 5 tikal alloy (meaning 65 per cent to alloy added).

————, *gyan*, half yowetnee (and half alloy).

* The Burmese Cake silver remains of the same weight and quality as stated by Prinsep, but it is always brittle from the presence of antimony and the alloys that render it quite unfit for coinage in its unrefined state.

Gold. The purity of gold is expressed by moos or tenths only: ten moos (*tshay moo*) (100 touch) being esteemed pure gold.

'King's gold,' or standard, is called *Ka-moo-ta-pe-leyowe*, (9 moos, 1 pe, 4 seeds,) or 9¾ moos fine.

'Merchants' gold,' is *Ko-moo-ta-be*, 9½ moos fine. Gold-mohurs are called 8½ moos fine by the Ava assayers."

As it may be of advantage to have always at hand a means of referring to the different Regulations which have from time to time been passed affecting the currency, the several Coinage Acts, and Orders of Government relative thereto, are subjoined:—

COINAGE ACTS.

Resolution, 2*nd June* 1766—Fixes the value of certain coins, and declares them legal tender.

Resolution, 24*th September* 1781.—Double, single, ½ and ¼ pyce to be coined.

Resolution, 28*th June*, 24*th October*, *and* 21*st November* 1792—Fixes the value of certain coins, and declares them legal tender.

Resolution XXXV. of 1793—19th Sun.*—Sicca rupees and mohur to be coined. Duty on gold only.

Resolution VI. of 1794—19th Sun.—Sicca rupees only to be received as revenue after 10th April 1795.

Resolution LXI. of 1795.—Wearage allowance on Sicca rupees 6 annas per cent. Its weights to be supplied by the Mint.

Resolution LXII. of 1795.—Moorshedabad Mint abolished.

Resolution III. of 1799—19th Sun.—Sicca mohurs and rupees only to be current in Sylhet, after 10th April 1798.

* This expression "Sun" refers to coins issued by individual monarchs of the Mussalman dynasty. It signifies "year of reign," also "æra," but has frequently a more extended signification. See Prinsep, pp. 19 & 21.

Resolution XLV. of 1803.—Furruckabad rupees or Lucknow—45th Sun.—Sicca rupees, with half and quarter, also pyce, to be coined, and the Furruckbad Mint established.

Resolution LIV. of 1803—19th Sun.—Sicca rupees and mohur only to be legal tender.

Resolution XI. of 1805.—Furruckabad rupees to be legal in the Dooab, &c.

Resolution XIII. of 1806.—Furruckabad rupees to weigh 173 grains, touch 95·. 5 pyce to weigh 284½ grains, and ½ pyce, 142¼ grains; 26 pyce = 1 Rupee.

Resolution IV. of 1807—Determines the value of rupees of sorts in the Jumna districts.

Resolution XIII. of 1807.—Relative to engagements for rupees or mohurs not of the established coinage.

Resolution X. of 1809.—Tirsoolee pyce for Benares, weighing 8 annas 9 pie of the 37th Sun, to be coined at Calcutta.

Resolution II. of 1812.—Duty on coining silver and gold.

Resolution VII. of 1814.—Tirsoolee pyce to be coined at Benares.

Resolution XXI. of 1816.—Furruckabad pyce of Regulation XLV. of 1803 reduced to 200 grains; and ½ pyce to 100; 32 and 64 = 1 Rupee.

Resolution XIV. of 1817.—Gold assay produce table.

Resolution XXV. of 1817.—Sicca single pyce to be coined of 100 grains.

Resolution XXVI. of 1817.—Furruckabad rupees circulation extended to the Ceded Provinces.

Resolution XIV. of 1818—Sicca weight of 19th Sun.—Sicca rupees and mohur changed. Refinage charge on gold.

Resolution V. of 1819.—Benares rupees withdrawn, and new stamped Furruckabad rupees to be coined.

Resolution VI. of 1820.—Sections of Regulation XLV. of 1803, empowering individuals to tender copper for coinage, at the Futtehghur Mint, rescinded.

Resolution V. of 1821—Settles exchange of Benares and Furruckabad rupees for Tirsoolee rupees.

Resolution II. of 1824—Abolished Futtehghur Mint.

Resolution VII. of 1821—Transfers the control of the Benares Mint to a Local Committee.

Resolution III. of 1831.—Sicca double pyce of 200 grains and pies of 33⅓ grains to be coined.

Resolution VII. of 1833.—Sicca rupees to weigh 1 tola of 180 grains. Refinage to be charged on silver.

Resolution XVII. of 1835.—Company's single, ½, ¼, and double rupee, and Company's mohur, ⅓, ⅔, and double to be coined, 11th and 12th June.

Resolution XXI. of 1835.—Company's single and double pyce and pies to be coined for Bengal.

Resolution XIII. of 1836.—Sicca rupees and Benares and Furruckabad pyce withdrawn from circulation in Bengal, Behar, and Orissa.

Resolution XXXI. of 1837.—The head of William IV. to continue on the coins until further orders.

Resolution XXI. of 1838.—Governor-General to direct the coinage of even sixteenths of a rupee.

Resolution XXXI. of 1839.—Punishment enacted for clipping, filing, &c., of coins.

Resolution of December 1840.—Ordering the coinage of Victoria rupees.

Resolution XIII. of 1844.—Tirsoolee pyce withdrawn from circulation, Benares.

Resolution XXII. of 1844.—Company's pyce, double pyce, and pies to be coined for all India.

Resolution VI. of 1847.—Cents, ½, and ¼ cents to be coined for the Straits Settlements.

Resolution XI. of 1854.—½ pyce to be coined.

Resolution XVII. of 1855.—Company's double, single, and ½ pyce to be legal tender in the Straits.

Resolution XIII. of 1862.—A new silver and copper coinage for British India. The rupee to be called the "Government rupee."

ORDERS OF GOVERNMENT TO THE MINT MASTER RELATIVE TO THE COINAGE.

July 1, 1833.—Authorizing the coinage of Furruckabad rupees of 180 grains at the Calcutta Mint.

July 1, 1833.—Authorizing the formation of a new system of weights with a tola of 180 grains as the unit.

December 1833.—To charge a duty of only 1 per cent on the re-coinage of rupees struck in any of the Government Mints in India.

May 15, 1834.—To credit the excess of fineness in rupees of the late coinage under the head of "gain in the assay of late standard rupees melted."

May 15, 1834.—Not to charge Collectors for the refinage of their under-standard coins.

June 1834.—Table of the intrinsic value of new gold and silver coins. Vide *Government Gazette.*

July 1834.—Mint Master to have power to levy duty of 4 rupees on gold and 2 rupees on silver withdrawn after assay.

March 1835.—Orders the introduction of the new system of weights in all the branches of the public service.

May 1836.—Government Regulation for the abolition of the Sicca rupees as a legal tender.

May 1836.—Mint open for the receipt of Tirsoolee pyce, 72 for 64 Company's pyce.

January 1837.—Constituting Mint Officers the judges of the fitness or unfitness of old pyce for circulation, and genuine old worn pyce are to be received at the Government treasuries from individuals.

April 1837.— To coin two-anna pieces of silver.

June 1837.—Court of Directors order a modification in the Resolution of Government of July 1834, and order fees to be invariably levied on bullion withdrawn after assay. The test of ringing should be always applied to coins issued from the Mint, but not to legal coin tendered by individuals.

August.—Collectors forwarding remittances to the Mint allowed the option of deputing a podar, appointing an agent in Calcutta, or leaving the charge of taking the remittances to Mint Officers.

August.—Not to manufacture any other weights than those of the legal standard.

November.—To reduce the seignorage on gold from 2 per cent to 1 per cent, and refinage charge only on actual cost.

November.—To grant licenses to podars for exchanging pyce.

February 1838.—Authorizing the Mint to issue to licensed podars 64½ pyce to the rupee, and to receive from them old pyce on the same terms, provided they sell to the public at 64, and authorizing them to purchase old pyce from the public at 65 for the rupee.

March.—To receive Madras rupees at par.

May.—To receive, free of duty, rupees coined in any of the Company's Mints, and still legally current in any part of India.

May 20, 1840.—Contains sundry directions regarding the copper coinage from the Court of Directors.

October 1840.—Court of Directors repeat their orders of June 1837, regarding the test of ringing, and that the fee for bullion withdrawn should be uniformly levied.

December 1840.—Government proclamation for the coinage of the new Victoria rupee.

January 1841.—The Mint has no right to reject any coins unless they are upon examination found unfit for coinage.

January.—The Court of Directors prohibit the Mint from trading in bullion, and direct that no other than the new standard gold-mohur be coined.

January.—Proclamation of Government notifying the device, weight, standard, wearage allowance, of the new gold coin.

July 1841.—Again authorizing the coinage of two-anna pieces.

August.—Directing that refining charges are to be levied according to the rates fixed in Regulation IV. of 1818 and VII. of 1838.

October.—To deduct in future from the profit of the copper coinage the loss arising from the re-sale of old copper coin.

January 1842.—To receive all legal pyce from any of the Government functionaries, having treasuries of receipt in Calcutta.

January 1842.—Prescribing one uniform rate of refinage charge for the Mints in India.

February 1843.—Directs Mint to receive all old copper pyce.

February 1843.—Directing the simultaneous issuing of assay certificates and Mint Master's advice to the Sub-Treasurer.

February.—To adopt measures for removing the Furruckabad and Madras rupees from circulation, and rules for the reception at the public treasuries.

October 1843.—The certificates for bullion delivered on the eve of holidays to bear date of the first working day.

February 1844.—To credit N. W. Collectors with the value at par of full weight rupees.

March 1845.—Authorizing the coinage of double pyce.

March 1845.—Government order for the reception of old pyce, to receive those that retain some portion of the Government inscription, and to reject those that have no trace of the original inscription.

September 1845.—To coin cents for the Straits Settlements.

February 1846.—To confiscate all base coins found in Collector's remittances.

May.—Not to return Collector's rejected pyce.

March 1847.—Base coins, when found in Collector's remittances, Remitting Officers to have the option of taking them back or leaving them at the Mint to be credited with their actual value.

April 1847.—All bullion (except Government coins) to be melted, instead of being cut and burnt, previous to receipt.

June 1848.—Orders all Government bullion (coins included) to be first melted, and the charges for converting them into ingots to be borne by the Mint.

February 1848.—The Court of Directors recommend the substitution of small silver coin for copper coin as much as possible.

March 1849.—Not to levy duty on Hyderabad rupees when received from public functionaries.

April 1849.—To have recourse to bazar refiners to refine all base coins.

April 18, 1849.—From the Mint Master in reply to Mint Committee, furnishing such information as it is in his power to afford regarding the copper currency of Bengal.

June 1852.—Government resolve, that minimum weights for the present rupees and half rupee, which have diminished by wear more than 2 per cent, be issued to Officers in charge of treasuries.

July 2, 1852.—Explains the cause of discrepancies in the size and embellishment of the silver coinages of the three Presidencies.

October 1852.—Mint Master recommending the coining of half and quarter pyce.

December 1852.—The Mint Committee recommends the above, as they will no doubt be acceptable to the public.

1854.—Half pyce are ordered to be coined.

1862.—The Mint authorized to sell pyce at 68 for the rupee.

Its Utility to the Country.

THE effects of Commerce upon the general civilization of the world are too manifest to escape observation. Wherever it has flourished, nations have enjoyed prosperity and plenty; and refinement and liberty have naturally followed. Commerce changes the character of a people: it dissipates crooked and mistaken notions: it produces a more expansive liberality of mind: it increases social intercourse, and teaches man his true rights. If this is, and has been the case with nations of the Western World, may not the same results be looked for here, at least so far as is compatible with the Asiatic character? It is true Europeans must be the pioneers:—but it is their privilege and *mission* to be so; and certainly, both to the philanthropist and merchant, there never was displayed a wider field than that now laid open by the removal of restrictions placed upon the general and extended colonization of the country.

The Commerce of India is undoubtedly increasing every year, but it has yet a wide range to accomplish. The internal trade is as backward as if it were still in its infancy; but it merely requires a period of tranquillity—a cessation from those intestine wars and commotions, which have hitherto kept the people both abject and poor, together with protection to property and person:—the usual concomitant of good government:—to give scope to enterprize and capital. Rich in soil, and in the productions of the earth, when properly attended to; with cheapness of labor, accessible rivers, and improved land carriage, affording convenience of transport—all that is required to stimulate the population to exert themselves, is capital, which, while reducing the usurious rate of interest, shall yet find a safe and profitable investment.

Nowhere is the investment of income more certain of good return, or more likely to be blessed than here. India has boundless resources, which merely require to be developed. If she has been hitherto a smaller producer than she might have been, it is owing to her being destitute of accessible markets for her surplus productions, in consequence of the *rudeness* of her productions. Every process, both in agriculture and manufactures, has been conducted with immense waste and want of ingenuity. The most simple methods of saving toil have been unknown. Husbandry is in a backward condition, and the implements both rude, primitive, and of the clumsiest construction. In fact, almost everything that is the produce of Indian rural labor is, when compared with that of people in a more civilized and favorable state of society, crude and unmarketable. There is, probably, no country in the world that has made such slow progress as India, when her antecedents are considered. Formerly, the natives of the soil, both morally and intellectually, stood higher than they do now, and excelled in all departments of science. But from this they have so completely, and for such a length of time declined, that it is difficult to believe that improvements in agriculture and manufactures were of very great antiquity in the provinces of Bengal.* Indeed, were there not evidences of the truth of this statement, it would be scarcely possible to view it in any other light than as a jest, so completely have the implements of husbandry and agriculture, as well as the manufactures of the country, been stationary for centuries.

The state of the useful arts is scarcely more advanced than agriculture—probably little more so than it was a hundred years back :—and it is hopeless to expect much improvement until European skill and science shall be more extensively diffused over the country. There is, however, no absence of natural genius, nor want of

* Adam Smith's "Wealth of Nations," lib. i., cap. iii.

conception in the people; and if only they will not allow their caste, (another name for idleness,) and their absurd religious prejudices, to raise difficulties and bar out the instructions of English science, an altered state of things may be anticipated. Until prohibitory rates of duty were placed on Dacca muslins—until Manchester and Paisley fabrics, of the same class, were admitted at lower rates of duty—what could compete with the former manufactures and the shawls of Cashmere, exquisitely delicate, and alike tasteful in fabrication and design? And what ingenuity could surpass the chaste workmanship of Delhi, Benares, Cuttack, and Trichinopoly in the precious metals?

"But for the future welfare of India," says a writer, "there is hope."* When the steam engine shall have traversed the country from one end to the other, satisfactory results may be looked for. New wants will be created: her myriads will look to our work-shops and factories for the implements of toil and the adornments of luxury: capital, which is necessary to promote production, will find an outlet: opportunities will be afforded of employing it safely and profitably; and internal trade will consequently be stimulated and enlarged. It is from the absence of capital, properly directed, and from the want of those aids and appliances which are absolutely essential to the success of every country, that the resources of India remain to this day almost unknown. Until the commercial and agricultural interests of the country are properly advanced: until a considerable improvement take place in the products of the soil and in the implements of labor—her manufactures have little chance of being placed on a par with those of Europe.

---

* Introduction to Nolan's "British Empire."

And, foremost in the rank of those means that require to be used for a thorough development of India's resources, railroads must, as already stated, take a promiment stand. Before this mighty innovator, the oppressive barriers of caste will be thrown down; races, hitherto unknown to each other, will be approximated; and the internal commerce of the country, for many years depressed, will be fully opened out. Under the vivifying influence of British energy and capital, which a wider colonization will introduce; with good roads, good tramways, good feeders, and a sufficiency of steam on the rivers—trade and manufactures must make a step forward. If the waste lands, which Lord Canning's statesmanlike Resolution made attainable on fee simple, be taken up and properly cultivated, the enterprize and skill, which will be brought to bear, will result in improvements such as European capital and energy can alone effect; and conduce to the material and moral advantage of large classes of the people. India has long suffered from the exclusiveness and monopoly of the East India Company. The senseless restrictions placed by that Corporation upon Europeans holding lands in the Mofussil, is one of the primary causes why the country has been retarded in her agricultural and commercial pursuits. Had there been a less restrictive policy, as well as less jealousy shown by the covenanted servants of the Company towards those whom *they* term *interlopers*, India would, at this time, have been in a position to render England independent of the United States' cotton. The fear of being dispossessed, and the dread of a too early enlightening of the natives, by leading the Government to oppose all attempts to improve the country, have obstructed the natural increase of capital, and, so far, tended to diminish the sum total of the revenue.

Colonization and capital then are the great *desiderata* for India.

By means of the former, the inland trade will be extended; commerce will increase commerce; and, although the area of territory is so vast, the progress of railways will influence both the money market and the development of the resources. By new facilities, new wants and new desires will be created; and neither climate, religion, nor long-established habits, will refuse the benefits thereof.

By means of the latter—both the cause and result of industry—improvements will be made: better machinery will be introduced, and appliances, which involve considerable outlay, will be brought to bear. Without money, commercial operations must, naturally, be stinted and embarrassed. It is too much, however, to expect that any individual who shall embark his capital, whether it be money, machines, instruments of trade or other materials, can, however extensive his means, carry on his plans, on any large scale, without pecuniary assistance. And here it is that the utility of Banks will be apparent, in rendering active and productive that capital which it is their province to accummulate and distribute. Dr. Smith says, "The judicious operation of Banking enables the dealer to convert his dead stock into active and productive stock; into materials to work upon; into tools to work with, and into provisions and subsistence to work for; into stock which produces something both to himself and to his country."* By "providing a sort of wagon way through the air, it enables the country to convert, as it were, a great part of its highways into good pastures and corn-fields, and thereby to increase, very considerably,

* "Wealth of Nations," lib ii., cap. ii., p. 131.

the annual produce of its land and labor."* But it will do even more in this country. Banking will step in and relieve the borrower from the crushing effect of usurious dealings with the native money-lenders—a class of people the most grasping, relentless, and unprincipled to be found in any country. It will counteract the mischievous consequences, and the pernicious habit—so congenial to the natives—of burying money, or convert-it into jewels for women and children—the fruitful cause of so many murders: it will bring forth and vivify millions of capital that lie dormant in the earth, or in secret hiding-places:† while, by increasing the

* "Wealth of Nations," lib ii., cap. ii., p. 131.

† The eagerness of the natives for gold and silver ornaments will account, in a great measure, for the great importation of silver, and its disappearance in India, which PLINY aptly terms "the sink of the precious metals." The extent to which hoarding has been, and, in the Upper Provinces, is still practised, is almost incredible. Money-lenders generally keep their whole fortune, in coin, hidden about the house, and merely produce it when needed. Rich natives hoard as well as poor. Some years back, the King of Oude had half a million sterling secreted in coin. At Benares, a Rajah had a quarter of a million. Runjeet Singh, in the Punjab, one million. The late King of Ava a million and a half. When Scindia's fort was taken, there was found at least a quarter of a million. At the siege of Bhurtpore, one million is said to have been found by the British troops. At the taking of Seringapatam one million was found: and, it is positively asserted, that when the Emperor SHAH JEHAN died, he left no less a sum, in coin, than 24 millions sterling, all wrung from his impoverished subjects.

In the early part of 1856, Colonel Sykes, the Chairman of the East India Company, published an interesting paper *on the External Commerce of British India*, in which occurs the following passage:—"The excess of exports (from India) over imports is constant, owing to the gradual improvement in the producing powers of the country, and the small wants and hoarding habits of the natives in their present low state of civilization. * * * Within the present century, India has received above 100,000,000 £ Sterling, which has never left the country." The silver received has been chiefly in coin, yet it has not in any appreciable manner affected prices. There is little doubt but that just before the mutiny of 1857-58, the expectation, throughout the country, of some great and terrific event, led to a more than ordinary absorption and secretion of the precious metals, which were converted into bracelets, anklets, ear-rings, necklaces, and waist-bands, as the safest mode in which treasure could be preserved. At the late sale of *Kirwee* prize property by Messrs. Hamilton and Co., there were to be found massive silver trappings of an elephant with chains sufficiently thick and large to serve as the ground tackling of a vessel of twenty-five tons.

advantages of accumulation, and making saving available, as well for immediate profit as for a future resource, it will add new strength to the spirit of industry and to the principle of cumulation.

Its Existing Condition.

THE increase of Banking Institutions in this country is one of the most remarkable characteristics of the age. No single feature in the Commercial aspect of the Asiatic Peninsula is more observable than the growth of these establishments, which are now assuming a very prominent place amongst the Colonial institutions of the Empire, and attracting the attention of a large and influential class in Europe—men who see, in this country, a luxuriant field for the culture of Banking.

The change we have alluded to has occurred at a time the most propitious for the investment of capital. Our internal improvements: our increased facilities of land and water carriage: a greater feeling of security in the country of our adoption, and the removal of many of those obnoxious restrictions upon trade and commerce, which formerly paralysed the exertions of the older settlers—encourage the investment of capital in undertakings holding out the promise of a good and safe return. Every rupee laid out on our railroads, rivers, and canal communication is sowing the country with the seeds of wealth—wealth equal to the Californian and Australian mines, and to be found in the yet undeveloped resources of this splendid Continent.

Banking establishments, from the facilities they afford for raising money, are well calculated to induce men of capital to embark in commercial and agricultural operations which promise fairly. India has, hitherto, been greatly deficient in Banking capital, and the jealousy of *interlopers*, ever shown by the covenanted servants of Government, has not tended to allure the independent capitalist from the shores of Europe. It is true much British capital has, of late years, found its way to India to the great advantage of both countries; but the best mode of introducing it is unquestionably by the application of a sound and liberal system of Banking, the first and best principle calculated to draw out the resources of a country, and to elevate it to commercial importance, affluence, and independence. Money affects, vitally, all questions, and if Banking be regarded as the medium of collecting and distributing money, every man must be satisfied of its importance.

It has always been a matter of surprise that, with the quantity of capital hitherto embarked in Banking in this country, the amount of deposits and circulation should have borne so low a proportion to those of the joint-stock Banks of England. Until the transfer of the Government business to the Bank of Bengal, the amount of its deposits seldom averaged over EIGHTY-FIVE LACS, or Pounds sterling 850,000—a trifle under 80 per cent on the paid-up capital—a vast difference between eight and eleven millions sterling generally held by the Union Bank of London, the London and Westminster Bank, and some few others. Possibly, a partial explanation is to be given in the peculiar commercial and social circumstances of India. A protracted residence in this country was, formerly, never thought of, and those who did expatriate themselves, looked around for some means whereby they might realize a rapid fortune or competency and go home. Hence numbers invested the savings of their salaries and other capital in various descriptions of productive employment, so that there was in fact no room for deposits in Banks, all surplus being taken from the country or locked up in the different loans opened by Government. But a more natural solution of the singularity may be found in the paucity of the European element in the country, relatively to the native: the preference shown by the natives for investments in landed property, (whereby their family status is advanced), and the practice of hoarding and burying metals in the earth, elsewhere referred to—a practice, doubtless, produced by a deep feeling of insecurity arising out of the tyranny and rapacity so frequently exercised by the native chieftains over the lower classes of the people. It has been noticed, as a remarkable fact, that the natives, who so greatly out-number Europeans, are not to be found—in their relative proportions—such extensive investors in the Government Stocks as our own countrymen, except for speculative or temporary purposes. This may be attributed to the practice above noticed, and to doubts of the stability of the British rule in India; but it may likewise be traced to the wider field they possess for investment, arising from their superior knowledge of details and localities, which enables them to place their funds more advantageously. It also accounts for the higher rate of interest among them. But whatever may be the cause, the consequences are most mischievous, both in the direct loss of capital which it involves, and still more in its indirect influence in preventing the formation of a spirit of emulation and enterprize.

Reverting, however, to the subject from which we have slightly departed—although the Banking profits in India have hitherto left nothing to desire, so far as the proprietary body are concerned—it must be clearly understood that these profits were not the consequence of deposits, but owed their existence to a high rate of interest, principally induced by a certain degree of risk, and the difficulty in obtaining securities of an unquestionable character. Everybody who has given the subject any thought must be aware that Banking deposits are a source of profit, and tend considerably to swell the earnings of a Bank. The well-known political economist *Ricardo* says:—" A Bank would never be established if it produced no other profits than those derived from the employment of its own capital: *the real advantage of a Banker commences only when he begins to employ the capital of others.*"* Capital is the moving power of commerce—the fuel which communicates to its machinery the means of propulsion. In order therefore to draw out the capabilities of a country and the energies of a people, there must be capital—not Bank paper, which, though only *currency*, and merely the representative of capital, is mistaken for one of the chief commodities of a Banker; but capital which consists of whatever is the net produce of former labor. The creators of Banking capital are various; timid people, who have not the disposition to enter personally into trading pursuits—the depositors of small sums—the owners of large credit balances, and the recipients of large incomes, whose accounts, at periodical times, present an available fund to the Banker. These are the people who supply him with the capital he administers, which

* "Principles of Political Economy," by D. Ricardo.

may be considered that part of the floating wealth of the country, not yet invested in trade, or otherwise locked up. Between themselves (the *non-producing* or lending class) and the *producing* (borrowing) class, Bankers are the middlemen, who, by means of funds raised from private capital (which may be reckoned as the paid-up capital), Banking capital (deposits and current balances), and circulation capital, carry on their business.

"The functions of a Bank in the Commercial body," says a writer, "resemble those of the heart in the human body. It attracts to itself capital, and propels it through all the arteries and channels of Commerce;"* and, further on, the same author remarks that the beneficial effects of Banking "are produced, not by the number of Banks, but by the number of people who keep Banking accounts."† The extension, therefore, of the Banking principle in India will afford to the native merchants and cultivators of the soil the means of safely and profitably investing their spare funds, without being exposed to any hazard whatever.

Having stated what the means are at the disposal of a Banker, it remains merely to show the channels through which ready capital operates. These are Cheques, Post Bills, Letters of Credit, Promissory Notes, and Bills of Exchange. The first are issued against ready capital in payment of commodities: the last absorb and employ ready capital to a great extent. With the deposits of their customers or their own notes (if Banks of issue), Bankers discount mercantile bills, and grant loans, from which they principally derive their profits. Some

* "Macleod's Theory and Practice of Banking," Vol. II., p. 209.

† Ibid, p. 216.

Banks, in order to encourage deposits, give interest upon the daily balance of their account current, and such are those generally carried on under the Scotch system. The advantage to the depositors in this system is great; for the money which would otherwise remain unemployed at home becomes productive to them.

The existing Banking establishments of India may be separated into two classes, *viz.* Banks of Deposit and Discount and Banks of Exchange and Remittance. Again, they may be divided into Banks located at the Presidencies and principal seats of Commerce, and those scattered over the interior of the country. The only Banks, strictly of deposit, are the Savings' Banks, which receive the deposits of their customers, but do not trade with them. *They* make no profit. The old Government Agency,* created in 1832, by Lord William Bentinck, to relieve the distress and anxiety caused by the Commercial Crisis of the years 1829—30, though not called a Bank, was, to all intents and purposes, one of deposit, making no profits. Its business was transferred to the Bank of Bengal in 1856. The Banks of Bengal, Madras, and Bombay, incorporated by Charter, and numbering among their shareholders the Indian Government, discharge the functions both of Banks of deposit and discount, and are engaged in supplying temporary advances to those engaged in trade or business, and discounting their bills: from these operations they make their greatest profits. They have not, in any sense, a monopoly of the business of Banking, but their long

* This Agency was actually established in 1810, under charge of the Accountant-General and Sub-Treasurer; but in 1832, after the failure of the large Agency houses, a separate Agent was appointed to give his whole attention to it. In 1855, the Agency was abolished under Government Orders published in the "Calcutta Gazette" of 27th January 1855.

connection with Government confers on them a certain prestige which operates in their favor, especially among the native community. The Oriental Bank Corporation—the Agra and United Service Bank*—the Commercial Bank of India—the Chartered Mercantile Bank of India, London and China—the Chartered Bank of Australia, India and China—the Central Bank of Western India—and the French Comptoir d'Escompte, though doing a considerable business in deposits and discounts, are principally Exchange and Remittance Banks, purchasing bills and drawing against them; and transmitting money, by means of their Agencies or Branches, as well as by their own bills. The Banks in the Mofussil—the Delhi Bank—the Simla Bank—the Punjab Bank—the Uncovenanted Service Bank—combine the character of the Presidency Banks. They are Banks of deposit and discount, exchange and remittance. All the present Indian Banks hold prominent places and are respectively entitled to the confidence of the public; not only from the high respectability of the proprietary body, whose confidence they enjoy, but from the honorable character of their conductors, who are second to none of the same profession in Europe. This is not saying too much nor more than strictly true, and is, we assert, due to them; for, after the discreditable failure of the Union Bank of Calcutta, the disgraceful fraud of the Benares Bank, the delinquencies of the North-Western Bank of India, and the rascality of the London and Eastern Banking Corporation (an offshoot

* We think it right to correct a very glaring mistake which Dr. E. W. Nolan has fallen into, in his work on the "British Empire in India," in stating that the establishment of the Agra Bank was followed by that of the Bank of Bengal.

of the Simla Bank)*—the Commercial and Banking morality of India—Calcutta in especial—have been loudly called in question.

The Banks of Bengal, Madras, and Bombay are closely connected with the Government, and are known as "Chartered or Government Banks." They receive deposits, advance money on tangible securities, discount bills, issue their own post bills, and engage in exchange operations *in India*, to which they are confined by their Charters.† By the agreement with Government (dated 3rd January 1862) they receive and make all payments, both at the Presidencies and all over the country, wherever they have established Agencies, and manage, to a certain extent, the Government currency at an annual charge. As an experiment, the Banks of Madras and Bombay have directed their Agencies to receive deposits on the system of the Scotch Banks, and to allow interest on them. The joint-stock, or unchartered Banks, deal largely in exchange operations in every quarter (from which they principally derive their profits), discount bills, and receive deposits at fixed rates of interest.

As the fullest particulars, in detail, will be given of all these Banks, with their working, in another part of this publication, we shall only now briefly notice in what respect their operations will be found beneficial to the country. The failure of the great Agency and Banking firms of Calcutta, the most extensively ruinous and

---

* No reflection on the Simla Bank is intended here. The object is merely to bring in the London and Eastern Banking Corporation as an *Indian* institution.

† The new Charter of the Bank of Bengal (Act IV. of 1862) allows the Bank to draw Bills of Exchange and grant Letters of Credit payable out of India for the use of their constituents in the Agency Department, and to buy Bills payable out of India for the purpose of remitting funds to meet such Bills or Letters of Credit. (Clause XXVIII. of the Charter.)

distressing series of mercantile calamities that probably ever fell upon a country, and the impress of which is still felt up to and even beyond Patna, inflicted on the Officers of the Civil and Military Services of the country, as well as on other residents, losses much greater than the entire capital of several of the Mofussil Banks, and withdrew a large amount of accommodation, which was already far too little for the wants of the country, and which could not well be spared. The gap was filled up by the Mofussil Banks, but as they were principally established with a view to assist the Services, they had no available capital for making advances to the mercantile and agricultural portion of the community, nor encouraging, by timely assistance, the increasing body of Europeans in the different professional pursuits in which they were embarking. At the high rate of interest charged by the native shroffs, recourse to them was out of the question, for no successful undertaking could have any chance of succeeding, or, at all events, of making a suitable return.

In the Mofussil, the Banks which formerly engrossed the whole monetary transactions of the interior will now divide the field with the Branches of the Chartered Banks, which are prepared to extend to all classes that accommodation, the want of which has been so long felt. By means of these Banks and Branches, the usurious rate of internal exchange will be broken down. Remittances can now be made all over the country; facilities will be afforded to the trader, the agriculturist, and the speculator; and thus will be at once removed the complaint against the Presidency Banks, that, having no Branches or subordinate establishments in any part of the country, the sphere of their operations is entirely limited to the scene of their formation. The day has gone by when the charge brought against the Chartered Banks of being notoriously incompetent to the proper transaction of the Banking affairs of India, can be maintained; at least, so far as the Bank of Bengal is concerned, we hesitate not to say that, under the present guidance, the future of this institution cannot but be prosperous. All who are engaged in raising indigo, sugar, silk, cotton, rice, and other staples of the country, as well as merchants purchasing goods in the interior, are short of capital, and require advances to enable them to prosecute their business. These advances Banks in the Mofussil will be in a position to give, until such time as the produce of their crops or sales comes to hand: not by an expensive transfer of specie from one part of a dangerous country to another at an enormous expense, but by the simplest of all means—discounting bills; by loans and cash credits; and by granting orders or credits on different parts of the country, thereby giving incalculable facilities to commerce. It is not therefore too much to assert that, sooner or later, these institutions will acquire a large proportion of the Mofussil business, which, for so long a period, has been confined to the native Bankers or *Shroffs*.

In former years,—before there were any European Banks in the interior,—the shroffs, who have their agents established in every important city, conducted their exchange operations by means of *hoondees*, which were the only currency not legalized, and as such superseded, in general payments, the use of metallic money. But when hoondees were not available, the medium of exchange was coin, and sealed bags containing 1,000 and 500 rupees were, and still are, even now in some parts, passed from place to place. These metallic payments were extensive, but there is scarcely an instance on record of the bags being found to contain less than the declared amount. The greatest difficulty therefore was experienced in procuring the necessary funds for manufacturing, &c., and merchants, who wished to place money in any particular district, were compelled either to purchase bills on the Government treasuries or hoondees. Remittance by bullion, in the case of private individuals or firms, was seldom resorted to, except where stations were contiguous to Calcutta, and communication easy of access. More than one case could be instanced in which the leading commercial firms of Calcutta had occasion, for years, to forward large sums to Moorshedabad and Kishnaghur, as well as to accept bills drawn on them from thence, for advances to their indigo and silk constituents. In almost all instances these constituents were compelled to draw at a considerable percentage as *shroffage*, or the firms were obliged to send up treasure under an escort. In nearly every instance, probably to the extent of *three-fourths* of the whole advances, the agents found it necessary to adopt the latter course, as from the scarcity of money with the native Bankers, the charges were most exorbitant. In one instance we could mention a premium of 3 rupees per cent per month, equal to 36 per cent per annum, has been paid for bills on a mercantile house in Calcutta, and the premium on Bank of Bengal Notes is known to have been as high as 6 and 8 annas per cent.

In regard to bills, it was not always that the Government were in a position to cash them, consequently hoondees were pretty extensively taken, and, in the absence of any thing better, proved a most convenient mode of remitting funds. The circulation of these hoondees—the most perfect portion of the Indian commercial system—was very great, and although millions were invested in them, the loss by bad debts, arising out of the dishonor of the instruments at maturity, was a most insignificant fraction per cent. The terms for which hoondees were, and still continue to be drawn, in the Upper Provinces, vary considerably. At Patna, for instance, the term is 41 days after date; Benares, Mirzapore, Lucknow, and Bombay draw at 51 days; Futtehghur, Furruckabad, and Delhi at 61 days; Lahore and Mooltan at 121 days. But these usances must, and will alter with the extension of the railroad.

The exchange is regulated here, as in every country, by the demand and supply; but we think it has been clearly shown that the placing of funds inland has averaged considerably over the same charge in England—a fact which can only lead to the inference, that a sufficient number of Banking establishments, possessing large Banking capital and other resources, are absolutely necessary to supplant the native exchanges, and to furnish a cheaper means of carrying on the commercial business of the country. The capacities of India are illimitable, and it requires no prophetic eye to see and appreciate the wonderful change which an enlarged system of Banking is destined to produce. The quelling of the mutiny of 1857-58 has done much towards enlightening the minds of the natives of this country, and if they *can* only be brought fairly to see that Banking, on an extended scale, affords new and unknown facilities for the accumulation of capital, they may be led to the conviction that the support of such institutions is alike conducive to their wealth, their tranquillity, and their security.

The Advantage of keeping a Banker.

A VERY few words may be necessary on this head before passing on to the history of the Indian Banks. The subject has been so often handled by able men, that it would be of little avail to notice it here, were it not that, this being we believe the first work of the kind that has been put forth in this country, it may not be out of place to treat of it.

A great advantage is gained by keeping a Banker. Formerly, before Banking was appreciated as it now is, people were in the habit, either of entrusting their money to the care of some specious speculative friend, or keeping it locked up at home, either in bank-notes or coin, by which they were subjected to all kinds of chicanery, and to losses by fire, robbery, &c. No such contingencies can by any possibility arise to those who employ Banking establishments for their deposits, and much good accrues to the rising generation by encouraging them in habits of economy, thoughtfulness, and prudence. In the case of Scotch Banks—or Banks carried on under that system—the depositor derives a double benefit; for every farthing he pays in earns a fixed rate of interest and goes to swell his savings. It is a great pity that the system of Scotch Banking is not more generally followed, for it tends, more than anything else, to the cultivation of industrious habits and sobriety of conduct. It has the effect of calling in all the surplus capital of a town or district, leaving merely what is sufficient for actual payment. In no part of the world has Banking thrived so much as in Scotland, and this is due to the effective manner in which it is carried on.*

* "General Principles of Banking," by W. J. Norfolk, p. 10.

The prudent clerk, the industrious trader, the careful agriculturist, and generally those of the saving class who are storing up funds for some definite purpose, are those who have their interests entwined with prudently conducted Banks. Their homes, their implements of husbandry, and their apparel, all testify to the improvement brought about by a resort to Banks.

But an equally important benefit to the depositor is the facility it gives in making payments. If he desire to transmit money from one part of the country to another, he can go to his Banker, who will either give him a draft on one of his Branches, or establish a credit for him with some agent, and thus is he saved all the trouble, anxiety, and risk of forwarding notes or coin. Again, in making his payments, he has only to draw a cheque against his account to the order of his creditor, and he is thus saved the chance of paying a bill twice over (which *has* happened in Calcutta); for the entry of payment is made in his pass-book, which, if he be not a methodical and business man, serves him as a cash-book, in which can be traced all his deposits and disbursements. If he has money to receive either in cheque to his order, or in bills, or in simple receipts of money payable to him as dividends by any Joint Stock Company, he has only to indorse the same to his Banker, who takes upon himself all the care and responsibility of collection, and becomes liable for any *laches*. When he requires money for his family expenses, he has only to draw a cheque for the exact amount he wants.

If this be the case with an individual, how much more important is it to the man, or firm of large dealings. These have another great advantage in keeping a Banker. If they are desirous of ascertaining the standing and character of a certain person, in some distant part of the country, who is anxious to enter into business relations with them, but is unknown, they ask their Banker to make the necessary enquiries, which he does from his agents, if he have any, or from some reputable person resident in the locality, who will never refuse to a respectable Banker the information thus solicited *under secresy.* If the depositor be about to take a journey, or leave his residence for a time, he is entitled to the utmost assistance from his Banker, who will take charge of his plate chest, title-deeds of property and other valuable papers, which there might be a risk in leaving behind him. If the depositor require temporary pecuniary accommodation, the Banker will refer to his deposit account, and consider his moral character; and if the investigation prove satisfactory, the Banker will seldom refuse the aid asked for in moderation. No Bank cares to have dealings with rogues, impostors, and immoral men, but will discourage them to the utmost. "It is thus," says Gilbart, "that Bankers perform the functions of conservators of the commercial virtues,"* and there are few, we think, who will dissent from us in the assertion with which we set out, that there is a GREAT ADVANTAGE IN KEEPING A BANKER.

On the Management of a Bank.

MANAGEMENT of a Bank! How much is involved in the expression. How difficult for those who are unacquainted

* "Practical Treatise on Banking," p. 12.

with the principles of Banking to understand the full import of the term. How much evil and misery would be avoided if shareholders would set themselves a little more attentively to consider what is required of Directors and Secretary before they are nominated.

"The Directors" are a body of men chosen by the shareholders, from amongst themselves, to undertake the control and supervision of their affairs. This body is termed a "Board," and they are generally selected from their weight and influence in their respective societies, whether European or native; their wealth and stake in the Bank; and the independence of their character, which will prevent their being led by the opinions of others against their own judgment. Before, however, they can be returned, it is absolutely necessary that they should qualify for the post by holding a certain number of shares, the amount of which is generally fixed in the Charter, Articles of Agreement, or whatever other covenant the shareholders enter into. Of course the greater the stake they hold, the greater the interest they feel in the success of the establishment.

The particular province of Directors is to inspect the accounts, to receive the report of the Manager or Secretary, and to take into consideration such matters as he may bring before them, affecting the welfare of the institution. For this purpose, they meet in consultation, on some stated day, when the operations of the week are laid before them. They then discuss questions affecting the money market, and the business in which the Bank is engaged. The Secretary, or chief officer, however designated, ought to be able to give correct information regarding the state of the money market during the previous week, and the general tone of business. He not merely records the decrees of the Board, but in every well regulated Bank his opinion is entitled to great weight in all the deliberations of the Board.

The Directors are responsible to the shareholders for what is done by their Secretary, and on very just grounds. They are bound to appoint a proper Manager, and if they give their official sanction to his proceedings, they adopt them as their own, and must abide by them. The shareholders, therefore, are perfectly right in paying peculiar attention to this appointment; for perhaps there is no other public act by which the Directors can exemplify their own fitness for office. The talents of Managers are very often a fair index of the talents of their Directors. If the Directors are a parcel of fools, the chances are a hundred to one that the Manager whom they appoint will also be a fool; for it is only by clever men that a clever man can be appreciated. As it is impossible for Directors to leave their own business pursuits altogether to attend to the Bank, they are compelled to entrust to their Manager or Secretary extensive discretionary powers, in the persuasion (from their estimate of his character) that he will not misuse them. Some Directors appoint one of their number to act as Managing Director, with a Secretary under him, but it is questionable whether the proceeding is a wise one; for it stands to reason that much must be left to the Secretary, and thus their offices may clash.

It is indispensable that every Bank should have a Consulting Committee to advise with the Manager, but beyond this they should not interfere. Practically speaking, the management *is* with the Secretary, *if* he can be confided in; but if his ignorance of business compel him, at every turn, to fly to a Director or the whole body for advice: in such case the Directors are justified in interfering more than is ordinarily expected of them. Directors are a sure shield to a Manager, for in carrying out any public measure, which may be open to animadversion, the *onus* rests on *them* and not on the Manager, who is absolved from all responsibility, because he can plead that he laid the question before the Board, and obtained their approbation and sanction.

In explaining the different duties and responsibilities of the delegate of the Directors, we shall use the terms Manager and Secretary as synonymous, confining ourselves to the *first*; for when a Secretary has no Managing Director over him, he is, to all intents and purposes, the chief officer—in fact, Manager; though he may be sometimes designated Secretary, Treasurer, or Cashier, Manager, and General Manager.

A Manager ought to be qualified, not only to subserve the interests of a monied establishment, but, if necessary, to lead the opinions of the Directors, who should not hesitate in placing the most implicit reliance on his judgment. He ought to be the referee in all cases of doubt or difficulty; in fact, to be the life and soul rather than the mere servant of a Bank—the prosperity of which depends, not upon the hastily acquired knowledge of an hour, but on the patiently and laboriously accumulated lessons of experience.

A Bank is not the mere bubble of a day—ascheme got up to satisfy some transitory caprice, or to effect some gigantic fraud; but an institution, the operations of which are defined by established principles, applicable to various phases of society. It requires an intimate acquaintance with these principles, not in their quiescent state, but in their active and efficient working, to qualify a person for the duties devolving upon the principal officer of a Banking establishment. He should know in what manner the funds of the institution can be most beneficially invested; whether in the promotion of commerce or in the encouragement of agriculture; and the exact proportion in which they ought to be supported. These capabilities can only be acquired by a long and patient investigation of the causes which influence the prosperity of nations, and the consequent motives which call into action the enterprize of individuals. A few months' poking into books, and referring to authorities, or even a little initiatory practice in detail,* are no more calculated to mould a man into a Banker, than a few months' drill in the mornings and evenings of the cold weather on the *maidan*, are calculated to mould a volunteer into a soldier.

The responsibilities of a Manager are multiform :—

1. His responsibility must be in proportion to his power. If a Manager be allowed no discretionary power—if he has only to obey the orders of the Directors, without taking any share in discussing their propriety or expediency, it is clear he cannot be made answerable for the wisdom or justice of those orders. If he be only a clerk in power, he can only be a clerk in responsibility. The constitution of a Bank assigns certain duties to the Manager, and certain other duties to the Directors. For the proper discharge of the duties assigned to him, the Manager is answerable, but not for the duties assigned to others.

2. A Manager is responsible for the exercise of his influential as well as his constitutional power. This

* We recollect hearing of an individual who, having for a few months kept some subsidiary book in a Bank, felt himself impressed with the belief that he was perfectly competent to undertake the management of a Bank.

influential power differs in many Banks. Much depends upon the personal character and qualifications of a Manager, as well as upon those of the Directors. We know institutions where the opinion of the Manager is deservedly received with the utmost respect, and with a conviction almost of its infallibility. In others it is treated with indifference or perhaps looked upon with suspicion and contempt. If, by the exercise of his influential power, a Manager bring the Bank into difficulties, he cannot turn round and defend himself by saying that he was merely the servant of the Directors.

3. A Manager is responsible for the soundness of his advice. It is the duty of a Manager to give advice to his Directors; and if he gives bad advice he is responsible for the result. He is not responsible, however, for the result of any measure which he may have advised, if as we have said a little higher up, the Directors adopted the measure, not *because* it was advised by the Manager, but because it seemed good in itself, and thus recommended itself for approval. The Manager, therefore, in such case, is responsible *only* to the extent to which his advice may have influenced the Directors. The Directors share in the responsibility, if, after examination, they become convinced of the propriety of the measure. But of course, if the Manager's advice did not influence the Directors at all, the Manager cannot *in the least* be considered responsibie.

4. A Manager is responsible for the measure he recommends as a whole. If a measure recommended by a Manager produces both advantages and disadvantages to the Bank, it is clearly unjust to reproach him for the bad effects of his advice, and give him no credit for those effects which are beneficial.

5. A Manager is responsible for the efficiency of those who are placed under his orders. This of course implies that he has the power of removing those who are *not* efficient—for power and responsibility must go together. And though it may not be proper, in all cases, that the Manager should have this power constitutionally, yet he must have it *influentially*, or his responsibility ceases. Having, however, procured the nomination of officers who are deemed efficient, he is not responsible for the mistakes, oversights, or frauds which they may commit, *unless* the previous character of the parties was such as ought to have awakened suspicion. Persons of respectability and of experience ought always to be obtained, and encouraged to remain in the establishment, by being rewarded in proportion to their ability and usefulness.* A Manager should himself be easy of access and agreeable in manners, carrying a mild persuasiveness about him that is of the utmost importance in communication with the public. He should be prompt, undecided in his measures, free from party influence, and firm in his purpose. Nothing makes a Manager look more silly or contemptible than a hesitating, dubious, and capricious manner. His answers ought to be prompt and satisfactory; he should say at once whether an act can be done or not; should appear free from restraint, and not disposed to alter an opinion when once formed.† He should consider it his duty to see that the customers are treated without insolence by the officers of the Bank; that expedition be used in the conduct of their business; and that any enquiries respecting their accounts be answered promptly

* "The Philosophy of Joint-stock Banking," by G. M. Bell, p. 72.

† Ibid, p. 41.

and civilly. It should be the object of the Manager and all those under his command, to attract business, and not, by insolence of office, to give customers a plea for not doing business with the Bank, or for withdrawing their existing accounts.

6. A Manager is responsible to his Directors, and not to the shareholders. He is appointed by the Directors, by whom he may be dismissed. It is clear, therefore, that he is responsible to *them*. It may be not only his right, but, occasionally, his duty to urge upon them his advice, to oppose their opinions, and even to protest against their proceedings; but, still he must, in all cases, obey their commands. In discharging his duty to the Directors, he does all that is required of him. Were he rendered responsible to the shareholders, the Directors would be virtually superseded, and the Manager rendered responsible to a body whose feelings, on many points, might be at variance with his own. It is only in the case of a very deficient Manager, and the supineness of the Directors, that the shareholders would be justified in interfering in order to ward off anticipated evils. Managers should not be too anxious to grasp at power, recollecting that by so doing they increase their responsibility. Directors should not be too anxious to abridge the power of the Manager, knowing that they thus take upon themselves the responsibility of which the Manager is relieved. When unfortunate events occur, shareholders should accurately discriminate as to the demerits of the respective parties, and be better able to "put the saddle on the right horse."

Finally, a Manager is bound to see that the system of book-keeping, in use in the Bank which he controls, is such as shall preserve a correct statement of the affairs of the Bank with the least possible trouble. A proper system of check is absolutely necessary, but it may be carried too far, and become annoying to the public. All Banks do not follow the same system; but there has been so much written, and there is so much known about it, that it is useless to go into details here. Still there *is* much ignorance abroad on the subject, and people of superficial acquirements are frequently to be found who condemn what they have not ability to fathom. The Scotch system is one of conciseness and beauty, and deserves the very high encomiums that have been passed upon it, from its readiness in affording the most immediate information of the state of every individual account.

The record of the frauds and delinquency of the Union Bank of Calcutta, the London and Eastern Banking Corporation, the Benares Bank, and the North-Western Bank, will, it is hoped, give some point to the above remarks. A good Manager is a blessing to a Bank; whereas an indifferent one, or one who is a mere tool in the hands of designing Directors, is a curse to an institution.

The Indian Banks.

In writing the history of the several Banks formerly and at present existing in the Presidencies of Bengal, Madras, and Bombay, in Ceylon, the Straits, and China, it will be more convenient to take them in the above order. We commence therefore with the

BANK OF BENGAL.

This Bank first opened for business on the 1st May 1806, under the name and style of the Bank of Calcutta, with a capital of Sicca Rupees 50,00,000, in five hundred shares of ten thousand Sicca Rupees each. The first Charter was granted on 2nd January 1809, during the government of Lord Minto, on which occasion the name was altered to that which it now bears, *viz.* The Bank of Bengal. Mr. J. W. Sherer, of the Bengal Civil Service, was appointed the Secretary.

The Charter declared :—

"That the affairs of the Bank shall be managed by nine Directors, *three* of whom shall be nominated by Government to represent their interest, (100 shares,) and *six* by the proprietors.

"That no person shall be entitled to vote who shall not be possessed of one share of the capital, registered as such in the Bank Books.

"That the presence of three Directors, at least, shall be necessary to constitute a Board to transact business.

"That dividends shall be determined by the Directors upon the grounds of the actual profits of the Bank, during the period for which such dividends shall be made.

"That upon giving only one year's notice, Government may put an end to the Corporation.

"That there shall be two General Meetings of the proprietors every year, when the Directors shall submit a statement of the transactions of the Bank."

The following gentlemen were the first Directors of the Bank under the Charter :—

HENRY ST. GEORGE TUCKER, ESQUIRE, *President.*
WILLIAM EGERTON, ESQ.
RICHARD WAITE COX, ESQ.

ALEX. COLVIN, ESQ.	JAMES ALEXANDER, ESQ.
JOHN PALMER, ESQ.	JOHN W. FULTON, ESQ.
GEORGE TYLER, ESQ.	MAHA RAJA SOOKMOY ROY.

The first three were the *ex-officio* Government Directors; the last six were elected at a public meeting, held at the Town Hall on 15th December 1808. Mr. W. Morton, C. S., whose name appeared on all the old notes of the Bank, was appointed Secretary on the retirement of Mr. Sherer. Mr. Henry Tyler was the first Accountant, and Ramchunder Rae the first Khazanchee.

The Bank is directly connected with, and, to a considerable extent, supported by the capital of the Government, who hold 275 shares of the value of Rupees 4,000 each. The management is vested in a Board of nine Directors. Of these, *six* are elected by the Proprietors, the other three being high officials of the Government, nominated, *ex-officio*, to watch over their interests. These last are, at the present time, the Secretary to Government in the Financial Department, the Accountant General to the Government of India, and a member of the Board of Revenue. Until the abolition of the General Treasury, the Sub-Treasurer to Government had always a place at the Board. The Directors meet, for the transaction of business, every Thursday morning, when they severally receive a fee of twenty-five rupees as a remuneration for the time and attention they give to the affairs of the Bank. The Secretary attends the weekly meetings.

A general meeting of proprietors is held, at the Bank, on the *first* Monday in the month of August, when the accounts of the Bank, closed to the 30th of June, are submitted.

Up to the close of February 1862, the Bank, under its old Charters, had the exclusive privilege of a circulation of bank-notes, which, although limited to two crores of rupees, seldom exceeded one crore and sixty lacs, except on a recent occasion, when it attained an average maximum of two crores and fifty lacs. For this infringement of the Charter, and to legalize the circulation to that extent, the Government passed a temporary Act, the Bank paying to the Government a commission of five per cent on the excess of the limit.

On 28th February 1862, the Government granted to the Bank a new Charter (Act IV. of 1862) without any limitation as to existence, Clause 2 declaring that "from and after the coming into operation of this Act, the present and future proprietors of the Bank of Bengal shall continue to be a body corporate with perpetual succession, and enjoy all the rights, privileges, and immunities incident to a corporation aggregate." On this occasion, the privilege of issuing notes was withdrawn from the Bank, Government having decided upon the introduction of a State Currency.

On the 1st March 1862, under special agreement with the Secretary of State for India in Council, and the Indian Government at Calcutta, the General Treasury at Calcutta was established at the Bank, in terms of the Notification published in the *Calcutta Gazette* of 3rd January 1862. Under this agreement, the business of receiving and paying money on behalf of the Supreme Government of India, and the Government of Bengal, heretofore transacted at the General Treasury at Fort William, was altogether vested in the Bank. From the same date an agency of issue was established at the Bank, which is now the agency for the Circle of Issue (of Calcutta,) under Act XIX. of 1861, for the issue, payment, and cashing of Government Currency Notes.

For this superintendence and management, the Bank is entitled to charge a commission calculated at the rate of three-fourths per cent per annum on the daily average amount of Government Currency Notes outstanding and in circulation through its agency at Calcutta. The Bank is bound to provide a separate office for the Head Commissioner of Issue, and may claim to be paid the cost of such office and any establishment that may be found necessary.

Much importance was very properly attached, by the mercantile and trading community, to the extension of a paper currency throughout India, but we think its advantages have been greatly over-rated. Confidence is of slow growth, and until the population get habituated to the new order of things, we do not look for a rapid or very large extension of the Government notes in the Mofussil. What India requires greatly, more than a paper currency, is a sound system of Banking, so as to break down the enormous internal exchange, and the usurious rates of interest, levied by the shroffs, as well as to aid the Goverment Currency. A permanent reduction in the rates of interest, hitherto exacted as a rule throughout India, would relieve commerce far more largely than any supposed advantages likely to arise from a note circulation. Capital would be greatly economised by the use of cheques and letters of credit. Facilities would likewise be afforded for the transaction of business which neither Government nor a Note Currency can ever afford. As matters recently stood, no one, looking to the amount of the exports and imports of India, can, for one moment, be in doubt as to the material progress made during the last twenty years, mainly with a silver currency. We question, indeed, if any other nation on the face of the earth can, during the same space of time, show like results. We are far from under-rating the convenience of a sound paper currency and the economy of capital, when freely confided in, which it affords; but we attach greatly more importance to an extension of Banking which we know, on the highest authority, has done so much for the material and social improvement of England and Ireland.

Under Clause 35 of the Charter the Bank commenced the establishment of Branches at Rangoon, Mirzapore, Benares, Patna, and Dacca. In the latter place there had been, for some time, an independent institution called the "Dacca Bank;" but, under the 37th Clause of the Charter, negociations were entered into with the shareholders, and the whole concern was purchased and taken over, the shareholders of the Dacca Bank receiving an equivalent for their shares in Bank of Bengal stock.

1809, January 7.—Rates fixed at 10 per cent per annum on Bills and Notes, and 9 per cent on Loans on deposit, with five per cent surplus. 19.—Under orders of Government, Securities of the East India Company, to the amount of 20 lacs, were indorsed to the Sub-Treasurer as a security for the credit given by Government to the Bank by the receipt of its notes. February 16.—Mr. Henry Stone appointed a Government Director in the room of Mr. Cox. July 6.—The Bank declared a dividend of nine and three-quarters per cent, or Sicca Rupees 488-4-6 per share.

From 1810 to the early part of 1812, the Bank dividends averaged about nine and three-quarters per cent per annum.

1812, July 2.—Dividend raised to ten per cent.

1813, September 4.—A fraud was brought to light. Eight bags, containing Rupees 1,200, were found missing from the treasure chests in the vaults. From this year to the early part of 1814, the rate of dividend did not exceed eight and a quarter, and eight and a half per cent.

1814, January.—Dividend eight and a half per cent. July 5.—Bank dividend increased to ten per cent.

1815, March 4.—Mr. Henry Wood, C. S., succeeded Mr. Morton as Secretary and Treasurer. Dividends this year ten and a half per cent. There was no change in the rates till 1818, when the dividends rose to twelve and three-quarters per cent.

1816, February 8.—Mr. Charles Morley, C. S., was appointed Secretary and Treasurer in place of Mr. Wood. Dividend ten and a half.

1819, January 7.—Bank dividend was at the rate of twelve and a half per cent. July 3.—At nine per cent.

1820, December 4.—Mr. W. H. Oakes, C. S., was appointed to officiate as Secretary and Treasurer during Mr. Morley's absence. The dividends this year averaged seven and three-quarters per cent.

1821, January 5.—Bank dividend reduced to a little under five and a half per cent. July 4.—Increased to six and a quarter per cent.

1822, March 12.—Mr. C. T. Glass was appointed to

officiate as Secretary and Treasurer. Dividends averaged six and a quarter per cent.

1823, January 2.—Mr. Glass was confirmed in the office of Secretary. The Bank Charter was renewed on 29th May (during the government of the Honorable John Adam), until the expiration of twelve months, notice to be given after the 31st December 1827, being an extension for five years. Dividends averaged over ten and three-quarters per cent.

1824, January 5.—In consequence of a fraud committed on the Bank, some time during the previous year, the dividends were reduced to two and a half per cent. One of the Company's Loan acknowledgments, upon which the Bank had advanced a sum of 40,000 rupees, was found to have been abstracted and re-pledged to the Bank, for the same amount, by a party representing himself as Soobul Chunder Dey. There was considerable mystery attending the circumstances, which neither Mr. Glass the Secretary, nor the Directors could fathom. The then khazanchee held jointly with the Secretary (as at present) the key of the iron chest in which the Company's Paper was deposited, but it is difficult to say how the abstraction occurred. In the investigation at the Police, suspicion rested on the head podar, one of the khazanchee's own people, but when the case came on before the Supreme Court, it was dismissed *from want of evidence.* The amount of the fraud was necessarily written off to Profit and Loss. Mr. Henry Henderson was appointed Accountant in the room of Mr. Tyler, who died. July 2.—Dividend a little over four and a quarter per cent.

1825, January 6.—Dividend under four per cent. July 7.—Dividend over eleven per cent.

The subjoined statement will show the average of the dividends during the following years:—

1826.—Fifteen and a quarter per cent.

1827.—Fourteen and three-quarters.

1828.—Ten and a quarter.

1829, January 5.—Dividend fourteen and a quarter. February 19.—Mr. J. A. Dorin, C. S., who had been officiating as Secretary and Treasurer, in the room of Mr. Glass, since 1826, was confirmed in the office. Rajkissore Dutt's forgeries attracted attention this year. The Bank advanced upon some forged Company's Papers tendered by him for loan. When the papers were taken, in the usual course, to the Secretary for the required advance, Mr. Dorin thinking he perceived some peculiarity in the printing, which excited his suspicion, sent the papers to the Treasury for examination, in accordance with an arrangement entered into with the Accountant General to the Government, in 1828, "that, as a security against fraud and forgery, as well as counterfeit securities, the Bank, before making any advance upon Government Promissory Notes, should send the notes themselves to the office of the Accountant General, to be verified by the Head Uncovenanted Assistant, who, after comparison with the office registers, was directed to certify to their correctness or otherwise." On their being returned with the assurance that all was right, Mr. Dorin, deeming further objection unjustifiable, passed them. The loan was renewed, but under the same precautions of that able officer, who still retained his suspicions. The result was the same. When the duplicate numbers turned up, the papers deposited with the Bank were *then only* discovered to be forgeries. The exactness of the signatures was so complete, that the public officers, whose names appeared on the papers, could not deny them to be genuine. It was very generally believed, at the time, that the signatures *were* genuine, but had been surreptitiously obtained; and in this opinion the Magistrate, who investigated the case, concurred. Mr. H. T. Prinsep, the Financial Secretary to Government, whose name was appended to the notes, when placed in the witness box in court, declared, when the notes were put into his hand, that he could not swear that the signatures were *not* his own. There is little doubt that duplicate notes were signed by him, and that, without looking at what he signed, he affixed his name to those *called* forgeries, which amounted to nearly seven lacs of rupees. Rajah * * * * * * * * *'s indorsement was on several of the papers, and there was sufficient evidence to show his signature to have been genuine, and that he participated in the amount raised on the notes. Government having declined to make good to the Bank the amount advanced upon the reputed forgeries, the matter was referred to the Court of Directors in England. July 2.—Dividend over fourteen and a quarter per cent.

1830, January 7.—Bank dividend nine per cent. July 8.—Eight per cent. These rates remained unaltered during the following year. August 26.—Mr. Richard Udny, C. S., was appointed to act as Secretary and Treasurer. November 4.—Mr. George Udny, C. S., succeeded his brother, who was compelled, by ill health, to resign his situation.

1832, January 5.—Dividend seven per cent. July 5. —Eight per cent.

1833, January 3.—Dividends seven per cent. Bank

discounted Government and Salary Bills at four per cent. Private Bills at six per cent. July 4.—Dividend reduced to six per cent.

1834, January 3.—Dividend six per cent. Bank discounted Government and Salary Bills at five per cent. Private Bills at seven per cent. February.—The Directors of the Bank having declined to receive and issue any more of the notes of the Union Bank, and determined upon confining themselves to their own issue, a protest, numerously signed by most of the mercantile and trading firms of Calcutta, was lodged at the Bank. The Directors, however, refused to yield, and explained the ground of their objection. June 30.—The Court of Directors of the East India Company having decided against the claim of the Bank to a refund of the amount advanced on Rajkissore Dutt's forgeries, no dividend was declared, the whole of the profits of the previous half-year being written off to Profit and Loss. The Bank brought its action against the Government in the Supreme Court, and lost it. A want of unanimity, however, on the part of the Judges, induced the Bank to appeal to the Privy Council, which confirmed the decision of the Lower Court. On its being known that no dividend would be made, Bank Stock fell from 6,000 rupees to 500 rupees premium, and even to *par*, so great was the consternation in the bazar. The excitement, however, was merely temporary, and tended only to benefit those who seized the opportunity to purchase all the Bank Shares they could meet with; for, the following year, the premium rose to its former standard. August.—Directors declined to close the Bank on occasion of the Hindoo holidays.—December.—Certain parties addressed the Government on the subject of Rajkissore Dutt's forgeries, requesting the executive to take into consideration the losses sustained by the public from the manner in which the Government of Bengal conducted the business connected with the Government Loans.

1835, January 5.—Dividend six per cent. Bank discounted Government and Salary Bills at six per cent. Private Bills eight per cent. 22.—Cash balance being much reduced, Directors raised the rates one per cent., except on Salary and Government Bills; and directed that Mint Certificates, having twenty days to run, should be taken as cash. April 6.—A General Meeting of Proprietors decided on reducing each share in the capital stock of the Bank from 10,000 to 5,000 rupees. A proposition was also made that three *additional* Directors be appointed for the 20 lacs additional to be added to the capital. 23rd.—The capital increased from 50 to 70 lacs of rupees. The Chamber of Commerce reported to the Bank that the Civilian Collectors of Districts refused to receive bank-notes as cash. The Directors intimated that the refusal must be solely on the part of the Collectors of Districts beyond the Provinces of Bengal and Behar, where it did not appear to be the wish of the Government that the notes of the Bank should be received into the public treasuries. The receipt of bank-notes, in payment of Government demands, is authorized by Government in the Lower Provinces, where the Calcutta *Sicca* rupee is current; but Collectors not permitted to exchange notes. July 2.—Bank dividend fourteen per cent. Bank shares selling at Sicca Rupees 16,000, or 60 per cent premium. Circulation, 1,16,00,000, one crore sixteen lacs. August.—A man named Ramcomul Singhee, convicted in the Supreme Court of altering a bank-note, was sentenced to seven years' transportation.

1836, January 4.—Bank divided eleven and a half per cent. Discounted Government and Salary Bills at four per cent. Private Bills at seven per cent. June.—The Court of Directors of East India Proprietors refused to compensate the Bank and other individual sufferers by Rajkissore Dutt's forgeries, on the grounds that compliance might lead to their being importuned, and that proper caution, which it is the duty of commercial men to exercise, was not used by the sufferers. They repudiated all negligence on the part of their own servants. July 7.—Dividend ten per cent. October 1.—In consequence of the change which had been made in the currency of these Provinces, it was deemed advisable that the capital stock of the Bank of Bengal, and every share of that capital stock should be expressed in Company's rupees, and should consist of such a number of Company's rupees as would admit of ready computation. The capital stock was therefore raised to Company's Rupees 75,00,000, being 20 lacs additional of Sicca rupees; and at the same time the amount of a single share was reduced to Company's Rupees 4,000, at which it now stands. New Charter granted by Lord Auckland, known as Act XIX. of 1836. 5.—Bank divided for three months at the rate of twelve and a half per cent. The total number of dividends declared from the 2nd January 1809 to the 30th September 1836, a period of twenty-seven years and nine months, was fifty-five, and the total amount of profit divided for the same period was Sicca Rupees 1,31,00,307-4-8, equal nearly to Sicca rupees nine and half per cent per annum on 50 lacs of Sicca rupees, which was the capital stock from the commencement of the Bank in 1809 to September 1836, when it received the augmentation before noticed.

Government send to the Directors a correspondence with some merchants in England, on the subject of establishing a new Bank to be called "The Bank of India," into which it is proposed the Bank of Bengal should merge.

1837, January 5.—Bank declared a dividend for three months at the rate of ten per cent. Discounted Government and Salary Bills at four per cent. Private Bills at seven per cent. July 6.—Dividends rose to seven per cent.

1838, January 4.—Dividend fourteen per cent. Discounted Government and Salary Bills at five per cent. Private Bills at nine per cent. In February of this year a very proper rule was passed by the Directors, that no bill or note of any Bank Officer should be taken for discount, except under the votes of a majority of the Directors. A new office of Deputy Secretary was created, and Mr. H. Henderson, the Accountant, was appointed to it. July 5.—Dividend fifteen per cent. September 22.—A fraud was practised on the Bank. A person representing himself as one "Robert Coombs," took a loan of Rupees 11,900, for three months, on deposit of Government Promissory Notes for Rupees 13,000. Those notes were stolen from the Government Agent's Office. The forged endorsements, which passed current at the Bank, were also passed by the Officer of the Accountant General's Office and the Treasury. November 1.—The capital stock of the Bank was increased by one-half its amount of seventy-five lacs of rupees. Market rates of Government Securities stood thus :—

Sicca rupees ...	... 4 per cent ...	6-12 discount.
Co.'s „	„ ...	6-12 „
Sicca „ 2nd and 3rd ...	5 „ ...	4 ans. to 2 rupees premium.

1839, January 5.—Dividend was ten per cent. Bank discounted Government and Salary Bills at four per cent. Private Bills at eight per cent. The paid-up capital increased to Company's Rupees 89,61,000. Under Act VI. of 1839, the Bank Charter was extended or renewed until the expiration of twelve months' notice to be given after the 1st day of May 1846, being an extension of eight years. The old Charter was variously modified, and permission given to the Bank to establish branches, subject to all the rules and restrictions imposed on the parent institution. July 4.—Dividend eight per cent. Amount of paid-up capital increased to Company's Rupees 96,65,000. Under the same Act (VI. of 1839) the Bank established an agency at Mirzapore for the conduct of its business, under the superintendence of Mr. Claude Hamilton. October 21.—Mr. J. B. Plumb appointed Deputy Secretary, in succession to Mr. Henderson deceased.

1840, January 6.—Dividends seven and quarter per cent. Amount of paid-up capital increased to Company's Rupees 100,44,000, under the same Act (VI. of 1839). 15.—Mr. Thomas Bracken was appointed Secretary in the room of Mr. George Udny resigned. The Government Directors protested against the withdrawal of the appointment from the Civil Service, and intimated that, if persevered in, Government would stop the allowance made by them in part of the Secretary's salary. July 6.—Dividend eight per cent. Amount of paid-up capital increased to Company's Rupees 107,00,000, under the same Act (VI. of 1839), in 2,675 shares of Company's Rupees 4,000 each. * * * * * August 3.—General meeting of Proprietors gives to the Directors power, under Clauses 23 and 26 of the Act (VI. of 1839), to make provision for the salary of the Secretary, consequent on the withdrawal of the portion heretofore paid by Government. August 10.—Government borrow from the Bank 25 lacs, for which they issue Treasury Bills bearing interest at four per cent per annum. August 26.—Directors make a difference of one per cent in interest charged on loans on goods deposited in the Bonded Ware-house and Government godowns, and those placed in private godowns. December 3.—Directors present Mr. McCann, Deputy Superintendent of Police, with a gold watch, in testimony of his services in discovering several gangs of forgers of bank-notes.

1841, January 7.—Dividend nine per cent. Discounted Government and Salary Bills at six, and Private Bills at eight per cent. April 3.—Bank raise the rates one per cent. April 8.—Bank's rates of advance.

On	5 per cent. Government Promissory Notes	...	Rs. 95
„ Co.'s 4	„ „ „ „	...	„ 85
„ Sa. 4	„ „ „ „	...	

The opening of the new five per cent. loan affected Government Securities. April 19.—A fraud was attempted by means of a forged cheque, purporting to have been drawn by one Joseph Abreo. February 2.—A fraud took place in the Bank-note Department. One Isserchunder Doss, who was employed in that Department, was the principal party implicated in the fraud. The following are the particulars:—

In the General Cash Department,—a department exclusively under the control and management of the khazanchee, and to which his own people are allowed to be appointed,—it is customary to receive and exchange bank-notes, which are subject to certain known processes before the party exchanging the notes can receive cash for them. Documents called chirkoots, or native cheques, are prepared by the khazanchee's people for the purpose of facilitating the business of the Department. These chirkoots bear the name of the party who brings either cash or bank-notes for exchange, and the description of notes received or paid. To these chirkoots the podar, who fills them in, signs his name, and they are then taken to another podar, who tells out the cash. On the day of the fraud, two chirkoots,—one for Rupees 16,000, and the other for Rupees 18,000, making a total of Rupees 34,000, were presented, for the purpose of being cashed, to the head podar, who, perceiving that the requisite verification to the chirkoots was not wanting, paid the money to the party presenting them. These chirkoots, after the payment of the money, are filed by the podar who issues them. Early on the morning succeeding the fraud, when the usual regular comparison of accounts between the different departments was made,* the deficiency was discovered. The books kept by the khazanchee were closely examined, but no entries corresponding with the above-mentioned payments were discoverable, nor could it be found that any notes equal in amount to the sum abstracted in coin had been received for exchange. The chirkoots, upon which the payment was purported to have been made, were then called for, but were not forthcoming. It would seem they had been destroyed. Directly the result of the investigation had been arrived at, notice was sent off to the Directors, who met the next morning, to take the affair into consideration. They found that the abstraction lay entirely with the khazanchee's people. In fact, it could be traced to nobody else. The scheme seems to have been concocted,

* The comparison is now made every evening and the balance tested.

matured, and perpetrated in the department, and to have had no ramification elsewhere. The khazanchee, who holds good securities for the podars, finding how matters stood, endeavored to make the securities responsible, but failed therein. Isserchunder Doss absconded, but was afterwards captured. Owing, however, to some extraordinary interference, all the parties implicated, who had been secured by the Deputy Superintendent of Police, slipped from his fingers, and justice was thereby frustrated. July 3.—Dividend ten per cent for the past half year. August.—The Bank of Bombay intimate their intention to open a branch at Calcutta.

1842, January 6.—Bank declared a dividend at the rate of ten per cent. March 24.—New rupees selling, at Mirzapore, at a premium of 3 rupees, and 3 rupees 8 annas per cent. July 4.—Dividend for the past half year at the rate of twelve per cent. October 6.—A forged cheque for Rupees 4,000, purporting to have been drawn by Mr. C. E. Schoene, in favor of one Obhoychurn Banerjee, was paid at the Bank. This was the last day before closing for the Doorgah Poojah holidays, and the crowd very great. The forgery was drawn on one of the cheques issued to Obhoychurn Banerjee, who was a constituent of the Bank. Obhoychurn absconded. December 22.—In consequence of the sudden relinquishment of his duties by the khazancheé of the General Treasury, Government solicited the Bank to undertake the payments until a new khazanchee could be appointed.

1843, January 5.—Dividend at twelve per cent. March 2.—Rates raised half per cent all round. A verdict was given against the Bank in the matter of General Lindsay's Company's Paper. The particulars of the case are these:—General Lindsay left his

Government securities with Messrs. Macleod, Fagan and Co., with power "to sell, indorse, and assign" the same for his behalf. Mr. A. D. Macleod, one of the partners, obtained a loan from the Bank on presenting the papers indorsed thus: *A. Lindsay by his Attorneys, Macleod, Fagan and Co.* When the loan was paid off, the Bank re-indorsed to Macleod, Fagan and Co., who subsequently failed, and in whose failure the amount was mixed up. 23.—Rates raised to seven per cent on Government Bills, and ten per cent on Private Bills. June 1.—Rates reduced one per cent. On Private Bills from ten to nine; on Government Bills from seven to six. July 3.—Dividend increased to fourteen per cent. August 3.—Rates reduced one per cent all round. November 2.—Rates reduced one per cent.

1844, January 4.—Dividend for the preceding half year nine per cent. July 4.—There was a further decline for the past half year, the Bank having only declared at eight per cent. Baboo Horeemohun Sen, the son of Baboo Ramcomul Sen, was appointed khazanchee in the place of his father resigned. Horeemohun Sen had, previously, been Dewan of the Mint. September 19.—Sicca four per cent paper selling at twelve annas discount. New five per cent held at ten and eleven rupees premium. December 19.—Reduced discount on Salary Bills from four to three per cent.

1845, January 3.—Dividend eight per cent. January 23.—Directors appoint a medical practitioner—one Gobind Chunder Goopto, to attend the amlah of the Bank. April 3.—Government decline to allow medicines to be dispensed to the native establishment of the Bank on the prescriptions of the native practitioner appointed by the Directors. May 15.—Rates raised one per cent all round. July 3.—Dividend eight per cent.—Several forgeries of opium passes having been discovered, Directors discontinue, for a time, making advances on the drug. November 6.—Reduced the rates one per cent on all descriptions of business.

For particulars of the dividends and alteration of rates from 1846, reference is made to a few pages further on. Mr. Thomas Bracken having resigned the Secretaryship in 1847, was succeeded by Mr. Charles Hogg, on whose retirement, in 1851, Mr. W. Grey, C. S., was nominated to the office. This gentleman having been appointed Secretary to the Government of Bengal in 1854, the Deputy Secretary, Mr. J. B. Plumb, was appointed. In 1856, all the Banks in Calcutta petitioned the Legislative Council of India for an enactment to protect them from the consequences of paying cheques bearing forged indorsements, similar to the Act in force in England, 16 and 17 Victoria, chapter 59, sec. 19.

In 1857 the Mutiny occurred, and led to great distrust on the part of the natives, and to an active demand for silver in exchange for notes. May 1.—Mr. Plumb resigned the Secretaryship. In 1860, Mr. George Dickson, Secretary and Inspector of the Caledonian Banking Company, was chosen, by the Directors, out of more than fifty applicants, one of a small number whose qualifications were enquired into by a Committee of retired Directors resident in England, and by them unanimously preferred to the vacant appointment. March 3.—The Right Honorable James Wilson, Financial Minister of India, announces, in Council, the intention of Government to issue a State Paper Currency for India, and to withdraw the right of issue hitherto enjoyed by the three Presidency Banks.

P

1862, January 3.—Government notify that the Government Treasury shall be made over to the Bank of Bengal on 1st March. February 28.—The Bank's new and modified Charter (Act IV. of 1862) received the assent of the Governor-General in Council. March 1.—The business of the Treasury of the Secretary of State for India in Council commences at the Bank.

In a connected form below will be found a list of the dividends of the Bank of Bengal for fifty-three years. The average has already been shown, in nine and a half per cent, up to 30th September 1836, a period of twenty-seven years and nine months. It remains, therefore, to start from the 1st October of the same year to arrive at the mean dividend for twenty-six years and three months. The result is that the Bank has divided, for this period, ten and a half per cent on an average of one year with another. The shareholders ought to be satisfied with this return for their money, especially as they have the advantage of belonging to a Chartered Bank, and are only liable to the loss of their capital, and not, as in some Joint Stock Banks, to the consequences of a limited responsibility in proportion to their shares, or of one altogether unlimited. On the occurrence of some severe losses in the exchange business of the Meerut Bank, in 1847, the Secretary pointed out to the shareholders that those of them who were in the Bank at its commencement had received annually, from dividend and bonuses united, twenty-two and half per cent per annum. The Agra Bank, about the same period, showed that the returns, for a very long period of years, and not merely for the brief existence of the junior institution, had been, on the whole, at the rate of twelve per cent. Returns, however, cannot be uniform, and the shareholders of the Bank of Bengal, who received fourteen per cent on their capital stock, and more than seven per cent on the market value of it, in 1862, have no reasonable cause for complaint.

Year.	Value of Share.	Rate of Dividend.
	Rs.	
1809 ...	10,000 ...	9¾ per cent.
1812 ...	" ...	9¼ "
1814 ...	" ...	8⅞ "
1815 ...	" ...	10½ "
1816 ...	" ...	10½ "
1817 ...	" ...	10¾ "
1818 ...	" ...	12¾ "
1819 ...	" ...	12½ "
1819 ...	" ...	9 "
1820 ...	" ...	7¾ "
1821 ...	" ...	5½ "
1821 ...	" ...	6¼ "
1822 ...	" ...	6¼ "
1823 ...	" ...	10¾ "
1824 ...	" ...	2½ Reduced by fraud.
1824 ...	" ...	4¼ per cent.
1825 ...	" ...	4 "
1825 ...	" ...	11 "
1826 ...	" ...	15¼ "
1827 ...	" ...	14¾ "
1828 ...	" ...	10¼ "
1829 ...	" ...	14¼ "
1830 ...	" ...	9 "
1830 ...	" ...	8 "
1832 ...	" ...	7 "
1832 ...	" ...	8 "
1833 ...	" ...	7 "
1833 ...	" ...	6 "
1834 ...	" ...	6 "
1834 ...	" ...	No divd., forgery.
1835 ...	" ...	6 per cent.
1835 ...	" ...	14 "
1836 ...	" ...	11½ "
1836 ...	" ...	19 "
1836 ...	" ...	12½ "
1837 ...	4,000 ...	10 "
1837 ...	" ...	17 "
1838 ...	" ...	14 "
1835 ...	" ...	15 "
1839 ...	" ...	10 "
1839 ...	" ...	8 "
1840 ...	" ...	7½ "
1840 ...	" ...	8 "
1841 ...	4,000 ...	9 per cent.
1841 ...	" ...	10 "
1842 ...	" ...	10 "
1842 ...	" ...	12 "
1843 ...	" ...	12 "
1843 ...	" ...	14 "
1844 ...	" ...	9 "
1844 ...	" ...	8 "
1845 ...	" ...	8 "
1845 ...	" ...	8 "
1846 ...	" ...	8-6 "
1846 ...	" ...	13-6 "
1847 ...	" ...	11-4 "
1847 ...	" ...	15 "
1848 ...	" ...	9 "
1848 ...	" ...	8 "
1849 ...	" ...	6 "
1849 ...	" ...	6 "
1850 ...	" ...	6½ "
1850 ...	" ...	8½ "
1851 ...	" ...	10¼ "
1851 ...	" ...	12 "
1852 ...	" ...	12 "
1852 ...	" ...	8-12 "
1853 ...	" ...	5 "
1853 ...	" ...	6 "
1854 ...	" ...	7 "
1854 ...	" ...	10 "
1855 ...	" ...	8 "
1855 ...	" ...	14½ "
1856 ...	" ...	20 "
1856 ...	" ...	16 "
1857 ...	" ...	6¼ "
1857 ...	" ...	11 "
1858 ...	" ...	14 "
1858 ...	" ...	12½ "
1859 ...	" ...	11 "
1859 ...	" ...	12 "
1860 ...	" ...	12 "
1860 ...	" ...	15 "
1861 ...	" ...	6½ "
1861 ...	" ...	10 "
1862 ...	" ...	9¼ "
1862 ...	" ...	14 "

The following table will show the rate of discount and interest on loans for the past twenty-one years:—

Rates from 5th April 1841.

DISCOUNT.—Government and Salary Bills, 6 per cent. Private, 8. 1 per cent more for each renewal.

INTEREST.—On deposit of Company's Paper, 7 per cent. On Opium and Salt, 7½. On Metals and Indigo, 7½; and on other Goods, 8. Credit on deposit of Company's Paper, 7. On Opium and Salt, 7½. On Metals and Indigo, 7½; and on other Goods, 8.

From 16th April 1841.

DITTO.—On deposit of Company's Paper, 6½ per cent. Credit on deposit of Company's Paper, 6½.

From 2nd December 1842.

DITTO.—On deposit of Opium and Salt, 8 per cent. On Metals and Indigo, 8; and on other Goods, 8½. Credit on deposit of Opium and Salt, 8. On Metals and Indigo, 8; and on other Goods, 8½.

From 2nd March 1843.

DISCOUNT.—Government and Salary Bills, 6½ per cent. Private, 8½. 1 per cent more for each renewal.

INTEREST.—On deposit of Company's Paper, 7 per cent. On Metals and Indigo, 8½. On Opium and Salt, 8½; and on other Goods, 9. Credit on deposit of Company's Paper, 7. On Opium and Salt, 8½. On Metals and Indigo, 8½; and on other Goods, 9.

From 23rd March 1843.

DISCOUNT.—Government and Salary Bills, 7 per cent. Private, 10. 1 per cent more for each renewal.

INTEREST.—On deposit of Company's Paper, 8 per cent. On Opium and Salt, 9. On Metals and Indigo, 9; and on other Goods, 10. Credit on deposit of Company's Paper, 8. On Opium and Salt, 9. On Metals and Indigo, 9; and on other Goods, 10.

From 1st June 1843.

DISCOUNT.—Government and Salary Bills, 6 per cent. Private, 9. 1 per cent more for each renewal.

Interest.—On deposit of Company's Paper, 7 per cent. On Metals and Indigo, 8. On Opium and Salt 8; and on other Goods, 9. Credit on deposit of Company's Paper, 7. On Metals and Indigo, 8. On Opium and Salt, 8; and on other Goods, 9.

From 3rd August 1843.

Discount.—Government and Salary Bills, 5 per cent. Private, 8. 1 per cent more for each renewal.

Interest.—On deposit of Company's Paper, 6 per cent. On Opium and Salt, 7. On Metals and Indigo, 7; and on other Goods, 8. Credit on deposit of Company's Paper, 6. On Opium and Salt, 7. On Metals and Indigo, 7; and on other Goods, 8.

From 2nd November 1843.

Discount.—Government and Salary Bills, 4 per cent. Private, 7. 1 per cent more for each renewal.

Interest.—On deposit of Company's Paper, 5 per cent. On Opium and Salt, 6. On Metals and Indigo, 6; and on other Goods, 7. Credit on deposit of Company's Paper, 5. On Opium and Salt, 6. On Metals and Indigo, 6; and on other Goods, 7.

From 12th January 1844.

Discount.—Private Bills, 6 per cent. 1 per cent more for each renewal.

Interest.—On deposit of Opium and Salt, 5 per cent. On Metals and Indigo, 5. Credit on deposit of Opium and Salt, 5; and on Metals and Indigo, 5.

From 19th December 1844.

Discount.—Government Acceptances, 3 per cent.

From 20th February 1845.

Ditto.—Government and Salary Bills, 4 per cent. Private, 7.

Interest.—On deposit of Company's Paper, 6 per cent. On Opium and Salt, 6. On Metals and Indigo, 6; and on other Goods, 8. Credit on deposit of Company's Paper, 6. On Opium and Salt, 6. On Metals and Indigo, 6; and on other Goods, 8.

From 15th May 1845.

DISCOUNT.—Government and Salary Bills, 5 per cent. Private, 8.

INTEREST.—On deposit of Company's Paper, 7 per cent. On Opium and Salt, 7. On Metals and Indigo, 7; and on other Goods, 9. Credit on deposit of Company's Paper, 7. On Opium and Salt, 7. On Metals and Indigo, 7; and on other Goods, 9.

From 10th November 1845.

DISCOUNT.—Government and Salary Bills, 4 per cent. Private, 7.

INTEREST.—On Company's Paper, 6 per cent. On Opium and Salt, 6. On Metals and Indigo, 6; and on other Goods, 8. Credit on deposit of Company's Paper, 6. On Opium and Salt, 6. On Metals and Indigo, 6; and on other Goods, 8.

From 26th December 1845.

DISCOUNT.—Private Bills, 8 per cent.

INTEREST.—On deposit of Company's Paper, 7 per cent. On Opium and Salt, 7. On Metals and Indigo, 7; and on other Goods, 9. Credit on deposit of Company's Paper, 7. On Opium and Salt, 7. On Metals and Indigo, 7; and on other Goods, 9.

From 22nd January 1846.

DISCOUNT.—Government and Salary Bills, 5 per cent. Private, 9.

INTEREST.—On deposit of Company's Paper, 8 per cent. On Opium and Salt, 8. On Metals and Indigo, 8; and on other Goods, 10. Credit on deposit of Company's Paper, 8. On Opium and Salt, 8. On Metals and Indigo, 8; and on other Goods, 10.

From 12th March 1846.

DISCOUNT.—Government and Salary Bills, 6 per cent. Private, 10.

INTEREST.—On deposit of Company's Paper, 9 per cent. On Opium and Salt, 9. On Metals and Indigo, 9; and on other Goods, 11. Credit on deposit of Company's Paper, 9. On Opium and Salt, 9. On Metals and Indigo, 9; and on other Goods, 11.

From 26th March 1846.

DISCOUNT.—Government and Salary Bills, 7 per cent. Private, 11.

INTEREST.—On deposit of Company's Paper, 10 per cent. On Metals and Indigo, 10; and on other Goods, 12. Credit on deposit of Company's Paper, 10. On Metals and Indigo, 10; and on other Goods, 12.

From 18th June 1846.

DISCOUNT.—Government and Salary Bills, 8 per cent. Private, 12.

INTEREST.—On deposit of Company's Paper, 11 per cent. On Metals and Indigo, 11. Credit on deposit of Company's Paper, 11. On Metals and Indigo, 11.

From 23rd July 1846.

DISCOUNT.—Government and Salary Bills, 7 per cent. Private, 11.

INTEREST.—On deposit of Company's Paper, 10 per cent. On Metals and Indigo, 10; and on other Goods, 11. Credit on deposit of Company's Paper, 10. On Metals and Indigo, 10; and on other Goods, 11.

From 20th August 1846.

DISCOUNT.—Government and Salary Bills, 6 per cent. Private, 10.

INTEREST.—On deposit of Company's Paper, 9 per cent. On Metals and Indigo, 9; and on other Goods, 10. Credit on deposit of Company's Paper, 9. On Metals and Indigo, 9; and on other Goods, 10.

From 6th November 1846.

DISCOUNT.—Government and Salary Bills, 5 per cent. Private, 9.

INTEREST.—On deposit of Company's Paper, 8 per cent. On Metals and Indigo, 8; and on other Goods, 9. Credit on deposit of Company's Paper, 8. On Metals and Indigo, 8; and on other Goods, 9.

From 17th December 1846.

DITTO.—Credit on deposit of Company's Paper, 8½.

From 1st February 1847.

DISCOUNT.—Government and Salary Bills, 7 per cent. Private, 11.

INTEREST.—On deposit of Company's Paper, 10 per cent. On Metals and Indigo, 10; and on other Goods, 11. Credit on deposit of Company's Paper, 10½. On Metals and Indigo, 10½; and on other Goods, 11½.

From 18th March 1847.

DISCOUNT.—Government and Salary Bills, 8 per cent. Private, 12.

INTEREST.—On deposit of Company's Paper, 11 per cent. On Metals and Indigo, 11; and on other Goods, 12. Credit on deposit of Company's Paper, 11½. On Metals and Indigo, 11½; and on other Goods, 12.

From 5th August 1847.

DISCOUNT.—Government and Salary Bills, 6 per cent. Private, 10.

INTEREST.—On deposit of Company's Paper, 9 per cent. On Metals and Indigo, 9; and on other Goods, 10. Credit on deposit of Company's Paper, 9½. On Metals and Indigo, 9½; and on other Goods, 10½.

From 28th October 1847.

DISCOUNT.—Government and Salary Bills, 6 per cent. Private, 10.

INTEREST.—On deposit of Company's Paper, 8 per cent. On Metals and Indigo, 9; and on other Goods, 10. Credit on deposit of Company's Paper, 8½. On Metals and Indigo, 9½; and on other Goods, 10½.

From 6th December 1847.

DISCOUNT.—Government and Salary Bills, 6 per cent. Private, 10.

INTEREST.—On deposit of Company's Paper, 8 per cent. On Opium, 9. On Metals and Indigo, 9; and on other Goods, 10. Credit on deposit of Company's Paper, 8½. On Opium, 9½. On Metals and Indigo, 9½; and on other Goods, 10½.

From 17th February 1848.

DISCOUNT.—Government and Salary Bills, 5 per cent. Private, 9.

INTEREST.—On deposit of Company's Paper, 7 per cent. On Opium, 8. On Metals and Indigo, 8; and on other Goods, 9. Credit on deposit of Company's Paper, 7½. On Opium, 8½. On Metals and Indigo, 8½; and on other Goods, 9½.

From 4th July 1848.

DISCOUNT.—Government and Salary Bills, 5 per cent. Private, 8.

INTEREST.—On deposit of Company's Paper, 6 per cent. On Opium, 7. On Metals and Indigo, 7; and on other Goods, 8. Credit on deposit of Company's Paper, 6½. On Opium, 7½. On Metals and Indigo, 7½; and on other Goods, 8½.

From 11th January 1849.

DISCOUNT.—Government and Salary Bills, 4 per cent. Private, 7.

INTEREST.—On deposit of Company's Paper, 5 per cent. On Opium, 6. On Metals and Indigo, 6; and on other Goods, 7. Credit on deposit of Company's Paper, 5½. On Opium, 6½. On Metals and Indigo, 6½; and on other Goods, 7½.

From 14th March 1850.

DISCOUNT.—Government and Salary Bills, 5 per cent. Private, 8.

INTEREST.—On deposit of Company's Paper, 6 per cent. On Opium, 7. On Metals and Indigo, 7; and on other Goods, 8. Credit on deposit of Company's Paper, 6½. On Opium, 7½. On Metals and Indigo, 7½; and on other Goods, 8½.

From 2nd May 1850.

DISCOUNT.—Government and Salary Bills, 6 per cent. Private, 9.

INTEREST.—On deposit of Company's Paper, 7 per cent. On Opium, 8. On Metals and Indigo, 8; and on other Goods, 9. Credit on deposit of Company's Paper, 7½. On Opium, 8½. On Metals and Indigo, 8½; and on other Goods, 9½.

From 4th January 1851.

DISCOUNT.—Government and Salary Bills, 6 per cent. Private, 10.

INTEREST.—On deposit of Company's Paper, 8 per cent. On Opium, 9. On Metals and Indigo, 9; and on other Goods, 10. Credit on deposit of Company's Paper, 8½. On Opium, 9½. On Metals and Indigo, 9½; and on other Goods, 10½.

From 9th January 1851.

DISCOUNT.—Government and Salary Bills, 7 per cent. Private, 11.

INTEREST.—On deposit of Company's Paper, 9 per cent. On Opium, 10. On Metals and Indigo, 10; and on other Goods, 11. Credit on deposit of Company's Paper, 9½. On Opium, 10½. On Metals and Indigo, 10½; and on other Goods, 11½.

From 13th March 1851.

DISCOUNT.—Government and Salary Bills, 6 per cent. Private, 10.

INTEREST.—On deposit of Company's Paper, 8 per cent. On Opium, 9. On Metals and Indigo, 9; and on other Goods, 10. Credit on deposit of Company's Paper, 8½. On Opium, 9½. On Metals and Indigo, 9½; and on other Goods, 10½.

From 26th February 1852.

DISCOUNT.—Government and Salary Bills, 5 per cent. Private, 9.

INTEREST.—On deposit of Company's Paper, 7 per cent. On Opium, 8. On Metals and Indigo, 8; and on other Goods, 9. Credit on deposit of Company's Paper, 7½. On Opium, 8½. On Metals and Indigo, 8½; and on other Goods, 9½.

From 25th March 1852.

DISCOUNT.—Government and Salary Bills, 4 per cent. Private, 8.

INTEREST.—On deposit of Company's Paper, 6 per cent. On Opium, 7. On Metals and Indigo, 7; and on other Goods, 8. Credit on deposit of Company's Paper, 6½. On Opium, 7½. On Metals and Indigo, 7½; and on other Goods, 8½.

From 29th April 1852.

DISCOUNT.—Government and Salary Bills, 4 per cent. Private, 7.

INTEREST.—On deposit of Company's Paper, 5 per cent. On Opium, 6. On Metals and Indigo, 6; and on other Goods, 7. Credit on deposit of Company's Paper, 5½. On Opium, 6½. On Metals and Indigo, 6½; and on other Goods, 7½.

From 4th November 1852.

DISCOUNT.—Government and Salary Bills, 3 per cent. Private, 6.

INTEREST.—On deposit of Company's Paper, 5 per cent. On Opium, 5½. On Metals and Indigo, 5½; and on other Goods, 6. Credit on Deposit of Company's Paper, 5½. On Opium, 6. On Metals and Indigo, 6; and on other Goods, 6½.

From 18th November 1852.

DISCOUNT.—Government and Salary Bills, 3 per cent. Private, 6.

Interest.—On deposit of Company's Paper, 4 per cent. On Opium, 5. On Metals and Indigo, 5; and on other Goods, 6. Credit on deposit of Company's Paper, 4½. On Opium, 5½. On Metals and Indigo, 5½; and on other Goods, 6½.

From 24th February 1853.

Discount.—Government and Salary Bills, 3 per cent. Private, 5.

Interest.—On deposit of Company's Paper, 4 per cent. On Opium, Metals, and Indigo, 5; and on other Goods, 6. Credit on deposit of Company's Paper, 4½. On Opium, Metals, and Indigo, 5½; and on other Goods, 6½.

From 30th June 1853.

Discount.—Government and Salary Bills, 4 per cent. Private, 5.

Interest.—On deposit of Company's Paper, 4 per cent. On Opium, Metals, and Indigo, 5; and on other Goods, 6. Credit on deposit of Company's Paper, 4½. On Opium, Metals, and Indigo, 5½; and on other Goods, 6½.

From 4th August 1853.

Discount.—Government and Salary Bills, 3 per cent. Private, 5.

Interest.—On deposit of Company's Paper, 4 per cent. On Opium, Metals, and Indigo, 5; and on other Goods, 6. Credit on deposit of Company's Paper, 4½. On Opium, Metals, and Indigo, 5½; and on other Goods, 6½.

From 8th September 1853.

Discount.—Government and Salary Bills, 3 per cent. Private, 5.

Interest.—On deposit of Company's Paper, 4 per cent. On other Goods, 5. Credit on deposit of Company's Paper, 4½. On other Goods, 5½.

From 22nd September 1853.

Discount.—Government and Salary Bills, 4 per cent. Private, 5.

Interest.—On deposit of Company's Paper, 4 per cent. On other Goods, 5. Credit on deposit of Company's Paper, 4½. On other Goods, 5½.

From 8th December 1853.

Discount.—Government and Salary Bills, 3 per cent. Private, 5.

INTEREST.—On deposit of Company's Paper, 4 per cent. On other Goods, 5. Credit on deposit of Company's Paper, 4. On other Goods, 5. No credit granted for less than Rs. 500 ; a commission to be charged at ¼ per cent on the amount of Credit opened.

From 5th January 1854.

DISCOUNT.—Government and Salary Bills, 4 per cent. Private, 6.

INTEREST.—On deposit of Company's Paper, 5 per cent. On other Goods, 6. Credit on deposit of Company's Paper, 5. On other Goods, 6½. ¼ per cent commission as above.

From 21st February 1854.

DISCOUNT.—Government and Salary Bills, 5 per cent. Private, 7.

INTEREST.—On deposit of Company's Paper, 5 per cent. On other Goods, 7. Credit as above, and ¼ per cent commission as above.

From 4th May 1854.

DISCOUNT.—Government and Salary Bills, 4 per cent. Private, 6.

INTEREST.—On deposit of Company's Paper, 5 per cent. On other Goods, 6. Credit as above ; a commission to be charged at ¼ per cent on the amount of Credit opened.

From 4th January 1855.

DISCOUNT.—Private Bills and Notes at or within three months, 9 per cent. Government Acceptances do. do., 7.

INTEREST.—On Fixed Loans and Cash Credits not exceeding three months, on deposit of Company's Paper, 8 per cent. On deposit of Goods, 9.

From 20th January 1855.

DISCOUNT.—Private Bills and Notes at or within three months, 11 per cent. Government Acceptances do. do., 9.

INTEREST.—On Fixed Loans and Cash Credits not exceeding do. do., 10 per cent. On deposit of Goods, 11.

From 8th February 1855.

DISCOUNT.—Private Bills and Notes at or within three months, 11 per cent. Government Acceptances do. do., 10.

INTEREST.—On Fixed Loans and Cash Credits not exceeding do. do., 10 per cent. On deposit of Goods, 11.

From 9th March 1855.

DISCOUNT.—Private Bills and Notes at or within three months, 12 per cent. Government Acceptances do. do., 11.

INTEREST.—On Fixed Loans and Cash Credits not exceeding do. do., 11 per cent. On deposit of Goods, 12.

From 5th April 1855.

DISCOUNT.—Private Bills and Notes at or within three months, 11 per cent. Government Acceptances do. do., 10.

INTEREST.—On Fixed Loans and Cash Credits not exceeding do. do., 10 per cent. On goods, 11.

From 10th May 1855.

DISCOUNT.—Private Bills and Notes at or within three months, 10 per cent. Government Acceptances do. do., 9.

INTEREST.—On Fixed Loans and Cash Credits not exceeding do. do., 9 per cent. On Goods, 10.

From 17th May 1855.

DISCOUNT.—Private Bills and Notes at or within three months, 10 per cent. Government Acceptances do. do., 8.

INTEREST.—On Fixed Loans and Cash Credits not exceeding do. do., 9 per cent. On Goods, 10.

From 9th August 1855.

DISCOUNT.—Private Bills and Notes at or within three months, 11 per cent. Government Acceptances do. do., 9.

INTEREST.—On Fixed Loans and Cash Credits not exceeding do. do., 10 per cent. On Goods, 11.

From 16th August 1855.

DISCOUNT.—Private Bills and Notes at or within three months, 12 per cent. Government Acceptances do. do., 10.

INTEREST.—On Fixed Loans and Cash Credits not exceeding do. do., 11 per cent. On Goods, 12.

From 23rd August 1855.

DISCOUNT.—Private Bills and Notes at or within three months, 12 per cent. Government Acceptances do. do., 11.

INTEREST.—On Fixed Loans and Cash Credits not exceeding do. do., 12 per cent. On Goods, 12.

From 28th February 1856.

DISCOUNT —Private Bills and Notes at or within three months, 12 per cent. Government Acceptances do. do., 10.

INTEREST.—On Fixed Loans and Cash Credits not exceeding do. do., 12 per cent. On Goods, 12.

From 15th May 1856.

DISCOUNT.—Private Bills and Notes at or within three months, 11 per cent. Government Acceptances do. do., 9.

INTEREST.—On Fixed Loans and Cash Credits not exceeding do. do., 11 per cent. On Goods, 11.

From 22nd May 1856.

DISCOUNT.— Private Bills and Notes at or within three months, 10 per cent. Government Acceptances do. do., 7.

INTEREST.—On Fixed Loans and Cash Credits not exceeding do. do., 9 per cent. On Goods, 10.

From 12th June 1856.

DISCOUNT.—Private Bills and Notes at or within three months, 9 per cent. Government Acceptances do. do., 6.

INTEREST.—On Fixed Loans and Cash Credits not exceeding do. do., 8 per cent. On Goods, 9.

From 3rd July 1856.

DISCOUNT.—Private Bills and Notes at or within three months, 7 per cent. Government Acceptances do. do., 4.

INTEREST.—On Fixed Loans and Cash Credits not exceeding do. do., 6 per cent. On Goods, 7.

From 24th July 1856.

DISCOUNT.—Private Bills and Notes at or within three months, 6 per cent. Government Acceptances do. do., 4.

INTEREST.—On Fixed Loans and Cash Credits not exceeding do. do., 5 per cent. On Goods, 6.

From 21st August 1856.

DISCOUNT.—Private Bills and Notes at or within three months, 5 per cent. Government Acceptances do. do., 3.

INTEREST.—On Fixed Loans and Cash Credits not exceeding do. do., 4 per cent. On Goods, 5.

From 27th November 1856.

DISCOUNT.—Private Bills and Notes at or within three months, 6 per cent. Government Acceptances do. do., 4.

INTEREST.—On Fixed Loans and Cash Credits not exceeding do. do., 5 per cent. On Goods, 6.

From 24th December 1856.

DISCOUNT.—Private Bills and Notes at or within three months, 7 per cent. Government Acceptances do. do., 5.

INTEREST.—On Fixed Loans and Cash Credits not exceeding do do., 6 per cent. On Goods, 7.

From 8th January 1857.

DISCOUNT.—Private Bills and Notes at or within three months, 9 per cent. Government Acceptances do. do., 7.

INTEREST.—On Fixed Loans and Cash Credits not exceeding do. do., 8 per cent. On Goods, 9.

From 22nd January 1857.

DISCOUNT.—Private Bills and Notes at or within three months, 10 per cent. Government Acceptances do. do., 8.

INTEREST.—On Fixed Loans and Cash Credits not exceeding do. do., 9 per cent. On Goods, 10.

From 29th January 1857.

DISCOUNT.—Private Bills and Notes at or within three months, 12 per cent. Government Acceptances do. do., 10.

INTEREST.—On Fixed Loans and Cash Credits not exceeding do. do., 11 per cent. On Goods, 12.

From 5th February 1857.

DISCOUNT.—Private Bills and Notes at or within three months, 14 per cent. Government Acceptances, having over 15 days to run, 12. Do. do., under 15 days to run, 10.

INTEREST.—On Fixed Loans and Cash Credits not exceeding do. do., 13 per cent. On Goods, 14.

From 26th February 1857.

DISCOUNT.—Private Bills and Notes at or within three months, 13 per cent. Government Acceptances, over 15 days, 11. Do. do., under 15 days, 9.

INTEREST.—On Fixed Loans and Cash Credits not exceeding do. do., 12 per cent. On Goods, 13.

From 5th March 1857.

DISCOUNT.—Private Bills and Notes at or within three months, 12 per cent. Government Acceptances, over 15 days, 10. Do. do., under 15 days, 8.

INTEREST.—On Fixed Loans and Cash Credits not exceeding do. do., 11 per cent. On Goods, 12.

From 16th March 1857.

DISCOUNT.—Private Bills and Notes at or within three months, 11 per cent. Government Acceptances, over 15 days, 9. Do. do., under 15 days, 7.

INTEREST.—On Fixed Loans and Cash Credits not exceeding do. do., 10 per cent. On Goods, 11.

From 19th March 1857.

DISCOUNT.—Private Bills and Notes at or within three months, 10 per cent. Government Acceptances, over 15 days, 8. Do. do., under 15 days, 6.

INTEREST.—On Fixed Loans and Cash Credits not exceeding do. do., 9 per cent. On Goods, 10.

From 2nd April 1857.

DISCOUNT.—Private Bills and Notes at or within three months, 9 per cent. Government Acceptances, over 15 days, 7. Do. do., under 15 days, 5. Mint Certificates, 5.

INTEREST.—On Fixed Loans and Cash Credits not exceeding do. do., 8 per cent. On Goods, 9.

From 16th April 1857.

DISCOUNT.—Private Bills and Notes at or within three months, 8 per cent. Government Acceptances, over 15 days, 6. Do. do., under 15 days, 5. Mint Certificates, 5.

INTEREST.—On Fixed Loans and Cash Credits not exceeding do. do., 7 per cent. On Goods, 8.

From 7th May 1857.

DISCOUNT.—Private Bills or Notes at or within three months, 7 per cent. Government Acceptances at do. do., 5. Mint Certificates, 5.

INTEREST.—On Fixed Loans and Cash Credits not exceeding do. do., 6 per cent. On Goods, 7.

From 11th June 1857.

DISCOUNT.—Private Bills and Notes at or within three months, 9 per cent. Government Acceptances at do. do., 7. Do. do., having 15 days or less to run, 7. Mint Certificates, 7.

INTEREST.—On Fixed Loans and Cash Credits not exceeding ninety days on deposit of Company's Paper, 8 per cent. On Goods, 9.

From 16th July 1857.

DISCOUNT.—Private Bills and Notes at or within three months, 9 per cent. Government Acceptances do. do., 7. Do. do., having 20 days or less to run, 5. Mint Certificates, 5.

INTEREST.—On Fixed Loans and Cash Credits not exceeding do. do., 8 per cent. On Goods, 9.

From 21st July 1857.

DISCOUNT.—Private Bills and Notes at or within three months, 11 per cent. Government Acceptances do. do., 9. Do. do., 20 days or less, 5. Mint Certificates, 5.

INTEREST.—On Fixed Loans and Cash Credits not exceeding do. do., 10 per cent. On Goods, 11.

From 3rd September 1857.

DISCOUNT.—Private Bills and Notes at or within three months, 11 per cent. Government Acceptances not having more than 30 days to run, 9. Mint Certificates, 5. Do. do., having less than 7 days to run, par.

INTEREST.—On Fixed Loans and Cash Credits not exceeding do. do., 10 per cent. On Goods, 11.

From 8th September 1857.

DISCOUNT.—Private Bills and Notes at or within three months, 11 per cent. Government Acceptances not having more than 30 days to run, 9. Mint Certificates, 5. Do. do., having less than 7 days to run, par.

INTEREST.—On Fixed Loans not exceeding do. do., 10 per cent. On Goods, 11.

From 15th October 1857.

DISCOUNT.—Private Bills and Notes at or within three months, 12 per cent. Government Acceptances not having more than 10 days to run, 10. Mint Certificates not having more than 10 days to run, 10.

INTEREST.—On Fixed Loans not exceeding 90 days, 11 per cent. On Goods, 12.

From 22nd October 1857.

DISCOUNT.—Private Bills and Notes at or within three months, 12 per cent. Government Acceptances not having more than 30 days to run, 10. Mint Certificates, 10.

INTEREST.—On Fixed Loans not exceeding do. do., 11 per cent. On Goods, 12.

From 29th October 1857.

DISCOUNT.—Private Bills and Notes at or within three months, 12 per cent. Government Acceptances not having more than 30 days to run, 10. Mint Certificates, 10.

INTEREST.—On Fixed Loans not exceeding do. do., 11 per cent. On Goods, 12.

From 19th November 1857.

DISCOUNT.—Private Bills at or within three months, 12 per cent. Government Acceptances do. do., 10. Mint certificates, 6.

INTEREST.—Fixed Loans not exceeding 90 days on deposit of Company's Paper, 11 per cent. Cash Credits not exceeding 45 days on do. do., 11. On deposit of Goods, 12.

From 14th January 1858.

DISCOUNT.—Private Bills at or within three months, 11 per cent. Government Acceptances do. do., 9. Mint Certificates, 5.

INTEREST.—Fixed Loans not exceeding do. do., 10 per cent. On deposit of Goods, 11. Cash Credits not exceeding do. do. on deposit of Company's Paper, 10. On deposit of Goods, 11.

From 28th January 1858.

DISCOUNT.—Private Bills at or within three months, 10 per cent. Government Acceptances do. do., 8. Mint Certificates, 4.

INTEREST.—Fixed Loans not exceeding do. do., 9 per cent. On Goods, 10. Cash Credits not exceeding do. do., 9. On deposit of Goods, 10.

From 4th February 1858.

DISCOUNT.—Private Bills at or within three months, 10 per cent. Government Acceptances do. do., 8. Mint Certificates, 4.

INTEREST.—Fixed Loans not exceeding 90 days, 9 per cent. On Goods, 10. Cash Credits not exceeding 45 days on do. do., 9. On Goods, 10.

From 11*th March* 1858.

DISCOUNT.—Private Bills at or within three months, 9 per cent. Government Acceptances do. do., 7. Mint Certificates, 3.

INTEREST.—Fixed Loans not exceeding do. do., 8 per cent. On Goods, 9. Cash Credits not exceeding 45 days on do. do., 8. On deposit of Goods, 9.

From 29*th July* 1858.

DISCOUNT.—Private Bills at or within three months, 8 per cent. Government Acceptances do. do., 6. Mint Certificates, 3.

INTEREST.—Fixed Loans not exceeding do. do., 7 per cent. On deposit of Goods, 8. Cash Credits not exceeding 45 days on do. do., 7. On Goods, 8.

From 5*th August* 1858.

DISCOUNT.—Private Bills at or within three months, 8 per cent. Government Acceptances do. do., 6. Promissory Notes with one name protected by security of Company's Paper, 6. Mint Certificates 3.

INTEREST.—Fixed Loans not exceeding do. do., 7 per cent. On Goods, 8. Cash Credits not exceeding 45 days on do. do., 7. On Goods, 8.

From 12*th August* 1858.

DISCOUNT.—Private Bills at or within three months, 7 per cent. Government Acceptances do. do., 5. Promissory Notes with do. do., 5. Mint Certificates, 3.

INTEREST.—Fixed Loans not exceeding do. do., 6 per cent. On deposit of Goods, 7. Cash Credits not exceeding 45 days on do. do., 6. On Goods, 7.

From 19*th August* 1858.

DISCOUNT.—Private Bills at or within three months, 7 per cent. Promissory Notes with do. do., 5. Government Acceptances do. do., 4. Mint Certificates, 3.

INTEREST.—Fixed Loans not exceeding do. do., 6 per cent. On deposit of Goods, 7. Cash Credits not exceeding 45 days on do. do., 6. On Goods, 7.

From 23rd December 1858.

DISCOUNT.—Private Bills at or within three months, 8 per cent. Promissory Notes with one name protected by security of Company's Paper at or within 90 days, 6. Government Acceptances do. do., 5. Mint Certificates, 4.

INTEREST.—Fixed Loans not exceeding do. do., 7 per cent. On deposit of Goods, 8. Cash Credits not exceeding 45 days on do. do., 7. On deposit of Goods, 8.

From 25th January 1859.

DISCOUNT.—Private Bills at or within three months, 9 per cent. Promissory Notes with do. do., at or within 90 days, 7. Government Acceptances do. do., 6. Mint Certificates, 5.

INTEREST.—Fixed Loans not exceeding do. do., 8. On deposit of Goods 9. Cash Credits not exceeding 45 days on do. do., 8. On deposit of Goods, 9.

From 27th January 1859.

DISCOUNT.—Private Bills at or within three months, 9 per cent. Promissory Notes with do. do., at or within 60 days, 7. Government Acceptances do. do., 6. Mint Certificates, 5.

INTEREST.—Fixed Loans not exceeding 60 days on do. do., 8 per cent. On deposit of Goods, 9. Cash Credits not exceeding 45 days on do. do., 8. On deposit of Goods, 9.

From 15th February 1859.

DISCOUNT.—Private Bills at or within three months, 9 per cent. Promissory Notes with do. do., at or within 60 days, 7. Government Acceptances do. do., 6. Mint Certificates, 5.

INTEREST.—Fixed Loans not exceeding 60 days on do. do., 8 per cent. On deposit of Goods, 9. Cash Credits not exceeding 45 days on do. do., 8. On deposit of Goods, 9.

From 3rd May 1859.

DISCOUNT.—Private Bills at or within three months, 9 per cent. Promissory Notes with do. do., at or within 60 days, 7. Government Acceptances do. do., 6. Mint Certificates, 5.

INTEREST.—Fixed Loans not exceeding 60 days on deposit of Company's Paper, 8 per cent. On deposit of Goods, 9. Cash Credits not exceeding 45 days on do. do., 8. On deposit of Goods, 9.

From 23rd June 1859.

DISCOUNT.—Private Bills at or within three months, 8 per cent. Promissory Notes with do. do., at or within 60 days, 6. Government Acceptances do. do., 5. Mint Certificates, 4.

INTEREST.—Fixed Loans not exceeding 60 days on do. do., 7 per cent. On deposit of Goods, 8. Cash Credits not exceeding 45 days on do. do., 7. On deposit of Goods, 8.

From 7th July 1859.

DISCOUNT.—Private Bills and Notes at or within three months, 8 per cent. Promissory Notes with one name protected by security of Government Paper, at or within 60 days, 6. Government Acceptances at or within three months, 5. Mint Certificates, 4.

INTEREST.—Loans not exceeding 60 days on deposit of Government Paper, 7 per cent. On Goods, 8. Cash Credits not exceeding 45 days on deposit of Government Paper, 7. On Goods, 8.

From 18th July 1859.

DISCOUNT.—Private Bills at or within three months, 7 per cent. Promissory Notes with do. do., at or within 60 days, 8. Government Acceptances at or within three months, 4. Treasury Bills No. 2, 4¾. Mint Certificates, 3.

INTEREST.—Loans not exceeding 60 days on do. do., 6 per cent. On Goods, 7. Cash Credits not exceeding 45 days on do. do., 6. On Goods, 7.

From 1st September 1859.

DISCOUNT.—Private Bills at or within three months, 7 per cent. Promissory Notes with do. do., at or within 60 days, 5. Treasury Bills No. 2, 4¾. Government Acceptances at or within three months, 4. Mint Certificates, 3.

INTEREST.—Loans not exceeding 60 days on do. do., 6 per cent. On Goods, 7. Cash Credits not exceeding 45 days on do. do., 6. Goods, 7.

From 19*th January* 1860.

DISCOUNT.—Private Bills at or within three months, 8 per cent. Promissory Notes with do. do., at or within 60 days, 6. Treasury Bills No. 2, 5¾. Government Acceptances at or within three months, 5. Mint Certificates, 4.

INTEREST.—Loans not exceeding 60 days on do. do., 7 per cent. On Goods, 8. Cash Credits not exceeding 45 days on do. do., 7. On Goods, 8.

From 26*th January* 1860.

DISCOUNT.—Private Bills at or within three months, 9 per cent. Promissory Notes with do. do., at or within 60 days, 7. Treasury Bills No. 2, 6¾. Government Acceptances at or within three months, 6. Mint Certificates, 4.

INTEREST.—Loans not exceeding 60 days on do. do., 8 per cent. On Goods, 9. Cash Credits not exceeding 45 days on do. do., 8. On Goods, 9.

From 11*th February* 1860.

DISCOUNT.—Private Bills at or within three months, 10 per cent. Promissory Notes with do. do., at or within 60 days, 8. Treasury Bills No. 2, 7¾. Government Acceptances at or within three months, 7. Mint Certificates, 5.

INTEREST.—Loans not exceeding 60 days on do. do., 9 per cent. On Goods, 10. Cash Credits not exceeding 45 days on do. do., 9. On Goods, 10.

From 1*st March* 1860.

DISCOUNT.—Private Bills at or within three months, 11 per cent. Promissory Notes with do. do., at or within 60 days, 9. Treasury Bills No. 2, 8¾. Government Acceptances at or within three months, 8. Mint Certificates, 5.

INTEREST.—Loans not exceeding 60 days on do. do., 10 per cent. On Goods, 11. Cash Credits not exceeding 45 days on do. do., 10. On Goods, 11.

From 5th April 1860.

DISCOUNT.—Private Bills at or within three months, 11 per cent. Promissory Notes with do. do., at or within 60 days, 8. Treasury Bills No. 2, 7¾. Government Acceptances at or within three months, 7. Mint Certificates, 4.

INTEREST.—Loans not exceeding 60 days on do. do., 9 per cent. On Goods, 10. Cash Credits not exceeding 45 days on do. do., 9. On Goods, 10.

From 17th April 1860.

DISCOUNT.—Private Bills at or within three months, 9 per cent. Promissory Notes with do. do., at or within 60 days, 7. Treasury Bills No. 2, 6¾. Government Acceptances at or within three months, 6. Mint Certificates, 3.

INTEREST.—Loans not exceeding 60 days on do. do., 8 per cent. On Goods, 9. Cash Credits not exceeding 45 days on do. do., 8. On Goods, 9.

From 26th April 1860.

DISCOUNT.—Private Bills at or within three months, 8 per cent. Promissory Notes with do. do., at or within 60 days, 6. Treasury Bills No. 2, 5¾. Government Acceptances at or within three months, 5. Mint Certificates, 3.

INTEREST.—Loans not exceeding 60 days on do. do., 7 per cent. On Goods, 8. Cash Credits not exceeding 45 days on do. do., 7. On Goods, 8.

From 3rd May 1860.

DISCOUNT.—Private Bills at or within three months, 7 per cent. Promissory Notes with do. do., at or within 60 days, 5. Treasury Bills No. 2, 4¾. Government Acceptances at or within three months, 4. Mint Certificates, 3.

INTEREST.—Loans not exceeding 60 days on do. do., 6 per cent. On Goods, 7. Cash Credits not exceeding 45 days on do. do., 6. On Goods, 7.

From 7th June 1860.

DISCOUNT.—Private Bills at or within three months, 6 per cent. Promissory Notes with do. do., at or within 60 days, 4½. Treasury Bills No. 2, 3. Government Acceptances, 3. Mint Certificates, 3.

INTEREST.—Loans not exceeding 60 days on do. do., 5 per cent. On Goods, 6. Cash Credits not exceeding 45 days on do. do., 5. On Goods, 6.

From 13th December 1860.

DISCOUNT.—Private Bills at or within three months, 6 per cent. Promissory Notes with one name protected by security of Government Paper, at or within 60 days, 4½. Treasury Bills No. 2, 3. Government Acceptances at or within three months, 3. Mint Certificates, 3.

INTEREST.—Loans not exceeding 60 days on deposit of Government Paper, 5 per cent. On Goods, 6. Cash Credits not exceeding 45 days on do. do., 5. On Goods, 6.

From 24th January 1861.

DISCOUNT.—Private Bills at or within three months, 7 per cent. Promissory Notes with do. do., at or without 60 days, 5. Treasury Bills No. 2, 4. Government Acceptances at or within three months, 4. Mint Certificates, 4.

INTEREST.—Loans not exceeding 60 days on do. do., 6 per cent. On Goods, 7. Cash Credits not exceeding 45 days on do. do., 6. On Goods, 7.

From 3rd April 1861.

DISCOUNT.—Private Bills at or within three months, 8 per cent. Promissory Notes with do. do., at or within 60 days, 6. Government Acceptances at or within three months, 5. Mint Certificates, 5.

INTEREST.—Loans not exceeding 60 days on do do., 7 per cent. On Goods, 8. Cash Credits not exceeding 45 days on do. do., 7. On Goods, 8.

From 1st August 1861.

DISCOUNT.—Private Bills at or within three months, 7 per cent. Promissory Notes with do. do., at or within 60 days, 5. Government Acceptances, 4. Mint Certificates, 4.

Interest.—Loans not exceeding 60 days on deposit of Government Paper, 6 per cent. On Goods, 7. Cash Credits not exceeding 45 days on do. do., 6. On Goods, 7.

From 12*th September* 1861.

Discount.—Private Bills at or within three months, 7 per cent. Promissory Notes with do. do., at or within 60 days, 5. Government Acceptances, 4. Mint Certificates, 4.

Interest.—Loans not exceeding 60 days on do. do., 6 per cent. On Goods, 7. Cash Credits not exceeding 45 days on do. do., 6. On Goods, 7.

From 26*th September* 1861.

Discount.—Private Bills at or within three months, 7 per cent. Promissory Notes with do. do., at or within 60 days, 5. Government Acceptances at or within three months, 4. Mint Certificates, 4.

Interest.—Loans not exceeding 60 days on do. do., 6 per cent. On Goods, 7. Cash Credits not exceeding 45 days on do. do., 6. On Goods, 7.

From 24*th October* 1861.

	Within 30 days.	Above 30 days.
Discount.—On Private Bills and Notes	5½	6
Drafts and Bills accepted by Local Banks ...	Uniform rate @ 4½	
Promissory Notes with one name protected by security of Government Paper or Railway Shares...	3½	4
Government Acceptances and Mint Certificates ...	Uniform rate @ 2½	
Interest.—On Fixed Loans on deposit of Government Paper or Railway Shares ...	4	4½
On deposit of Goods ...	5½	6
Cash Credits on deposit of Government Paper or Railway Shares	4	4½
On deposit of Goods ...	5½	6
From 13*th February* 1862.		
Discount.—On Private Bills and Notes	6½	7
Drafts and Bills accepted by Local Banks ...	Uniform rate @ 5	

	Within 30 days.	Above 30 days.
Promissory Notes with one name protected by security of Government Paper or Railway Shares ...	4½	5
Government Acceptances and Mint Certificates ...	Uniform rate @	3½
INTEREST.—On Fixed Loans on deposit of Government Paper or Railway Shares ...	5	5½
On deposit of Goods ...	6½	7
Cash Credits on deposit of Government Paper or Railway Shares ...	5	5½
On deposit of Goods ...	6½	7

From 20th February 1862.

DISCOUNT.—On Private Bills and Notes	7½	8
Drafts and Bills accepted by Local Banks ...	Uniform rate @	6
Promissory Notes with one name protected by security of Government Paper or Railway Shares ...	5½	6
Government Acceptances and Mint Certificates ...	Uniform rate @	4½
INTEREST.—On Fixed Loans on deposit of Government Paper or Railway Shares ...	6	6½
On deposit of Goods ...	7½	8
Cash Credits on deposit of Government Paper or Railway Shares ...	6	6½
On deposit of Goods ...	7½	8

From 27th February 1862.

DISCOUNT.—On Private Bills and Notes	8½	9
Drafts and Bills accepted by Local Banks ...	Uniform rate @	7

	Within 30 days.	Above 30 days.
Promissory Notes with one name protected by security of Government Paper or Railway Shares ...	6½	7
Government Acceptances and Mint Certificates ...	Uniform rate @ 5½	
INTEREST.—On Fixed Loans on deposit of Government Paper or Railway Shares ...	7	7½
On deposit of Goods ...	8½	9
Cash Credits on deposit of Government Paper or Railway Shares	7	7½
On deposit of Goods ...	8½	9

From 8th May 1862.

DISCOUNT.—On Private Bills and Notes	8½	9
Drafts and Bills accepted by Local Banks ...	Uniform rate @ 7	
Promissory Notes with one name protected by security of Government Paper or Railway Shares ...	6½	7
Government Acceptances and Mint Certificates ...	Uniform rate @ 5½	
INTEREST.—On Fixed Loans on deposit of Government Paper or Railway Shares ...	7	7½
On deposit of Goods ...	8½	9
Cash Credits on deposit of Government Paper or Railway Shares ...	7	7½
On deposit of Goods ...	8½	9

From 22nd May 1862.

DISCOUNT.—On Private Bills and Notes	7½	8
Drafts and Bills accepted by Local Banks ...	Uniform rate @ 6	

	Within 30 days.	Above 30 days.
Promissory Notes with one name protected by security of Government Paper or Railway Shares ...	5½	6
Government Acceptances and Mint Certificates ...	Uniform rate	@ 4½
INTEREST.—On Fixed Loans on deposit of Government Paper or Railway Shares ...	6	6½
On deposit of Goods ...	7½	8
Cash Credits on deposit of Government Paper or Railway Shares ...	6	6½
On deposit of Goods ...	7¾	8

From 12*th June* 1862.

	Within 30 days.	Above 30 days.
DISCOUNT.—On Private Bills and Notes	6	7
Drafts and Bills accepted by Local Banks ...	Uniform rate	@ 5
Promissory Notes with one name protected by security of Government Paper or Railway Shares ...	5½	6
Government Acceptances and Mint Certificates ...	Uniform rate	@ 4½
INTEREST.—On Fixed Loans on deposit of Government Paper or Railway Shares ...	6	6½
On deposit of Goods ...	7½	8
Cash Credits on deposit of Government Paper or Railway Shares ...	6	6½
On deposit of Goods ...		7½

The distinction between the terms of 30 and 60 days was done away with on 28th August. Further alteration 4th and 25th September 1862.

THE ORIENTAL BANK CORPORATION.

In July 1842 a Company was formed at Bombay, under the name and title of the BANK OF WESTERN INDIA, having for its basis a capital of fifty lacs of rupees (or £500,000 Sterling) in 10,000 shares of five hundred rupees each. The chief object of this institution was to supply the want of a Bank for the conduct of Exchange and other legitimate Banking business, from which the Bank of Bombay was excluded by its Charter. The office opened for business in October 1842, and, subsequently, branches were established at Colombo, Calcutta, Hong-Kong, and Singapore. The operations embraced Exchange, Loans, Deposits, and all legitimate Banking, under certain restrictions set forth in the bye-laws embodied in the deed of co-partnery.

1845, April.—Shares at a premium of 40 to 42 per cent. May.—The shareholders being desirous of bringing the Company under the provisions of the Joint Stock Bank Act—(7 and 8 Victoria Regina, Chapter 113)—for the purpose of obtaining Royal Letters Patent to enable the Bank to sue and be sued in a corporate capacity, formed themselves, by a fresh deed of settlement, into a new Company, under the name of THE ORIENTAL BANK; the principal feature of the new deed being the transfer of the government of the Bank from Bombay to London, at which place the general meetings were appointed to be held. At the same time the capital was doubled by the creation of 10,000 new shares, and by doubling the amount of each share to Rupees 1,000.

The entire management and superintendence of the Company is vested in Directors: those in London being called "the Court of Directors;" while those in

Bombay, who are intrusted with the affairs there, are termed " The Board of India Directors." At each of the branches, local Directors are appointed at the discretion of the London Board, to whom they are subject. The executive management of the affairs of the Company is conducted by the Chief Manager in London and the Inspector of branches, who are amenable to the London Directors, to whose control the Bombay Managers are also subject.

1846.—The Bombay shareholders being dissatisfied with the expense and conduct of the London Directors, resolved to put an end to that direction. This movement was somewhat premature, for no alteration could be made in the constitution of the Bank without the express consent of a general meeting of the shareholders, English as well as Indian.

1847.—This year was remarkable for the most extraordinary commercial and financial events, and for a series of disasters affecting Banking establishments, such as probably had not occurred since the memorable year of 1825. The Bank did not emerge scatheless from the crisis; the violent convulsion (which some of the highest firms in England were unable to withstand) having re-acted upon India, and led to the loss of about Rupees 5,70,000, principally the bills of insolvent firms at Bombay, Ceylon, and Calcutta.

In order to guard against similar contingencies for the future, it was determined to increase the reserve fund, and to make new laws and regulations for the more efficient management of the concern. The Directors charged the whole amount of the loss to the reserve fund, arranging to replace the sum abstracted by a deduction of one per cent from the current profits of each year, until the whole should be cleared off; without however reducing the dividend, at any time, to a sum below *six* per cent per annum. Dividends this year at the rate of 8 per cent per annum. The paid up capital

Amounted to	£898,007	10	0
Reserve Fund.................	„ 128,380	19	6

1848.—The commercial crisis, before referred to, depreciated the Bank Stock to 8 and 10 per cent discount. Still the operations of the Bank were satisfactory and encouraging, the profits divided from the establishment of the Bank of Western India having amounted to no less a sum than Rupees 21,49,726-7-9. The following statement will show the rates of dividend, *viz.* :—

For half-year to	5th August 1843 ...	@ 5	per cent per annum.
„ „	5th February 1844	@ 7 „	„
„ „	5th August 1844	@ 7 „	„
„ „	5th February 1845	@ 7 „	„
„ „	5th August 1845	@ 8 „	„
„ „	1st March 1846	@ 8 „	„
„ „	1st September 1846	@ 8 „	„
„ „	Ditto	Bonus	
„ „	1st March 1847...	@ 8 „	„
„ „	1st September 1847 ...	@ 8 „	„
„ „	1st March 1848...	@ 9 „	„
„ „	1st September 1848... ...	@ 7 „	„

The Bank applied to the Supreme Government of India for a legislative enactment similar to that granted to the Union Bank of Calcutta, but could not succeed in obtaining it.

Some modifications were made in the provisions of the deed to enable proprietors to pledge their shares to other parties, and to have the dividends payable wherever there should be an office of the Bank. At the same time it was arranged that the owners of India shares might have them converted into English shares at the exchange of 2*s*. the rupee, provided the holders were resident in Europe. Dividends paid, March 1, nine per cent per annum; September 1, seven per cent. December 1st—the paid-up capital

Amounted to £903,182
Reserve Fund .... „ 128,381

1849.—All the applications of the Bank at the Treasury and India House having failed to secure for them a Charter, an arrangement was made with the Bank of Ceylon to take over the business of that institution; the stipulation being that the capital of the Oriental Bank should be reduced by the amount of capital required by the Charter of the Bank of Ceylon. The capital was accordingly reduced to £642,725. The object of this arrangement was to secure the Charter of the Bank of Ceylon, which conferred privileges connected with limited liability, and placed the Bank in a position to command the business of Colombo free of rivalry. Dividends at 7 per cent per annum.

1850.—The Bank sustained a loss through the failure of Mr. T. R. Richmond, of the firm of Richmond and Co., of Bombay. He was agent for the Ganges Company, and, in that capacity, borrowed from the Bank money which he stated to have been for and on account of the Ganges Company, who, however, repudiated the debt, alleging that the loan had *not* been appropriated to the purposes of the Company. Dividends for the year 7 per cent.

1851.—The Bank sustained some heavy losses this year through robbery and forged Bills of Exchange, Hoondees and Cheques. The most remarkable of these occurrences was the robbery, in February, of about one lac of rupees, principally in notes of the Bank of Bombay, taken from the cashier's safe, where they had been safely deposited on the Saturday night, but from which they were found missing on the following Monday morning. The investigation at the police office elicited nothing at the time: but nearly the whole of the property was recovered two months subsequently, through the instrumentality of one Ali Ackbar Khan, a Moonshee, previously in the employ of Sir Charles Napier. The robbery caused a great sensation in Bombay, particularly in the bazar, where the alarm was very great, lest the Bank of Bombay should refuse to cash its notes. The immediate consequence was that the notes of that Bank were showered in upon it until a guarantee was given.* March.—A forged Bill of Exchange for Rupees 15,000 was successfully negotiated at the Bank. An action was brought in the Supreme Court of Bombay, against the supposed drawer, but the Bank were cast. The Bank made provision for these losses, which were chiefly caused by misplaced confidence in individuals filling situations in which confidence could not be withheld. June.—The arrangements made by the Directors in the matter of the adoption of the Bank of Ceylon were confirmed. October.—A Royal Charter was granted to the Bank, constituting it a Bank of Issue in Ceylon and China, and empowering it to carry on exchange, deposit, and remittance business anywhere to the east of the Cape of Good Hope. The amalgamation of the Bank of Ceylon, with the Oriental Bank, led to an alteration in the name

* Full particulars of this case, and of the proceedings of the Governor's Council, will be given under the head of the "Bank of Bombay."

of the latter, which became thenceforth THE ORIENTAL BANK CORPORATION, with a

Paid up capital of .... £ 600,000
in shares of £25 each.
And a Reserve Fund (invested in Government Securities) of .... „ 112,000

The leading features of the Royal Charter of Incorporation are:—

"1. The liability of shareholders is absolutely limited to double the amount of their respective subscriptions.—2. No debts ascertained to be bad may be retained in the assets, but must forthwith be written off, and no dividend may be paid out of the capital.—3. Power is given to wind up the Corporation if, in the opinion of the Auditors appointed by the shareholders, there shall at any time occur a loss of one-third of the paid-up capital.—4. Three Directors retire annually—one only being immediately re-eligible; the remaining two cannot be elected till the following year.—5. The most stringent rules are laid down for the keeping of accounts. Monthly statements are required to be made out, and copies thereof to be furnished to the Lords Commissioners of Her Majesty's Treasury, who may, at pleasure, order such further returns or information as they may deem expedient—6. The business of the Corporation is confined to banking, exchange, deposit, and remittance; and it is declared unlawful to advance money on the security of houses, lands, ships, or other immoveable property, or to deal in goods or merchandise.—7. A minimum reserve of specie, equal to one-third the amount of notes in circulation, must be held by the Corporation in each colony where an issue is permitted, and the same has to be examined and verified by the governor of such colony, or as he may direct; and a statement of the circulation and the specie in reserve, so verified, must be published in the official gazette.—8. There is also a provision made for a reserved fund to be kept up, and although the amount is not defined by the Charter, it is thought desirable to maintain it at a sum equal to 20 per cent on the paid-up capital."

On the occasion of the first meeting after the amalgamation, an additional capital of £200,000 was called up on 8,000 shares of £25 each, being half the amount authorized by Treasury Warrant.

Dividends for the year at seven per cent per annum.

1852, May.—The Directors created 10,046 new shares of £25 each, which they issued at £30. November.—The Bank established a branch at the Mauritius, and agencies at Melbourne and Sydney. December.—9,873 of the new shares were taken up. The amount of capital actually paid was as follows:—

On 24,000	Shares........................	£ 600,000
„ 8,214	„	„ 205,350
„ 532	„	„ 7,980
„ 1,127	„	„ 5,635
On 33,873	Shares........................	£ 818,965

Reserved surplus Fund, increased by premium on new shares .... £ 169,365

Dividends for the year, 1st, ten per cent; 2nd, ten per cent per annum, and bonus five per cent.

1853, March.—The Directors created 3,800 additional shares, which they issued at £30, and at the rate of one new share for every nine old. April.—The allotment of new shares and the payment in full of the shares of the former issue brought the capital up to ... £ 942,450

The Reserve Fund (invested in East India Government Securities) standing at .... £ 188,440.

1854, June 30.—Dividend ten per cent per annum. July 1.—Under warrant of the Lords of the Treasury the Bank were authorized to call up £500,000 additional capital on 12,579 shares, but they only called up £250,000. Bank suffered a loss of £24,000 by the sinking of two vessels, the *Essex* and *Madagascar.* The amount not having been insured through the carelessness of a clerk, he was dismissed, and the amount written off to profit and loss. December.—Dividend ten per cent.

Paid-up Capital	....	£ 1,080,235
Reserve Fund	.... ,,	225,415

1855.—Dividend ten per cent, bonus two per cent last half.

1856.—Dividend ten per cent. Bank sustained a loss of 27,000 dollars through fire in China.

Paid-up Capital	....	£ 1,260,000
Reserve Fund	.... ,,	252,000

at which they now respectively stand.

1857.—1st dividend ten per cent. 2nd dividend ten per cent., and bonus two per cent. The Bank's Indian Branches, with the concurrence of the other Banks at Bombay and Calcutta, took over charge of the affairs of the London and Eastern Banking Corporation, in order to wind them up, the Bank having advanced that Corporation £10,000, to relieve them from pressing liabilities.

1858.—1st dividend ten per cent, 2nd dividend ten per cent, and bonus two per cent, equal to £1-15 per share, or 7 per cent on the capital of the Company. Bank received from H. M. Government a Supplemental Charter, permitting shares to be held in two or more names. The branches of the Bank amount to fourteen, beyond which it is not intended to increase them. Mr. Charles Stuart was appointed to succeed Mr. W. W. Cargill as Chief Manager. The Insurance Fund was reported to amount to £50,000.

1859.—1st dividend ten per cent per annum, 2nd dividend ten per cent, and bonus two per cent, equal to twelve per cent on the capital.

1860.—1st dividend ten per cent per annum, and bonus seven per cent. The Bank instituted a friendly suit in the Court of Exchequer, in London, to try the question of the Indian double income tax. The case was given in their favor, but they could not recover the tax already deducted. 2nd dividend five per cent, and bonus four per cent, equal to nine per cent.

1861.—1st dividend equal to fourteen per cent, 2nd dividend to 31st December five per cent for the half year, and a bonus of three per cent. Bank closed the two experimental Branches in New Zealand. The fund created by the contributions of the officers of the Bank, which was intended to answer as a guarantee fund, and to relieve those requiring relief, was reported to continue at £50,000.

The Bank do not issue their own notes in India, but those of the State currency. In Ceylon and China, as well as at Singapore, they issue their own notes.

1862.—The number of partners amounted, this year, to 1,240. The following are the particulars of the Head Office, Branches, and Agencies, corrected to up October 1862:—

Head Office, London.

THREADNEEDLE STREET, &c.

Established in 1845.

COURT OF DIRECTORS.

HARRY GEORGE GORDON	...	*Chairman.*
WILLIAM SCOTT BINNY	...	*Deputy ditto.*
C. J. F. STUART	...	*Chief Manager.*
PATRICK CAMPBELL	...	*London Manager.*
FRANCIS A. CARGILL	...	*Secretary.*
JOHN MACNAB	...	*Chief Accountant.*
JAMES WILSON	...	*Accountant.*

Branches.

BOMBAY.

Opened October 1842.

COLUMBO (CEYLON).

Opened December 1843.

Sub-Agencies.

GALLE AND KANDY.

CALCUTTA.

Opened February 1844.

Wm. Anderson	...	*Agent.*
James Galloway	...	*Sub-Agent.*
Henry J. Stewart	...	*Accountant.*
Geo. Harper	...	*Sub-Accountant.*

MADRAS.

Opened March 1853.

SINGAPORE.

Opened May 1846.

HONG-KONG.

SHANGHAI.

Opened April 1845.

MAURITIUS.

MELBOURNE.

J. Stewart	...	*Manager.*
A. G. Meison	...	*Sub-Manager.*
G. Faulkner	...	*Accountant.*

SYDNEY.

G. K. Ingelow	...	*Manager.*
Stewart Murray	...	*Sub-Manager.*
W. F. Russell	...	*Accountant*
W. M. Elles	...	*Inspector.*
Wm. Mather Anderson	...	*Assistant Inspector.*

The business of the London Office is confined to Agency for the Branches, and for parties connected with the East, and making or receiving their remittances.

Bills of Exchange are bought and sold, and deposits taken for fixed periods of 3, 6, and 12 months. Constituents of the Bank *abroad* have the privilege, on going home, of keeping accounts current with the Head-Office, a privilege not accorded to the general public. For some years past a Branch has been established in Edinburgh for the purpose of drawing deposits, which they succeed well in doing, as their rates are generaly 2 to 3½ per cent above what the Scotch Banks can afford to allow.

THE BANK OF MADRAS.

Previous to the establishment of the present institution, there existed, at Madras, a Bank known as the *Government Bank,* which conducted business on a very small scale, and had a circulation of very limited amount. It was administered by the three *ex-officio* financial Officers of Government at that Presidency. As it was not suited to the wants of the second Presidency in India, it was determined to start an institution almost in every respect on the plan of the Bank of Bengal. An act of incorporation (Act No. IX.) was passed by the Supreme Government in 1843, and the Bank came into operation on 1st July of the same year. The capital fixed, to commence with, was thirty lacs of rupees, whereof three lacs were to be the property of the Governor in Council of Madras, for the time being, on behalf of the East India Company. The number of shares subscribed for was three thousand, of one thousand rupees each.

The shareholders at present number 260.

No addition has been made to the capital.

The business of the Bank is managed by nine Directors, of whom three are appointed, and removeable by the

Governor in Council at Madras, and the remaining six are elected by a General Meeting of Proprietors. It is expressly provided by Charter:—

That the Bank of Madras shall not be engaged in any kind of business, except the kinds of business hereafter specified; that is to say—

1*st.*—The discounting of Negotiable Securities.

2*nd.*—The keeping of Cash Accounts, including the realization of dividends and interest on Government Securities to the credit of constituents of the Bank.

3*rd.*—Buying and selling of Bills of Exchange payable in India.

4*th.*—The lending of money on short loans.

5*th.*—The buying and selling of bullion.

6*th.*—The receiving of deposits.

7*th.*—The issuing and circulating of Bank Post Bills.

8*th.*—The selling of property or securities deposited in the Bank as security for loans and not redeemed, or of property or securities recovered by the Bank in satisfaction of debts and claims.

The average amount of the circulation previous to its suppression was between 15 and 16 lacs. At one time it reached 30 lacs, and in the negotiations of the Bank with Government for a maximum and minimum they struggled hard to fix the former at 25 and the latter at 20 lacs. The average was finally fixed at 10 and 15 lacs. With the exception of the year 1860 the circulation was always under 20 lacs, though in that year it rose to 24½ lacs, the surplus being principally held by the Treasury and the other Banks at Madras. The arrangement with Government had an extraordinary effect upon the shares of the Bank. In 1861 they were quoted at fourteen per cent premium. In October and November 1862 they were saleable at eighty-five premium, and even reached 100. At fourteen they were too cheap. At the latter figures they are at their full value. The Bank does but a small agency business comparatively. The agency houses monopolize it. The quantity of paper which the Bank have got enfaced for payment of interest in England has always been very trifling.

In April 1862, the privilege of issuing bank-notes was withdrawn from the Bank, Government currency notes being substituted. In November 1862, the circulation of the Government issue had reached 35 lacs, which is just double the Bank's issues of its own notes.

In June 1851 these amounted to ... Rs. 11,06,395
In June 1861 ditto ... „ 15,93,845

In the issue of Post Bills there was a most remarkable difference between the years 1852 and 1862. In the former year the issues amounted to .... Rs. 2,158
In the latter year to .... „ 78,534

The following tabular statements will furnish all particulars connected with the business of the Bank from its establishment.

STATEMENT.

U

Statement showing the Dividends paid and the

DIVIDEND PAID.				RATES OF		
Half Year ending			Rate.	Year.	Government Bills.	
					Range.	Mean.
1843	December	31 ...	3½ p.c.	1843	5 p.c.	5 p.c.
1844	June	30 ...	6½ „			
	December	31 ...	6½ „	1844	4 „	4 „
1845	June	30 ...	6½ „			
	December	31 ...	6½ „	1845	4 @ 6 „	5 „
1846	June	30 ...	6½ „			
	December	31 ...	6 „	1846	5 @ 7 „	6 „
1847	June	30 ...	6 „			
	December	31 ...	5 „	1847	3 & 10 „	6½ „
1848	June	30 ...	5 „			
	December	31 ...	5 „	1848	3 & 5 „	4 „
1849	June	30 ...	6 „			
	December	31 ...	5¾ „	1849	5 „	5 „
1850	June	30 ...	7 „			
	December	31 ...	7 „	1850	5 & 9 „	7 „
1851	June	30 ...	10 „			
	December	31 ...	10 „	1851	5 & 12 „	8½ „
1852	June	30 ...	10 „			
	December	31 ...	5 „	1852	3 & 12 „	7½ „
1853	June	30 ...	4 „			
	December	31 ...	4½ „	1853	3 „	3 „
1854	June	30 ...	5 „			
	December	31 ...	5 „	1854	3 & 5 „	4 „
1855	June	30 ...	8 „			
	December	31 ...	10½ „	1855	6 & 10 „	8 „
1856	June	30 ...	12 „			
	December	31 ...	5 „	1856	3 & 12 „	7½ „
1857	June	30 ...	5 „			
	December	31 ...	7½ „	1857	4 & 7 „	5½ „
1858	June	30 ...	7 „			
	December	31 ...	6 „	1858	4 & 7 „	5½ „
1859	June	30 ...	10 „			
	December	31 ...	8½ „	1859	3 & 10 „	6½ „
1860	June	30 ...	9½ „			
	December	31 ...	5 „	1860	5 & 9 „	7 „
1861	June	30 ...	8 „			
	December	31 ...	5 „	1861	4 & 10 „	7 „
1862	June	30 ...	9½ „			

N. B.—The present value

Rates of Interest charged by the Bank of Madras.

INTEREST CHARGED.

Private Bills.		Loans.		Cash Credits.		Average.	Rate per cent of actual produce on average business.
Range.	Mean.	Range.	Mean.	Range.	Mean.		
6 p.c.	6 p.c.	5½ p.c.	5½ p.c.	6 p.c.	6 p.c.	5·62	5·95
6 ,,	6 ,,	5 ,,	5 ,,	5 & 5½ ,,	5¼ ,,	5·06	5·6
7 & 8½ ,,	7¾ ,,	5½ @ 7 ,,	6¼ ,,	6 & 7½ ,,	6¾ ,,	6·44	6·33
7½ & 11 ,,	9¼ ,,	6½ & 9 ,,	7¾ ,,	7 & 9½ ,,	8¼ ,,	7·81	7·44
8½ & 12 ,,	10¼ ,,	6 & 10½ ,,	8¼ ,,	7 & 11 ,,	9 ,,	8·5	8·94
6 & 8½ ,,	7¼ ,,	5 & 6 ,,	5½ ,,	6 & 7 ,,	6½ ,,	5·81	5·87
7 & 8½ ,,	7¾ ,,	6 ,,	6 ,,	7 ,,	7 ,,	6·44	6·53
7 & 11½ ,,	9¼ ,,	6 & 10 ,,	8 ,,	7 & 11 ,,	9 ,,	8·31	7·45
8 & 12 ,,	10 ,,	7 & 12 ,,	9½ ,,	8 & 12 ,,	10 ,,	9·5	9·38
6 & 12 ,,	9 ,,	5 & 12 ,,	8½ ,,	6 & 12 ,,	9 ,,	8·5	8·2
6 & 7 ,,	6½ ,,	5 ,,	5 ,,	6 ,,	6 ,,	5·12	5·78
5 & 8 ,,	6½ ,,	3½ & 6 ,,	4¾ ,,	6 & 7 ,,	6½ ,,	5·44	5·54
8 & 12 ,,	10 ,,	6 & 10 ,,	8 ,,	8 & 11 ,,	9½ ,,	8·87	9·03
7 & 12 ,,	9½ ,,	5 & 12 ,,	8½ ,,	6 & 13 ,,	9½ ,,	8·75	9·03
8 & 11 ,,	9½ ,,	6 & 10 ,,	8 ,,	7 & 11 ,,	9 ,,	8·	7·79
8 & 11 ,,	9½ ,,	5 & 10 ,,	7½ ,,	6 & 11 ,,	8½ ,,	7·75	6·91
8 & 13 ,,	10½ ,,	5 & 11 ,,	8 ,,	6 & 12 ,,	9 ,,	8·50	8·49
7 & 12 ,,	9½ ,,	5 & 10 ,,	7½ ,,	6 & 11 ,,	8½ ,,	8·12	7·85
7 & 13 ,,	10 ,,	5 & 11 ,,	8 ,,	5 & 11 ,,	8 ,,	8·25	8·14

of shares is Rs. 1,995.

Comparative Statement showing Maximum, Minimum,

INVESTMENTS.									
Date.	Maximum.			Minimum.			Average taken out monthly.		
1843	24·19·199	..	..	16·89·555	..	..	20·91·397	..	..
1844	35·09·405	..	..	17·17·508	..	..	26·71·932	..	..
1845	34·61·889	..	..	29·71·211	..	..	32·72·089	..	..
1846	37·89·417	..	..	23·83·496	..	..	32·60·315	..	..
1847	38·29·730	..	..	21·67·042	..	..	30·95·020	..	..
1848	33·55·117	1	2	26·48·770	6	7	31·62·788	..	..
1849	35·59·660	6	4	25·84·691	..	..	31·28·443	..	..
1850	38·90·116	2	5	29·70·107	7	7	33,56·446	..	..
1851	43·27·965	7	10	31·09·143	8	2	36·93·983	..	..
1852	42·69·195	8	5	23·73·773	6	2	32·11·711	..	..
1853	32·46·470	12	2	22·85·668	5	11	26·85·383	..	..
1854	36·45·739	12	8	26·79·884	14	5	32·27·582	..	..
1855	45·63·761	1	1	36·47·104	10	11	40·19·666	..	..
1856	44·40·851	15	6	24·42·971	3	7	34·19·323	..	..
1857	36·86·544	12	2	24·51·525	15	7	31·02·378	..	..
1858	48·60·645	14	8	25·54·220	14	2	38·44·742	..	..
1859	49·54·797	7	7	37·25·695	10	7	44·46·864	..	..
1860	52·85·518	..	..	30·00·617	..	..	39·55·416	..	..
1861	47·08·604	..	..	29·70·016	..	..	37·19·756	..	..

Government

Amount held on	31	December	1848,	4·86·619	0	2
„	31	„	1849,	6·86·631	2	3
„	31	„	1850,	4·86·619	0	2
„	31	„	1854,	5·00·000	0	0

and Average of Investments and Lodgments.

LODGMENTS.														
Maximum.			Minimum.			Average taken out monthly.			Maximum required by Charter.			Minimum required by Charter.		
....	..	..	....	..	..	....	..	..	....	..	..	....	..	..
....	..	..	....	..	..	....	..	..	....	..	..	....	..	..
....	..	..	....	..	..	....	..	..	....	..	..	....	..	..
....	..	..	....	..	..	....	..	..	....	..	..	....	..	..
....	..	..	....	..	..	....	..	..	....	..	..	....	..	..
13·35·108	7	10	8·98·137	2	4	10·14·502	..	..	7·36·925	13	11	5·68·780	10	9
12·45·871	13	10	8·59·485	12	2	10·28·693	..	..	6·67·760	8	2	5·32·806	7	..
10·37·980	15	..	7·08·948	11	7	8·51·946	..	..	6·56·048	7	7	4 75·329	4	4
12·81·118	8	6	6·86·809	12	..	9·17·453	..	..	6·37·509	10	2	4·57·633	12	1
14·85·275	11	1	6·70·804	13	9	9·87·921	..	..	7·32·440	12	4	4·90·157	14	10
22·44·158	8	8	10·84·462	11	9	15·63·437	..	..	9·92·381	3	4	5·98·927	14	6
32·56·219	11	3	17·35·803	14	2	26·77·810	..	..	12·24·565	6	2	8·09·572	7	10
23·43·894	7	5	10·81·333	15	1	15·31·217	..	..	10·14·121	3	3	5·88·819	1	10
24·34·319	12	9	12·29·548	15	4	16·83·320	..	..	10 57·206	3	3	6·68·374	5	2
23·80·144	2	8	10·68·960	8	6	16·27·100	..	..	10·62·764	8	6	7·22·748	15	6
27·05·664	10	9	16·06·741	5	3	21·67·111	..	..	11·41·105	1	8	7·59·219	15	5
33·21·825	7	8	15·55·667	5	11	21·89·249	..	..	13·68·530	3	8	7·60·701	4	2
33·32·827	..	..	14·16·642	..	..	20·88·724	..	..	13·94·394	..	..	9·87·072	..	..
29·89·896	..	..	29·11·09·093	..	..	19·71·599	..	..	13·48·193		..	7·38·522	..	..

Securities.

Amount held on	31	December	1855,	5·00·000	0	0
„	31	„	1859,	7·00·000	0	0
	31	„	1860,	4·87·200	0	0
„	31	„	1861,	1·08·056	13	0

Comparative Statement showing Maximum, Minimum,

SPECIE.									
Date.	Maximum.			Minimum.			Average taken out monthly.		
......	....	..	..	....	..	..	....	..	..
......	....	..	..	....	..	..	....	..	..
......	....	..	..	....	..	..	....	..	..
......	....	..	..	....	..	..	....	..	..
......	....	..	..	....	..	..	....	..	..
1848	31·60·678	13	11	15·66·168	6	9	19·35·013	..	..
1849	21·86·526	3	4	13·24·746	1	7	16·63·967	..	..
1850	19·06·991	5	3	7·05·434	6	8	12·13·054	..	..
1851	20·63·242	5	3	5·52·562	9	6	13·78·566	..	..
1852	35·13·156	10	2	8·10·787	2	1	21·70·924	..	..
1853	37·43·685	8	9	19·75·129	10	1	28·87·389	..	..
1854	43·03·801	13	4	25·79·361	14	11	34·87·720	..	..
1855	27·08·178	10	..	11·94·383	6	..	17·73·883	..	..
1856	46·43·695	15	2	12·76·681	11	5	28·65·647	..	..
1857	45·10·252	5	1	24·68·598	3	7	32·15·862	..	..
1858	43·04·783	8	9	17·23·066	13	..	29·41·868	..	..
1859	36·00·570	11	8	12·97·985	..	2	23·93·856	..	..
1860	42·41·192	..	..	13·69·321	..	..	31·43·967	..	..
1861	40·79·203	..	..	13·51·967	..	..	29·77·118	..	..

Government

Amount held on	31	December	1848,	4·86·619	0	2
"	31	"	1849,	6·86·631	2	3
"	31	"	1850,	4·86·619	0	2
"	31	"	1854,	5·00·000	0	0

and Average of Investments and Lodgments.—(Continued.)

CIRCULATION.									AGGREGATE BUSINESS.					
Maximum.			Minimum.			Average taken out monthly.			Receipts.			Payments.		
....	..	..	....	..	..	....	..	..	....	..	..	....	..	..
....	..	..	....	..	..	....	..	..	....	..	..	....	..	..
....	..	..	....	..	..	....	..	..	....	..	..	....	..	..
....	..	..	....	..	..	....	..	..	....	..	..	....	..	..
....	..	..	....	..	..	....	..	..	....	..	..	....	..	..
16·12·600	..	..	13·31·850	..	..	14·80·610	..	..	411·49·550	10	11	4·27·58·748	8	5
15·19·025	..	..	10·86·605	..	..	13·24·366	..	..	461·58·200	4	11	4·54·558	15	8
17·30·485	..	..	10·35·970	..	..	12·85·512	..	..	540·42·912	..	1	559·18·458	3	6
15·65·480	..	..	10·26·735	..	..	11·99·641	..	..	675·70·842	11	6	669·97·714	4	9
17·26·700	..	..	11·26·125	..	..	13·69·145	..	..	668·25·834	..	10	650·27·306	..	8
19·11·960	..	..	11·87·020	..	..	14·74·649	..	..	735·36·139	11	9	7·43·21·728	13	2
18·95 910	..	..	13·59 655	..	..	15·70·886	..	..	875·46·430	4	..	891·78·201	13	10
18·19·905	..	..	10·49·900	..	..	13·32·656	..	..	754·22·317	8	5	761·86·368	15	8
22 52·840	..	..	12·72·035	..	..	16·06·000	..	..	799·81·803	10	4	782·60·176	15	9
21·08·410	..	..	14·14·345	..	..	17·16·565	..	..	858·89·554	13	3	853·39·349	14	9
20·51·530	..	..	12·62·490	..	..	16·40·521	..	..	001·21·845	15	..	1000·31·784	..	..
26·99·470	..	..	13·21·125	..	..	19·17·249	..	..	12·18·98·976	13	10	121·731·664	13	3
30·14·275	..	..	17·43·050	..	..	24·37·740	..	..	11·14·77·779	..	..	113·060·146	..	..
28·48·610	..	..	14·81·770	..	..	19·81·841	..	..	962·17·159	9	5	908·91·204	6	7

Securities.

Amount held on	31	December	1855,	5·00·000	0	0
„	31	„	1859,	7·00·000	0	0
„	31	„	1860,	4·87·200	0	0
„	31	„	1861,	1·08·058	13	0

Year.				Dividend.	Average Rates.
1843	December	31	...	3½ p. c.	5·02%
	From 1844 to 1854, average			6⅔ „	7·20%
1855	June	30	...	8 „	
	December	31	...	10½ „	9·03%
1856	June	30	...	12 „	
	December	31	...	5 „	9·05%
1857	June	30	...	5 „	
	December	31	...	7½ „	7·79%
1858	June	30	...	7 „	
	December	31	...	6 „	7·75%
1859	June	30	...	10 „	
	December	31	...	8½ „	8·50%
1860	June	30	...	9½ „	
	December	31	...	5 „	8·12%
1861	June	30	...	8 „	
	December	31	...	5 „	8·25%
1862	June	30	...	9½ „	

The following are the present Directors and Staff of the Bank :—

H. A. MANGLES, ESQ., *Accountant-General,*	*ex-officio* Govt. Dirs.
Colonel C. A. ORR, *Mint Master,*	
Honorable C. PELLY, *Board of Revenue,*	
Honorable R. O. CAMPBELL,	Elected by the Proprietors.
JOHN VANS AGNEW,	
A. T. BROWN,	
A. J. BYARD,	
H. FOLQUETT,	
F. AGNEW,	
JOHN McIVER ...	*Secretary and Treasurer.*
T. E. FRANCK ...	*Deputy ditto ditto and Chief Accountant.*
W. T. G. IRVINE ...	*Deputy Accountant.*
A. MACKINTOSH ...	*Assistant ditto.*
JOHN FLETCHER ...	*Chief of Bond Department.*
WM. FITZGERALD ...	*Chief of Correspondence ditto.*

Agencies.

COCHIN BRANCH.

I. C. WINCONSIN ...	*Agent.*
LONDON CORRESPONDENTS...	*Bank of England.*
CALCUTTA DITTO ...	*Bank of Bengal.*
BOMBAY DITTO ...	*Bank of Bombay.*

THE BANK OF BOMBAY.

It is a remarkable circumstance in the history of Banking in India, which cannot fail to excite attention, that although a public Bank was established in Calcutta in 1770, no attempt, that we are aware of, was made to establish a similar institution in Bombay until more than sixty years afterwards.

The Banking of Bombay appears to have been from time immemorial in the hands of a very limited number of large capitalists, and to break through the monopoly these virtually possessed, the effects of which were sensibly felt, but against which it was difficult to contend, about the close of the year 1836 a proposition was brought forward for establishing a Chartered Bank at Bombay, which was to be based on the most liberal principles. For this purpose, after much deliberation, a public meeting of the community was convened, at which it was resolved, that the rapid extension of the Commerce of Bombay, and the great increase of the capital within the Island, ready for profitable investment, rendered that period particularly fitted for the establishment of a Chartered Bank. The want of such an institution had been long felt by the Commercial Community, and the Government, by withdrawing the privilege of making deposits and transfers at the Treasury, increased it to a considerable degree.

As the question of establishing a Bank was then interesting, chiefly in its commercial bearings, personal application was made in the first instance to every respectable firm in the place to ascertain their sentiments on the projected institution. Amongst the first applied to were the three oldest Mercantile Houses, which, under the old system, had enjoyed almost the whole business appertaining legitimately to a public Banking institution, and whose hostility proved afterwards but too successful in protracting every succeeding step. Solicited upon public grounds to co-operate in the proposed measure, and appearing for a while inclined to that course, it was soon found that they had secretly addressed Government, praying for an issue of treasury notes payable on demand, and stating that, "if the accommodation now solicited is granted, nothing further is wanted to put the monetary system of Bombay upon a good and convenient footing: nor do the subscribers conceive that any advantage can flow from the establishment of a Bank, while numerous evils would undoubtedly arise from the issue of paper notes."

The concession of such a prayer would have not only impeded the new proposal, but have in all probability prevented its revival at any future period. Government, to its honor be it spoken, rejected the insidious suggestion, and the indignant re-action of the public mind from that moment imparted to the new enterprize an almost irresistible impulse. Civil and Military Officers vied with one another, and with the Mercantile Community, in approving and supporting the scheme. A meeting was held, a Committee nominated, a Prospectus adopted, a Charter was applied for from the Local Government, and instantly granted; an Agent was at great cost despatched to London to communicate with the Court of Directors and the Board of Control, and to procure their sanction to the Charter already granted by the Bombay Government. The Government also addressed the Court in favor of the infant establishment, stating not only its unqualified approval of the objects set forth, but substantially manifesting its interest by taking for itself, subject to the approval of the higher authorities, 300 shares.

To this address the Court of Directors replied, that they did not object to the establishment of a Bank at Bombay, upon the same principles in every respect as those which were recently sanctioned for the re-incorporation of the Bank of Bengal, and they directed the Government of India to prepare a similar Act for incorporating a Bank at Bombay, the only points of difference being those which related to the amount of capital, and the proportion to be subscribed by Government. They approved of 50 lacs as the amount of the capital of the Bank of Bombay, three lacs of which were to be subscribed by the Government, and it was required, as at Calcutta, that three of the nine Directors should be Officers of Government. On the draft being adopted by the Proprietors in all its provisions, and the capital paid up, the Government of India were empowered, without further reference to the Court, to pass the requisite Act of Incorporation.

Notwithstanding, however, this support of the Local Government, and the sanction of the Court of Directors, such was the influence of those who were opposed to the Bank, that from various delays and references the Charter of the Bank of Bombay, Act III. of 1840, was not passed until February 1840, and the Bank was enabled to commence business on the 15th April in the same year, nearly four years after it was first projected.

Although it was originally intended that the capital of the Bank should be only thirty lacs of rupees, yet such was the demand for shares, that the Provisional Committee was obliged to increase the amount to Rupees 52,25,000, so as to meet the wishes of the numerous applicants. This amount was divided into 5,225 shares of one thousand rupees each; and the following analysis of the shareholders in 1840 shows the proportion of capital subscribed by the different classes of the community, and the number of shareholders of each denomination :—

1840.

173	Europeans resident in India	3,261	Shares.
12	Native Christians	49	„
3	Mahomedans	55	„
109	Parsees..........................	1,233	„
35	Hindoos	327	„
	The Bombay Government...	300	„
332	Shareholders.	5,225	Shares.

1848.

91	Europeans, resident in India...	1,473	Shares.
95	Ditto, non-resident	2,365	„
13	Native Christians	62	„
1	Mahomedan	18	„
88	Parsees	877	„
25	Hindoos..............................	130	„
	The Bombay Government ...	300	„
313	Shareholders.	5,225	Shares.

The present number of shareholders is 342.

From the above comparative statement, it appears that the European shareholders, chiefly Officers in the Civil and Military Services, have increased from 173 holding capital stock for Rupees 32,61,000, in 1840, to 186 holding capital for Rupees 38,38,000, in 1848, and that a corresponding decrease has taken place in the number and amount of capital of the native shareholders. In 1860 there were 159, with Rupees 19,64,000 of capital, and in 1848, only 127, with Rupees 13,87,000 of capital.

It also appears that about one-half of the Europeans

who first subscribed for shares have, in the usual changes to which Indian society is liable, retired, and are now settled in England; and it is very probable that in the course of a few years the largest proportion of the capital will be held by parties resident in England.

The Bank is governed by a Board of Directors consisting of nine members, who receive no remuneration for their services. Three are appointed by the Government, and are generally the Chief Secretary to Government, the Accountant General, and the Secretary to Government in the Financial Department. The other six are elected by the proprietors, and the qualification is that each should be possessed of 12 shares in his own name. Two go out by rotation annually on the second Monday in December, and are not re-eligible.

The Directors at their first meeting in every year choose from among themselves a President, who has the casting vote in all cases of an equal division of votes at meetings either of Directors or Proprietors.

The following is a list of the present Directors appointed by Government:—

S. D. Birch, Esq., *President.*

R. W. Lodwick, Esq. | J. B. Peile, Esq.

Elected by the Proprietors.

John Baumbach, Esq.
Hon'ble M. H. Scott, Esq.
George Poggo, Esq.
Robert Hannay, Esq.
Hon'ble Rustomjee J. Jejeebhoy, Esq.
Cowasjee Jehanjier, Esq.

The Directors have the power of appointing all Officers to the Bank and of fixing their salaries, provided that the whole expense of the establishment is not to exceed sixty thousand rupees in any one year, without authority from a general meeting of the proprietors.

The undermentioned are the present Officers, and they all give security for the faithful discharge of their duties—

OFFICERS OF THE BANK.

JAMES BLAIR	...	*Secretary and Treasurer.*
JOHN H. RYLAND	...	*Deputy Secretary.*
D. ROBERTSON	...	*Chief Accountant and Inspector of Branches.*
S. W. READ	...	*Accountant.*
W. FRASER	...	*Registrar of Securities.*
W. S. JOHNSTON	...	*Assistant.*
WILLIAM BULLOCK	...	*Ditto.*

Three Branches

Established in 1862.

AHMEDABAD.

WILLIAM WILSON	...	*Agent.*
G. J. HYNES	...	*Accountant.*

POONA.

WILLIAM F. HUNTER	...	*Agent.*
A. S. HARRISON	...	*Accountant.*

SURAT.

WILLIAM WATSON	...	*Agent.*
R. H. WILSON	...	*Accountant.*
INSPECTOR OF BRANCHES	...	————

Under the provisions of the Charter, the Bank is prohibited from engaging in any kind of business, except the kind specified, *viz.*:—

1.—The discounting of Negotiable Securities.

2.—The keeping of Cash Accounts.

3.—Buying and selling Bills of Exchange payable in India.

4.—The lending of money on short loans.

5.—The buying and selling of bullion.

6.—The receiving of deposits.

7.—The issuing and circulating of Bank Post Bills.

8.—The selling of property or securities deposited in the Bank as security for loans and not redeemed.

The Bank is obliged at all times to keep cash in its Treasury equal to at least one-fourth of all claims outstanding against it, and payable on demand. It is prohibited from lending more than 7½ lacs of Rupees to Government, or more than 3 lacs to any one party, except upon deposit of security.

The note circulation of the Bank has now been withdrawn, and the Government currency notes substituted in the same way as with the Banks of Bengal and Madras. The circulation was limited to two crores of rupees, but the highest point it ever reached was Rupees 1,28,12,000. The amount of Post Bills the Bank issues is not large, the average scarcely exceeding Rupees 32,000 in a year.

Extensive forgeries of the bank's notes were detected in the years 1848 and 1851, whereby at least four-fifths of the entire circulation was temporarily reduced. It speedily recovered however, and continued to increase until February 1862, when it was withdrawn by Government.

The subjoined statement, showing the rates of discount and interest, and the dividends paid, will be found useful.

STATEMENT.

Rates of Discount and Interest from 1840.

Date.				On Government Bills.	On Private Bills.	On Fixed Loans.	Cash Credits.	Advances on Goods.
1840	April	15	...	5 p.c.	7½	6	6½	7½
„	July	15	...	4 „	6	5	5½	6½
1841	February	15	...	6 „	7	6	6½	8
„	June	10	...	5 „	6	5	5½	7
„	December	23	...	5 „	6	6	6½	8
1842	January	11	...	6 „	7	6	6½	8
„	„	20	...	6 „	8	6	6½	8
„	„	27	...	7 „	9	7	7	9
„	July	2	...	6 „	7	6	6½	8
„	„	28	...	5 „	7	5	6½	8
„	September	15	...	5 „	7	5	6½	8
„	November	24	...	6 „	7½	6	6½	8½
„	December	22	...	6 „	8	6½	7	8
1843	June	8	...	5 „	7	5½	6	7
„	July	20	...	5 „	6½	5½	6	7
„	August	24	...	5 „	6	5	5½	6
1844	April	18	...	5 „	7	6	6½	7
„	August	1	...	4 „	6	5	5½	6
1845	February	27	...	4 „	7	6	6½	7
„	March	20	...	4 „	8	6½	7	8
„	April	3	...	5 „	9	7	7½	9
„	July	17	...	4 „	7	6	6½	7
„	September	18	...	4 „	6	5	5½	6
„	November	27	...	5 „	8	7	7½	8
„	December	4	...	5 „	9	7	7½	9
„	„	11	...	5½ „	9	8	8½	9
„	„	20	...	6 „	10	9	9½	10
1846	March	6	...	6 „	12	9	9½	12
„	April	2	...	7 „	12	9	9½	12
„	June	4	...	6 „	10	8	8½	10
„	July	30	...	6 „	9	8	8½	9
„	September	30	...	5 „	8	7	7½	8
„	October	8	...	4 „	7	5	6	7
„	„	15	...	5 „	9	7	8	9
1847	January	7	...	4 „	8	6	7	8
„	„	28	...	5 „	9	7	8	9
„	February	25	...	6 „	10	8	9	10
„	March	16	...	6 „	11	9	10	11

Rates of Discount and Interest from 1840.—(Continued.)

Date.				On Government Bills.	On Private Bills.	On Fixed Loans.	Cash Credits.	Advances on Goods.
1847	July	22	...	6 p.c.	10	8	9	10
„	August	19	...	5 „	8	6	7	8
„	December	16	...	6 „	9	7	8	9
1848	January	27	...	7 „	10	8	9	10
„	February	10	...	8 „	12	10	11	12
„	March	23	...	8 „	11	9	10	11
„	April	6	...	7 „	10	8	9	10
„	May	11	...	6 „	9	7	8	9
„	June	8	...	5 „	7	5	6	7
„	November	23	...	6 „	8	6	7	8
1849	January	1	...	5 „	8	6	7	8
„	February	22	...	5 „	7	6	7	8
„	April	26	...	4 „	6	5	6	6
„	November	8	...	4 „	6	4	5	6
„	December	20	...	5 „	7	5	6	7
1850	January	4	...	5 „	8	6	7	8
„	„	10	...	6 „	9	7	8	9
„	February	21	...	7 „	10	8	9	10
„	March	14	...	7 „	9	8	9	10
„	„	28	...	6 „	9	7	8	9
„	May	2	...	5 „	7	5	6	7
„	July	2	...	4 „	7	5	6	7
„	November	7	...	5 „	8	6	7	8
„	December	5	...	6 „	9	7	8	9
1851	January	9	...	7 „	10	8	9	10
„	May	29	...	6 „	9	7	8	9
„	July	3	...	5 „	8	6	7	8
„	„	31	...	4 „	7	5	6	7
1852	January	8	...	4 „	6	4	5	6
„	April	22	...	4 „	7	5	6	7
„	June	3	...	3 „	6	4	5	6
„	August	26	...	3 „	5	3	4	5
„	November	11	...	3 „	6	4	5	6
1853	July	1	...	4 „	7	5	6	7
„	August	25	...	3 „	6	4	5	6
1854	March	2	...	4 „	7	5	6	7
„	April	13	...	5 „	8	6	7	8
„	„	27	...	6 „	9	7	8	9

Rates of Discount and Interest from 1840.—(Continued.)

Date.				On Government Bills.	On Private Bills.	On Fixed Loans.	Cash Credits.	Advance on Goods.
1854	May	25	...	5 p.c.	8	6	7	8
„	June	15	...	4 „	7	5	6	7
„	July	20	...	3 „	6	4	5	6
„	November	16	...	4 „	7	5	6	7
„	December	7	...	5 „	8	6	7	8
„	„	14	...	6 „	9	7	8	9
„	„	21	...	7 „	10	8	9	10
1855	May	25	...	6 „	9	7	8	9
„	June	7	...	5 „	8	6	7	8
„	„	16	...	6 „	9	7	8	9
„	July	19	...	5 „	8	6	7	8
„	August	16	...	4 „	7	5	6	7
„	November	1	...	5 „	8	6	7	8
„	December	13	...	6 „	9	7	8	9
„	„	27	...	7 „	10	8	9	10
1856	January	3	...	8 „	11	9	10	11
„	„	17	...	10 „	12	11	12	12
„	April	3	...	8 „	10	9	10	11
„	May	8	...	7 „	9	8	9	10
„	„	29	...	6 „	8	7	8	9
„	June	12	...	4 „	7	5	6	7
„	August	7	...	4 „	6	4	5	7
„	October	31	...	5 „	7	5	6	8
„	November	5	...	6 „	8	6	7	9
„	December	4	...	7 „	9	7	8	9
„	„	18	...	8 „	10	8	9	10
1857	March	12	...	7 „	9	7	8	9
„	„	26	...	5 „	8	6	7	8
„	April	2	...	4 „	7	5	6	7
„	May	14	...	6 „	9	7	8	9
„	„	19	...	7 „	10	8	9	10
„	June	4	...	8 „	11	9	10	11
„	„	12	...	9 „	12	10	11	12
„	July	29	...	9 „	12	10	11	12
„	August	6	...	7 „	10	8	9	10
„	„	20	...	6 „	9	7	8	9
„	November	5	...	7 „	10	8	9	10
„	„	11	...	8 „	11	9	10	11

Rates of Discount and Interest from 1840.—(Continued.)

Date.				On Government Bills.	On Private Bills.	On Fixed Loans.	Cash Credits.	Advance on Goods.
1857	November	12	...	9 p.c.	12	10	11	12
1858	January	28	...	8 ,,	11	9	10	11
,,	February	4	...	7 ,,	10	8	9	10
,,	,,	18	...	6 ,,	9	7	8	9
,,	March	15	...	7 ,,	10	8	9	10
,,	,,	18	...	8 ,,	11	9	10	11
,,	April	15	...	9 ,,	12	10	11	12
,,	May	13	...	8 ,,	11	9	10	11
,,	,,	20	...	7 ,,	10	8	9	10
,,	,,	27	...	6 ,,	9	7	8	9
,,	June	3	...	5 ,,	8	6	7	8
,,	,,	17	...	4 ,,	7	5	6	7
,,	November	11	...	5 ,,	8	6	7	8
,,	,,	25	...	5 ,,	9	7	8	9
,,	December	7	...	6 ,,	10	8	9	10
,,	,,	16	...	7 ,,	11	9	10	11
,,	,,	30	...	8 ,,	12	10	11	12
1859	January	28	...	8 ,,	12	11	12	12
,,	March	24	...	8 ,,	12	10	11	12
,,	April	7	...	7 ,,	11	9	10	11
,,	May	19	...	9 ,,	12	10	11	12
,,	June	8	...	8 ,,	11	9	10	11
,,	,,	16	...	6 ,,	9	7	8	9
,,	,,	22	...	5 ,,	7	5	6	7
1860	January	12	...	6 ,,	8	6	7	8
,,	,,	19	...	7 ,,	9	7	8	9
,,	February	4	...	8 ,,	10	8	9	10
,,	,,	10	...	10 ,,	12	10	11	12
,,	,,	16	...	9 ,,	11	9	10	11
,,	,,	23	...	8 ,,	10	8	9	10
,,	March	15	...	7 ,,	9	7	8	9
,,	,,	22	...	6 ,,	8	6	7	8
,,	April	19	...	5 ,,	7	5	6	7
,,	May	31	...	3 ,,	5	3	4	5
,,	November	15	...	5 ,,	7	5	6	7
,,	,,	29	...	6 ,,	8	6	7	8
,,	December	6	...	7 ,,	9	7	8	9
,,	,,	27	...	9 ,,	11	9	10	11

Rates of Discount and Interest from 1840.—(Continued.)

Date.				On Government Bills.	On Private Bills.	On Fixed Loans.	Cash Credits.	Advance on Goods.
1861	January	10	...	10 p.c.	12	10	11	12
„	April	17	...	11 „	13	11	12	13
„	„	20	...	9 „	11	9	10	11
„	May	2	...	7 „	9	7	8	9
„	„	9	...	6 „	8	6	7	8
„	June	6	...	5 „	7	5	6	7
„	„	13	...	4 „	6	4	5	6
„	July	18	...	3 „	5	3	4	5
„	October	3	...	5 „	7	5	6	7
„	„	24	...	6 „	8	6	7	8
„	November	7	...	8 „	10	8	9	10
„	April	3	...	6 „	8	6	7	8
„	May	8	...	4 „	6	4	5	6
„	„	29	...	4 „	5	4	5	6
„	June	4	...	3 „	4	3	4	5
„	September	4	...	4 „	5	4	5	6
„	„	18	...	5 „	6	5	6	7
„	October	3	...	6 „	7	6	7	8
„	„	9	...	8 „	9	8	9	10

DIVIDENDS.

Dividends paid since 1840.

1841	June	30	...	5 p.c.	1852	June	30	...	5½ p.c.
"	December	31	...	5 "	"	December	31	...	5½ "
1842	June	30	...	7 "	1853	June	30	...	6 "
"	December	31	...	7 "	"	December	31	...	6½ "
1843	June	30	...	7 "	1854	June	30	...	6 "
"	December	31	...	7 "	"	December	31	...	7½ "
1844	June	30	...	7 "	1855	June	30	...	9 "
"	December	31	...	7 "	"	December	31	...	9 "
1845	June	30	...	7 "	1856	June	30	...	10 "
"	December	31	...	7 "	"	December	31	...	8 "
1846	June	30	...	7 "	1857	June	30	...	7 "
"	December	31	...	7 "	"	December	31	...	9 "
1847	June	30	...	8 "	1858	June	30	...	9 "
"	December	31	...	8 "	"	December	31	...	9 "
1848	June	30	...	8 "	1859	June	30	...	9 "
"	December	31	...	7 "	"	December	31	...	11 "
1849	June	30	...	6 "	1860	June	30	...	11 "
"	December	31	...	6 "	"	December	31	...	10 "
1850	June	30	...	6 "	1861	June	30	...	10 "
"	December	31	...	6 "	"	December	31	...	10 "
1851	June	30	...	6½ "	1862	June	30	...	9 "
"	December	31	...	5½ "					

Previous to the establishment of the Bank, all payments were made in coin, and a note circulation was almost unknown at this Presidency. But the advantage of bank-notes as a medium of exchange is now so apparent, and so fully appreciated by all classes of the community, that the proportion used may be estimated at about eighty-five per cent. All the European Merchants, and a great majority of the natives keep accounts with the Bank, and settle their transactions by cheques.

An account of the profits is taken half-yearly, on the 1st day of January and 1st July, and a dividend thereof declared as soon after as conveniently may be, generally about the 15th of the month. The following is a summary of the profits realized from the commencement, and the amount of dividends paid in each year; also the fluctuations in the value of the shares.

The Directors have the power of setting apart out of the profits a sum not exceeding Rupees 2,61,250, or five per cent upon the paid-up capital of the Bank, as a *Reserve Fund* against contingencies.

Summary of the Profit and Loss Accounts.

Date.	*Net Profits.*	Dividends paid.		*Reserved Fund.*	*Premium on Shares.*
		Amount.	*Rate per cent.*		
1840	Rs. 84,548	Rs. 51,559*	...	Rs. 32,989	44 per cent.
1841	" 253,778	" 261,250	5	" 25,517	22 "
1842	" 360,595	" 365,750	7	" 20,362	23 "
1843	" 361,512	" 365,750	7	" 16,125	40 "
1844	" 392,711	" 365,750	7	" 43,087	52 "
1845	" 385,516	" 365,750	7	" 62,855	48 "
1846	" 416,117	" 365,750	7	" 113,221	40 "
1847	" 411,210	" 418,000	8	" 56,431†	86 "
1848	" 220,341 half year	" 209,000 half year	8	" 67,773	85 "

* The preliminary expenses of forming the Bank were paid out of the profits of the first year.

† The decrease in the Reserved Fund is in consequence of a depreciation to the extent of fifty thousand rupees in the value of Government Securities sold, and a loss of Rupees 10,000 sustained by forgeries on Captain Thornhill, Joint Remount Agent's account.

From the analysis of the shareholders, it appears that nearly four-fifths of the capital belongs to Europeans, and these chiefly Officers in the Civil and Military Services, who invest their savings in Bank stock, as yielding a larger return than the Government Loans, and this may in some measure account for the fact that the value of the shares is not influenced to any great extent by a pressure on the money market. Their value appears to be regulated more by the value of Government Securities; thus we find that in 1843-44, after the 5 per cent Loan of 1841-42 closed, and 4 per cent Paper was at par, Bank shares were at a premium of fifty-two per cent; and in 1846-47, when the 5 per cent Loan was re-opened, the shares fell to thirty-six per cent premium, although during the latter year the dividend was increased from seven to eight per cent.

The following abstract of the Assets and Liabilities is made up from the published accounts on the 31st December in each year, from the commencement of the Bank:—

	Liabilities.		Assets.		
Date.	*Deposits and Circulation.*	*Total including capital. Rs.52,25,000*	*Government Securities and Cash.*	*Loans, Credits, and Bill discounted.*	Total.
1840	34,27,434	86,52,434	75,48,908	11,03,526	86,52,434
1841	34,56,167	86,81,167	43,48,497	43,52,670	86,81,167
1842	43,31,156	95,56,156	41,93,338	53,62,768	95,56,156
1843	104,64,083	156,89,083	136,07,222	20,81,861	156,89,083
1844	74,95,110	127,20,110	94,24,121	32,95,989	127,20,110
1845	68,01,979	120,26,979	69,03,940	51,23,039	120,26,979
1846	66,24,608	118,49,608	83,43,448	35,06,160	118,49,608
1847	66,34,248	118,59,248	71,86,768	46,72,480	118,59,248
1848	63,29,654 30th June	115,54,654 30th June	73,44,524	42,10,130	115,54,654

THE UNION BANK.

This Bank was first established in 1829. Mr. John Carr was its first Secretary. It principally owed its existence to the Proprietors of the *Commercial* and *Calcutta* Banks, who, in order to make room for it, by mutual consent, contracted their circulation. The main object of this establishment was to fill up the space in the money market, left vacant, as it were, by the restrictions imposed on the Bank of Bengal by its Charter. It was intended, at first, to call the institution the Commercial Bank, but there was a prejudice against the name, and it was over-ruled. It was finally settled that it should be called the UNION BANK. It was the only one of which the capital was wholly furnished by individuals on the principle of a Joint-Stock Bank. It had no Charter. It was formed avowedly as a Commercial Bank, to be managed by commercial men. The Directors, from its opening, were chosen as commercial men from the leading Commercial Houses in Calcutta, to afford pecuniary facilities to commerce, which the regulations of the semi-Government Bank of Bengal did not permit.* By the deed of copartnership, clause 2nd, its circulation was restricted to *one-fourth* of the paid-up capital. Its notes, however, not being received into the Government Treasuries, the circulation was limited to about six lacs, and confined to Calcutta and its immediate vicinity. It commenced operations on the 17th August 1829, with a capital of Sicca Rupees 15,00,000

* McCulloch, in his Commercial Directory, Article Calcutta, second edition, page 215, says: "In 1843, the Union Bank is the only private Bank in Calcutta, the Bank of Hindostan, Commercial Bank, and the Calcutta Bank, having all discontinued business. Its main object was to fill up the space in the money market, occasioned by the restrictions imposed on the Bank of Bengal by its Charter."

(equal to Company's Rupees 16,00,000), consisting of 600 shares, of Sicca Rupees 2,500 each, which were held by all classes of the community. The Bank had contemplated an issue of *one thousand* shares, of Sicca Rupees 2,500 each, but, up to 1835, no more than the 600 shares had been taken up. Note circulation on 31st December was Rupees 6,48,050.

1830.—Bank-note circulation, Rupees 3,63,020.

1831.—Note circulation, Rupees 3,15,860.

1832, July 15.—The Bank declared a first dividend of six per cent. The previous profits of the Bank had been set off against the preliminary expenses of the institution. There was no alteration in the rate of dividend for three years. Note circulation, Sicca Rupees 5,87,034.

1833.—Note circulation, Sicca Rupees 3,69,771.

1834.—Note circulation, Sicca Rupees 4,88,088.

1835, July 15.—This second half year's dividend was at ten per cent. Note circulation, Sicca Rupees 5,26,145.

1836, January 15.—The Bank divided ten per cent. This month, consequent on the change in the currency, it was deemed advisable to raise a further sum of Rupees 20,000, in order to make the amount of shares an even sum, and this was done by calling for an additional subscription of Rupees 33-5-4, which made the amount of each share Rupees 2,700, and augmented the capital to Rupees 16,20,000. In May of this year, 600 supplementary shares were created, of Rupees 900 each, which made the total capital Rupees 21,60,000. July 15.—The Bank declared a dividend of twelve per cent for the previous half year. Note circulation, Rupees 7,05,175-7-5.

1837, April.—The capital of the Bank was again further increased to Rupees 32,00,000 in shares of Rupees 1,000 each.

This month the Bank divided fourteen per cent for the previous half year. Note circulation, Rupees 5,01,218-3-2.

1838.—This year the dividends fell to twelve per cent. In January, a further increase of Rupees 8,00,000 was made to the capital by the creation of 800 new shares of 1,000 each, which made the capital 40,00,000. In May, a further augmentation was effected by means of 4,000 new shares of Rupees 1,000 each. This brought up the capital to Rupees 80,00,000. Note circulation, Rupees 4,57,855-8-3.

1839, January 15.—The dividend was eleven per cent, one per cent less than the previous half year. In June, the capital received a further increase of Rupees 20,00,000, by means of 2,000 new shares of Rupees 1,000 each, which brought up the capital to Rupees 100,00,000, equal to one million of pounds sterling. July 15.—The dividends reduced to eight per cent. This great and sudden increase of the Bank's capital occasioned considerable anxiety in the Bank parlour, as to the way in which it might be profitably invested, and the means by which good dividends would be insured to the subscribers. An Agency was established at Mirzapore this year. It commenced working on the 26th March, under the direction of Mr. George Stuart Dick. In September, Mr. George James Gordon, formerly of the firm of Mackintosh and Co., was appointed Secretary to the Bank. The close of this year witnessed the introduction of that pernicious system of advances upon indigo factories, other blocks, and the personal security of the borrower, which so deeply preyed upon the vitals of the Bank, and led to its failure in 1847-48, under circumstances the most disgraceful and dishonorable to all concerned. On the 31st December the *paid-up* capital amounted to Rupees 94,77,000, and the whole Rupees 100,00,000 was soon after paid up. This year the deed of partnership was altered to enable the Directors to issue Bank Post Bills for cash. Note circulation, Rupees 4,74,839-8-10.

1840.—The dividends this year did not exceed seven per cent. This year the Bank commenced the business of buying and selling Bills of Exchange on London. July 25th.—The Agency at Mirzapore not being found to answer, was closed. In September of this year, full publicity was given to one of the most successful frauds ever perpetrated. The delinquent was Mr. A. H. Sim, for many years the Accountant to the Bank.

The following is the report read at a special meeting of shareholders, held on the 14th of August 1840.

Towards the end of May 1839, it was discovered that the accounts of several constituents of the Bank were apparently overdrawn; and upon Mr. Sim being questioned on the subject, he admitted his responsibility for those irregularities, and immediately discounted some Bills, the proceeds of which, amounting to about Rupees 64,000, were appropriated by him to the rectification of these accounts. It was almost immediately afterwards made apparent that, though in some instances *bonâ fide* accommodation had been given by Mr. Sim on his own responsibility, assets had, in the majority of cases, come to his hands, which he had, for a time, appropriated to his own use, instead of bringing the amount to the account of the respective parties in the books of the Bank.

Mr. Sim being from severe illness unable to attend office, the native writer of the ledger was now strongly pressed on the subject of the correctness of Mr. Sim's own account. For two days he was employed in bringing it up, when it exhibited a sum of only 12 or 13,000 rupees due by him. The balance corresponded exactly with that exhibited by the Bengallee ledger kept in the office of the Treasurer; and that fact would naturally have set suspicion at rest for the time, had not another native writer given private information to Mr. DaCruz, the present Accountant, that the English and Bengallee ledger writers were in collusion, and that they both falsified their books, so that they might be found always to correspond.

Having assured himself that fraud had been actually committed in some of the accounts that had been paid up, and fortified in his suspicion of further fraud by the information privately received, Mr. DaCruz roundly taxed the ledger writer with falsification of the accounts, saying he was well assured that, instead of 12,000 rupees, Mr. Sim had overdrawn Rupees 1,20,000. Upon this the writer retired to a private room with Mr. DaCruz, and acknowledged that his suspicions were well founded, as far as regarded the fact of Mr. Sim having overdrawn his account to a much greater extent than was exhibited by the ledger; handing to him, at the same time, a memorandum of the particulars of the false entries, the amount of which turned out to be exactly the sum guessed at by Mr. DaCruz. The items were eight in number. The first false entry was on 12th October 1836; when, by the prefixing of 10, a payment of Rupees 592-1-4 was converted into one of 10,592-1-4, and in the same way the other entries were falsified by prefixing or altering one or more figures.

The ledger credits being entered from the daily

cash (book), these accounts are, when fair copied, handed over to the ledger writer. Anticipating the possibility of a scrutiny, by comparison of the entries in the cash book with those in the ledger, the writer of the ledger altered the entries in the cash book while in his possession, so as to correspond with the false entries in the ledger; while the balances at foot of the page were allowed to remain unaltered. At the end of each half year, the Accountant, whose duty it is to see the striking of the half-yearly accounts, rectified the balance by falsifying the addition of a particular class of accounts, so that the errors on both sides mutually compensating, the general balance came out correct.

But though by the alterations of the Cash Book entries, the writer of the ledger might expect to be able, in case of need, to throw the charge of falsification on the writer of the cash book, he made two slips that brought detection home to him. In one entry in the cash book, three receipts upon one day are added together, their true sum, namely Rupees 19,469-6-5, is written beneath, and yet the sum carried out into the adjacent general column is Rupees 49,469-6-5, the left-hand figure 1 being altered to 4. In another instance the original entry in the cash book was, by some oversight, allowed to remain unaltered, so that the falsification of the ledger stands unsupported. In the first case, the inconsistency between the additions and the sum carried out might be plausibly attributed to mere inadvertence in servilely copying the corresponding entry in the cash Book; but in the case, when the ledger alone was falsified, it was impossible to frame any excuse; and the writer, a very intelligent and active assistant, though a rogue, was dismissed accordingly. Until those facts were pointed out, the ledger writer persisted in asserting that the falsifications originated with the writer of the cash book, a native, who is now dead, alleging that he ascertained the particulars of the fraud, of which he gave information to Mr. DaCruz, by comparing the ledger with the waste book.

The better to escape detection, Mr. Sim did not allow an account in his name to be opened in the *check ledger;* but without the connivance of the ledger writer, he could not have appropriated to himself the payments made by constituents for a longer time than during the intervals between the balancing of the Bank books. The writer of the check ledger has also been dismissed. Further, as the correspondence of the Bengallee with the English ledger left no doubt of the participation of the writer of the former in the guilt of falsification, he was at once dismissed by the Treasurer.

To this system of frauds, the late Accountant must have been tempted by the permission to have dealings on his own account. This indulgence appears to have been granted to him by the late Secretary, on the precedent of a similar indulgence having been enjoyed by the former Accountant* of the Bank of Bengal, who was allowed to speculate, or to act as a broker in the purchase and sale of Company's Paper, Bank Shares, and Bills of Exchange. Mr. Sim appears to have, at first, confined himself to dealings of that description, but afterwards to have entered into other transactions requiring a large and continued command of money. His success in gaining over to his purposes three of the native officers of this establishment, whose collusion was indispensable

* Mr. Henry Henderson.

to his success, was a contingency so extraordinary, that it is no wonder that it was not anticipated nor provided against.

However much the Accountant might have been suspected, it was not likely to have occurred to any one that he could have got a principal assistant in another department, that of the Treasurer, a man with whom, in the routine of business, he had no communication, to collude with him; and, even now, after the whole system has been unravelled, it is difficult to say by what course of investigation the fraud could have been detected, had not the particulars been divulged by the accomplices.

The attention of the Directors was, however, immediately addressed to the prevention of a recurrence of similar fraud. With this view, it was ordered that no officer of this establishment should engage himself in any trade or business that requires pecuniary accommodation; and secondly, that no officer of the Bank should have any account in the books, except for the amount of his salary. The rigorous observance of this rule is insured by the appointment of an Assistant Secretary, one of whose offices it is to see and to order payment of all cheques; and who, besides, examines, every morning, the receipts and payments of the preceding day. Besides this, the great increase of the Bank's business has rendered indispensable numerical additions to the former establishment in every department, so that a much more extensive combination than formerly would be requisite for the success of any fraudulent attempt, while the dangers of detection would be multiplied in the same proportion.

The bank-note circulation amounted on 31st December of this year to Rupees 7,48,629-6-8. This year the Bank established an Agency at Singapore under the conduct of Mr. A. G. Paterson, some time the Deputy Secretary. It commenced operations on 23rd October, and was intended, principally, to engage in the buying and selling Bills of Exchange.

1841, January 16.—Bank declared a dividend of nine per cent. February.—A motion was made in the Bank parlour to the effect that no loans on landed property, or on blocks of indigo factories, or houses, or factories of any kind, be granted in future. The motion was lost. July 17.—Dividend nine per cent. December.—Mr. Henry William Abbott, appointed Agent of the Singapore Branch, took charge from Mr. Paterson, who returned to Calcutta, and resumed his seat as Deputy Secretary. Bank-note circulation, Rupees 3,56,855.

1842, January 15.—Dividend ten per cent. July 16.—Dividend declined to eight per cent. Note circulation, Rupees 1,43,975.

1843, January 21.—Dividend eight per cent. July 15.—Same rate. This month the proprietors passed a resolution, authorizing expressly, and as an exceptional thing, the outlay of twenty-five lacs per annum in indigo cultivation, for the use of those firms which had hitherto depended for this aid on the Bank. December.—Mr. James Calder Stewart, who was one of the earliest Directors, was appointed Secretary in the room of Mr. George James Gordon, resigned. Note circulation, Rupees 1,81,930.

1844, January 20.—Dividend seven per cent. May 1st.—Mr. Abbott, the Agent at Singapore, was appointed to officiate as deputy Secretary during the absence of Mr. Paterson in England. July 21.—Dividend the same. Note circulation, Rupees 2,20,975.

1845, January 18.—Dividend seven per cent. May 1st.—Mr. Abbott was confirmed in the office of Deputy

Secretary, in the room of Mr. Paterson, who resigned and returned to Calcutta, to establish a new house of business. July 19.—Dividend the same. Note circulation, Rupees 2,05,525.

1846, January 17.—Dividend seven per cent. July 18.—The same. Note circulation, Rupees 1,23,380.

1847, January 16.—Dividend seven per cent. Mr. Abbott, the Deputy Secretary, was appointed Secretary on the resignation of Mr. James Calder Stewart. Mr. William Hay, a clerk in a mercantile house of this City, was nominated to the Deputy Secretaryship. On 30th June of this year, the Bank's Agency at Singapore was brought to a close. July 17.—Dividend seven per cent. Note circulation contracted to Rupees 55,910

1848, January.—The Bank stopped payment. This event had long been foreseen, but many perseveringly closed their eyes to the possibility of such an event, until the crash came upon them. For some years previously, it was well known to those accustomed to look carefully into the published accounts, that the Bank was in a hopelessly insolvent state, and that the dividends it declared, and of which it made so great a parade, were taken, not from the capital, for that had gone long before, but from the deposits that people were still confiding enough to make. No Bank has probably ever failed under circumstances so discreditable, and so humiliating to those who were the cause of the stoppage. The following remarks will give a pretty clear insight into the iniquities of the Union Bank parlour. The failure of the Union Bank of Calcutta, and the unfortunate situation of its victimised shareholders, have occupied the attention of the community of Calcutta, and created in England a strong sensation of disgust at the unprincipled conduct which brought about the catastrophe.

In 1839, the capital of the Union Bank having been increased to one million sterling, we have seen that anxiety was felt to find profitable employment for its own funds, and the deposits of its customers.* The system was then adopted of making advances to the indigo houses of Calcutta, on the deposit of title deeds of their factories, and assignment of the annual produce. To this system some opposition was raised. But this was not all. Another scheme was to introduce into the Bank the Scotch system of lending money on cash credits, to be granted on the personal security of the borrower, with the addition of such collateral security, real or personal, as might be thought sufficient; such loans were not like those hitherto granted to be debited to the borrower in one sum, and to be repaid by him at a time certain,

---

* The failures of Commercial Houses from 1830 to 1833, had reduced the number of merchants out of whom to select Directors, neither Civil nor Military Officers of the Company being allowed to take a seat in the Direction of a private Bank.

But the list at foot shows that in 1838 every Director was connected with a Commercial House, or in business, and so it continued for the next ten years, until the Bank's failure.

DIRECTORS IN 1833.

D. Tagore.
R. S. Thomson, Druggist.
Promothonath Day.
Prosunnocomar Tagore.
W. Martin (Cockerell and Co.)
W. C. Hurry (Assignee of Alexander and Co.)
K. R. McKenzie (Gilmore and Co.)
Radamadub Bannerjee.
James Cullen (MacKillop, Stewart and Co.)
W. Horn, Merchant.
T. Holroyd, (Assignee of Alexander Mackintosh and Co.)
J. W. Cragg (Bruce, Shand and Co.)—*Facts explanatory of the connection with the late firm of Cockerell and Co.*

but were to be drawn for, from time to time, as his necessities required, and repaid as his returns became available.

The deed of partnership offered an obstacle to this scheme, inasmuch as the deed prohibited loans for a longer term than four months; but this was got over by taking the borrower's note of hand at three months' date, giving him an assurance that on his paying up the interest, his note would be renewed, unless the Bank gave him six weeks' notice to the contrary.

The first advance on this sort of security was in December 1839, when a loan of Rupees 2,50,000 was made to the Calcutta Docking Company, collaterally secured by deposit of the title deeds of the docks. In February 1840, a large loan was made to the owners of certain collieries, on the collateral security of coals at their depôts, and the deposit of title deeds of the mines. Soon after a loan was made on the collateral security of some buildings near Calcutta. And later again, a proposition was favorably received by the Directors for granting such cash credits to Calcutta tradesmen.

In January 1840, the following proposition of a Director, regarding advances on indigo factories, was circulated among his colleagues—

"If a Planter and Agent conjointly deposit deeds of a block worth one lac, and agree to consign the whole produce to the Bank at the end of the season, I would advance a regulated portion of the value of the block, say two-thirds, at the commencement of the season, and increase the advance to full value, or even to a portion of the produce, say two-thirds, on the Planter's certificate that he had such in his godowns."

In fine, it was determined, by the Directors, to make

advances on cash credits collaterally secured by mortgages, and among others by mortgages of indigo factories.

Those engaged in the cultivation of indigo were not slow in availing themselves of the accommodation thus offered them. In June 1841, there were outstanding on the security of indigo factories, sums due to the Bank, amounting to Rupees 43,15,000, and in the year 1842, *the credits granted* on such securities amounted to Rupees 1,37,85,477 (equal to one million, three hundred and seventy-eight thousand, five hundred pounds sterling). On the 31st December of that year there was due to the Bank on these accounts Rupees 56,37,000, above half a million sterling.

This system was not introduced without deliberation and much discussion. In February 1841, a motion was made in the Bank parlour to the effect that no loans on landed property, or on blocks of indigo factories, or houses or factories of any kind be granted in future. The reasons urged against granting loans on such securities, generally, being that, under the deed of partnership, the Bank could not hold such collateral securities, except in cases where a debtor had failed to make good his prior obligation; and against such loans on indigo factories in particular, it was urged, that advancing money on such securities, involved the probability of the Bank being compelled to carry on the concern at its own risk, as without the growing of indigo on it were continued, the property pledged would become intrinsically worthless.

The motion was lost, and another to the effect that all existing loans of the above description be gradually wound up, was withdrawn, while a counter-motion was carried, to the effect, that the system of making advances on cash credits, with a deposit of title deeds by way of collateral security, was not inconsistent with the deed of partnership, was safe and profitable, and ought to be continued. In February of the subsequent year 1842, it was resolved that no accommodation should be granted on the collateral security of any real property, except with the view to the production of staple articles of produce; and that the extent of such accommodation should not exceed the estimated value of the property alone, or that of the average produce of the property. A week or two before it had been resolved that in the case of all future loans on indigo factories, the amount advanced should not exceed such sum as might reasonably be expected to be repaid from the produce of the season.

Of the two systems introduced into the Bank, that of buying and selling Bills of Exchange on London, appears to have been introduced by the proprietors. It was held, that under the old deed of partnership, the Bank could not do such business, and an alteration in the deed became necessary to allow it to do so. The question of introducing the system of cash credits on a deposit of title deeds of property as collateral security not being held to be fettered by the terms of the deed of partnership, the opinion of the proprietors was not expressly asked before the system was introduced by the Directors, who appear to have looked on it as a matter falling within the scope of their own discretionary powers.

In 1842, the loans and credits on deposit of goods and other securities, under which title these cash credits were comprised, amounted to Rupees 96,43,320-13-1.

Some attention to them appears about this time to have been directed by the proprietors; some failures had taken place, and questions were asked respecting the losses which the Bank might sustain by them, and respecting reports, that the greater part of the assets of the

Bank were appropriated to the accommodation of a few favored houses. At the half-yearly meeting on the 16th July 1842, the amount due under the same head had increased to Rupees 97,62,935-13-10. The detail will show what portion was invested in goods in the Bonded Warehouse, what amount in the cultivation of indigo and other factories, and what in other property.

Credits to Planters and Agents on the security of deposit of title deeds of indigo and saltpetre concerns	Rs.	57,70,135	13	1
Ditto on silk filatures ...	,,	1,57,500	6	0
Ditto on collieries	,,	2,84,270	2	6
Ditto to tradesmen on joint and several personal securities	,,	3,89,265	12	6
Ditto to public bodies ...	,,	2,54,756	0	0
Ditto on goods	,,	20,54,766	2	5
Ditto on shares, &c.	,,	8,52,241	4	4
	Rs.	97,62,935	13	10

In the interval, say between 1841 and 1843, or, to speak more positively, at the close of 1842, by the failure of indigo houses, (Messrs. Fergusson Brothers, Gilmore and Co., and others) 60 lacs of rupees, say £600,000 sterling, were locked up in indigo concerns, about £300,000 sterling in claims on indigo houses, partly only secured by factories, and nearly an equal sum, say £250,000, required for annual expenses of cultivation.

Two firms alone owed the Bank above 30 lacs of rupees, (three hundred thousand pounds,) leaving nothing but indigo factories to the Bank as security for this debt.

These 60 lacs of the Bank's capital were in fact sunk, and the question was, how could they be got out again?

This question, which was fairly brought before the proprietors, in January 1843, was felt to be a difficult one. The opinion of the proprietors having been taken, it was found to be in favor of withdrawing their capital from indigo investments as soon as they could.

Other indigo houses, besides those which had failed, partook of advances under this system: and after mature deliberation, the Directors and the Proprietors, who were present at the meetings of January and July 1843, and made acquainted with the state of these concerns, agreed not to sacrifice the indigo properties the Bank held, but to carry them on, limiting the advances as much as possible, and gradually disposing of the factories themselves. The proprietors also considered that it would be unfair by the houses who had hitherto enjoyed the advances given under this system, abruptly to withdraw all assistance, and a large sum was altogether appropriated to the maintenance of the system so adopted in 1840-41.

That this was an unwise decision, subsequent events may be supposed to have proved. The system adopted by the Bank was decidedly opposed to all sound banking principles.

In 1843, it was no longer a question whether indigo factories were securities on which it was prudent to invest the Bank's money; 60 lacs of Rupees of that money was at that time invested in those securities, and it was erroneously believed, that by limiting all advances to what was necessary for cultivating the lands, and by appropriating the produce, the Bank might gradually relieve its mortgages, so as to enable it to get rid of what was virtually its own property at no very heavy loss, and to enable its debtors to pay it off. Miserable fallacy! There was not a season in which the produce of these factories paid the cost of cultivation.

It would excite surprise to see under how very few names the enormous cash credit accounts on indigo for 1842 (nearly a million and a half of money) were comprised. When the Bank began to contract these accounts, the first names which disappeared from the books were those under which the smallest amounts of such credits were comprised, and the residue were left in proportionately much fewer hands than the whole had been originally distributed among. Gilmore and Co., Fergusson Brothers and Co., Alex. Rogers, Colville Gilmore and Co., Cockerell and Co., and Carr Tagore and Co., were soon almost the only houses with whom these accounts were open, and after the failure of the two first, such accounts were confined to the cases of the three last houses, and to some few cases where they had been opened with purchasers of indigo property, which had been thrown on the Bank. It soon came to this, that the demands on account of the securities to which alone the Bank could look for payment of large debts, proved as much as it could meet; and the necessary consequence of these debts being due upon a small number of accounts was, that the Bank's money fell to be distributed among few parties.

As a pretty fair specimen of the manner in which the Directors, who were members of the above-mentioned firms, helped themselves to the Bank money, it may be mentioned that Colville Gilmore and Co. were debtors, at one time, of twenty-four lacs of rupees, one-fourth part of the whole capital of the Bank; and that Cockerell and

Co. took cash credits to the amount of sixteen lacs of rupees. After 1843, when the Bank became desirous of withdrawing its money from these investments, it became usual to keep the sums due on such accounts under two heads, *viz.*, one comprising the outstanding balance, due on former advances, which retained its old name of "Advances on Securities;" the other comprising what was advanced for the cultivation of the season, which was called "Discounts on Security." Besides these, Cockerell and Co. had their ordinary discounts at the Bank, limited, like those of other houses in good repute, to three lacs of rupees, and they were in the habit of getting loans from the Bank, from time to time, on the deposit of Bills of Exchange drawn by them on their London Correspondents under special credits.

The following Abstracts show the accommodation granted them by the Bank in the respective years since 1843, in which year—1842-43—they had,

Cash Credits on indigo factories to the amount of		Rs. 16,70,000
In 1843-44.		
1. Advances on Security	4,30,000	
2. Discounts on Security	5,00,000	
	9,30,000	
3. Loans on deposit of London Bills	3,00,000	
4. Ordinary Discounts	3,00,000	
		15,30,000
In 1844-45.		
1. Advances on Security	3,00,000	
2. Discounts on Security	5,00,000	
Carried over ...	8,00,000	

	Brought forward ...	8,00,000	
3.	Loans on deposit of Bills ...	3,00,000	
4.	Ordinary Discounts	3,00,000	
		14,00,000	
	To this ought to be added advances on Khalboliah factory, which now fell into their hands, and was afterwards sold, separate advance on this	5,00,000	
			19,00,000

In 1845-46.

1.	Advances on Security	2,00,000	
2.	Discounts on Security	5,00,000	
		7,00,000	
3.	Loans on deposit of Bills ...	3,00,000	
4.	Ordinary Discounts	3,00,000	
5.	New Loan on Bonded Warehouse Shares	62,000	
6.	Ditto on Bengal Indigo Company's Shares	50,000	
			14,12,000

In 1846-47.

1.	Advances on Security	2,00,000	
2.	Discounts on Security	4,00,000	
		6,00,000	
3.	Loans on deposit of Bills ...	3,50,000	
4.	Ordinary Discounts	3,00,000	
5.	Loans on Bengal Indigo Company's Shares	2,50,000	
			15,00,000

In the above is omitted loans on goods, or on indigo actually made.

Fergusson Brothers and Co. failed in 1842, owing the Bank, on one consolidated account on the security of indigo factories, Rupees 21,00,000. The Bank sold great part of the property, on credit, to the original mortgager, and had to provide the yearly outlays, receiving the whole produce. It would have saved money if, on the failure of Fergusson Brothers and Co., the whole debt of Rupees 21,00,000 had been written off to profit and loss.

A very important branch of the Bank's business was its London Exchange business. The plan adopted was, for the Bank to buy here Commercial Bills on London, remitting them for realization to a London banker, and to sell here its own Bills drawn on such banker; its profit being the difference between what it bought Commercial Bills at, and what it sold its own Bills for, less the charges on the transaction. This profit, apt to be regarded as interest on money employed frequently only for a few hours, between the time of the Bank's paying for the Bills it bought, and receiving for the Bills it sold, was in truth an Insurance on the risk run; the main risk being that of the Bills remitted not being available assets for meeting the Bills drawn, and that risk dependent, not on the fact of whether the Bills bought were good or bad here, and at the time they were bought, but whether they would be good or bad in London, at the time they would become due, ten months afterwards.

Mr. Stewart said he had the management of this business, in his own hands entirely, from January 1844 till August 1846; *after which date,* he never purchased a Bill for remittance home, on his own responsibility, but invariably took the Directors' instructions what Bills to buy. During the two years and a half, in which this branch of the business was confided to his management, he said he remitted to Messrs. Glyn and Co. Bills exceeding a million sterling in amount, and never remitted them one bad penny. Mr. W. P. Grant said, the bad Bills remitted by the Bank amounted in all to about £280,000.

A great part of the advances to Colville Gilmore and Co., as much certainly as ten lacs, and probably more, consisted of Post Bills. So did a great part of the advance to Cockerell and Co. The six lacs advanced to them, on security of indigo at the factories, did so consist; so did a part, and probably the whole of their advance on deposit of London Bills, and a great part of their advance on Bengal Indigo Company's shares. When Post Bills were first made use of this was the common way in which they were taken. A person applied for a cash credit on certain security. He got this on certain terms of interest. He took the amount in Post Bills, bearing another lower rate of interest, and, when the Post Bills appeared at the Bank for payment, he paid the amount and the difference of interest on the account. Besides, the issues of Post Bills to Colville Gilmore and Co., and Cockerell and Co., which, in the abstract of their accounts with the Bank, have been included as cash, there were some others on securities which the parties might, under the rules of the Bank, have obtained on cash, to Hickey Bailey and Co., and some others.

It is not perhaps generally known to the public, what the nature of the India trade had been, since the breaking up the monopoly of the East India Company. All agricultural produce in India is generally raised by borrowed capital, the amount possessed by such cultivator is very small. A person in Bengal is said to be a large farmer, who has more than £20 to work with. Advances are made to agents, and by them to manufacturers and cultivators. For money so advanced, eight to ten, and even twelve per cent interest is paid, besides other advantages in commission, &c. In such a state of society, the intervention of the European capitalist is the only mode by which any of the staple* productions of India can be raised for export to this country, *viz.*—indigo for our manufactures—sugar for home consumption—silk, cotton, and other various minor articles, which form the export trade of the East, and are the means of paying for British manufactures, which have superseded those of the East. The capital is supplied *month by month,* until the produce is brought for shipment to the port, and many months' outlay must be paid, before the article has assumed a merchantable shape. Ever since the Company's Revenue has ceased to be employed in investments of produce, it has been to the European capitalist that the native producer has looked for the means of carrying on his cultivation and his manufacture. The rich natives have always been, and still are indisposed to give directly such advances; they prefer dealing in money in the bazars, and supplying the wants of Government by investment, in their Loans.†

Bearing in mind the above statement, the decision of the Union Bank Functionaries has been termed not so erroneous as it might otherwise have been considered. "Once stop the advances, and the debt and the proper-

* See "Evidence before the Select Committee on East India Matters in 1840."

† See "Correspondence and Documents relating to the suspension of W. P. Grant, Esq.,"—also "Facts explanatory of the connection with Cockerell and Co."

ties themselves are destroyed. Continue them—and an average crop, and fair prices, especially of an article like indigo, of which Bengal enjoys, to a considerable extent, almost a monopoly, and the debt is recovered, and the value of the property maintained." It is very well for an ex-Director, and one who was mixed up in the transactions of the Bank, to talk thus; but the safest course would have been to withdraw, as soon as it was found to be a losing concern, all capital from indigo investments. Of this, however, there was no chance, while the Directors were men who were heavily and hopelessly indebted to the Bank. The keeping up the factories they had mortgaged, enabled them to ward off, to an indeterminate period, the fatal day of insolvency. When very heavy claims of the Bank were, year after year, treated as good debts, without being paid off—when interest was added to the large sums hopelessly lost, and, the whole returned as tangible assets, can we wonder that the proprietors were deceived? And yet the remark is coolly hazarded, that no shareholder can in fairness complain of the general system the Directors pursued. We blame the shareholders for not looking more narrowly into their affairs, but we blame the Directors much more: they were the trustees of the shareholders, and in appropriating the funds of the Bank to any other purpose than that of legitimate banking, they shamefully violated their trust. A few favored houses absorbed nearly all the money the Bank possessed. It is not a question whether, had the usual advances been refused to the indigo houses from 1844 to 1847, the interests of the Bank would have suffered materially, from the diminished value of all indigo concerns, including those which belonged to the Bank; but whether the business the Bank was doing, was or was not in strict accordance with the principle of banking. The Bank's ruin is said to be attributed to dealing in *Bills of Exchange*, and to indigo engagements entered into as far back as 1840, and not to subsequent mismanagement: but the former Secretary, Mr. Stewart, asserted,* that it was owing to excessive credit given to a few particular houses in the form of indigo advances, and to the purchase of their Bills in 1847, and to other accommodation to them long after they were insolvent, that the Bank's ruin is truly to be attributed. This we are quite prepared to believe. ***The banking principle should not have been departed from, and, we should not have had to chronicle such disgraceful proceedings.*** As there is no breach of trust more flagrant than that of the Directors of Joint Stock Company helping themselves to the capital in the shape of advances, so there is no punishment sufficiently severe for such unprincipled robbery.

THE BANK OF HINDOSTAN.

The Bank of Hindostan, established by the late firm of Messrs. Alexander and Co., about 1770, was the oldest institution of the kind in India. Though it was a branch of the business of one of the first firms of the period, yet, that its operations were entirely distinct from their trading business, it may be assumed, from the fact that Mr. Barretto, of the firm of Barretto and Co., who had no interest in the houses, was a partner in the Bank for a few years. The circulation of its notes was confined entirely to Calcutta and the immediate neighborhood, the Government having refused to allow their reception into their Collectors' Treasuries in the Mofussil. They

* See "Facts and Documents relating to the Union Bank of Calcutta," page 11.

also refused to recognize them on the spot as a legal tender. The amount of the issues of this Bank was very fluctuating; sometimes not exceeding two or three lacs; at others reaching to twenty or twenty-five lacs, according to the state of the market. On two occasions this Bank most successfully supported very severe runs upon it. One in 1819; when in consequence of some forgeries, the proprietors issued a notice to the public, pointing their attention to the mode of distinguishing the genuine from forged notes. Some evil-disposed persons gave to this notice a false character, and spread reports among the natives, that unless the notes were brought in by a certain day, they would not be paid. The consequence was an immediate run, which brought in all, or nearly all the notes then outstanding,—about 18 lacs; which being cashed without difficulty, and the real tendency of the notice explained, were issued again within a few hours. The second occasion was in January 1829, when the failure of Messrs. Palmer and Co. spread the greatest alarm among the inhabitants of Calcutta. The Bank of Hindostan met the demand with the utmost promptness to the extent of about 20 lacs of Rupees. It continued its operations till the month of December 1832, when the most awful commercial crisis that ever visited India, by drawing into its vortex all the old firms, necessarily caused the stoppage of this Bank; for although it had commenced operations as an independent institution, and quite distinct from Messrs. Alexander and Co., it had latterly become so closely mixed up with the trading part of their business, as to be unable to weather the storm that wrecked the firm. Very few of its notes, however, were in circulation at the time the house failed.

THE COMMERCIAL BANK.

This institution, which partook somewhat of the character of a Joint Stock Bank, commenced operations on the 1st of May 1819. Its partners were the members of the firm of Mackintosh and Co., J. Melville and P. Reirson, Esquires, of the firm of Fergusson and Co., Edward Brightman, Esq., Gopeymohun Thakoor—the members of the firm of Joseph Barretto and Co., and Messrs. Mendietta Uriarte and Co. Although it was generally supposed to have been a constituent part of the firm of Mackintosh and Co., it was, in fact, a perfectly distinct establishment. Like that of the Bank of Hindostan, its circulation fluctuated according to the state of the market. The *average* amount of its notes in circulation was about 16 lacs; its operations continued uninterrupted till about the close of the year 1828, when in consequence of the failure of Messrs. Barretto and Co., and some of the other partners quitting Calcutta, the Bank contracted its circulation. In 1829 the Union Bank was projected, and finally established; and as this new institution was raised principally by the partners of the Commercial Bank, whose place it was intended to supply, its operations were gradually narrowed till 1833, when the failure of Messrs. Mackintosh and Co. took place. The settlement of the affairs of the Bank then devolved upon Baboo Dwarkanath Tagore, the only solvent partner, who finally adjusted all claims against the Bank.

THE CALCUTTA BANK.

This Bank was established in 1824 by Messrs. Palmer and Co. Its operations, as a Bank of Issue, ceased in 1829, before the failure of the house, in consequence of the arrangements which were then on foot for the establishment of the Union Bank; the Calcutta Bank's circulation averaged 20 lacs. Its notes were refused by the Government. Treasuries on the same grounds as were those of the Bank of Hindostan and the Commercial Bank.

THE BANK OF MIRZAPORE.

Nobody appears to be aware of the existence of such a Bank, and some have confounded it with the branch of the Bank of Bengal formerly established, prior to the present Agency, at the large commercial Town of Mirzapore.

In 1835-36, Mr. Bathurst, a young man, from England, of plausible manners, suave address and gentlemanly appearance; the son, or otherwise near relative of a highly respected Civil Servant, whose name is still a bye-word at Mirzapore, determined upon striking out for himself a new business which was to make his fortune. He announced the establishment of a Bank to be called "THE BANK OF MIRZAPORE." In connection with this undertaking he came to Calcutta, had the necessary plates engraved, and a large stock of notes printed. With these—other materials, and the promise of support from a highly respectable firm in Calcutta, if he went on cautiously, he returned to Mirzapore and commenced business. As may be supposed, the native mahajuns did not, at first, readily enter into his views; but Mr. Bathurst's ingenuity soon supplied him with all the sinews of war, and obtained for his bank-notes a limited circulation. He appointed an Agent in Calcutta, to whom he remitted funds to be applied in the payment of Bills on Calcutta, which he negotiated at

Mirzapore. The punctuality which characterized these transactions for a time, inspired the mahajuns with confidence, and they began to lend him money and take his notes, of which he had sent a goodly supply to Calcutta to be put into circulation. The public, however, had not the same confidence in them as in the notes of the Bank of Bengal, and Mr. Bathurst's expectations were disappointed. In 1837 the Bank collapsed, and the originator was compelled to leave India, to avoid unpleasant proceedings. The place of business at Mirzapore was the large house known as Bathurst's, occupied, before the mutiny, by Mr. James Hunt, of Hunt and Emsley, and, during that most eventful period, turned into a Fort. Some of the notes of the Mirzapore Bank are, we believe, still to be met with in the Upper Provinces; but they are now merely looked upon as curiosities.

THE AGRA AND UNITED SERVICE BANK "LIMITED."

ESTABLISHED IN INDIA, JULY 1833.

Incorporated June 1857, *by Royal Charter, under* 7 *and* 8 *Victoria C.* 112.

This Bank, which dates its rise from the breaking up of the great Calcutta Agency houses in 1829-30, and is, to a certain extent, founded on their *debris,* made its first debut as a Mofussil institution. The intention, in getting it up, was to supply the place of those private banking houses which, in their character of Bankers and Agents, were accustomed to receive, at a high rate of interest, the accumulated savings of people of all grades in the Civil and Military Services of the East India Company. The ruin which struck far and wide, and left on the minds of the Indian Community a furrow which it will require more than half a century totally to efface, appeared perfectly remediless, until it was suggested that the best course the Services could take was to start an institution which should not only receive, as did the Agency houses, their monthly savings, but should employ the contributed funds in such business as would, in a small degree, repay the very heavy losses they had sustained. A plan was promulgated by an eminent member of the Civil Service for a general United Service Agency.* The plan itself was not carried out, but gave birth to the scheme of a Joint Service Bank at Agra. A preliminary meeting was held at Agra on the 4th March 1833, when the necessary arrangements having been made, the institution started into life on the 1st July following, under the denomination of THE AGRA BANK, with a capital of Rupees ten lacs (10,00,000 of rupees) in 4,000 shares of Rupees 250 each, the whole of which was paid up by the 31st December 1836. It was placed under the management, for some time, of experienced commercial gentlemen, and watched over with no little care by a Committee of the shareholders. Under such management, the shares, which were principally held by gentlemen of the Services, rose to a premium.

The first Directors were—

Sir W. RICHARDS, K. C. B.	J. S. BOLDERO, ESQ., C. S.
M. W. WOOLLASTON, ESQ.	CAPT. JAS. GRAHAM.
CAPT. J. F. BLOIS.	H. H. BELL, ESQ.

In addition to the usual business of Joint Stock Banks, the Bank was to advance money, for certain terms, to the Officers in the Services, on the security of approved sureties, and to grant loans to regiments

* Its origin is attributed to Dr. Henderson.

to facilitate the establishment and maintenance of messes, bands, libraries, and other regimental purposes.

The Secretaryship was held, in the first instance, for a few months, by Mr. J. O. Beckett, and subsequently by Mr. Geo. J. Gordon, who, on joining the Union Bank of Calcutta, was succeeded by Capt. R. G. Macgregor as Secretary; Kishen Chund being Treasurer, and C. G. Mansell, C. S., General Pollock, and Captain the Hon'ble H. B. Dalzell being the Trustees. The proprietors were always respectable, numbering, as they still do, in their ranks, the best and most influential men in the Services, including many high Civilians, General Officers, and other persons of capital and reputation.

The original rules of the Company declared :—

Business of the Company.

"That the business and concerns of the said Company shall consist in issuing Promissory Notes; in the purchase, sale, and negotiation of Bills of Exchange, which said Promissory Notes and Bills of Exchange shall be payable on demand, or at such time after date or sight as the Directors for the time being shall fix, to parties who shall require the same.

In discounting Bills, Hoondies, and Promissory Notes. In discounting Salary Bills of persons in the service of Government after the same shall have become due.

In lending money repayable within such periods as may be determined by the Directors, and making advances on the security of personal property, or on the security of two or more individuals, covered also, if considered expedient, by an insurance on the life of the borrower.

In making advances on the security of Government Stock or Paper endorsed to the Bank.

In making advances on assignments of the salary of persons in the public service.

In making advances on cash accounts to persons giving undoubted security or giving guarantee of another party or parties, or a mortgage of real property in the Division of Agra, or in the immediate neighborhood of any other place where the Bank may hereafter be established, provided that the aggregated sums advanced on mortgage of real property shall never exceed one-fifth of the subscribed capital of the Bank.

In the purchase and sale of coin and bullion and of Government Securities.

In receiving deposits of cash and allowing interest thereon when the same shall to the Directors seem expedient.

In money Agency and other branches of business usually transacted by Bankers, subject always to such rules and restrictions as the proprietors at any general meeting may from time to time direct as hereinafter more particularly provided for."

A great deal has been written and said about the evils caused by the provincial Banks in fostering extravagance, and hopelessly embarrassing young men. There is certainly much truth in many remarks that have been made, but there has been unjustifiable clamour and vituperation. By the failures of the large Agency houses, all the married men were ruined, hundreds of widows and orphans were left destitute, family remittances were dishonored, to the great loss and serious distress of those at home: numbers were prevented from retiring from the Service, by which promotion was greatly impeded, and the Orphan and other funds suffered much injury. On the other hand, the Mofussil Banks drew into productive operation the various sums of money which would otherwise lie useless in the hands of individuals, and were useful as places of security for the deposit of money. The establishment of these Banks has been a source of great loss to the Calcutta Agency houses. The opium, indigo, and sugar speculators severely felt the want of capital invested in them, and hence the soreness manifested.

1837.—In the summer of this year, Mr. Thomas Bracken, (afterwards Secretary to the Bank of Bengal,) was solicited by the Directors of the Agra and United Service Bank at Agra, to undertake the formation, at Calcutta, of an Agency of this Bank, (the first it ever had) which he settled and took charge of, in the capacity of Agent, on 13th November 1838.

The origin of the Agency was this. At Agra, the season for purchasing Hoondies and Bills to any large amount was limited to six or seven months of the cold weather, while the sale of the Bank's Bills continued pretty equally throughout the year. By necessity, therefore, a portion of the remittances accumulated in Calcutta, over and above the Bills drawn against them, and, for this surplus, existing for five or six months, employment of course was desirable. The total amount of exchange operations this year were estimated in round numbers at thirty lacs, and the proportion available for temporary employment at six or seven lacs. The Union Bank refused to allow on the Agra Bank's Funds more than one per cent interest. Hence the idea of an Agency, conducted under a Committee of shareholders resident in Calcutta; and the result, as far as can be judged, was favorable. Some intention existed of employing a mercantile house, but objections were raised on the ground of a confliction of interests. As Mr. Bracken had no connection, direct or indirect, with any commercial establishment in Calcutta, the situation was offered to him unsolicited, and his services in it met with the cordial approbation of the Directors and shareholders. The Calcutta Agency was maintained at a cost of about Rupees 1,200 a month, and was of material service in a class of operations increasing in importance. The Directors negatived a proposition to decrease the salary of the Calcutta Agent, on the ground of the intelligence, worth, and active usefulness of the then Agent. The Agra Bank Directors offered Mr. Bracken the Secretaryship of that establishment, which he declined, although on the last occasion, it was intimated to him that the salary would be raised to 25,000 rupees and a house.

1839, June.—Some of the Directors being dissatisfied with the small measure of good that was then derived, the stock was doubled by call for an additional payment of 250 per share, the shares being raised to Rupees 500 each, thus making the capital 20 lacs. The expectations, however, which were entertained of a large accession of work in commercial transactions and in exchanges, failed; the loans at the same time were considerably enhanced in extent, and still constitute the grand staple of the Bank's profits. Mr. Bracken resigned the Calcutta Agency, being succeeded by Mr. F. R. Hampton.

The following augmentations of capital took place :—

1841	 1,000	shares.
1842	 3,000	,,
1844	 1,000	,,
1845	 2,000	,,
1846	 1,000	,,
1847	 1,555	,,

1843.—A branch was opened at Madras under the management of Mr. J. I. Geddes.

1845.—A branch was opened at Bombay by Mr. H. W. I. Wood, the Deputy Secretary at Agra, and remained under his charge until his departure for England in 1847, when Mr. J. G. H. Brown succeeded.

Paid-up Capital	Rs.	45,00,000
Number of Shares	„	9,000
Par value of Share	„	500
Number of Shareholders	„	427

Secretary ...	CAPTAIN R. G. MACGREGOR.
Accountant ...	J. W. URQUHART, ESQ.
Agents in London ...	MESSRS. COUTTS AND CO.
Agent in Calcutta ...	F. R. HAMPTON, ESQ.
Agent in Madras ...	J. I. GEDDES, ESQ.
Agent in Bombay ...	H. W. I. WOOD, ESQ
Agent in Mirzapore...	W. LIDDELL, ESQ.

Market value of Shares......... Rs. 775 to 800

As the establishment of the Bombay Agency completed, in India, the chain of establishments necessary for the satisfactory conduct of the Bank's affairs, much benefit was anticipated from the measure.

1846, May 1.—A branch was established in London under Mr. F. R. Hampton, who was deputed from Calcutta by the Directors. Directors consider the expediency of rendering the stock of the Bank transferable in England. Reserve Fund, Rupees 1,20,000.

1847, July 1.—Paid-up capital, Rupees 60,00,000, in 12,000 shares of Rupees 500 each. The expenses of management being about two per cent on the paid-up capital. The dividends paid up to this time, were, on an average, equal to 11 per cent per annum. Mr. F. R. Hampton, having decided upon joining the firm of Mackenzie, Lyall and Co., Calcutta, retires from the London Agency, being temporarily succeeded, as official Agent, by Mr. H. W. I. Wood from Bombay. On this occasion, the London Committee of the Agra Bank directed the following record of their sentiments to be conveyed to him:

"Mr. F. R. Hampton, having this day reported his retirement from the management of this Agency, the Committee cannot deny themselves the gratification of recording the high sense they entertain of his valuable services. With thorough habits of business, a complete identification of his own interests with those of the Bank, and a perfect knowledge of the duty of his office, Mr. Hampton has ever brought to the performance of them such facilities of explanation, so sound a judgment, and such obligingness of disposition, as have justly obtained for him the unqualified respect and hearty good wishes of every individual connected with the establishment."

Mr. F. R. Neilson, the Calcutta Agent, appointed Secretary whenever Captain R. G. MacGregor should leave to take charge of the London Agency. Mr. H. W. I. Wood appointed Agent in Calcutta. December 31.—Reserve Fund, Rupees 1,89,895-7-1. Paid-up capital, Rupees 67,77,500, in 13,555 shares. Some losses were sustained, but none to excite uneasiness. A general meeting adopts the Resolution of the Directors to make the stock transferable in England. The Directors, at Agra, submit their accounts, for the first time, to an independent audit.

1848.—Some losses were sustained, attributable, partly, to the failure of consignees, before arrival, of the shipments against which Bills were drawn, thus throwing upon the Bank the additional expense of duty, freight, and charges; and, partly, to the advances on Union Bank shares, upon the security of a party believed to be individually competent for a much larger amount, but who was ruined by the insolvency of the Bank. A violent and indiscriminating panic, affecting all financial relations, and depreciating all securities, public and private, seriously affected the value of the stock of the Bank in the local market, and particularly in Calcutta and Bombay. In consequence of a period of commercial disaster, Captain MacGregor consented, on the wish of the Directors, and at considerable sacrifice and self-denial, to continue at his post.

A general meeting passed the following resolutions:—

"That in conformity with the recommendation of the Bank's Counsel the 1st clause of the deed of partnership be altered as follows:—

That the business and concerns of the said Company shall consist in issuing Promissory Notes payable to bearer on demand, for any sums not less than Rupees one hundred and not exceeding Rupees ten thousand, and Bills of Exchange, including the purchase, sale and negotiation thereof, payable either to bearer or order, on demand, or at sight, or at such date or sight as the Directors for the time being shall fix to parties requiring the same. Provided that such Promissory Notes and Bills of Exchange shall purport to be signed 'FOR THE AGRA AND UNITED SERVICE BANK,' and shall be made, drawn, or accepted, respectively, either by the Secretary or Acting Secretary or one of the Local Agents of the said Bank. Provided that no securities shall be issued by the said Bank or any of its Branches other than such as are hereinbefore specified.

In discounting Bills, Hoondies and Promissory Notes. In discounting Salary Bills of persons in the service of Government after the same shall have become due.

In lending money repayable within such periods as may be determined by the Directors, and making advances on the security of personal property, or on the security of two or more individuals, covered also, if considered expedient, by an insurance on the life of the borrower.

In making advances on the security of Government Stock or Paper endorsed to the Bank.

In making advances on assignments of the salary of persons in the public service.

In making advances on cash accounts to persons giving undoubted security or giving guarantee of another party or parties, or a mortgage of real property in the Division of Agra, or in the immediate neighborhood of any other place where the Bank may hereafter be established, provided that the aggregated sums advanced on mortgage of real property shall never exceed one-fifth of the subscribed capital of the Bank.

In the purchase and sale of Coin and Bullion and of Government Securities.

In receiving deposits of cash and allowing interest thereon when the same shall to the Directors seem expedient.

In money agency and other branches of business usually transacted by Bankers, subject always to such rules and restrictions as the Proprietors at any General Meeting may from time to time direct as hereinafter more particularly provided for; and it is hereby declared and provided that the Secretary, or Acting Secretary, and also the several Local Agents of the Bank, with the knowledge and consent of a majority of the several Local Committees respectively, have and shall have full power and authority to discount, sell, negotiate, pledge, endorse, and transfer all securities whatsoever belonging to the said Bank standing in the names of such Officers respectively or endorsed to them respectively, either in their names individually, or in their names with the addition of such office or capacity, and that such sales, pledges, endorsements, and transfers shall be fully and effectually binding upon the said Bank."

The following were the position and staff of the Bank, 1st January 1848:—

Reserve Fund................	Rs.	2,11,638	4	2
Paid-up Capital..............	„	67,77,500	0	0
Number of Shares............	„	13,555	0	0
Par value.......................	„	500	0	0
Number of Shareholders...	„	624	0	0

Secretary	...	CAPTAIN R. G. MACGREGOR.
Accountant	...	J. W. URQUHART, ESQ.
Agent in London,	Under the control of Proprietary Committees.	H. W. I. WOOD, ESQ.
Agent in Calcutta,		F. R. NEILSON, ESQ.
Agent in Madras,		J. I. GEDDES, ESQ.
Agent in Bombay,		J. G. H. BROWN, ESQ.
Agent in Mirzapore	...	J. S. PELLETREAU, ESQ.

1849, January.—The Directors considered it necessary to address the Government with the view of obtaining a legislative enactment for the Bank. Certain requisitions were accordingly sent to the Bengal Government, requiring :—

"1. A power to enable the Bank to sue and to be sued in the name of the Secretary of the Company for the time being, at its head office, and in the names of the duly appointed Agents for the time being of its several Branches in India, namely, at Calcutta, Madras, and Bombay.

2. A power restricting the liability of the Proprietors to the amount of the share or shares held by each respectively.

3. A power authorizing the Governor-General of India in Council to appoint (from a list comprising, at the Head Office, six names, and at each of the Branches three names, such lists being framed by the Directors of the Bank for the time being) two Directors at the Head Office and one member of Committee at each of the Branches, in addition to the ordinary number of six Directors elected by the proprietors, and in the case of Branch Committees to the members nominated by the Director; such additional Directors and Committee men being in virtue of such appointment considered thenceforward as Directors on the part of Government, and vested with all powers and privileges appertaining to such office, the same as if they were ordinary Directors chosen by the proprietors at large.

4. That, whereas at present, in particular cases, the Bank is subjected to a double or doubtful jurisdiction of the Supreme Courts of Judicature at the Presidencies on the one hand, and of the Company's Courts in the Mofussil on the other, some new legislative provision be made, whereby it may be secured from the consequences of such anomaly and injustice; for instance, that it be subject at the Presidencies to the jurisdiction of the Supreme Courts alone; and where located in the Mofussil to that of the Mofussil Courts only, or at least, that, after having satisfied the decree of one Court, it shall not also be subjected to the power of the other."

August.—Directors reported probability of considerable loss being incurred at Bombay, in consequence of deficient, or rather disputed security held in three cases of advances made on Oriental Bank stock. This business had previously been very profitable, but the wish to act, in consequence, with liberality towards good and old customers had been allowed, as events proved, too great a weight. Unaware however of the distant, costly, and hazardous speculations, beyond their personal control, into which the parties alluded to had entered, the Directors had no sufficient reason to doubt their continued competency, and no apprehension was entertained that any part of the security for their advances was liable to question.

The following was the position and staff of the Bank, 30th June 1849:—

Reserve Fund	Rs. 3,69,139	10	0
Paid-up Capital	„ 67,77,500	0	0
Number of Shares	„ 13,555	0	0
Par value	„ 500	0	0
Number of Shareholders...	„ 608	0	0

Secretary	...	CAPTAIN R. G. MACGREGOR.
Assistant Secretary	...	T. H. FALKLAND, ESQ.
Accountant	...	J. W. URQUHART, ESQ.
Agent in London,	Under the control of Proprietary Committees.	H. W. I. WOOD, ESQ.
Agent in Calcutta,		F. R. NEILSON, ESQ.
Agent in Madras,		J. I. GEDDES, ESQ.
Agent in Bombay,		J. G. H. BROWN, ESQ.

1850, December 31.—Reserve Fund, Rs. 4,65,563-3-11. A general meeting passed the following resolution relative to the Secretary, Captain MacGregor:—" That the proposed early retirêment of Captain R. G. MacGregor from the office of Secretary to the Agra and United Service Bank, and his contemplated assumption of the duties of Agent of the Institution in London, to which he has been appointed, call for the expression of the sentiments of the general body of proprietors on his executive administration of the affairs of the Bank during a period of ten years. They feel bound to declare their high opinion of the zeal, integrity, and unwearied assiduity which has progressively, in that period, raised the Bank from its limited sphere of private and public advantage and utility to its present prosperity; and persuaded that the same spirit which has ever animated him in the exercise of his official duties, will continue to be exerted with unabated interest, in the new position for which he has been selected, for the benefit of the concern which owes so much to his exertions, they hereby tender him sincere thanks for his previous valuable services, and express the fullest confidence in his effective management of the new charge into which he is about to enter." Directors announce that they had purchased in, and cancelled 367 shares of the Bank at a discount varying from five to ten per cent.

1851, February.—Paid-up capital, Rupees 63,64,500, in 12,729 shares. Number of shareholders, 547. The difference between this and the year 1848 is accounted by the fact that the shares of several deceased persons were bought by the Bank and cancelled. Reserve Fund, Rupees 4,65,563-3-11. Mr. H. W. I. Wood voluntarily terminates his connection with the Bank. Considerable anxiety being felt to know the true position of the Bank, three Auditors were appointed to examine and report, which they did satisfactorily.

1852, June 30.—Directors fix 28th September to consider the question of the transfer of the Head Office to Calcutta. The Secretary, Mr. Neilson, inspected the branches at Bombay and Madras prior to his removal to Calcutta. Mr. Mackintosh Balfour, the Calcutta Agent, appointed to be Branch Agent at Agra.

1853, February 15.—Since the last general meeting transfer of the Head Office of the Bank from Agra to

Calcutta has taken place. The Directors establish an Agency at Lahore, which, they conceive, will be of great service to the Bank's constituents in the Punjab. Directors purchase the premises occupied by the Bank in Council House street.

1854.—A general meeting confirms the resolutions of a special general meeting, held 10th January, to increase the capital to 70 lacs of rupees, and to establish a Branch of the Bank in China. Mr. Cardno appointed to the Agency at Canton.

1855.—Last general meeting limited the dividends to nine, afterwards ten per cent, until the Reserve Fund should amount to 15 lacs. General meeting confirms resolution to increase the capital 20 lacs more.

1856.—Reserve Fund, Rupees 13,73,906-15-4. December 31.—Paid-up capital, 75,00,000. The Chinese, at Canton, burned down the Bank house, together with all the factories. The books, papers, cash, &c., belonging to the Bank had been previously removed and placed in safety. The Agency temporarily located at Hong-Kong.

1857.—Directors contemplate removal of the Head Office of the Bank from Calcutta to London. A general meeting awards to Mr. Neilson, on his departure from India to take charge of the London Office, a testimonial to the amount of £300, in approbation of his conduct of the Bank's affairs in India. This year was marked by serious and unprecedented disturbances in India, owing to the mutiny of the East India Company's troops.

1858.—The first ordinary general meeting was held in London in April. Steps are taken to procure the registration of the Bank, as a Bank with limited liability. May.—A Branch was opened at Shanghai. December 31.—Paid-up capital, £1,000,000. Reserve Fund, £164,535-13-0.

1859.—Directors state that the Bank's claim for compensation, to the extent of 21,784 dollars, for destruction of its property at Canton, by the Chinese in 1856, had been passed by Her Majesty's Consul, subject to confirmation.

1860.—Reserve Fund, £190,000. Directors apply £3,000 to open a superannuation fund account, considering that provision for this eventual liability should be gradually made by moderate appropriations from the yearly profits. In order to provide further for the heavy and fast increasing duties of the Head Office, Mr. William Shipman is appointed London Manager. Mr. F. R. Neilson, General Manager, dies at Boulogne.

1861.—Reserve Fund, £200,000. The Bank established a Branch at Kurrachee. Mr. Mackintosh Balfour, the Manager of the Calcutta Branch, appointed General Manager in the place of the late Mr. Neilson, retaining, while in India, the duty of Inspector of Branches. Paid-up capital, £1,000,000 sterling. The claims of the Bank against the London and Eastern Banking Corporation stated to amount to £16,000 and upwards, against securities of £13,000.

1862.—Mr. John Cardno, formerly the Manager at Shanghai, appointed Chief Manager in India, with Mr. H. G. Dunlop, Deputy Manager at Calcutta. A Branch of the Bank opened at Edinburgh. A general meeting awards Major R. G. MacGregor an annuity of £500 per annum, on his retirement from the Chair. April 23.—Mr. Dunlop appointed Manager at Calcutta.

1863, January 1.—Mr. E. A. Flinders, Accountant of the Eastern Bengal Railway Company, appointed Deputy Manager.

The following is a detailed statement of the dividends declared by the Bank:—

1833 ... 2nd half-year, at the rate of	8	per cent per annum.
1834 ... 1st ditto ditto	10	ditto ditto.
„ ... 2nd ditto ditto	10	ditto ditto.
1835 ... 1st ditto ditto	10	ditto ditto.
„ ... 2nd ditto ditto	12	ditto ditto.
1836 ... 1st ditto ditto	12	ditto ditto.
„ ... 2nd ditto ditto	14	ditto ditto.
1837 ... 1st ditto ditto	12	ditto ditto.
„ ... 2nd ditto ditto	16	ditto ditto.
1838 ... 1st ditto ditto	12	ditto ditto.
„ ... 2nd ditto ditto	11	ditto ditto.
1839 ... 1st ditto ditto	10	ditto ditto.
„ ... 2nd ditto ditto	9	ditto ditto.
1840 ... 1st ditto ditto	11	ditto ditto.
„ ... 2nd ditto ditto	10	ditto ditto.
1841 ... 1st ditto ditto	11½	ditto ditto.
„ ... 2nd ditto ditto	12	ditto ditto.
1842 ... 1st ditto ditto	11	ditto ditto.
„ ... 2nd ditto ditto	12	ditto ditto.
1843 ... 1st ditto ditto	11½	ditto ditto.
„ ... 2nd ditto ditto	11	ditto ditto.
1844 ... 1st ditto ditto	11	ditto ditto.
„ ... 2nd ditto ditto	11	ditto ditto.
1845 ... 1st ditto ditto	12	ditto ditto.
„ ... 2nd ditto ditto	11	ditto ditto.
1846 ... 1st ditto ditto	12	ditto ditto.
„ ... 2nd ditto ditto	12	ditto ditto.

1847	... 1st half-year, at the rate of	12	per cent. per annum.
„	... 2nd ditto ditto	10	ditto ditto.
1848	... 1st ditto ditto	10	ditto ditto.
1849	Dividend	8	ditto ditto.
1850	„	8	ditto ditto.
1851	„	9	ditto ditto.
1852	„	9	ditto ditto.
1853	„	9	ditto ditto.
1854	„	10	ditto ditto.
1855	„	10	ditto ditto.
1856	„	10	ditto ditto.
1857	„	10	ditto ditto.
1858	„	10	ditto ditto.
1859	„	10	ditto ditto.
	Bonus 1 £ per share.		
1860	... Dividend	10	ditto ditto.
	Bonus 1 £ per Share.		
1861	... Dividend	12	ditto ditto.

Giving an average dividend of a fraction above eleven per cent per annum. The shares had generally risen in value, from the first establishment of the Bank, until the period of commercial difficulty in connection with the failure of the Union Bank, when they fell to par. The Bank has no bank-note circulation in India. Mr. G. J. Gordon, when Secretary, tried very hard to establish one, but it was discountenanced by Government; and, had it been allowed, would have failed in its effect, for the natives would not have used the notes to a sufficient extent.

In addition to the dividends, bonuses to a large amount have, at different times, been divided amongst the proprietors. The following will show the present state and Staff of the Bank.

Paid-up Capital, £1,000,000 (One Million Sterling).

Subscribed Capital, £2,000,000 (Two Million Sterling), in 20,000 Shares of £100 each.

Number of Shareholders (whose Names are published Annually)—612.

Reserve Fund, £200,000.

Head Office,

27, Cannon Street, London, E. C.

Branches at Calcutta, Bombay, Madras, Agra, Lahore, Umritsur, Kurrachee, Shanghai, Hong-Kong, and Sydney.

General Manager ... MACKINTOSH BALFOUR.
Secretary ... T. J. MACRITCHIE.
Accountant ... G. B. DALBY.
Inspector of Branches ... JOHN CARDNO.
Manager at Calcutta ... H. G. DUNLOP.
Deputy ditto ... E. A. FLINDERS.
Manager at Bombay ... H. B. MACCULLOCH.
Manager at Madras ... EDWARD MORRIS.
Manager at Agra ... WILLIAM BIRKS.
Manager at Lahore ... HECTOR GUNN.
Manager at Umritsur ... T. BAILEY.

Manager at Kurrachee	...	R. E. W. BAKER.
Manager at Shanghai	...	HENRY TURNER.
Manager at Hong-Kong	...	HENRY NOBLE.
Manager at Sydney	...	ALEXANDER CAMPBELL.

Auditors, WM. NEWMARCH and J. H. WILLIAMS.

Solicitors, MESSRS. LACY and BRIDGES, 19, *Kings' Arms Yard.*

Calcutta Branch.

Office, No. 2, Council House Street.

Under the Management of a Committee of Resident Shareholders.

Hours of business, 10 A. M. *to* 3 P. M. *On Saturday to* 1 P. M.

No Cash receipt or payment after 3 P. M.

Manager	...	HAMILTON G. DUNLOP.
Deputy Manager	...	E. A. FLINDERS.
Accountant	...	J. PARSICK.
Assistants	...	W. C. SMITH, W. Y. PODE, and J. T. MENZIES.
Assistant Accountant	...	OMBERKACHURN SOOR.
Treasurer	...	MODOOSOODUN SEN.

NORTH-WESTERN BANK OF INDIA.

This Bank was originally established at Mussoorie, as a private bank, in January 1840, by Mr. Solaroli, Mr. Troup, and Major Angelo, on a capital of Rupees 50,000, for merely local discounts, and other local purposes, under the designation of the MUSSOORIE BANK.

In 1841, the capital was doubled, and seven other gentlemen joined the Bank; but, finding this was not sufficient for the wants of the rising settlement, it was converted, in January 1844, into a Joint Stock Bank, with a capital of 5 lacs of rupees, divided into 1,000 shares of Rupees 500 each, under the superintendence of a board of six Directors, and three Trustees.

On the 1st January 1844 the co-partnership was renewed and extended for a term of ten years, under the same title and denomination of the Mussoorie Bank, with power to alter the title, at any period within the ten years, should it be deemed necessary. The Articles of Agreement for the conduct of the Company provided:—

"That the business of the said Company shall consist in issuing Promissory Notes, in the purchase, sale and negotiation of Bills of Exchange, which said Promissory Notes and Bills of Exchange shall be payable on demand or at such time after date or sight, as the Manager, for the time being, shall fix to parties who shall require the same.

In discounting Bills, Hoondies and Promissory Notes, in discounting Salary Bills of persons in the service of Government, after the same shall have become due.

In lending money repayable within such periods as may be determined by the Manager, and making advances on the security of personal property, or on the security of two or more individuals, covered also, if considered expedient, by an Insurance on the life of the borrower.

In lending advances on the security of Government Stock, or paper endorsed to the Bank.

In making advances on assignments of the salary of persons in public service.

In making advances on cash accounts to persons giving undoubted security, or giving guarantee of another party or parties, or a mortgage of real property in the settlement of Mussoorie, or in the immediate neighborhood of any other place where the Bank may hereafter be established, provided that the aggregated sums advanced on mortgage of real property, shall never exceed one-fifth of the subscribed capital of the Bank.

In the purchase and sale of coin and bullion and of Government Securities.

In receiving deposits of cash and allowing interest thereon, when the same shall to the Manager seem expedient.

In money agency and other branches of business usually transacted by Bankers, subject always to such rules and restrictions as the proprietors, at any general meeting, may, from time to time, direct as hereinafter more particularly provided for."

1844, July 1.—The capital was increased 1,000 shares more, making it 10 lacs.

1845, January 1.—The capital was increased 2,000 shares, making it 20 lacs.

1846, January 1.—The capital was increased 2,000 shares, making it 30 lacs.

1847, May 1.—The capital was increased 1,000 shares, making it 35 lacs.

September 1, was again increased 1,000 shares, making it 40 lacs.

The manner in which these increases were made were as follows, and the dividends paid since 1st January 1842, are also detailed :—

Memo. of the several dates of Increase, and of the Distribution of the Stock of the North-Western Bank of India.

1st January 1844...	1,000 shares...	Rs. 5,00,000	0	0	
1st July 1844...	1,000 „ ...	„ 5,00,000	0	0	To shareholders, according to their previous holding, giving one new for every old share.
1st January 1845...	2,000 shares...	Rs. 10,00,000	0	0	
	2,000 „ ...	„ 10,00,000	0	0	400 shares to Reserve and 1,600 to shareholders, giving four-fifths of a new for every old share.
1st January 1846...	4,000 shares ..	Rs. 20,00,000	0	0	
	2,000 „ ...	„ 10,00,000	0	0	400 to London. 400 to Calcutta. 200 to Bombay. Total 1,000 to Reserve. 1,000 to shareholders, giving one-fourth new for every old share.

1st May 1847 ...	6,000 shares...Rs.30,00,000 0 0		
	1,000 " ... " 5,00,000 0 0	500 to Reserve and 500 to shareholders, giving one-twelfth new for every old share.
1st Sept. 1847 ...	7,000 shares...Rs.35,00,000 0 0		
	1,000 " ... " 5,00,000 0 0	500 to Reserve, and 500 to shareholders, giving one-fourteenth new for every old share.
	8,000 shares ... Rs. 40,00,000 0 0		

The following dividends were declared from 1842:—

1st January	to 30th June 1842	10 per cent.
1st July	to 31st Dec. 1842	10 per cent.
1st January	to 30th June 1843	12 per cent.
1st July	to 31st Dec. 1843	14 per cent.
1st January	to 30th June 1844	10 per cent.
1st July	to 31st Dec. 1844	10 per cent.
1st January	to 30th June 1845	10 per cent.
1st July	to 31st Dec. 1845	10 per cent.
1st January	to 30th June 1846	10 per cent.
1st July	to 31st Dec. 1846	12 per cent.
1st January	to 30th June 1847	12 per cent.
1st July	to 31st Dec. 1847	8 per cent.
1st January	to 30th June 1848	8 per cent.

1847, December.—The drafts of the Bank on Messrs. Glyn and Co., the London Bankers, were refused acceptance, in consequence of the securities received by Glyn and Co. being insufficient to cover the amount of drafts drawn. Mr. James Watson, the London Agent, however, gave protection to all presented. The paid-up capital, at this date, was Rupees 40,00,000, with a Reserve Fund of Rupees 3,00,000. On the arrival of the mail, Glyn and Co. accepted the drafts refused.

1848, June 30.—The Calcutta Committee recommended that Rupees 60,000 out of the profits should be reserved to meet chances of eventual deficiencies on the

E 1

realization of Bills on England returned. Dividend declared at eight per cent per annum.

1849.—Declared dividend at eight per cent per annum. Reserve Fund, Rupees 2,19,143-2-9. August 20.—A meeting of proprietors was held at Meerut, when it was resolved to reduce the capital to THIRTY LACS in accordance with the resolution of the Directors. October 25.—A special meeting confirmed this resolution. About this time also the establishment of a Branch in Calcutta and London was determined on, for the protection of the interests of retired shareholders in Europe, the safe remittance of their funds, and for the service of the public generally. Local Committees were also formed, and the practical workings of their Branches proved most conducive to the interests of shareholders and the public.

Mr. R. J. R. Campbell, the Managing Director in Calcutta, was appointed to proceed to take charge of the London Agency. Mr. Campbell's services having been gratuitous, the Directors present him with a piece of plate of the value of £200. Mr. Gollan, who had been acting as Calcutta Agent, retired, and was succeeded by Mr. C. B. Wood, the Deputy Secretary to the Bank, until the return of Mr. Watson from England.

The following were the staff of the Bank at this period:—

DIRECTORS.

T. F. Blois.	J. Linton.
F. Lloyd.	R. Willis.
J. Abercrombie.	G. C. Ponsonby.
T. C. Plowden.	

Secretary	... Major Frederick Angelo.
Deputy Secretary	... Charles B. Wood.
Accountant	... F. Whitehead.

The Bank established the following branches:—

CALCUTTA BRANCH,

No. 2, Mangoe Lane.

Agent ... JAMES WATSON.
Treasurers ... BANK OF BENGAL.

MUSSOORIE BRANCH.

Agent ... MAJOR W. FREETH.

LAHORE BRANCH.

Agent ... J. O'BRIEN TANDY.

LONDON BRANCH,

No. 19, King's Arms Yard.

Manager ... R. J. R. CAMPBELL.
Accountant ... F. McNAGHTEN.
Treasurers ... GLYN, HALLIFAX, MILLS AND CO.

1850.—The Directors of the Bank, conjointly with those of the Delhi Bank, the Simla Bank, and the Cawnpore Bank, address a memorial to the Governor-General of India, calling his attention to the imperfect state of the law affecting Joint Stock Bank shareholders in India, and requesting a new law to remedy the evils complained of.

1851.—Certain delinquencies in the Bank are the subject of general comment, involving charges brought against one of the Directors, and the Secretary. Fraudulent entries are proved to have been made in the books, and the panic is so wide spread, that people demand a general and independent audit of all the Joint Stock Banks. A Court of Enquiry assembles at Meerut, under orders from Army Head Quarters, to investigate the connection of certain Officers with the delinquencies committed. Captain Blois' justification is considered most satisfactory, and it is said that no blame attaches to Captain Watt on account of the transaction in which *he* was concerned. Mr. John O'Brien Tandy, the Agent at Lahore, is appointed Secretary and Manager, on the resignation of the Secretary, Major Angelo. This gentleman, whose alleged indiscretions are also the subject of official enquiry, and who was residing at Cossipore, suddenly leaves Calcutta on sick certificate, postponing a promised full and ample explanation of the *mistakes* in the Bank's book-keeping.

1853, February 1.—Mr. Robert McKim appointed London Agent. He finds all in order, with exception only of the accounts left unadjusted by Mr. R. J. R. Campbell. June 30.—Dividend seven per cent per annum, or fourteen per share upon the capital stock of Rupees 22,05,600. Several irregularities are proved to have been committed in the London accounts, for which a general meeting impounds the dividends of the London Committee. In addition to these irregularites, a direct embezzlement by a clerk of £2,353-11-11 was brought to light. The aggregate loss sustained by the Bank was Rupees 1,29,889-11-10. Serious charges are brought against Mr. R. J. R. Campbell, the late London Agent, of trading in indigo with the Bank's funds, and of the London Committee being cognizant thereof. Mr. R. J. R. Campbell addresses the shareholders of the Company in refutation of the charges made against him, and refers to a favorable record of him by a general meeting on 7th January 1851, to this effect:—

"Mr. Campbell intimated that it would not suit him to continue his services in an institution where such gross neglect and deception, by the Secretary, could be allowed and countenanced by the Directors, in the face of his and his Committee's repeated protests for eighteen months. Mr. Campbell was earnestly requested to defer his resignation for the present, which he only consented to do out of consideration for his friends in the Bank."

1856.—Mr. Rich, the Bombay Agent, proceeds to England on sick leave, an arrangement having been entered into with Mr. J. E. MacLachlan, formerly connected with the Commercial Bank, to officiate as Mr. Rich's *locum tenens*. A general meeting removes Mr. Robert McKim from his office of Agent for the Bank in London, on or after three months from the date upon which the resolution shall be notified to him. Mr. Rich, on leave to England, is instructed to officiate as London Agent in the room of Mr. McKim.

1857, April 30.—Mr. J. O'B Tandy tenders his resignation of the Secretaryship, which is accepted by the Directors, who record their sense of his services in a very flattering minute.

1859.—The affairs of the Bank are put in liquidation; Mr. J. H. Fergusson being appointed to the office of Winding-up Manager.

1862—September 1.—Mr. Fergusson publishes his Eighteenth Report to the proprietors of the North-Western Bank of India in Liquidation, in conformity with the resolutions of the special general meeting of the 20th of August 1859, and the decree of the Supreme Court of Judicature of Fort William in Bengal, dated the 26th of September 1859.

GENTLEMEN,

The following is a Statement of your Assets and Liabilities made up to 31st August:—

ASSETS.

Cash in hand... ... Rs.	131 10 1	
Ditto in the Bank of Bengal	27,622 5 10	
		27,753 15 11

				Brought forward ...	27,753	15	11					
Government Five per cent Paper applicable to the second dividend...	Rs.	600	0	0								
Ditto ditto to the fifth dividend ...	„	2,400	0	0								
Ditto in hand, Rs. 70,000 valued at 5-8 per cent premium ...	„	73,850	0	0								
Interest due on Government Paper for Rs. 70,000 to date, less Income Tax	„	1,680	0	0								
					78,530	0	0					
									1,06,283	15	11	

London and Eastern Banking Corporation balance unpaid after receipt of first and second dividends, and after deducting amount of interest and charges disallowed by the Vice-Chancellor, Exchange 2 shillings per Rupee	Rs.	1,54,717	7	4
Balance of Loan on House Property in the Upper Provinces and other Securities	„	13,036	6	0

LIABILITIES.

Floating Deposits still unclaimed ...	Rs.	21,585 10 10		
Ditto on account of fifth dividend ...	„	2,299 0 0		
Ditto on account of previous dividends	„	3,179 8 2		
Payable in Government Five per cent Paper on account of the second dividend unclaimed	„	600 0 0		
Ditto on account of the fifth dividend	„	2,400 0 0		
			30,064 3 0	
Sixth dividend at Rs. 12 per share, after deducting the amount transferable to credit of sundry debtors to the Bank, being also shareholders, payable in cash on and after the 10th instant		Rs.	61,512 3 0	
Reserved for Law Charges	Rs.	5,000 0 0		
Ditto for Rent and Commission ...	„	2,500 0 0		
Ditto for Dependencies and Contingencies	„	1,500 0 0		
			9,000 0 0	
				1,00,576 6 0

I have now the pleasure to report the settlement of the Equity Suit with the estate of the late Mr. Featherstonhaugh, and that I have received under it, by order of the Supreme Court, the sum of Rupees 31,435-11-3, and have since paid the costs of the Bank's Solicitors in that suit. This has enabled me to declare a sixth dividend in further part of capital, payable in cash on and after the 10th instant, of Rupees 12 per share, which has been duly advertized, making, with previous dividends declared by me, payable partly in cash, and partly in Government Five per cent Paper, Rupees 182 per share.

The winding-up of the affairs of the Bank being now nearly completed, and it being uncertain how soon we may be able finally to close them, principally on account of the claim on the London and Eastern Banking Corporation, I have thought it desirable that my accounts up to hand should be audited. The resolutions and order of Court, under which I was appointed, do not provide for this: but with the sanction of the Committee of shareholders, and in anticipation of the approval of the shareholders generally, I have arranged for the audit. I trust this arrangement will be satisfactory to all parties concerned.

Owing to the lamented death of Colonel Cuthbert Davidson, C. B., the late Resident at Hyderabad, since the date of my last Report, there is a vacancy in the Committee of Proprietors appointed by the order of the Supreme Court to co-operate with me in the wind-up, and if it be thought necessary by the proprietors a meeting can be called for the purpose of filling up that vacancy.

Mr. M. R. Gubbins, the other member of the Committee, has proceeded to England on account of his health for a few months, but is expected back before the end of the year, and he is represented, under the arrangement sanctioned by the order of the Supreme Court, by Mr. William Anderson, of the firm of Gordon Stuart and Co. of Calcutta, who holds his Power of Attorney.

DELHI BANK CORPORATION LIMITED.

This Bank was established at Delhi, in September 1844, under the designation of the DELHI BANK. The number of shares at first subscribed for was 2,400, of Rupees 500 each:—subsequently increased to 4,800.

Dividends have been declared as follows, *viz.*:—

21st July 1845	... ...	8	per cent.	per annum.
20th January 1846	... ...	3	ditto	ditto.
14th July 1846	... ...	9	ditto	ditto.
1st February 1847	... ...	10	ditto	ditto.
28th July 1847	... ...	10	ditto	ditto.
10th February 1848	... ...	10	ditto	ditto.
1st August 1848	... ...	10	ditto	ditto.

The commercial crisis in 1847-48 very injuriously affected the value of the shares of this, in common with those of every other institution of the kind. The present paid-up capital stock of the Bank is Rupees 20,00,000. The par value of each share Rupees 500. Reserve Fund, Rupees 60,000. The Bank has no charter; nor any note circulation.

In 1860 the Bank applied to be registered under the Limited Liability Act, on which occasion the style and designation was altered to that which it now bears, namely THE DELHI BANK CORPORATION LIMITED.

For several years its operations and influence were purely local, but it has now established Branches at Allahabad, Calcutta, Lucknow, and Mussoorie.

The following are the staff of the Bank :—

TRUSTEES.

COL. F. GAITSKELL, C. B., *Royal Artillery.*
J. C. MURPHY, *Civil Judge, Umritsur.*
LALLA CHOONNA MULL, *Banker, Delhi.*

Manager	...	J. C. PARRY.
Deputy Manager and Secretary	...	H. P. HEALY.
Sub-Deputy Manager and Accountant	...	C. H. RUSHTON.
Agent in London	...	UNION BANK OF LONDON.
Agent in Calcutta	...	DAVID LANCASTER.
Agent in Allahabad	...	CHARLES F. VAUGHAN.
Agent in Lucknow	...	W. B. THOMPSON.
Agent in Mussoorie	...	JOHN HEALY.
Agents in Bombay and Madras	...	AGRA AND U. S. BANK.

Calcutta Branch,

Office, No. 6, *Government Place.*

Agent	...	DAVID LANCASTER.
Assistant Agent and Accountant	...	W. H. TROTTER.
Cashier	...	SIB CHUNDER DUTT.

DACCA BANK.

This Bank was established on the 1st July 1846, with a capital of 5 lacs, in shares of Rupees 1,000 and 500 each: of these 400 rupees per share were paid up. The projectors of the Bank were: George Lamb, Esq., Superintending Surgeon, Dacca; Captain H. M. Nation, Assistant Superintendent for the Suppression of Thuggee, Dacca; Kajeh-alleemoollah of Dacca; Josiah Patrick Wise, Esq., of the firm of Wise and Glass, Dacca; and Baboo Nundlall Dutt of Dacca; John Dunbar, Esq., Commissioner of Revenue, Dacca; Doctor Thomas Alexander Wise, Civil Surgeon of Dacca; and Khajeh Abdool

Gunni of Dacca, the three latter being *trustees*. The deed of settlement recited that

"The capital of the said Company at present consists of Company's Rupees five hundred thousand, divided into one thousand shares of Rupees five hundred each. The capital may, however, at any time be increased by sanction of a majority of shareholders, holding a proportion of two-thirds of stock; such new stock to belong to the existing proprietors ratably.

No member of the Company can possess shares to a larger amount than one-fifth of the capital of the Bank, whatever that may be, or may become.

The present partnership shall be and continue for and during the term of ten years from the date of this deed, but may be enlarged at the will of existing shareholders.

In case the Company shall at any time previous to that period sustain a loss one-fourth of its capital, the affairs of the Company shall be wound up.

In issuing Promissory Notes; in the purchase, sale, and negotiation of Bills of Exchange; in discounting Bills and Notes; in lending money on the security of individuals, and of personal or real property; in granting Cash Credits; in the purchase and sale of coin and bullion and Government Securities; in the receipt of cash at interest; in money agency; and any other branches of business commonly carried on by bankers."

Its very limited business gave it nothing more than a purely local interest. It had no charter, nor did it issue notes. Its dividends, which were declared on the 30th June and 31st December respectively, ranged from six to ten per cent. In the early part of 1862, the following were the staff of the Bank :—

Secretary	... G. M. Reily.
Accountant	... Kistocoomar Seal.
Assistant	... Chottun Kissen Bysack.
Treasurer	... Bungo Chunder Roy.
Calcutta Agents	... Surroopchunder and Modhoosoodun, Poddars, *Burra bazar*.

In February of the same year, the Bank of Bengal, under the 37th clause of the Charter Act, purchased and took over the whole concern, the shareholders of the Dacca Bank receiving an equivalent for their shares in Bank of Bengal stock. Mr. G. M. Reily, the Secretary, was retained as Agent, but, resigning in 1863, his place was supplied by Mr. D. Kennedy, the Accountant to the Rangoon Branch.

THE BENARES BANK.

This Bank, which has earned an infamous notoriety by its failure, was established in 1844-45, chiefly by the influence of *Colonel Pew,* who, some years back, was a man of large fortune and unbounded credit. He was seized with a mania for speculating, however, and the Benares Bank was one of the results of his madness. When the Bank was commenced in 1845, its capital was proposed to be Rupees 5,00,000, raised by the sale of 1,000 shares at Rupees 500 each. The first instalment, of Rupees 250 each, was all that was ever paid on the shares, and even this was done on many occasions, by borrowing the amount from the Bank, on the security of its own scrip. Unable to call up the full price of the shares, the Bank determined on issuing new ones.

1848.—The Bank continued to issue new shares till the total amount was 6,000, giving a nominal capital of Rupees 15,00,00, of which, however, no more than Rupees 9,00,000 was ever paid up, much of it having been so by loans from the Bank.

1849.—Formidable irregularities discovered in the management; the Directors having purchased their stock with money borrowed from the Bank. They held their ground by the value of the votes of parties who had not paid up their shares, and who had paid their first instalments by loans from the Bank at twelve per cent interest. When the Bank stock was selling in the market at from thirty to fifty per cent discount, the Directors purchased in the stock of their friends at par, and cancelled the shares. They also invested nearly the whole capital in the Ganges Steam Navigation Company, from which, under any circumstances, it could not have been withdrawn, if desired, and which pursued a ruinously losing career. As nearly all the Directors belong to the Army, the matter undergoes a strict investigation. July 19.—A meeting of the shareholders of the Benares Bank was held at the Bank House.

"PRESENT:

Rev. J. A. Shurman, Major Stewart, Lieut. Stewart, Dr. Butter, Dr. Brander, Dr. Berwick, Dr. Edlin, Mr. Bason, Baboo Hurree Chund, Lala Sumbhoonauth, Narain Rao Trebeenlo, Hunmunt Rao, Kushi Nutt Biswass, Umbeeka Churn Biswass, Deo Sunker Sylhet, Purostum Doss, Koorsheid Bahadoor, Buloder Doss, Goorshoy Mull, Gunshorun Doss, Ram Chund, Doorga Dial Sing, and Lala Gobind Narain.

On this occasion most of the absent shareholders were represented by proxy.

The Rev. J. A. Shurman having been unanimously called to the Chair, read the following requisition convening the meeting: Agreeable to a requisition from shareholders representing one-tenth of the capital of the Bank, a special meeting of shareholders will take place at the Bank House on Monday, the 9th July, at 11 A. M., to consider the propriety of forthwith winding up the affairs of the Benares Bank, and to concert measures in respect to the same.

By order of the Directors,

E. G. Dunbar, *Secretary*.

Benares, 16*th June* 1849.

He said, that the purpose for which they had met was one of deliberation ; and they must take time and exercise patience, to come to a sound conclusion, and concert to advantage. He had no doubt some official information had been prepared by order of the Directors, and if the meeting pleased, he would call on the Secretary to read the statement of their affairs.

Mr. Dunbar, the Secretary, read the following, as his professional opinion and suggestions :—

Benares Bank, 9*th July* 1849.

The following scheme for adjusting the accounts of the Bank's proprietors is submitted for consideration :—

Out of the capital of			Rs. 15,00,000
The amount standing in the name of parties who have no paid-up shares is		Rs. 3,74,450	
The amount standing in the names of parties who have both paid and unpaid shares is Rs. 6,95,575, of which there is unpaid		„ 4,21,253	
The Bank holds nominally shares to the amount of		„ 1,42,200	
Total unpaid		„ 9,37,903	
The amount held by parties whose whole stock is paid-up is	Rs. 2,87,775		
Amount held by parties who also have unpaid shares as above	„ 2,74,322		
Total paid up...		Rs. 5,62,097	
			15,00,000

The amount paid up has been considerably more in reality, being at one time Rupees 7,42,650, but, as several parties, holding both paid and unpaid shares, are indebted, in cash account, on inadequate security, and all of them are liable for interest on their unpaid shares, a proportionate amount of their paid shares is struck out, and considered as unpaid, to cover their liabilities under these heads.

Of the amount now reckoned to be paid up on shares, say		Rs. 5,62,097
Premising that the funds on hand will nearly suffice to meet the Bank's engagements to third parties, it is estimated that there may be realised from debtors on other than share accounts, within the next two months, about	Rs. 63,000	
And within the following four months about ... ... „	1,37,000	
		2,00,000
Thus leaving an apparent deficiency		Rs. 3,62,097

which is just about equal to what is due by one party, in his individual capacity, and, conjointly with others, for loans taken for the use of a Steam Company and two Sugar Companies.

It is uncertain whether any large proportion of this sum will be eventually recovered, and, as, in any case, the time when it may be realized is likely to be distant, it would appear expedient to pass this amount of Rupees 3,62,097 to a suspense account, and apportion the deficiency ratably among shareholders, subject to any future mode of adjustment that may be determined on.

The number of shares among whom the deficiency would be devisable is	6,000
Less shares held by the Bank	$568\frac{4}{5}$
viz.	$5,431\frac{1}{5}$

which would give, on each share, a deficiency of about Rupees 67, but, as some of the shareholders are not in a position to pay, the deficiency may be reckoned moderately at 75 rupees per share, or thirty per cent when thus apportioned.

At this rate, the amount of deficiency that would devolve to the unpaid shares of those who also have part of their stock paid up would be ... ... Rs. 1,26,375

Of which, however, some parties hold so large a proportion of unpaid that, after giving credit for the whole of their paid shares at their estimated value of seventy per cent, there would be due from them, for the difference between that value and the deficiency chargeable to them, upwards of ... ... Rs. 73,190

Leaving to be borne by others who have a large surplus on their paid-up shares taken at their estimated value over and above their quota of deficiency ... ... Rs. 53,185

While the deficiency devolving to those whose whole stock is unpaid would be ... ... Rs. 1,12,335

It would hence appear the fairest mode of adjusting these accounts, to write off altogether the shares held by the Bank, and to give credit to the extent of seventy per cent for all other unpaid shares with which parties now stand charged, requiring those whose whole stock is unpaid to make up the remaining thirty per cent at once with the interest that may be now due from them on the amount of their shares, and to continue from time to time to pay the future interest that may accrue on such portion of the said amount as would correspond, taken ratably, with the sum remaining due on each paid-up share, after deducting the dividends that may be distributed thereon. The like course would be advisable in the case of those whose quota of the deficiency exceed the estimated value of their paid-up shares, who should, therefore, be called on to pay up such excess, together with the future accruing interest on their unpaid shares, calculated on the plan above indicated. On the other hand, as regards those whose paid-up shares would, at their estimated value, more than cover the deficiency on their unpaid stock, together with the future interest thereon, reckoned in the manner just described, it would seem sufficient to allow the dividend devolving to their paid-up shares to be carried to their credit as a set-off against such deficiency and interest, until the same shall have been cleared off; and thereafter those parties would be entitled, on the declaration of further dividends, to be placed, as respects their paid-up shares, on the same footing with those whose whole stock may be paid up. Were the recoveries alluded to effected nearly in full, the holders of paid-up shares would get within thirty per cent of the original amount thereof, and the expenses of winding up would, at the same time, be defrayed from the interest proposed to be charged on unpaid stock; provided, of course, that heavy law charges are not incurred, while whatever amount was realized on the sums transferred to suspense account, would be divisible ratably among the entire number of shares that contributed, on due proportion, to the payment of the estimated deficiency, including the paid-up shares, though it would be necessary to retain the dividends on the unpaid, derived from this source, to await the final adjustment of accounts. For in the event of any large proportion of the deficiency being irrecoverable from parties having no paid-up shares, or those whose quota of deficiency greatly exceed the estimated value of their paid-up shares, there would, of course, be a heavier quota of the deficiency devolving to the fully paid-up stock-holders, and those having a larger proportion of paid to unpaid shares, and it may happen that in such event, several, in the latter category, may have the entire dividends on their paid-up shares swallowed up in the increased quota of deficiency falling on their unpaid shares. Whatever sum, however, might be realized on the amount transferred to suspense account would, under these circumstances, be divisible among these two classes alone, as having been the parties by whom the deficiency would have been borne, and if considerable, would probably render their ultimate loss comparatively light.

E. G. DUNBAR,
Secretary of the Benares Bank.

The Secretary said the following had been sent to be laid before the meeting by Dr. Butter:—

Chairman—please to read it.

DR. BUTTER TO MR. DUNBAR,
Secretary, Benares Bank.

DEAR SIR,—Lest I should be prevented from fulfilling my intention of being present at the Bank meeting to-day, I beg that this note may be taken as my written vote for the winding up of the Bank on the score of the impossibility of finding Directors to carry it on.

The Bank's pecuniary difficulties will now probably have a speedy termination. I have ever since the commencement of the agitation recommended abstinence;—that Colonel Pew and the Ganges Steam Navigation Company would themselves act fairly by all their creditors; and a letter from Colonel Pew, dated the 2nd instant, which Captain Fagan, on Saturday evening, authorised me to communicate to the Directors, fully justifies, I think, that recommendation.

Colonel Pew states, contrary to the newspaper report of the trial, that he, Major Stewart, and Dr. Duncan, had the Oriental Bank's suit decreed against him and others *personally*. That the Oriental Bank is forcing through the Court, another suit, for Rupees 1,17,000, surreptitiously taken by Richmond, from the Oriental Bank, as if for the purposes of the Ganges Company; that Mr. Blake is bringing a third action for coals, Rupees 32,031; and that to prevent his private assets from being seized in satisfaction of these claims against the Ganges Company, Colonel Pew has determined immediately to throw his affairs into the Insolvent Court, and thus to act fairly by all his creditors, by having his estate wound up more favorably than it could be done by any private individual, and by dealing summarily with Richmond, who has, among other property of Colonel Pew's, misappropriated 406 Oriental Bank shares (Rupees 2,03,000).

Colonel Pew adds that his balance sheet, drawn up under legal advice, looks well, and that the Ganges would VERY SOON pay off all their debts, if its creditors allowed them to run their five boats, (*to Bulloah only*,) in the dry season, instead of bringing actions against their Managing Directors. An enclosed note from Mr. Stopford states that the *Patna*, *Benares*, and *Mirzapore* are now making large profits; that the *Ghazeepore* was ready for a trial of her engines, which had at the date of his note been deferred only on account of the rain; and that Robinson and Co. had agreed to abide by the arbitration of Colonel Forbes regarding the fifth boat, the *Chunar*.

I congratulate the Directors on this most favorable prospect for the Bank, although it is impossible for any one, who looks for the advancement of India, by the application of British captial and enterprise, to regard, without regret and apprehension, this termination of Colonel Pew's useful and self-denying career.

Yours faithfully,

D. Butter.

A murmur of approval.

Dr. Butter himself arrived about this time.

The Chairman said, it would be prudent to refresh Colonel Pew's memory, which was much burdened (a laugh), with an exact account of the amount of his debts to this Bank, previous to his going into the Insolvent Court. The Secretary was desired to transmit such a document to the Colonel without delay.

Dr. Edlin begged permission to ask the Secretary several formal questions, the answers to which might be satisfactory to the shareholders at large.

Who are our present official Trustees?

Baboo Hurri Chund and the Rev. J. A. Shurman.

Have they been duly elected, and in strict conformity with clauses 7, 8, and 9 of the deed?

The Secretary read the clauses aloud, and said the Trustees had been *formally and duly elected.*

Have any bad or doubtful debts been contracted since the last half-yearly meeting?

No, scarcely any business had been attempted since February.

Who were the *Managing* Directors from the commencement of the Bank to this time, specifying dates of appointment and resignation?—It was essential to have precise information on this point, as one and another said, I was a *Director*, but not a *Managing* Director; I was a Director, but not an *original* Director.

Dr. Butter rose, and begged to protest against such a statement being made, if, as it clearly appeared, its object was to throw exclusive odium and responsibility on the *Managing* Directors. All the Directors did know, or might have known all the affairs of the Bank, and must share in either general credit or blame.

Dr. Berwick perfectly agreed, and thought Dr. Edlin took too much on himself, &c.

The Chairman moderated.

Dr. Edlin said, Dr. Berwick might spare him; his sentiments on the subject were those of Dr. Berwick himself and of Dr. Butter:

but he had an express reason for putting the question in a form which would bring on a plain discussion. He had been asked by a near connexion of Major Stewart to point out, publicly, that Major Stewart was not a '*Managing*' Director, and stress had been laid on it, in the newspapers, as they knew.

Major Stewart said, all he wished to have the public aware of was, that he was not a participator in the unequal cancelling that had been so justly condemned on all sides. He expressed his readiness to share in all the other responsibilities of the original Directors, and confessed that a strong distinction could not be drawn between *Directors* and *Managing* Directors.

Dr. Edlin pointed out that Lala Sumboo Nauth, an original Director, had applied in vain to have some of his shares cancelled. This looked very bad. He could not have known the affairs; and Mr. Charles distinctly, by his minutes at the time, or as soon as he became acquainted with the state of the case, showed that he was no party to it, but on the contrary condemned the cancelling. Dr. Butter's minutes also showed that he was surprised at Captain Fagan's conduct in cancelling four-fifths of the stock he held; and Colonel Pew's cancelling 591 out of 991 shares. Let Dr. Butter's minutes be referred to.

Dr. Berwick said, when he came into the direction, and understood matters, he disapproved of and put a stop to further cancelling, which accounts for the Lala's shares not having been cancelled. He was a creature of Colonel Pew.

Mr. Bason pointed out and called particular attention to Mr. Charles, his partner, not having been informed of Colonel Pew's and Captain Fagan's intention to cancel. He first heard of it when Dr. Butter's proposition came round, and was much astonished.

Dr. Edlin said it was quite proper on Dr. Berwick's part to put a stop to cancelling, but why was not the wrong and injury already perpetrated redressed; and equal justice done to the Lala Sumboo Nauth and other applicants for relief? Why was it left for him (Dr. Edlin) to make a question about it so long afterwards as the middle of May? Dr. Berwick might fancy such notoriety was pleasant to him (Dr. Edlin): he begged to say he did not like it at all.

At the end of the discussion the sense of the meeting was clearly with Dr. Butter, that the document formally required by Dr. Edlin, to single out the *Managing* Directors for shafts, should not be given.

Dr. Edlin was glad it was so settled; but, in correspondence with himself, one of the late Directors had laid great stress on, 'I am not a Managing Director now.' He thought the excuse a paltry one when he heard it. He would never for his part be a Director of anything of which he would not make a point to know all about.

Major Stewart now requested permission to read an explanation of his views and conduct.

I trust I may be permitted to say a few words regarding my own individual connexion with this Bank, both as a shareholder and for a long period Director, although never a Managing Director.

The present state of this Bank is, we all know, alone attributable to the derangement of Colonel Pew's affairs; for, had he been able to meet his heavy liabilities there would have been no necessity for this meeting. The Bank might have met with losses from other quarters, but not sufficient to affect its stability. Colonel Pew came among us with the reputation of being a man of unbounded wealth, whose limits no one seemed able to determine. He was known to be the largest shareholder in several florishing banks, and, such was his name as a Banking Capitalist, that, when he adopted the Benares Bank as his own particular bantling, it was supposed that nothing could tend more towards its credit and influence. When he first became a debtor to the Bank, at a time when there was some difficulty in employing its funds, I do not exaggerate when I say that it was considered a subject of congratulation that they were in such excellent keeping. The progressive increase of his debt, caused principally, I believe, by the accumulation of new shares, which he did not pay up, caused no alarm. He might have sold them at a good premium, and then have diminished his debt, but, strange to say, he did so to a very limited extent, declaring his intention of keeping them as a permanent investment, for which he certainly believed he had ample means. Even when his securities became depreciated no one doubted his ability to replace them. For my own part, it was not till a very late date,—not, indeed, till he was on the point of leaving Benares, that I could believe his misfortunes elsewhere had utterly paralized his efforts to do so. I do not defend, and never did approve of his being allowed to become so heavy a debtor. I only mean to say that no one considered the safety of the Bank compromised by it. In proof of the sincerity of my own belief, I need only say that from the day the Bank was established up to the last half-yearly meeting, every farthing I could save from my pay has, month after month, been faithfully devoted to the payment of my shares. I have even purchased shares at a premium when able to do so, and have taken up and paid for all the new shares allotted to me, with the exception of a portion of the last two issues, which I had not time to pay for up to the period of cancellation. There were others better able to judge of the prospects of the Bank who participated with me in this security. The late Secretary,* who is my near connexion, and in right of his wife a considerable shareholder, purchased into the Bank at a premium, and has taken up and paid for all his new stock. His daughter, also a shareholder, has done the same. My own son, acting under my advice, invested his batta, earned in the battles of the Sutledge, in shares purchased at a premium, and has devoted all his savings towards the payment of his new stock. Unless you can believe that we wilfully threw away our money, you must at least give us credit for sincerity and good faith towards the Bank, however we may have deceived ourselves as to its prosperity. Even after I began to entertain doubts of Colonel Pew's ability to meet his liabilities, I heard that the present Directors were making strenuous endeavors to remedy the disasters, and believed that with the suspension of a few dividends, and a little time given to the principal debtors, it might have survived them; but credit and confidence having gone it is perhaps as well as it is.

When I first heard that the Managing Directors, in consequence of being unable to obtain payment of the last two increases of stock, injudiciously made in the face of a falling market, were about to cancel a corresponding amount of capital at par, I did not consider they were conferring any valuable privilege either on themselves or any one else. I declare to you, gentlemen, and strange as it may now appear, that at the time the measure commenced, I would have refused for the shares I possessed. I had paid four per cent premium towards the Reserve Fund for my new stock, and should not have consented to sacrifice so much by selling only at par. I supposed that all Bank stock was suffering only from a temporary depression, and

* Major Debnam.

that prices would rise with better times. Had I applied in October, when the cancellation began, I suppose my shares would have been cancelled as well as those of others; but, instead of that, I continued paying for my new stock up to the 31st January, and then only consented to the remainder being taken over with reluctance. Although aware of the inequality with which the permission to cancel was accorded, I did not consider that my interests as a paid-up shareholder were in any way affected by it, nor do I yet believe that the Managing Directors contemplated taking any advantage over their co-partners, by cancelling so many of their own: at all events, when made aware that they had done so, not a voice was raised against the annulment of the whole proceeding.

In winding up, according to the design proposed to the meeting, I trust matters will not be found so unfavorable as many anticipate. A considerable portion of the amount placed to a suspense account will ultimately be recovered, although it may take some time to do so. From recent information, I am in hopes that Colonel Pew's estate will not turn out so very unfavorably, and the Ganges Steam Company, which seems lately to have started into new life, ought soon to be in a position to meet all its liabilities. Should this anticipation prove correct, even the shares of that Company, now so valueless, may eventually yield some return.

In conclusion, I have only to express a hope that you, Mr. Chairman, in conducting the business of this meeting, will interpose your authority to prevent all unnecessary and uncalled for remarks; also in common justice that no shareholder here present will report any translation of a Hindoostanee speech, unless it has either been interpreted to the meeting, or previously submitted in its translated form.

Dr. Butter said he objected to the last advance of capital that was made to the Ganges Steam Navigation Company; but regrets that he did not record that firm protest he should have done. The Doctor confessed the Directors had been to blame, but not in the way some would make it appear. They acted in good faith, however much deceived in Colonel Pew's resources, and erroneous in their banking system.

Dr. Edlin was sorry to intrude so often on the meeting, but he must, in rejoinder to what Major Stewart had read, request to be permitted to refer to some of his own correspondence with the Directors, in self vindication, in some respects, he might say. He was accused of wanting to BEAR the whole Joint Stock market, as much as others had wished to BULL it.

He thought Major Stewart's remarks most manly and to the purpose. The effect *must* be to lessen if not disarm opposition and animosity. It was a pity others had not before adopted this method. Major Stewart's candour and sense enabled one to carry on a discussion with him with some satisfaction. Even though there might, after all, be a great deal of difference of sentiment, where there is a frank admission of obvious error, he would be the last to impugn motives, and he would like to be done by, as he was willing to do.

DR. EDLIN TO MAJOR DEBNAM.

Secretary to the Benares Bank.

Calcutta, 4th September 1848.

DEAR SIR,—Will you do me the favor to obtain for me early answers from the Directors to my propositions and suggestions about the Bank, that is, so far as a proprietor may claim attention.

I have to acknowledge your letter of the 7th August, mentioning the receipt of a draft for 500 rupees, and promising a reply when the busy time of the annual meeting had passed.

More particularly I wish to hear what is said to the objections against the Bank's lending money on its own shares, these shares being *unnegotiable*—a fact only too clear, seeing that, even with your aid, I have not been able to sell a single share at any rate of premium *or discount*, in the course of a year and a half, nor can I find any body who will lend money on the Bank's stock in Calcutta.

I wish also to know if the Benares Bank will not follow the example of the Commercial Bank of Bombay, and cancel the shares that seem to glut the market. I propose the cancelling of the last batch. I never accepted my quota, and I demur very much to the cash credit at twelve per cent. It never formed part of my plan on joining the Bank, and in the event of the Bank's not seeing fit to cancel the shares, and not relieving me of the reponsibility of them, a responsibility thrust upon me *nolens volens*, and one which I never took on myself, can you tell me what price the shares would *command.* I have not thought it well to advertise, owing to the *unjust* depression of all stock of the sort; but time goes on, and I cannot flatter myself the

Benares Bank shares will rise while the Bank lends on its own shares.

It seems to me that the rate of interest, twelve per cent, is too high. Does the Bank *never* intend to lend cheaper? Why is it higher than the Delhi? Other Banks lend at nine or ten per cent, and while the Bank lends on its own shares *at all*, it must count the security first-rate. It cannot therefore charge the higher rate, owing to the poorness of the security. *Are there two rates for credits and loans?* I am sure I do not know how the Ganges Steam Navigation Company can make a profit, if it pays the Bank twelve per cent on the large sum lent to it.

That reminds me to remark that it may admit of question whether Colonel Pew, who is a Director of the Ganges Steam Navigation Company, should be also a Director of the Bank; at least it was something of the sort which eat the core of the late Union Bank.

I write to the Directors plainly, *and direct*, preferring that course to publicly addressing them in a pamphlet, or in the newspapers, though I am no enemy to publicity, and all the subscribers may know my transactions with the Bank. I saw a letter signed WIDE AWAKE in the *Delhi Gazette*. Pity he does not write in his own name, whatsoever he is. If there had been a little more 'pernicious publicity,' the Union Bank might have been spared. The Benares Bank, professing more correct banking than other Banks, we necessarily look for more from it, in candour of statement.

Will you please tell me if the Directors have taken, or will take, any measures to obtain a Charter; or to secure the non-resident, non-interfering shareholders from more responsibility, than the amount of their shares. One more word to remind you to reply to enquiry. How long will the Directors give me to pay off my cash credit? I am willing to make efforts to pay up the last batch of shares but one, *but not the last*, of Rupees 6,500. I want the annual revenues of my shares to use, and particularly wish to avoid encreasing my stock in a Bank which lends on its own shares. Present my respects to the Directors to favor me with a full reply.

Yours faithfully,

EDWARD EDLIN,

Shareholder.

Before it was done, Dr. Berwick asked 'with dismay' if Dr. Edlin was to be allowed to read all that great bundle of letters. He must again complain, and enter a protest against the line of conduct and assumption of Dr. Edlin. The Chairman moderated, and stopped to remark that Dr. Edlin had been interrupted. He (the Chairman) had not observed any impatience in the meeting on listening to Dr. Edlin, but that, if Dr. Berwick wished, it should be formally put that Dr. Edlin be stopped!

This was not pressed.

After Dr. Berwick had sat down, the Chairman observed that these documents seemed calculated to modify Major Stewart's statement, and should therefore accompany it. Perhaps Dr. Edlin did not intend to read *all* those letters which he held in his hand. (A laugh.)

Dr. Berwick complained of the encroachment upon his time. He wished to know if any body had got any resolution to wind up the affairs of the Bank, and allow him to depart. The Baboos and others might then sit and talk as long as they pleased.

The Chairman said, they were not in a hurry:—a patient and even protracted discussion on this particular occasion, for it was not a common one, might be particularly useful in accommodating differences of opinion and removing wrong impressions, and enabling them to understand the true state of affairs. Would Dr. Edlin have the goodness to go on, and oblige Dr. Berwick by coming speedily to the end?

Dr. Edlin said, he had not the slightest intention to read all those letters. They were all of one purport, written last year, to warn the original Directors of their danger. He need not add, written—in vain. He must read this answer of Major Debnam's, for it was the only piece of bread to all that sack he sent to the Directors.

THE SECRETARY, BENARES BANK, TO DR. EDLIN.

Benares Bank, 1*st October* 1849.

DEAR SIR,—In reply to your letter of the 27th ultimo, this being Sunday, and having a little leisure time, I beg to reply to your enquiries.

My time would be much more occupied than would be compatible with the working of the Bank, had I to attend to all the wishes of all the shareholders; but I am most willing to satisfy you on all points as far as lies in my power, though, were all the shareholders to address the Directors on the numerous points you do (some of them relating to the future, which is unknown to them), it must be obvious to yourself that it would be impossible to reply to them, much as they wish to satisfy all parties.

The Directors have not taken any steps regarding a charter, but if you or any of the proprietors will preface a matured and well digested measure on the subject, they will be happy to take it into consideration, and, if desirable, submit it for the consideration of the body of shareholders.

When the shares were allotted to you on the several occasions of increase, you never declined taking them.

The Bank's rate of interest is twelve per cent per annum on the deposit of Company's Paper.

The rate of interest has recently been again under the consideration of the Directors, and they have thought it right to adhere to those.

You will have seen by the Bank's circulars of the 23rd ultimo how it is intended to liquidate the debts on security of shares.

Shares are not saleable at all, I therefore can fix no price.

I can assure you no discourtesy has been intended to you.

Circumstances have so changed of late, together with the changeable times and unparalleled events, that I find it difficult to give suitable answers to all questions.

Yours truly,

R. J. Debnam.

And this, said Dr. Ellin, was the only reply, and all the satisfaction I got on my numerous serious warnings to the Directors, on lending to Colonel Pew, a Director, to such an extent, and on lending on their own shares.

And, (a shrug from Dr. Berwick, who commenced to read the newspaper,) he would read this one letter also. Let the shareholders and the public judge if he had been precipitate, and whether he had, or had not given the Directors good notice and warning, and applied first to themselves for redress. Till he arrived here, 12th May, he thought the *capital* all safe at all events, and Mr. Charles, on whom he called, was the first to undeceive him. His first objections to the cancelling (or sale to the Bank) were on the ground of *inequality*. He afterwards learned the much worse offence in the rate or price for which the 2,000 shares were sold to the Bank, 1,067 being the three Managing Directors' own shares.

Dr. Edlin to the Secretary, Benares Bank.

Camp Goojrat, 9th March 1849.

Dear Sir,—I have just received the printed reports of the last half-yearly meeting.

2,000 shares cancelled.

This, in proportion, would have entitled me to *have* cancelled all the debts that now remain in my name in the books of the Bank.

I think all should have equal chance of ridding themselves of unsaleable Stock. Is it too late for me to benefit in fair and equal proportion? The Bank agreed to cancel 26 of my shares, (I remember all the circumstances,) but if a larger proportion were allowed to others, why not to me? Now—will the Bank cancel all my shares beyond 120, leaving a par capital of 30,000?

Otherwise, will they lower the enormous rate of interest, twelve per cent, on the loan in their own stock. To divide eight and charge twelve is too much discrepancy. I cannot consider I get fair play at that rate. I wish to be assured that, at all events, equal measure is dealt to all; and if others of parallel security are charged twelve per cent, I must submit; but the news of 2,000 shares being cancelled, one-third of the whole capital, while only one-sixth of mine is cancelled, and a debt at a penal interest remains against me,—this news, I say, staggers my faith.

Respectfully begging that the Directors (considering that I was charged twenty-five per cent premium, *which turned out* to be fifty, for some of my shares) will consider my hard case, and do something to re-assure my mind that the absent are not taken advantage of.

I remain, yours faithfully,

Edward Edlin.

The following resolutions were then put and carried:—

1st Resolution.—Proposed by Baboo Hurree Chund, seconded by Baboo Hunmunt Rao—that in consequence of the insolvency of several of the Benares Bank's principal debtors, there is every reason to fear that more than one-fourth of the capital of the Bank is lost.

The seconder, Baboo Hunmunt Rao, had some remarks drawn up in English, which he begged the Secretary to read. The Secretary could not well make the paper out, so the Baboo read it himself.

His speech was received with mingled murmurs and merriment.

Dr. Berwick objected to such a speech altogether, both on account of its detailing the private banking affairs of the original Directors and others, and also on account of the personal reflections on those parties.

Baboo Kashinath Biswas objected to the reflections on Colonel Carpenter in a well written minute, which he read. He heard, it seems, Baboo Hunmunt Rao's remarks read previous to the meeting. Perhaps Baboo Hunmunt Rao would modify his remarks.

Lieut. Stewart objected to the personalities, but smiled at the fun.

Baboo Hunmunt Rao offered to modify, though he was not ashamed of anything he had said in the paper now in the Chairman's hand. Last time he spoke in Hindoostanee, and that did not do. This time he wrote in English, and *that* did not do. Some people were difficult to please.

Dr. Berwick called on the Chairman to reject it summarily.

The Chairman remarked that Hunmunt Rao's written paper was supposed to be spoken in free discussion, and *had* been spoken; and though there might be good reasons for not publishing such private accounts of the banking transactions, gentlemen of the 1st and 2nd parts, as the Baboo has facetiously called them, still he would not take upon himself to put the Baboo down altogether; let the meeting decide it.

Major Stewart pressed that the paper should not be allowed to be modified, but be accepted or rejected (on reference he meant to publication with the other documents), just as it was. The Baboo could use his discretion what to print; but it was another thing if read, and put forth by the meeting with their stamp and sanction.

Rejected unanimously.

Baboo Hunmunt Rao expressed himself quite well pleased with the conclusion come to. He would use the liberty given. He thought he might have had the usual privilege to modify his remarks: It is true, they *were* personal.

2*nd.*—Proposed by Persotum Dass, seconded by Doorga Dial Singh—that in conformity with clause 5 of the deed of settlement, the affairs of the Benares Bank be immediately wound up, and that the Benares Bank be termed the Benares Bank in liquidation.

Before this was put, a letter was read from Captain Graham from Dacca, and considered. The Chairman observed Captain Graham's wishes had been in a great degree anticipated. Also a complaint by Dr. Edlin, about the rate of fifty per cent premium charged for certain Benares Bank shares. It was not merely a private, it was also a general question. He had told the Secretary he would buy at twenty-five and he was charged fifty. They *called* it twenty-five, and it turned out fifty in the bill.

A poet had been found to chronicle this grievance in the *Benares Recorder* of the 30th instant last:—

In the Bank on the Burna water,
Ere shares began to fall,
Some shares for a spec I bought, ah!
Would that I could recall.

TWENTY-FIVE per cent was the ticket
They sold to me that day,
I could not believe them so wicked,
For FIFTY *they* made me pay.

At Major Stewart's suggestion, both of these cases were agreed to be referred to the Committee, which might eventually be appointed to wind up the affairs of the Bank. As the Bank was not Insolvent to its creditors, a deed and trustees would not be necessary. A Committee of independent shareholders could transact the business. Major Stewart, when he entered the Bank, expected the shares were to be 500 rupees each, but it did not turn out so.

3rd.—Proposed by Kashinath Biswas, seconded by Umbika Churn Biswas—that pending the receipt of advice from Counsel, and pending deliberation concerning the election of a suitable Committee for winding up the affairs of the Bank, the Directors of the Bank for the time being be instructed to take measures for the immediate liquidation of existing liabilities, and the realization of assets.

Introduced by its proposer with arguments and persuasions at some length.

4th.—Proposed by Dr. Edlin, seconded by Baboo Deo Sunker Sylhet—that the proceedings and minutes of the Direction, so far as they elucidate the principles on which the Bank has been from the first conducted, and correspondence with shareholders of general interest—*mere private accounts being carefully omitted*—be printed for the general information of the shareholders, and that a Committee, consisting of two shareholders and the Secretary, be hereby appointed to carry this resolution into effect. And that the pamphlet, before it be sent to press, be submitted to the original Directors and old Secretary on the spot, that any explanatory remarks they may have to make, or additional matter from the records, be also published in the form of an Appendix. But no note or comment to be added by the Committee; and that the cost be limited to twenty-eight copies, to be charged to each shareholder for this purpose.

Dr. Berwick rose to protest and oppose, impugning the motives that prompted the resolution, the same he had complained of throughout. The Chairman wished Dr. Berwick would contrive to express his sentiments without imputing motives, and without such direct personalities.

Dr. Berwick said it might be argued that it would be lifting up a beacon to other Banks, to publish a statement, and public good would thereby accrue. For his part he did not profess to be so patriotic; other Banks might take care of themselves. He had three reasons against the proposition; it would be of no service in collecting the assets, and that was the principal thing with him. *2nd.*—It would be a waste of money. Yes, 2-8 was 2-8 (two rupees eight annas was two rupees eight annas), much more than he wished to waste. *3rd.*—It would be merely feeding Dr. Edlin's love of notoriety. Besides, why should it be wished to expose those who injured us. He appealed to Christianity, especially to Evangelical Christianity. They ought to be forgiven seventy times *seven*. Had Dr. Edlin never heard that? (A laugh.) There was really too much vindictiveness, party spirit, and prejudice—but he hoped the shareholders would reject the proposition. Charity required it. He had too much charity to wish to see what Dr. Edlin proposed carried out.

Dr. Edlin hoped they would all appreciate Dr. Berwick's appeal to Christianity. He was glad to hear him make it. He (Dr. B.) had pointed to the side of the table, where there sat himself and seven native gentlemen, upon whom he feared it might be thrown away. He had better therefore take it all to himself.

But Dr. Berwick assumed two things; first, that a publication, such as he suggested, *would* expose the original Directors; and, secondly, that his (Dr. Edlin's) motive was vindictive in the proposition he had made.

Dr. Berwick stood alone in advancing the first. It was not proved; and he (Dr. Edlin) was not prepared to grant him the second. The public had a right to know.

See the fairness with which he desired the Directors to be judged of by their own words! No malicious note or comment of his was to be introduçed! If the Directors of the Benares Bank had not *achieved* success, it might be seen, when all came to be known, that "they had done more; that they had deserved it." (A laugh.)

Did the old Directors *so* shrink from publicity? One was present, (Dr. Butter had left a short time previously,) what did he say?

Major Stewart being appealed to, said, he rather agreed with Dr. Berwick. He did not care about it very particularly, but he thought the publication might possibly have the effect of exposure or something like it. He did not expect any *credit* to accrue to any body.

Dr. Brander said, that though he coincided very much with Dr. Berwick in this point, he did not see why the old Directors should shrink from the publication under circumstances so favorable to themselves. It was better that way, than that garbled or *ex-parte* statements should go forth, as otherwise they might do. It was so far a field for vindicating themselves, and the Directors should make the best of it.

Dr. Edlin continued—He would ask Dr. Berwick one question. Were Christians (Evangelical Christians) the only parties who were to have no redress from the laws? It might be laws against fraud, or laws against anything else. For his part he thought it was difficult to say what was honest in money transactions in India. The Judges must settle it, and if people *did* traverse the laws, they must pay the penalty. He was willing to stand that test himself. Dr. Berwick was very hard upon the original Directors.

There was a correspondence, by-the-bye, between Dr. Berwick himself and Colonel Pew, which the distant shareholders ought to hear. It was far from uninteresting. Colonel Pew got much the worst of it, Dr. Berwick would remember. If fame did not belie Dr. Berwick, he had at that time agitated, and published not a little.

Dr. Berwick explained he *had* agitated, and published in the newspapers too; but it was for the good of the Bank; whereas what he (Dr. E.) proposed would only gratify his own vanity and vindictive feelings. He was sorry, but he must speak his mind.

The Chairman again moderated.

As an argument for his resolution, Dr. Edlin said, a full and fair report of all the minutes would place the Directors' conduct in a just light, with respect to each other. Dr. Butter had a shower of virtuous indignation very unjustly poured on his head by a colleague, because he had not procured for the Bank a formal lien on the securities he had (how foolishly it seems!) given to it. It would seem universal suspicion had sprung up in joint-stock affairs, and liens were seized on every side for collateral securities. Dr. Butter gave security but not the lien. It was seized by the Bank for obligations of a tertiary sort. Other parties, especially the party accusing, gave neither security *nor* lien, though *his* debt to the Bank now amounts to upwards of five and thirty thousand rupees. Whatever might have been said, he thought Dr. Butter's conduct would, at least, as well bear looking at as Captain Fagan's own, or the other Managing Directors. Concerning that question of the lien, he believed Dr. Butter, when that gentleman declared he had acted in good faith in tendering the security. The procuring the lien was an after and unforeseen difficulty.

Dr. Berwick feared Dr. E.'s notice was less to defend Dr. Butter than indirectly to accuse Captain Fagan. Now the subject had been introduced, he was forced to say he had shared Captain Fagan's views about the lien on Dr. Butter's securities. He had not been pleased with Dr. Butter's conduct in reference to that matter.

Major Stewart and the Chairman said they gave Dr. Butter credit for acting in good faith about the lien.

Dr. Edlin said.—Dr. Berwick was well aware his accusations of Captain Fagan were not of an *indirect* sort. No one had better reason to know that than Dr. Berwick. He accused Captain Fagan openly. He listened, however, with respect to what Dr. Berwick said in favor of Captain Fagan's conduct of the Bank; and, while he spoke against Captain Fagan's acts, and Captain Fagan's conduct in banking transactions, he forebore to impugn Captain Fagan's *motives*, and wished Dr. Berwick would spare his. This, if any, was the place; and now, if ever, was the time to speak out. He denounced

Captain Fagan's conduct. The discussion being ended, the Chairman asked Major Stewart to explain to the Native gentlemen the exact purport of resolution 4.

Somebody present said—It could soon be done. Dr. Berwick voted for *choop* (conceal), Dr. Edlin for *chop* (print). Now the Native Gentlemen should not be *choop*, but just say whether they voted for *choop* or *chop*, and so settle it.

Carried for *chop* (to print).

5th.—Proposed by Baboo Hunmunt Rao, seconded by Baboo Koorshed Bahadoor—that a Committee, consisting of Messrs. Shurman and Edlin, with Mr. Dunbar, the Secretary, be appointed to carry out the above resolution.

6th.—Proposed by Major W. M. Stewart, seconded by Kashinath Biswas—that this meeting do adjourn till Monday, the 30th instant, by which time the vote of all the shareholders concerning the appointment of a Committee of five, two Europeans and two Natives, with the Secretary, for winding up the affairs of the Bank, may be expected to be fully made known, and plans submitted for carrying resolution 2nd fully into effect to the best advantage. The votes of the Proprietary to be taken as in the case of election of Directors.

7th.—Proposed by Doctor Brander, seconded by Major W. M. Stewart—that thanks be given to the Rev. J. Shurman for his able conduct in the Chair.

The Meeting lasted four hours. Though the discussion was often animated, good humour prevailed. The confession and justification of Major Stewart and Dr. Butter were, we thought, well received by the Meeting."

October 1.—A second meeting of the Benares Bank in liquidation took place.

"The Rev. J. A. Shurman was called to the chair. Discussion occurred concerning the transfer of certain shares from Dr. Berwick's to Colonel Pew's account, in December last, whereby the Bank lost a large sum of money; also on the past management of the Bank in reference to paper votes, jobbing in stock by the Directors, the payment of profits out of capital, and the usurpation of power by the Sub-Committee. A correspondence was read at the desire of some of the shareholders between the Rev. Mr.

Shurman and Brevet-Captain C. G. Fagan. The latter gentleman had made an attempt to deprive the shareholders of Mr. Shurman's services. The ex-Directors were represented by Dr. Butter, who, however, said little. The attendance of shareholders, both European and Native, was larger than usual. A dividend of twenty per cent was declared to the fully paid-up shareholders only, *not* on all paid-up shares. Rupees 58,000 suffices for this. Some of the largest *bonâ fide* proprietors having so many of the shares forced on them, by the creation of new stock unpaid (and the loss of forty per cent is calculated on all shares), that they are not participators. The securities held by the Bank have not been disposed of, except 2 Agra Bank shares, the only stock of that Bank, which had not been redeemed. The rate obtained (through the Agency of the Agra Bank) was 460 rupees per share. The Committee of Adjustment announced that their work would be ended by 1st November, and recommended that the affairs after that time should be left to Mr. Dunbar, controlled by Trustees.

1st Resolution.—Proposed by Thomas Wilson, Esq., seconded by Baboo Hurree Chund—that the proceedings of the last meeting be confirmed, and that the printed report (a copy of which is on the table) be entirely approved. Carried.

2nd.—Proposed by Mr. J. Alone, seconded by Thos. Wilson, Esq.—that this meeting adopt and confirm the opinion entertained by the Committee of Adjustment, that Dr. Berwick is not liable for any loss arising from the transfer of 196 shares from his account to that of Colonel Pew, and accordingly absolve him from all liability; and that the opinion of Counsel be obtained, whether with reference to the minutes of the Managing Directors, Dr. Butter and Captain C. G. Fagan, any redress can be had against such Managing Directors, for the loss occurring to the Bank by such transfer. Carried.

3rd.—Proposed by T. Wilson, Esq., seconded by Dr. Edlin—that legal opinion be sought for to ascertain what redress, and of what nature, pecuniary or other, is obtainable by shareholders, in consequence of the injury supposed to have been sustained by the irregular use of paper votes, the jobbing in stock, in 1846-47, and the division of profits out of capital. Carried.

4th.—Proposed by Mr. Charles, seconded by Mr. Bason—that the opinions of the Proprietary be taken as to the expediency of adopting the suggestion of the Committee of Adjustment to entrust the affairs of the Bank to Mr. Dunbar, *controlled* by two or more Trustees, from November next. Carried.

5th.—Proposed by T. Wilson, Esq., seconded by Hunmunt Rao—that this meeting consider the attempt of Captain Fagan (whose conduct in this Bank is undergoing official investigation) to put down the Rev. Mr. Shurman, who was appointed a member of the Committee of Adjustment by the free votes of honest and paid-up shareholders, highly unbecoming, and his insult to the Rev. gentleman reprehensible. That the correspondence just read be published with this day's proceedings. Carried.

6th.—Proposed by Kashinath Biswas, seconded by Baboo Deosunker Sylhet—that the estimated deficiency of forty per cent be called for, and collected from the unpaid shareholders without any further delay. Carried.

7th.—Proposed by Mr. W. Bason, seconded by Mr. John Alone—that the reports of the proceedings of the meetings of shareholders on the 11th June, and 9th July, as they appeared in the *Delhi Gazette*, be adopted and included in the pamphlet now being printed, under the authority of the 4th resolution of the meeting of the latter date; and that the clean proof of the pamphlet, as shown, be approved, and that the Committee be allowed to make any additions they deem necessary. Carried.

8th.—Proposed by Rev. J. A. Shurman, seconded by Lalla Sumboonath—that this meeting be adjourned to the 22nd instant, for the transaction of business. Carried.

The Rev. Mr. Shurman left the chair, when the matter in which he was concerned began to be discussed; and, on the motion of Mr. Charles (one of the ex-Directors), Dr. Edlin was voted into it.

The documents read were voluminous, and the meeting lasted for five hours."

November 3.—Colonel Pew came up for the benefit of the Insolvent Act this morning, before Sir L. Peel.

"Mr. Dickens and Mr. Theobald supported him.

Mr. Morton and Mr. Edlin opposed him, on behalf of Captain Graham, Dr. Edlin, and Baboo Hunmunt Rao, shareholders of the Benares Bank.

Mr. Ritchie also held a brief on behalf of the Managing Committee of the Benares Bank.

On the Insolvent appearing, the Commissioner desired Mr. Edlin, who was the only Counsel for the opposition then in Court, to inform him upon what grounds the opposition was based, that he might know how to apply the evidence.

Mr. Edlin replied, that the grounds were grossly improper dealing with the assets of the Benares Bank, contraction of debts thereto by means detrimental to the interests of the shareholders, and scandalous breach of trust. Mr. Edlin added that he relied upon the 51st section of the Insolvent Act.

Mr. Morton, who arrived afterwards, with Mr. Ritchie, opened his case more at length. He said—I have been instructed on the part of Captain Graham, Dr. Edlin, and Baboo Hunmunt Rao, shareholders of the Benares Bank, to oppose the Insolvent upon the ground of breach of trust, with respect to the mode in which certain debts were incurred by him to the Benares Bank. The Schedule contains four or five entries of these debts. The first is—'Benares Bank, Mr. E. G. Dunbar, Secretary, Rupees 4,98,000. This account is of some standing. Admitted. Borrowed by me upon the security of the following joint stock shares:—63 Cawnpore Bank shares, 100 Dacca Bank shares, 163 Ganges Steam Company shares, 50 Benares and Mirzapore Steam Company shares, 17 Nischindpore Sugar Company shares, 300 Sylhet Coal Company shares (I am unable to state the present market value of any of these shares), and 647¼ Benares Bank shares.' The next entry of a debt to the Benares Bank is as follows:—'Benares Bank, Mr. E. G. Dunbar, Secretary, about Rupees 42,000. This account was opened in 1847. Due jointly from me and the other partners of the Nischindpore Sugar Company.' The third entry is—'Benares Bank, Mr. E. G. Dunbar, Secretary, Rupees 29,000. This account was opened in 1847. Admitted. Due jointly from me and the other partners of the Richmond estate.' The fourth entry is—'Benares Bank, Mr. E. G. Dunbar, Secretary, Rupees 1,08,000. This account was opened in 1846. Admitted. Due jointly from me and the other partners of the Ganges Steam Navigation Company.' The fifth and last entry is—'Benares Bank, Mr. E. G. Dunbar, Secretary, about Rupees 3,500. This account was opened in 1846. Due jointly from me and the other partners of the Mirzapore Coal Company.' These several debts aggregate Rupees 6,80,500. My opposition is chiefly directed to the first, which is due by the Insolvent individually, and in the creation of which, as I am instructed, he has been guilty of a breach of trust.

Colonel Peter Lawrie Pew examined by Mr. Morton.—I am a Colonel of Artillery. I was a Director of the Benares Bank and nominally a Trustee; but nothing was ever made over to me in trust. The Bank was established on 1st August 1845, but I was not in Benares at the time. I was not a Director originally. My battalion was moved down from Cawnpore to Benares about the end of August in that year. It was about September 1845 that I became a Director of the Bank. The original paid-up capital of the Bank was 2,50,000 rupees, divided into 1,000 shares, of the nominal amount of Rupees 500 each, but of which Rupees 250 only was paid up. The remainder, Rupees 250, was never paid up. A thousand new shares were afterwards created. They were precisely similar shares. There were altogether five increases subsequent to the original issue of the first stock. The second half of the first 1,000 shares was never paid up, 250 rupees upon each share of the second issue was paid up. After the last issue of new stock, the total number of shares was 6,000, on none of each of which more than 250 rupees had been paid. I do not know whether any payment whatever had been made on some. I believe the Bank had paid for them all, taking other security for the money advanced.

The subsequent shares were issued at par to the old proprietors. If all the shares were paid up at 250 rupees, the total capital of the Bank, after the issue of the sixth and last instalment of stocks, would be 15 lacs. I left Benares in March last on sick certificate. I continued a Director from September 1845 to March in the present year. The Benares Bank suspended payment on the 1st August last. I think some bye-laws were made by the Directors for the purpose of regulating advances by the Bank. In lending on personal security, the practice of the Bank was to require two personal securities besides the applicant for the loan. I do not remember that any limit was assigned to the extent of the money lent on personal security. The Directors would be guided by the supposed means of the applicant and personal sureties. In lending on the shares of other joint-stock companies, the Directors generally allowed the whole par value. There were seven Directors with myself in the Benares Bank. A Managing Committee of three was formed, of which I made one. Captain Fagan and Dr. Butter were the other two. All loans required the sanction of the three members of the Managing Committee at least—sometimes the sanction of all the seven Directors. There were no personal securities for the Rupees 4,98,000 due by me to the Benares Bank. The securities given consisted of joint-stock shares. There were 63 Cawnpore Bank shares, at par value; 100 Dacca Bank shares, on which 300 rupees each had been paid up; 163 Ganges Steam Company shares, on each of which 1,500 rupees had been paid up; 50 shares in the Benares and Mirzapore Steam Company, on which 250 rupees had been paid up; Nischindpore Sugar Company shares, on which 3,000 rupees each had been paid up; 300 Sylhet Coal Company shares, on each of which 300 rupees had been paid up; and 647 Benares Bank shares (my own), on each of which 250 rupees had been paid up. I had given no money payment, but other security for these 647 Benares Bank shares, and the Bank paid them up. I gave for them what was considered good security by the Bank Directors at the time. Some portion of the money due on them I paid into the Bank myself. I cannot say precisely how much, having kept no regular books;—but I believe it was about 80,000 rupees. The total number of my shares in the Benares Bank was 991; and upon these I think I paid about 80,000 rupees. Upwards of 490 of my shares in the Benares Bank were cancelled in the cancellation in December last. I was not present at the Bank when this took place, being sick at the time.

Mr. Morton.—You applied for the cancellation, I presume, or am I to understand that it was done against your consent?

Colonel Pew.—I don't think I gave any vote on the occasion. I did not object to the cancellation certainly. But I expressed no wish on the subject, either way. The Directors generally expressed a wish for the cancellation. I don't know whether they did so, because they wished their shares cancelled. Captain Fagan and Dr. Butter had some of theirs cancelled.

Mr. Morton.—You were indebted to the Bank for these shares?

Colonel Pew.—The Bank had paid upon them for me.

Mr. Morton.—Well, then, the cancellation had the effect of adding a lac of rupees to the credit side of your account with the Bank?

Colonel Pew.—It had—but only for a time. The transaction did not take effect ultimately.

Mr. Morton.—I presume you mean the shareholders resisted it. From what date did it begin to take effect?

Colonel Pew.—I think the cancellation took effect from the 1st of August 1848.

Mr. Morton.—In the meantime, between that and the date of cancellation, you had voted in respect of the whole 991 shares that you held? In August 1848, for instance. Here is a half-yearly report which may refresh your memory.

Colonel Pew looks at the report, and admits that he voted in that month, in virtue of all his shares, *viz.*, 991.

Mr. Morton.—There were half-yearly dividends declared up to last February—were there not?

Colonel Pew.—I can only speak to August in last year, when dividends were declared at an average of twelve per cent on the paid-up part, *viz.*, 250 rupees a share. I did not draw dividends on the whole 991 shares, but I was credited with them in the Bank's books. I considered the shares I held to have been paid up, having given good security for the purchase-money.

Mr. Morton.—Did you get dividends on the shares for which you had not paid?

Colonel Pew.—Yes. I received dividends on the shares for which the Bank had paid, and for which I had given security: that is to say, I was credited with them in the Bank's books, and I drew on the account as I required.

Mr. Morton.—You have said that Rupees 250 were paid for the whole 6,000 shares issued. Do you mean that the aggregate of Rupees 15,00,000 was actually paid up, or that some shares were in the same predicament as those for which you had only given security?

Colonel Pew.—I cannot say how many shares were in this predicament. The 80,000 rupees which I had paid up, represented 300 shares. The others I gave good security for. On the whole 6,000 shares, about 8 or 9 lacs were paid up.

Mr. Morton.—Of this 8 or 9 lacs, I see you got about 7 lacs yourself! What security did you give for the debt to the Bank of Rupees 42,000 due by yourself and the other partners of the Nischindpore Sugar Factory.

Colonel Pew.—There were three personal sureties, who gave a

bond. Major Stewart and Dr. Duncan were the sureties besides myself. They were Co-Directors of mine in the Benares Bank. I do not know that they are unable to pay the debt. The debt of Rupees 29,000 due to the Bank by himself and the other partners of the Richmond estate jointly, was borrowed in the same way upon the names of myself, Captain Fagan, and Dr. Butter. I say the same of the debt of Rupees 1,08,000 due jointly from me and the other partners of the Ganges Company. We were all three (*i. e.*, Major Stewart, Dr. Duncan, and myself), I think, Directors of the Bank at the time of these loans. I am not certain about Dr. Duncan. He was a Director for some time. The debt to the Bank of Rupees 8,500, due jointly from myself and the other partners of the Mirzapore Coal Company, was borrowed on the security of Mr. Hamilton of Mirzapore, Major Stewart, and myself. I thought the Dacca Bank shares were always considered of good marketable value. The Dacca Bank is not only in existence yet, but is doing well.

Mr. Morton.—Well, then, as to the Ganges Steam Navigation Company shares. Is that Company flourishing too? I see it put down in your schedule for a debt due for coal supplied. Is it unable to pay for coals?

"Mr. Dickens.—If the credit of other Companies, not represented here, is to be attacked in this way, I must request that the Court will assign some limit to the nature and extent of Mr. Morton's questions. I cannot object to his asking whether the Ganges Steam Company was a paying Company at the date of the loan from the Benares Bank; but the Court will not admit a question as to its present position, which has nothing to do with the circumstances under which the particular advance was obtained.

The Commissioner.—I think the question put is a proper question. The Court must know what the value of the shares of the Ganges Company was at the time they were pledged as securities to the Benares Bank.

Mr. Dickens.—No doubt the Court must know this; but Mr. Morton's question refers, not to the time of the deposit, but to the present day. It is to this I object. The Ganges Steam Company is a numerous body, and is not represented here;—why, then, should any unnecessary question be put which might tend to affect their credit?

The Commissioner.—A Company may be perfectly solvent, and

yet its shares may be such that it would be extremely dangerous for Directors of a Bank to advance loans upon them, especially without a good margin.

Mr. Dickens.—Granted: then let Mr. Morton's question be restricted to the saleable value of the shares at the time they were pledged.

Colonel Pew to Mr. Morton.—The Benares and Mirzapore Company, which started the *Kashejee*, is still in existence. Mr. Stopford runs the *Kashejee* as the Agent of the Company; 3,000 rupees was paid upon each share of the Nischindpore Sugar Company. I do not know what they had sold for in the bazaar. I never knew that they were for sale in the bazaar. In the Mirzapore Coal Company there must be at least twenty partners, or more. The shares of this Company were sold in the market. I believe I may have voted for loans that I myself applied for; but I do not remember that I did. My vote was not requisite. The other two members of the Managing Committee constituted a majority, and passed the loans. I do not know that Captain Fagan and Dr. Butter were always in favor of my applications. Captain Fagan and Dr. Butter are indebted to the Bank for shares. In August 1848, there was an election of Directors. In answer to your question, whether we three voted each other in as Directors, I can only say there was a limited field at Benares, and there were none others there qualified for the Direction. Captain Fagan, Dr. Butter, and myself were therefore elected. There was a proposition for the appointment of Auditors in August last. I do not know that I opposed, and succeeded in negativing it. I think I must have opposed it. [He is shown a copy of the report.] Yes, I did oppose it. The proposition was rejected. I dare say it was known to the shareholders that 600 of my shares had not been paid for, except by the Bank itself, who took security. I must have approved of the half yearly reports of the Directors published during my connection with the Bank as Director. The reports represented that the paid-up capital was 15 lacs. Although 8 or 9 lacs was the amount of capital actually paid up, I thought this no misrepresentation, for I considered that the money lent to the people who bought shares upon security was the Bank's capital lent. I cannot say whether in every case where the Bank lent in this way, money really passed. If the Bank lent me money on good security, and I purchased shares with the money so lent, I should consider the shares paid for. The practice of purchasing shares upon security was generally understood among the shareholders I believe. Captain Graham was a shareholder of the Bank. He entered the Bank on my recommendation. He applied to me for my advice, and I told him I thought that the Bank was a very good institution. He frequently applied to me to purchase shares for him. I sold him some of my own. On one occasion, I sold them to him at a premium of twenty-five per cent. This was the rate the Bank fixed. I do not suppose that any other person would sell his shares in the Bank at the time at a smaller rate of premium. The seven Directors decided that a few shares that remained over at the end of a half year, should be divided among themselves at a premium of ten per cent.

The twenty-five per cent which I charged Captain Graham was calculated on the par value of each share, and not on the 250 rupees paid up; so that it is true that the premium was really fifty per cent. This letter to Captain Graham is in my handwriting:—

My Dear Graham,—Though very busy, here is a line in reply to your last. Firstly, you are down for 42 shares, and we could not well alter our books. Secondly, the total number of your shares should divide by 3—and 20 would not divide 3. Thirdly, were we to cut you down to 20, you would hereafter repent, for on the 31st January next you will get 8 new shares at par—being one in 3; again, on 31st July next you will get 8 new shares—one in 4; and on 31st January 1848, you will get 8 more new shares—one in 5; and so on for perhaps the next ten half years,—so you have made a deuced good bargain.

You should strain every nerve to come into this Bank largely, now, before a number of shares be created; you would not only be getting thumping dividends, but new stock, at par, every half year. Bring in all your rich friends—for 'twill be the best of Banks, with a glorious business.

Very sincerely yours,

P. L. Pew.

Benares, 24*th September* 1846.

Don't at all inconvenience yourself about payments—Debnam will lend you funds, as long as you require them.

Mr. Morton.—What was the glorious business that the Bank was doing at the date of this letter?

Colonel Pew.—The Bank was doing great discount business at the time—it was discounting sugar Bills chiefly. It was then under pretty considerable advances to me—not so much as 1 lac, however, I think. I look at these three other letters—

MY DEAR GRAHAM,—In reply to yours of the 27th ultimo, I say, yes; I advise you to buy as many more shares as you *possibly can*, for this will be a glorious Bank—and no mistake, and I think I may promise you old *shares* carrying new as on 31st January last on the same terms on which you got your last; but you must be quick in writing me your wishes, that I may instruct the Secretary, who will lend you *any* sum you may need to pay for them, and you can repay him by instalments, big or small, as may suit your perfect convenience. In haste,

Sincerely yours,

P. L. PEW.

7th February 1847.

MY DEAR GRAHAM,—Thanks for yours of the 30th ultimo—I have got you 12 old shares at twenty-five per cent premium, and 4 new shares at par—a deuced good bargain for you, as you escape the two per cent *premium* on those *new* shares. However, I'd always do *a deal* to get steady men like yourself into the Bank. Its a grand point—we are doing the most splendid business—and our onset dividend *may* be a *whacker*, if we like to divide *all* or nearly *all* the profits. Debnam will send you a memo. of your account. Just repay the Bank when most prefectly convenient to yourself and not before. Let me know if I can be of further use to you here or hereabouts. You have now a decent stake in the Bank, but you should still increase it—for this will be *the* Bank of Banks, and no mistake. We shall go on steadily, giving new stock *every half* year, and this of itself, leaving *fat* dividends out of the question, should make people join this Bank in preference to others. We could employ 100 lacs of capital at all seasons, to admirable advantage.

Very sincerely yours,

P. L. PEW.

13th April 1847.

"MY DEAR GRAHAM,—I thank you for yours of the 22nd instant. It's true your remittances monthly for six months won't quite cover the 18 new shares, but then recollect the dividend. This will never be less than twelve per cent, I may venture to say—as to a high rate of interest you are paying it to *your own* Bank, and getting it back in the shape of fat dividends. I made a deal of money *by borrowing to buy Bank stock*—and if you can get tick in this Bank or elsewhere, my advice to you is, 'borrow and buy Bank stock ere it rise.' You got the stock of this Bank in *the two last instances of your purchase* on very easy terms, see as follows:—

		Premium only.
3	old shares at twenty-five per cent premium.........	375 Rs.
1	new share, no premium	000
	Premium paid on 4 shares	375
	Equal to each	93¾

Or equal to eighteen and three-quarters per cent premium.

I believe I could still promise you a few more shares on the same favorable terms, if you be sharp about it; but whether you take them up or not, you have now got a fair stake in *this very rising Bank*. Stick to it, and your fortune is *sure*. By the time you think of going home your purse will be a *long* one—no doubt of it.

Easterly winds here and *very* hot—adieu.

Believe me,

Yours very sincerely,

Benares, 2nd *May* 1849. P. L. Pew.

Colonel Pew.—The greater part of the money lent to me was my own stock. It was not money taken from the Bank. The shares divided among the Directors at ten per cent premium were a few that remained over at the end of a half year. The Bank was anxious to sell, and I do not think the Directors were anxious to buy, but for the convenience of the Bank they did buy. At the same time that the Directors were dividing the remaining shares at a premium of ten per cent amongst themselves, I sold to Captain Graham some of my shares at a premium of twenty-five per cent. But I am not prepared to say that the shares I so sold, were part of those divided amongst the Directors at a premium of ten per cent. They may have been; but I have already told you that I held 991 shares in the Bank.

Mr. Ritchie.—I appear on behalf of the gentlemen connected with the management of the Benares Bank, to examine the Insolvent upon certain points.

Mr. Dickens.—If Mr. Ritchie appears on behalf of individual shareholders, I do not dispute his *locus standi:* but if he comes here to represent the general body, I, as the husband of one interested in the Bank, deny that be has a place of standing here, or that the Management have the right to spend one cowrie of the Bank's assets in taking a part in this opposition.

Mr. Ritchie.—I appear on behalf of the Management *de facto*, whether *de jure* or not, is another question, which need not be entered into now.

The Commissioner.—The Management *de facto* have a right to join in this opposition, if they conceive they have sufficient grounds. As to the question of expense, it is one which cannot be considered at present: for the Court cannot say now by which party the costs should be paid. I should like to hear from Mr. Ritchie to what ultimate object he proposes directing his opposition.

Mr. Ritchie.—My grounds apply to the mode in which the Insolvent has contracted certain portions of his enormous debt to the Benares Bank, and to the state of his assets as set out in the schedule.

The Commissioner.—Supposing your case proved, I shall have considerable difficulty in applying a penal clause of the Act against the Insolvent. The trust deed of the Benares Bank, unlike that of the Union Bank, assigns no limit to the terms upon which loans are to be advanced by the Directors; and, therefore, the making of the loans in question in the manner shown, does not amount to a breach of trust in that sense. It may be possible to show that there has been such gross misconduct on the part of the Directors, that, upon a bill filed in Equity against them, and a full investigation of the transactions and accounts, the Court would pass a decree requiring them to pay all the shareholders in full. But then, before I could decide that such would be the decree of a Court of Equity, I would have to go into an examination of the whole transactions of the Bank, and conduct the enquiry as in a Chancery suit. This being so, what am I do in this Court? If I enter upon such an enquiry, I must sit here from this time until the remainder of my residence in India, before I could bring it to a termination. Without such an enquiry, on the other hand, I should be unable to apply the 51st section of the Insolvent Act, supposing that I adopt your view of the case—under that section, I could only tell the Insolvent that he was entitled to the benefit of the Act, except as to his opposing creditors, and that he should not be discharged as to them, until after imprisonment at their suit for a certain period, and for a certain sum, which I must specify.

This sum I cannot ascertain, for it is in respect of a transaction which cannot be made to result in any liquidated sum in this Court. The opposition, therefore, if directed to my object at all, should rather be directed to the dismissal of the Insolvent's petition.

Colonel Pew to Mr. Ritchie.—A great many of the different joint stock shares which I have entered as assets in my schedule, are among those that are pledged. I have stated this distinctly in my schedule. There are 10 shares in the Pew estate (a coffee estate in the Malabar Coast) worth Rupees 70,000, and 5 Ganges Steam shares, on which Rupees 7,700 have been paid up. There are some Oriental Bank shares, of which the par value is Rupees 50,000, in pledge for Rupees 15,000. A large sum of money was paid into the Benares Bank on account of Dr. Berwick for the purchase of 249 shares. I acted as Dr. B.'s agent in that matter. The purchase was at seventeen per cent premium. A part payment was made on account of Dr. Berwick, *viz.*, Rupees 20,000, and the remainder, Rupees 76,000, was carried to the debit of Dr. Berwick in the Bank books on the security of the very shares purchased. Dr. Berwick subsequently seemed to think that I had exceeded my powers, and disputed his liability. But I and the Directors denied this, and insisted on his paying the balance of Rupees 76,000. I believe Dr. Berwick was doing great harm among the native shareholders. I believe there were some private meetings convened by him. Upon the advice of a friend I took over Dr. Berwick's shares, and the balance due, in consequence of this agitation. The Directors consented to this—at least three of the Directors must have done so. The shares were made over to me, and the balance of 76,000 rupees was carried to Dr. Berwick's credit in the Bank's books. I took the shares at seventeen per cent premium. I paid no money and gave no security for them. They were put into the Bank. I was not aware that I was in embarrassed circumstances in December 1848. I suspected then that an agent had made away with funds of mine, but I was not sure. My agent failed with my funds in June 1848. I was pressed for debts which I could not pay in December 1848. I dare say the premium realised from Dr. Berwick, in December 1847, entered into the accounts of the Bank as part of the profits, and was divided as such. I believe Dr. Berwick is solvent. In August 1848, I used all the votes I was entitled to, to elect Captain Fagan and Dr. Butter—I voted on 786 shares,

Captain Fagan on 400 odd shares, and Dr. Butter on 700 odd. Dr. Butter's and Captain Fagan's shares were not all paid in cash, like some of mine; security had been given for them. I do not recollect a clause in the trust deed prohibiting votes on unpaid shares. I considered that the shares for which I had given security had been paid for. I was not aware that the dividends up to August 1848 came out exclusively of the capital.

Mr. Dickens.—If Mr. Ritchie's object is to prove mismanagement of the Bank's affairs, I do not see what bearing such proof can have on the 51st section of the Insolvent Act.

The Commissioner.—I cannot say, until the inquiry has been further pursued.

Mr. Dickens.—Mr. Ritchie must not forget that Colonel Pew has already stated that he drew no portion of the dividends declared upon his shares. They were only carried to his credit in the Bank's books. Whether this was a good style of banking, or a good style of book-keeping, is not the question. Was it a breach of trust?

Colonel Pew to the Commissioner.—I believe the other Directors made cash payments into the Bank occasionally. I did not make cash payments regularly—only occasionally. These payments went to the relief of my *general* account. They aggregated, as I have said, about Rupees 80,000.

Mr. Ritchie to Colonel Pew.—You had 991 shares, on which Rupees 250 was to be paid up. That would be in the gross Rupees 2,47,750. Then you paid about Rupees 80,000. That would leave a balance of Rupees 1,67,750. But your debt to the Bank is Rupees 4,98,000. Did you draw the difference between Rupees 1,67,750 and Rupees 4,98,000 on your own account?

Colonel Pew.—If my shares were taken at par, my debt to the Bank would be Rupees 2,47,750: add the premium and interest, and you will increase it to Rupees 3,30,000.

Mr. Ritchie.—Your present debt is Rupees 4,98,000. Then you have paid Rupees 80,000. Add both these sums, and you have Rupees 5,78,000 as the sum which you originally owed to the Bank. Then you borrowed on your own account upward of Rupees 2,00,000 from the Bank? Is this so?

Mr. Dickens objects to such questions, saying that the Management have the Bank's accounts in their own custody.

The Commissioner to Colonel Pew.—What sort of business did the Bank carry on?

Colonel Pew.—Chiefly discount on sugar and commercial bills. The Bank realized large profits on these bills. There were losses also.

The Commissioner.—To what do you attribute the losses of the Bank?

Colonel Pew.—Chiefly to a party in Benares.

The Commissioner.—Were there many who had deposits in the Bank?

Colonel Pew.—A good many.

The Commissioner.—What proportion did their deposits bear to the actual payments made for shares?

Colonel Pew.—I cannot answer with any accuracy. I may mention that I also attribute the losses of the Bank to the general depreciation of security in 1847.

The Commissioner.—Then how did the Directors continue to declare dividends? I cannot understand what means they could provide for the payment of dividends, with outstandings unrealized, and losses accruing.

Mr. Dickens.—Colonel Pew has shown that there were no actual payments of dividends. The matter was managed by a mere entry at debit and credit in the books of the bank. The names of the Directors were inscribed to a certain number of shares, with the amount of which they were debited in account, and the dividends payable thereon were carried to their credit: so that the affair was all in the house.

Colonel Pew to Mr. Ritchie.—I have seen the printed statement of Mr. Dunbar. It was a very long business, and, being in ill health, I did not examine it; so that I cannot say whether it is correct or not.

Mr. Ritchie had intended to show from Mr. Dunbar's statement, that dividends were declared out of the capital of the Bank in August 1848; but as Colonel Pew was not prepared to admit its accuracy, he did not pursue his examination.

Colonel Pew to Mr. Ritchie.—When I pledged the Ganges Steam Company shares to the Benares Bank, they were at twenty per cent premium. They made a ready sale at that time. I was Chairman of the Ganges Steam Company. The Dacca Bank shares, when I pledged them, were sold at twenty per cent premium. The Cawnpore

Bank shares were then sold at twenty per cent premium. Both Dacca and Cawnpore Banks registered the transfer of my shares, in their respective Banks to the Benares Bank. The Sylhet Coal Company shares were, I believe, sold then at some premium. They were certainly then in the market at par. The Nischindpore Sugar Company shares were never in the market for sale. I executed a bond to the Benares Bank on the occasion of borrowing sums from it. The whole debt due by me to the Bank is secured by a bond.

To Mr. Theobald.—The Ganges Company is paying its debts very fast. I was told by one of the Directors, about twenty days ago, that in the course of three months its boats had cleared a profit of 70,000 rupees In the course of its business, I think it will pay its debts. Its property consists of five iron steamers, coal-depôts, wharfs, engines, stores, &c. The Nischindpore Company had been in business two years before I pledged its shares. It was managed by Gisborne and Co. of this town. I suppose the Cawnpore Bank will pay half the capital on those shares which I have pledged to the Benares Bank. The shares pledged by me were considerably above the loans which they secured. Joint-stock property generally is saleable in the Mofussil. Among officers of the Company, there are large sums invested in joint-stock shares. If at the end of 1847, I had, with the consent of the pledgees, sold the securities I had mortgaged, there would have been a very considerable surplus in my favor. The surplus would have exceeded the debts due to the Benares Bank by two lacs.

The Commissioner.—Could these shares, considering their large number at that period, have been sold in the market, without depreciating their value?

Colonel Pew.—The Benares Bank shares might have been depreciated, but not the others. In my own opinion, 506 Oriental Bank shares, held by me, have been misappropriated as security for a debt. The amount of the shares is above Rupees 2,50,000.

Captain Fagan, Mr. Charles, Captain Hobday, Major Carpenter, and Dr. Butter were co-Directors with me of the Benares Bank. They all took certain portions of shares that remained over at the end of a half-year, at the ten per cent premium. The new stock created was always made with the consent of the shareholders. The Secretary collected the votes on the increase by writing to the shareholders far and near. I think the Directors did not vote at all, and that the shareholders had only one vote each. The surplus amount of all my property, pledged and unpledged, if sold at a premium in December 1847, would be 16 lacs above my debts.

To the Chief Justice.—I believe the half-yearly meetings of the Bank, under the 20th section of the deed, were regularly held for declaring dividends to the shareholders. At those meetings, I do not think that any particular accounts were submitted showing that the Directors were debtors to the Bank. The shareholders had no information submitted to them that the shares created from time to time were not paid for by the Directors to whom they were appropriated. They might have ascertained, however, if they had taken the trouble of looking at the books. There would have been no difficulty in procuring money from the Cawnpore Bank on deposit of Agra Bank shares, or *vice versa.* I had no particular reason for applying for the loan to the Benares Bank. These advances to me were before the general crash here. The value of the shares pledged was depreciated at that crisis. Captain Fagan and Dr. Butter were in the habit of receiving advances from the Bank. Dr. Butter is now indebted to the Bank to a considerable. amount—Captain Fagan a little. They were holders of shares to a considerable amount in the Benares and other Banks. The advances to them had the same margin as those to me. A large number of shareholders, not Directors, were debited for shares for which security had been given, as in my own case.

Mr. Dickens.—That, I contend, was notice of the practice to the shareholders at large.

The Commissioner to Mr. Ritchie.—I remarked during a previous stage of these proceedings, that you should direct your opposition to the dismissal of the Insolvent's petition. But now that further evidence has been elicited, it appears to me, as at present advised, that the dismissal of the petition would not be for the benefit of the general creditors. There is a large number of securities in pledge, belonging to the Insolvent. It may be that these securities are under a cloud at this moment, and are either unsaleable, or of low value ; but it is not impossible that the Benares Bank may retrieve its affairs by more prudent and judicious management; and if its position *is* bettered at any future period, the securities now held in deposit from Colonel Pew, will rise in value again, and their sale may yield a large surplus, after payment of the claims which they secure, for division among the creditors at large. If, however, I dismiss the petition for insolvency, these securities will necessarily pass beyond the control of the Official Assignee; and the interests of the general body of creditors would thus be left unprotected.

Unless, therefore, I am asked to apply the penal clauses of the Act, my opinion at present is that I cannot deal with the case. But, as I have pointed out, there is a difficulty as to the mode of applying the penal clauses in this Court. Suppose that the Insolvent has contracted his debts to the Benares Bank by means of a breach of trust: the result of the transactions on which the debts have accrued, cannot be reduced to a liquidated amount, except by a Bill filed in equity, accounts taken, &c. This course cannot be pursued here. There is not the machinery in this Court for the purpose. Any order of mine, therefore, based upon penal clauses, would be idle—a mere nullity. I could only tell the Insolvent that he was entitled to the benefit of the Act as to all claims, except those of his opposing creditors, with respect to which he would not be discharged, until he should be in custody for a certain space of time at the suit of the parties, *for the specific sum due*, which sum I cannot give.

I must take this opportunity of remarking, that I do not at all approve of the course which the counsel for Captain Graham, and the other shareholders have adopted in conducting their opposition. Mr. Edlin began by stating the grounds of his opposition with a warmth of language which nothing could justify; and Mr. Morton, in examining the Insolvent, pursued his enquiries upon a point of the utmost importance to Colonel Pew, to a limited extent. This should not have been. The Court is no scene for the indulgence of angry feelings. The object of this enquiry is to ascertain whether the Insolvent is the victim of reverses, and entitled to the benefit of the Act; or whether he has come under heavy liabilities to the Benares Bank by breach of his duty as a Director, and of the trust reposed in him as such by the shareholders. In conducting his part of the enquiry, Mr. Morton contented himself with asking about the *present* value of the joint-stock shares lodged by the Insolvent as security for his debt to the Benares Bank. The learned counsel stopped there, which was stopping at the very point at which he should have proceeded. He should have gone on, to ask what was the value of these shares at the time they were deposited—whether they were then convertible into money by sale or pledge;—for this, and not the market value of the present day, must be the test of the Insolvent's object and motives at the time he incurred the debts. If the shares were convertible into money at premium or at par, or were generally considered valid, and sufficient security for loans at the time, then the deposit, though not a payment in form, was still a substantial payment. If, on the other hand, they were of no value, the deposit was a mere evasion, and the whole transaction was of a most reprehensible character. Mr. Morton asked no questions on the point; and the Court, in the exercise of its duty, put some to elicit the truth, when it came to its turn to examine Colonel Pew.

Mr. Edlin, in reply to the very first question I put to him as to his grounds of opposition, stated, in terms expressive of strong condemnation, what he conceived to be the nature of the breach of trust charged. This was perfectly gratuitous and unnecessary. It was for the Court, if it came to the same conclusion with Mr. Edlin, to characterize the nature of the offence; certainly, not for counsel to assume at the very outset the fact to be decided.

I mean to impute no wilful misconduct to either Mr. Morton or Mr. Edlin. I know they are both incapable of it. But I must say that they have laid themselves open to blame for error of judgment by the course they have taken. It should have been remembered that the object of this opposition was to apply penal clauses of the Act against the Insolvent; and the case for the opposition should have been conducted as in a criminal prosecution.

Mr. Morton was not in Court when the Commissioner made these remarks.

Mr. Edlin, who was present, said—I beg to disclaim any angry feeling on my own part. Colonel Pew can confirm me, when I say that, before the case was opened this morning at all, I asked him to impute nothing that I might say during the progress of the case to any personal feeling towards him.

The Commissioner.—No one personally acquainted with you, Mr. Edlin, can suppose that you would act with bad taste, or in a manner unbecoming you professionally. I desire thoroughly to examine the schedule and my notes before I pass any judgment in this case. I shall therefore defer my judgment to Monday, when I must sit again in the Insolvent Court to dispose of the other petitions; and I enlarge the *ad interim* protection order of Colonel Pew to that day.

Mr. Dickens.—I beg to address a very few words to the Court on behalf of the Insolvent.

Mr. Morton, who had now returned into Court.—In that case I apply that I should be heard first.

Mr. Dickens.—I do not know the practice under the new Act; but I am prefectly willing that my friend should be heard on his side. Under the old Act, the counsel for the opposing creditor did not address the Court at all on the evidence produced by himself.

The Commissioner.—Mr. Morton may address the Court first. An opposition of this kind is in the nature of a criminal prosecution; and it is only fair, therefore, that the Insolvent's Counsel should have the last word.

Mr. Morton.—I submit that the examination of the Insolvent shows, that the debt inserted as due by him to the Benares Bank, or a portion of it, was created by means which a Court of Equity would consider a breach of trust. It certainly is extremely difficult to say, at this moment, what is the extent of the debt so created; but it does not appear to me that it is necessary the Court should express an opinion on the subject, if it is satisfied that any portion of the gross debt to the Bank has been incurred in the manner charged. The difficulty, therefore, of ascertaining the liquidated sum due, is immaterial, in so far as a knowledge of such sum could guide the decision of this Court. It would, certainly, be extremely difficult to specify the liquidated sum in this case. But if a Union Bank Director, applying for the benefit of the Act, were shown systematically to have evaded the deed, and advanced loans in defiance of its most stringent provisions, no shareholder could have made out a case for a Common Law action against him, and he would likewise have found it difficult to apply a penal clause of the Insolvent Act to him. It is precisely so in the case of Colonel Pew. It would be very difficult for a shareholder of the Benares Bank to obtain a judgment or decree against him, under which he could put him into gaol, except by filing a Bill in Equity, making all the proprietors parties to the suit, and thus proving a breach of trust. But the point I submit, and the only one upon which I purpose to offer any observation, is this—whether the examination of Colonel Pew has not elicited the fact that *some* portion—it is difficult to ascertain what—of the debt due by him to the Bank has been contracted by means which a Court of Equity would treat as a breach of trust.

I do not mean to contend that every description of mismanagement of a Bank's affairs, is, in the absence of bad faith, a breach of trust, even supposing that such mismanagement result in the ruin of the institution. But I contend that, upon the showing of the Insolvent himself, there is evidence of such reckless and improvident dealing for his own benefit, as to establish a breach of trust upon which to apply the 51st section of the Insolvent Act against him.

I admit that the Trust Deed of the Benares Bank does not, like that of the Union Bank, prescribe a limit to the nature and extent of the loans which the Directors are to advance, or the sort of security they are to take. On the other hand, however, we have it upon the authority of Colonel Pew himself, that the Directors laid down certain rules for the regulation of the securities to be taken ;—and it further appears that these rules were violated, inasmuch as some portion of the advances to the Insolvent were made virtually upon the personal security of a single individual, which the deed prohibits.

Besides, even where the rules are silent as to the extent to which the Directors might use the Bank's capital in particular loans, leaving the matter to their discretion, a Court of Equity would assign some reasonable limit with respect to the margins necessary upon advances made on property of uncertain value, such as joint-stock shares, especially where such loans have been made to the Directors themselves. Here there have been cross loans from the Benares Bank between three of its own Directors. These, it seems, constituted a Managing Committee. Dr. Butter, one of the members, is indebted to the Bank to the extent of upwards of Rupees 2,00,000—at least to a considerable amount, for the precise sum has not transpired to-day ; Captain Fagan, the other member, is in the same situation, and Colonel Pew, the third member, owes to the Bank about Rupees 5,00,000 individually, and about Rupees 2,00,000 more, jointly with others.

I have forborne speculating at much length upon the causes which led to the ruin of this Bank. The institution was established only in 1845, and we have letters dated in February 1847, under the hand of the Insolvent, representing it to be in so flourishing and "glorious" a condition, that the writer asked the party with whom he was communicating, not only to strain every nerve to join the Bank by borrowing money at any rate of interest, but to bring all his rich friends into what, he said, would be the 'the best of Banks, and no mistake!' Yet, two years and a half after this representation, the Bank comes to wreck and ruin. How can we account for such a catastrophe in so short a period? I submit that it was owing, in a very great measure, if not entirely, to these enormous sums loaned by members of the Direction amongst themselves—to two of three Directors passing loans to the third, in expectation of obtaining similar accommodation from their fellow-members in turn. Taken by itself, this is, perhaps, no evidence of a breach of trust; but when considered in connection with the enormous amount advanced, I submit that it does afford proof upon which the 51st section of the Insolvent Act may be applied. When the sixth instalment of shares was issued, the total amount of the paid-up capital of the Bank would be Rupees 15,00,000, supposing 250 rupees to have been paid on each share in ready money. But, in point of fact, the amount of capital actually paid up was Rupees 8,00,000, or 9,00,000; for Colonel Pew admits that there was a large number of shares on which even the 250 rupees had not been paid, and which, consequently, were delusively described as representing part of the paid-up capital. Of the Rupees 8,00,000 or 9,00,000, it appears that Rupees 7,00,000 went to Colonel Pew himself. It lay upon Colonel Pew to show that he had contracted this monstrous debt by fair means. Had the borrower of this Rupees 7,00,000 been a most disinterested, and mere outside party, the fact that so enormous a loan had been advanced to him under the circumstances under which Colonel Pew obtained the amount, would have been a case of gross indiscretion, and a Court of Equity would have treated it as a breach of trust against the shareholders. What, then, must the judgment of the Court be when it sees that the whole of this Rupees 7,00,000 has been lent by Colonel Pew, the Director, to Colonel Pew the borrower?

The *onus* of accounting satisfactorily for such extraordinary dealing with the Bank's funds, then, lay upon the Insolvent; but, supposing that the *onus* lay upon me, the evidence, when carefully considered, shows that very considerable indiscretion has been exercised in the loans to Colonel Pew. That gentleman has said, that if the different shares he pledged to the Benares Bank were sold at their par value, there would be a surplus of Rupees 2,00,000, in his favor. When Colonel Pew said this, I believe he meant to say that this surplus would include the full value of his Benares Bank shares. But the fact is that more than a lac of Rupees is deficient upon these shares. Their full value is Rupees 500 per share: the sum actually paid is

Rupees 250 per share; and, having been thrown in as a make weight for a deposit, it does not require much logic to show that it was really no additional security for the loan raised. If this be so, upwards of Rupees 1,00,000 must be taken to be deficient, even calculating all the rest at par value.

Supposing, then, that in this state of things, there was a run upon the floating deposits. The securities lodged might have been of any nominal value you please: but if they were not of an actual value, for which they might be converted into money at any time, the loans advanced upon them might have had the effect of swamping the Bank entirely.

For many other reasons, it seems to me that it was extremely unreasonable and injudicious to take the par value of joint stock shares as a proper basis of security. I certainly did not minutely enquire, during my examination of the Insolvent, about the value of shares of the Cawnpore Bank, and one or two other Institutions, at the time they were deposited in pledge. I am perfectly willing to take it for granted, that these were saleable then at par. As to the Nischindpore Sugar Factory bills, I did ask the Insolvent what he thought their value was. His reply was, that they were valued at par at the time of the pledge, with reference to the price paid for them: but that he never knew them for sale in the market. Surely this was not a description of security on which so enormons a sum as Rupees 7,00,000, out of a total paid-up capital of Rupees 9,00,000, should have been advanced as a loan.

Under these circumstances, I submit that, on the first item in the schedule alone, a portion of the Insolvent's debt to the Benares Bank has been contracted by such an extraordinary violation of the ordinary rules of banking,—a violation which Colonel Pew does not seem to have been guilty of to accommodate any third outside party—that there is ample evidence of a breach of trust upon which to apply against him the 51st section of the Insolvent Act.

Mr. Dickens.—I really cannot see in what way Mr. Morton's last observations bear upon the case before the Court; but if he means to press the point he is now urging, I must say that he has not heard Colonel Pew's evidence respecting it. Mr. Morton wishes to show, that none others besides the Insolvent, or his co-Directors, had shares assigned to them on security. This is inconsistent with the evidence of Colonel Pew, who has stated that shares were so assigned to shareholders, not Directors.

Mr. Morton.—I am only speaking of the extent of the loans obtained by the Directors, and of the margin on which they were obtained by them. The margin appears to me to have been nothing. The securities Colonel Pew pledged, were calculated at their full value. I imagined that Mr. Dickens would show, at least, that the same indulgence had been extended to others not Directors. But he has tendered no such evidence; and I contend that the circumstance of Colonel Pew, a member of the Managing Committee, having obtained such heavy loans on such easy terms, is pregnant with presumptive evidence that he used his power as Managing Director to contract the debt to the Bank by means of a breach of trust.

With respect to the other items mentioned in the Schedule as those upon which money was due to the Bank from the Insolvent jointly with others, the parties, to my mind, have barely kept within the letter of the rule, and certainly gone very wide of the spirit. No less than three amounts, aggregating about Rupees 2,00,000, were lent to them by the Bank, without a particle of real or tangible security. Nominally, the loans may have been for the use of the different public Companies named: in reality, they were made to the self-same individuals, *viz*., Dr. Duncan, Major Stewart, and Colonel Pew. Those moneys were actually paid out of the little that was in the coffers of the Bank, to three who were Directors at or about the period; so that three loans, aggregating Rupees 2,00,000, in addition to the loan to Colonel Pew individually, were advanced to members of the Direction of the Bank jointly,—a transaction coming, no doubt, within the letter of the rule, which requires that there should be one applicant for a loan, and two sureties, but unquestionably evading the spirit.

Mr. Dickens.—If Mr. Morton urges this point, I would ask the Court to enquire of the Insolvent, whether the money lent by the Benares Bank to Dr. Duncan, Major Stewart, and Colonel Pew, was not lent upon a bond in which the borrowers expressly stated that the money was raised by them as Managing Directors of the Ganges Steam Navigation Company, and whether it was not duly appropriated to the purposes of that Company? Indeed, the Company is now defending an action for the amount of the loan, on the alleged ground that Messrs. Pew, Duncan, and Stewart exceeded their authority in borrowing it.

Mr. Morton.—No doubt all this is so; but I was arguing upon the Insolvent's own statement upon oath before the Court to-day, that he borrowed the three sums I have been alluding to, on the personal security of himself, Major Stewart, and Dr. Duncan, who joined in a bond. If Rupees 2,00,000 was lent upon a bond in which Colonel Pew, Major Stewart, and Dr. Duncan had joined, why then Colonel Pew, Major Stewart, and Dr. Duncan were indebted to the Bank for the amount, and not the Ganges Steam Company or any other party besides.

Here, then, we find Rupees 7,00,000 out of an aggregate paid-up capital of Rupees 9,00,000 lent out by a Director to himself and two fellow-Directors, who, again, borrowed in their turn, relying upon him and each other for the sanction of their loans.

The Insolvent has stated that he was a Trustee of the Benares Bank only nominally; and Mr. Dickens has suggested that the Trustees were appointed simply for the purpose of suing in the name of the Bank. I shall, therefore, make no comment upon that part of the case, beyond this, that it seems to me that a Director or any office-holder, being charged with the protection of the funds of an Institution, becomes a *Trustee* by virtue of such trust, and is guilty of a breach of trust when he uses the funds of the Institution in a manner so grossly improvident and improper, as Colonel Pew appears from his own evidence to have done, and with no other object than his own gain.

Mr. Ritchie.—I shall not address the Court on behalf of the Committee of Management of the Benares Bank. I will only call the attention of the Court to the cancellation of the debt due by Dr. Berwick. I do not wish to press the point against the Insolvent, nor will I address the Court upon it. My wish is simply to draw the attention of your Lordship to it.

The Commissioner.—But how do you propose that it should be construed into evidence of breach of trust?

Mr. Ritchie.—In this way. A certain number of shares were purchased by Dr. Berwick, whom the Insolvent himself has described as a solvent partner.

Mr. Dickens.—I deny that his solvency has been proved before the Court. Having been relieved of the payment of the 76,000 Rupees due from him for the purchase of the Benares Bank shares, he was solvent, no doubt, and Colonel Pew believed him to be so;—but query

—would he be solvent, had the payment of the Co.'s Rs. 76,000 been insisted on?

Mr. Ritchie.—I am only repeating what the Insolvent has said. He has said that Dr. Berwick bought a certain number of shares, through him, at twenty per cent premium, that 20,000 rupees was paid in part for them, and that Dr. Berwick was in solvent circumstances. The next half-year, the premium, plus the interest that had accrued upon the amount of the unpaid purchase-money, although unrealised in fact, went into the account of profits actually earned, and out of it a dividend was declared. In December 1848, Dr. Berwick disputed the validity of the purchase of the shares on which 20,000 rupees had been paid, and repudiated his liability for the balance of Rupees 76,000. Against this, both the Insolvent and the other Directors protested. Dr. Berwick, upon this, commenced an agitation into the affairs of the Bank. The Insolvent, according to his own admission, to put a stop to this agitation, took over, with the assent of all his co-Directors, the shares on which the 20,000 rupees had been paid, and carried the balance of 76,000 rupees to the credit of Dr. Berwick in the Bank's books; thus cancelling the debt which was unquestionably due from Dr. Berwick as such, as if he had received the 76,000 rupees in hard cash from the Bank. Colonel Pew did this with the assent of the other Directors; and the act was, therefore, binding on the shareholders.

The Commissioner.—I do not see how the Directors could exonerate Dr. Berwick from his original responsibility to the Bank. Supposing Colonel Pew had the power to purchase shares for him, which he says he had, and did purchase, as agent, the principal was bound by that act, so done. But suppose, on the other hand, that the agent exceeded his authority, and that, wishing to get rid of an objecting principal, he transferred the shares purchased, to his own name, the transfer would give him a derivative title to the shares, and, therefore, entail upon him the liability for the purchase-money due. It would not be an extinction of the debt *ab origine*. The Directors of a Bank have no authority to cancel debts due to the Bank.

Mr. Ritchie.—If the Court holds that opinion, I have nothing further to urge."

1850.—Further disclosures made about the irregularities in the management. From the investigations before the Insolvent Court, it appears that Colonel Pew is the principal debtor to the Benares Bank, having, as the chief Director, advanced enormous sums of the Bank's capital to himself; of course without available security, and he came up as an insolvent debtor chiefly to be relieved of his debts to the Bank. The sole business of the Bank was money-lending—the maximum interest drawn by it ten per cent, and out of this, dividends of twelve per cent were proposed to be paid! The selling price of shares was fixed by the Directors, who sold their own at premiums of from twenty-five to fifty per cent. When they found they had more of this than they could manage, a vast mass of them were cancelled—that is, sold at ten per cent premium to the Bank, from which they had been bought at par, and paid for with the Bank's money. Colonel Pew's share of this transaction realised for him Rupees 1,00,000 in a forenoon. Out of Rupees 9,00,000, *the entire assets of the Bank,* Rupees 7,00,000 *to* Rupees 8,00,000 *were borrowed by him.* The Insolvent Court, notwithstanding, saw no fraud in the case, and threw its protection over his person. Probably the Judge thought that the acts of Colonel Pew were rather to be attributed to ignorance than fraud. The letters, however, which were read during the progress of the case, show the absurd idea entertained of what could be realised as banking profits. Colonel Pew speaks of the Bank paying dividends of eighteen or nineteen per cent, while, in fact, the establishment never could receive more than ten in the way of interest; for, at this rate, private money-lenders in abundance were ready to do business. It could do next to nothing in the exchange market, and was, at that very time, unable to get its spare funds, limited as they were, invested, affording any such return as even the rates obtained by private money-lenders. The letters, therefore, which are recorded in the proceedings of the Insolvent Court, are either the result of disgraceful ignorance, or infamous fraud.

Colonel Pew in this case, it is said, knew perfectly well that he was taking a man of straw into the Bank. Captain Graham was buying shares with the Bank's own money; did he never think of where the eighteen per cent was to come from, when he and other borrowers were only paying ten? Colonel Pew assures his dupe that the Bank could safely invest a crore of capital! There cannot be a doubt of it—a hundred crores for that matter, so long as they were ready to create stock *ad libitum*, and to advance to proposing purchasers the price of their shares on the security of their scrip. These are the kind of dealings which have raised the cry against Banks lending on the security of their own stock. The stock in this case was unsaleable at any price: purchasers for it would only be found when the Bank lent the money; and in the general market no man would have a gift of it. How Bank Directors should desire to create useless paper of this sort would seem inexplicable, were the matter not cleared up by the executors. The Directors sold their own shares to their dupes, nominally at twenty-five, but, in reality, at fifty per cent premium. Shares for which no money had ever been paid to the Bank, or which is exactly the same thing, which had been paid for by the Directors of the Bank out of the coffers of the Bank, were made over to other parties,—the Directors who so made them over receiving one-fourth more for them than they had themselves paid or promised to pay! Nothing can remove transactions such as these from the category of impudent frauds.

The *Bombay Times*, in commenting on the Insolvent's examination, says—" The only reason that can be assigned for advancing money to intending shareholders to pay their stock is, that it enabled previous holders to dispose of theirs to advantage: the only explanation that can be given of the creation of new stock when that originally subscribed for was only half paid up—much of even this half payment being from the coffers of the Bank—is, that it induced dupes to come in and bring occasionally something in the shape of hard cash along with them. By this device the Rev. Mr. Shurman, Major Stewart and his son, seem to have been ruined. The grand object of the Bank seems to have been to secure loans to Colonel Pew and his brother Directors, and, before this could be effected, actual capital must be obtained from some quarter or other. The sale of shares by the Bank, for which the Bank had to pay, brought nothing to the treasury. If these assumptions be at all correct, the Benares Bank Directors, or a portion of them at all events, were quite on a par, in point of integrity, with their brethern of the Union—or, for that matter, of the Bunder Gang. The deed of settlement provided that votes should only be given on shares that were paid up—that is, on which Rupees 250 had been paid; but Colonel Pew and his brother Directors voted on all their shares, as if paid up, and thus carried their own election. The cancelment transaction comes out on the examination in a light something new: the shares purchased from the Bank, and with the Bank's own money, at par—that is at Rupees 500, half of which was paid up—were sold to the Bank at ten per cent premium, so that Colonel Pew, by this turning over of his capital (?) just realized a lac of Rupees. 'I'll buy your shares,' says Pew to the

Bank, 'if you will lend me the money.' 'Certainly,' says the Bank: so the shares are bought. 'Now,' say the Directors, 'we shall declare the shares worth ten per cent premium.' 'Then,' says Pew, 'I'll sell mine to the Bank and pocket the ten per cent.' 'So shall we,' say his co-Directors—and the shares are sold: so is the bank—so are the shareholders. Had the 250 rupees been paid on each of the 6,000 shares, the capital of the bank would have amounted to fifteen lacs of rupees; as it was, however, it amounted to no more than nine, and of this Colonel Pew obtained on loan seven to his own hand! While borrowing and lending wholesale amongst each other, the Directors might well strive to induce their dupes to purchase new stock, and see and bring something in the shape of hard cash to their coffers."

These discreditable transactions could not be slurred over, and a COURT MARTIAL was held at Simla on the 7th of May 1850, when Captain *Christopher George Fagan*, of the 8th Regiment of Light Cavalry, and Surgeon *Donald Butter*, *M. D.*, who had been Directors in the unfortunate and mismanaged Bank of Benares, were brought to trial on the following charges:—

"For conduct highly unbecoming the characters of officers and gentlemen, in the following instances:—

"1*st.*—In having, at Benares, between the 16th of February 1848, and the 21st of February 1849, they being at the time Directors of the Benares Bank, in concert with other Directors of that institution, put forth one or more false reports of the state of the Bank, and thereby deceived the shareholders.

"2*nd.*—In having, at Benares, during the month of August 1848, assumed an improper influence in the management of the affairs of the Benares Bank, by having voted as the holders of shares, notwithstanding that they had not paid for the same, and well knew that they had no right to vote upon them.

"*3rd.*—In having, at Benares, during the month of December 1848, cancelled, at their par value, shares in the Benares Bank, held by themselves, notwithstanding that the market value of the said shares was at the rate of about twenty-five to thirty per cent discount, thereby causing injury to the shareholders at large, and gaining themselves an unfair advantage."

The Court found both the prisoners *guilty* of the above charges, with a slight modification of the wording of the charges, and pronounced the following sentence:—

"*Sentence.*—The Court, having found the prisoner guilty as above specified, do adjudge him, the said Captain Christopher George Fagan, of the 8th Regiment of Light Cavalry, and Deputy-Paymaster, Benares Circle, to be cashiered.

Approved and confirmed,

(Signed) C. J. NAPIER, *General,*
Commander-in-Chief.

Head Quarters, 6th May 1850."

"*Recommendation.*—The Court, having awarded a sentence which they deem adequate to the offences of which they have found the prisoner guilty, do now most earnestly recommend him to the clemency of His Excellency the Commander-in-Chief, on the grounds of the very high character he, Captain Fagan, has borne during his service of twenty-two years."

Remarks by His Excellency the Commander-in-Chief.

"The Court have convicted the prisoner of falsehood and deceit in his dealings with a brother officer, who seems to have confided in him; yet eleven members of the Court recommend the prisoner to mercy, 'on the grounds of high character.' Such recommendations add much to the pain of those whose duty it is to inflict punishment; but I must decline complying with the request of those members who concur in this recommendation. When violence of temper, error in judgment, or the thoughtlessness of youth, lead men into culpable conduct, their high character bears great and honorable weight, excusing human frailty. High character is also justly appealed to when concurring circumstances cast suspicion on yet unblemished reputation; but, when the charge is dishonor, and, that dishonor proved, former high character vanishes, and is nothing.

(Signed) C. J. NAPIER, *General,*
Commander-in-Chief."

The *Bombay Times* makes the following remarks on the above case: —

"Captain Fagan and Dr. Butter have, we observe, been found guilty of the charges laid against them in the matter of the Benares Bank, and been sentenced to be cashiered. The sentence, though severe, cannot be considered too much so: the Directors of the Benares Bank were all, on their own showing, guilty of raising money on false pretences, to be invested for the accommodation of one of their number, in breach of the regulations of the Bank. The second of these two errors is comparatively venial; the first implies the highest degree of moral guilt. There is no evidence stronger than their own solemn declarations required to convict the Directors—out of their own mouths are they condemned. They were for years in the habit of inducing parties to purchase additional stock, by holding out to them that the speculation was an eminently profitable one, and, that all they required to bring it to the highest pitch of prosperity, was a little more capital in cash. While doing this, they knew that they were pushing, at the most desperate risks and against all the first principles of banking, an unprofitable trade; that instead of requiring more capital, they had not the means of investing profitably that which they originally possessed. There never, in fact, had been any occasion for the establishment of a Joint Stock Bank at Benares at all, and there was no outlet, at once safe and remunerative, for the investment of their cash. Before they could secure the semblance of a return at bazaar rates of interest, they put up with securities the money-lenders in the bazaar would have laughed at. They were not speculating against hope, but in the teeth of knowledge; there was no room for faith in better times even in the bosom of the most sanguine—they knew that the promises they held out could not be realised—that the concern was based on delusion, and that delusion was maintained by unceasing prevarication. We are of those who not only see no reason why Company's servants should not invest their savings in any way that seems most for their advantage, provided the investment be honorable and becoming; but, we go greatly beyond this, and hold, that such connections, on the part of the members of the Service are, in the great majority of cases, of the utmost value to the commonwealth, while they occasion no injury to the public service, and no diminution of dignity to its members. It is to the thrift and the exertions of the Officers of the Service that we owe all that is really excellent and valuable in joint stock banking—all we enjoy in the way of railway prospects—much of what we possess in efforts for the general improvement of the country. But, while members of the Service, engaged in this way, are, in all things, deserving of countenance and encouragement, forgetfulness of what is due to themselves and their position merits no mercy. They occupy a position where conduct becoming the character of a gentleman is demanded of them at their peril; they are looked up to and confided in as guaranteed by their rank against the commission of anything that is unworthy; the principles which regulate the conduct of the Service are judged of by many from the manner in which its members disport themselves in secular affairs; and, on all these grounds, they are specially bound to circumspection—specially deserving of punishment when forgetful of their duty. All that is wanted is uniformity of treatment; that there should be one law and one judgment for all; that fraud and falsehood, when fairly proved, should, when knowingly and deliberately committed, be visited with the severest punishment, however great or small the occasion, however exalted or insignificant the transgressor."

SIMLA BANK LIMITED.

This Bank commenced business on 19th November 1844. The first Secretary was Dr. Carte. He was succeeded by Mr. Arnold H. Matthews, who continued attached to the Bank till 1854, when he was appointed Agent for the Agra United Service Bank at Agra.

The head quarters of this Bank are at Simla. It has

Agencies at Umballa, Calcutta, Lahore, Mussoorie, Delhi, Agra, Bombay, and Madras. Mr. R. D. Turnbull was appointed Agent at Umballa, but was afterwards nominated Deputy Secretary at the Head Office; Mr. W. Charde succeeding him as Agent at Umballa.

1847.—The following is an abstract of the Balance Sheet for this year:—

Capital and Profits	Rs.	8,38,280
Liabilities	„	1,32,710
Cash and Government Securities	Rs.	95,950
Other Securities	„	8,75,040

The commercial crisis in 1847-48, and the calamitous failure of the Union Bank, combined, lowered the value of the shares of this Bank, in common with all other Joint Stock Associations in India. The Bank has no charter, nor any notes in circulation.

One thousand shares were first subscribed for, of 500 rupees each. Three increases took place, one of 600 shares, and two of 800 shares each. The subscribed capital in 1848 was 16 lacs of rupees, of which 14,62,000 rupees were paid up.

The business of the Bank consists chiefly in Indian Exchange and Loans to the Services, and is little more than local in its influence.

1849.—A Branch was established at Murree. For a time, Mr. L. Carmichael transacted the business of the Calcutta Agency, when it was taken up by Mr. John Morgan; both of these gentlemen being paid by a percentage on the disbursements. The Bank drew on Coutts and Co. When better arrangements were made,

Mr. John McKellar was appointed Agent in Calcutta, with Mr. R. D. Turnbull as Accountant. On account of the calamitous failures both in India and in England, and the numerous commercial disasters, the Directors recommend a large increase to the Reserve Fund as essential to the safety and stability of the Bank.

1852.—A Government Order, which prohibits Government servants from taking any active part in the management of Banks in India, causes, a considerable stir amongst all interested in those institutions.

1854.—A Branch is established in London under the Agency of Dr. J. E. Stephens, of the 10th Hussars, and Surgeon to Lord Gough. A proposal to remove the head quarters of the Bank to London leads to a disagreement among the shareholders, and to a division of capital; one-half keeping up the Simla and Umballa Bank, with its Branches at Umballa and Murree:—the other half opening a Bank in London, under the style and denomination of THE LONDON AND EASTERN BANKING CORPORATION, with Branches in Bombay and Calcutta.

The Simla Bank, of the present day, has a paid-up capital of Rupees 6,38,500, in 1,277 shares of Rupees 500 each, and is registered under Act XLIII. of 1850.

The following are the dividends which have been declared :—

1st	dividend	of 10 per cent	declared	1st May 1845.
2nd	ditto	of 8 per cent	ditto	25th November 1845.
3rd	ditto	of 8 per cent	ditto	25th July 1846.
4th	ditto	of 9 per cent	ditto	30th January 1847.
5th	ditto	of 9 per cent	ditto	3rd August 1847.
6th	ditto	of 9 per cent	ditto	1st February 1848.
7th	ditto	of 8 per cent	ditto	10th August 1848.

The present staff, &c., of the Bank are:—

Secretary	...	F. Peterson.
Deputy Secretary	...	Francis D. Daly.
Agent at Umballa	...	———
Agent at Rawul Pindee and Murree	...	P. Butler.
Agent at Calcutta	...	———

THE LONDON AND EASTERN BANKING CORPORATION.

It has been stated, that this Bank arose out of the schism between the proprietors of the Simla and Umballa Bank in 1854. It started with a nominal capital of £500,000, of which £50 per share was paid up, or supposed to be paid up. The number of shareholders was 98. In 1855 the first half-yearly meeting of shareholders took place, when a dividend was declared at the rate of six per cent. It was explained, that the amount to be distributed had been realised from the operations carried on at the Head Office in London, the accounts from India not having been prepared. It was further announced, that they had Branches at Calcutta and Bombay, and had been joined by some influential and wealthy shareholders. Dr. J. E. Stephens was the Manager, under whose magic wand this Corporation was doomed to attain a degree of unenviable notoriety, equal to, if not supassing that of the Royal British Bank, the Tipperary Bank, and the Benares Bank.

1856, July 4—Second annual meeting was held, when the successful result of the operations for 1855 was noticed. The accounts, audited by experienced London Accountants, showed a nett profit of £25,378, exceeding ten per cent. The assets and liabilities of the Bank, as published in the *London Gazette*, were referred to in proof of the Bank's prosperity. The Chairman, the Hon'ble J. C. Erskine, eulogized the Directors and other Officers of the Company.

1857, March 17.—The banking and commercial community of London are astounded by the announcement, that the Bank is in liquidation, and that the circumstances connected therewith are of a most discreditable character. The conduct of the Directors and Managers is stated to be deserving of the severest reprobation. It is said the charter was fraudulently obtained. The statements put forth at the last meeting are declared to have been deceptive. While the paid-up capital was £250,000, it appears that £237,000 had been lent, upon mortgage, on estates belonging to Colonel Waugh, one of the Directors, at Beddington, in Surrey, and Branksea-castle, Dorsetshire; while other advances, to a very serious extent, have been made to Directors and to the Manager, and this at a time when money could have been profitably invested in Calcutta at twelve per cent interest, and one per cent commission on Government Securities of the Five per Cent Loan. The failure of the Royal and British Bank in Scotland having caused a pressure on the London and Eastern Bank, and Dr. Stephens not having funds to meet the same, the paid-up capital of the Bank having been advanced to Colonel Waugh, a most dishonorable course was adopted. Bills were drawn on the Calcutta Branch, the Manager whereof, Mr. McKellar, was made to believe that some extensive exchange operations were in course, and that large funds would be remitted in time to meet them, whereby a handsome profit would be derived by the Bank. The promised funds never came, and Mr. McKellar, to meet the drafts, was compelled to draw on Dr. Stephens, which Bills were dishonored, and led to the close of the Bank. At the meeting to-day, Mr. John Carnac Morris, the Chairman of the Company, presided, and that gentleman admitted he was indebted £12,000 to the establishment, against which the Bank held securities on houses, &c. Mr. Fendall, a Director, was understood to have borrowed £5,350 on the security of his own shares; Colonel Curtis, a Director, £5,500 on steam shares worth £3,000; and Mr. Stephens, the Manager, £27,000 on various securities. During the proceedings, Mr. Guedalla, a shareholder, inquired upon what pretext, or temptation, £237,000 could have been sunk in mortgages, when the legitimate business for which the concern was established offered safe, regular, and heavy profits. The reply that ten per cent was paid upon the mortgages caused a strong feeling of indignation, since the very fact of such a rate being offered should have been a warning of their questionable character. Captain Corfield, another shareholder, pointed out the deceptive character of the clause in the charter providing for a meeting upon a fourth of the capital being lost, and maintained that those by whom it had been disregarded deserved heavy punishment. The direct liabilities of the Bank were stated by Mr. Coleman, the Accountant, to be £397,734; and it was intimated that, after allowing for large losses, the assets may yield £413,450, which will leave about £16,000 to meet the shareholders' paid-up capital of £250,000. Four Indian Banks—the Oriental, the North-Western, the Mercantile of Bombay, and the Agra, were stated to be willing to advance the amount necessary to meet immediate liabilities in India, about £104,000, and also to give time upon such bills of the London and Eastern Bank as are at present in their possession, on condition that certain assets shall be handed over to them, and that the shareholders shall give their notes of hand for the fifty per cent of capital still remaining uncalled. This arrangement seemed to be regarded as a fair and desirable one; and a Committee, consisting of Sir William Gomm, Colonel Yates, and Mr. Beville, was ultimately formed to promote it. It is stated that the Oriental Bank Corporation hold no bills or obligations of the London and Eastern Company, but are influenced to interfere in the matter, with the hope of saving the unfortunate shareholders (some of whom are shareholders and constituents of the Corporation) from the disastrous consequences of the litigation which would be likely to arise from a judicial winding up of the affairs of the London and Eastern Bank.

April 8.—General meeting of shareholders took place, when a report was read regarding the steps taken for the winding up. The shareholders are asked to confirm, by resolution, what has hitherto been done, both at, and since the meeting of the 25th March, and to authorise and sanction the arrangement made with the Oriental Bank Corporation on behalf of themselves and the other assisting Banks, and the Directors will be prepared, at the next half-yearly meeting, to be held in pursuance of the Letters Patent, to make a report of the progress of their administration.

The annexed resolutions were adopted:—"That the report of the Directors be received and confirmed, and this meeting declares its approval and confirmation of the measures taken to provide funds to meet the Company's engagements.—That this meeting does not think it proper that the Company should be dissolved.—That Colonel Yates, Mr. Thynne, and Captain Beville be requested to continue members of the Committee, and that Archibald Frederick Arbuthnot, Esq., and Samuel Smith, Esq., be requested also to become members of the Committee, and that the Committee be authorised and empowered to superintend the Board of Directors, and that the Board be authorised and enjoined to act under the direction of the Committee, and to carry out, on behalf of the Corporation, any measures which the Committee may direct, and to authorise and confirm any acts which may be done by Mr. Stuart, as Manager, under the authority of the Committee.—That the cordial thanks of the shareholders be conveyed to the Directors and Managers of the Oriental Bank Corporation, and the other assisting Banks, for their prompt and liberal assistance.—That thanks be also given to Mr. Stuart for undertaking the office of Manager, and for the services already rendered by him to the shareholders.—That the thanks of this meeting be given to the Committee and to Mr. Arbuthnot for their valuable advice and assistance."

July 26.—Another meeting of shareholders was held.

"A letter addressed to the Chairman, received from Captain Tucker, in which he recommended that every exertion should be used to bring the Directors to justice, appeared to meet approval, and it was stated that a subscription would cheerfully be raised to carry out the requisite measures. With regard to the affairs of the Bank, it will be noticed that the liquidation is making steady progress, and that the liabilities have been reduced from £340,240 to £282,700. The assets, which, on the 14th of April, were estimated at £234,010 are now taken at £169,996. It is found that the deficiency, after absorbing the shareholders' capital, which was placed at £6,020, will be increased to £12,710. This arises, however, not from any miscalculation, but through the loss occasioned by the drawings from the Head Office upon the Indian establishment when the exchanges were unfavorable. An announcement of this character created serious indignation, as it furnished additional evidence of the reckless steps adopted by the Directors and Managers to avail themselves of the general resources. The late Manager, Mr. Stephens, has, it is alleged, disputed his liability; but it can scarcely be believed, unless legal difficulties interpose, that he will prove successful; for, in no case have the Directors or Officers, who are indebted to the Bank, made arrangements for payment; and some questions put respecting Colonel Waugh's estate were not fully entered into, owing to the approaching sale of the Branksea property. The information elicited by Mr. H. Guedalla, and other shareholders, from the Chairman, Mr. Peachey, the Solicitor, and Mr. J. E. Coleman, the Accountant, was not of a description to produce satisfaction, and the amount of ultimate sacrifice remains to be ascertained. Every claim made upon the Bank has been promptly met, and it is hoped that the final liquidation will encounter no interruption. Subjoined are the Report and Accounts:—

Report to the Shareholders of the London and Eastern Bank, made at the General Meeting, held on the 20th July 1857, by the Committee of Liquidation:—

Since the last Report, advice has been received that the Managers of the Bank in India have, in conformity with the instructions sent them, made over charge of the Branches at Bombay and Calcutta to the Agents of the Oriental Bank Corporation, by whom the Indian affairs are being wound up as expeditiously as possible.

It is due to the Managers of these Branches to state that so far as the Committee can ascertain, the Indian business has been conducted prudently, and with due regard to the interests of the shareholders, the only operations resulting in loss being those originated at the Head Office. This loss has arisen chiefly from heavy drawings in London on the Branches in Calcutta and Bombay, and consequently re-drafts between these Branches and England at disadvantageous exchanges; and by these operations the balance of £42,700, now appearing in the accounts as to be received from India, will be reduced to less than £20,000.

In pursuance of the arrangement with the Oriental Bank Corporation, promissory notes of shareholders, on account of unpaid capital, for the sum of £206,150, have been handed to that Corporation; who have also received in Calcutta calls or security for the payment of calls amounting to £1,320. A second call of £15 per share has been made payable on the 1st of August next, and steps will be taken to enforce this and the previous call of £15 per share, payable on the 24th of April ultimo, against those shareholders who have not given their promissory notes for unpaid capital.

The Statement of Accounts now laid before the meeting, embraces the result of the liquidation from the 11th April, the date of the last account to the 11th instant, and shows that the liabilities of the Bank have been reduced from £340,240 to £282,706.

In addition to the assets actually realised and applied in reduction of liabilities as above, considerable progress has been made in arranging and bringing into a definite shape many outstandings of a complicated and doubtful character.

When the last report was made the estimated deficiency was £6,320; and by the present statement the deficiency appears to be £12,710. This arises, not from too high a value having been formerly made of the assets, but from loss on Indian exchange, as previously explained.

It is hoped that the out-turn of the general assets will fully bear out the present estimate; but the final result of the liquidation must entirely depend on the realisation of the securities held for Colonel Waugh's debt.

Statement of the Affairs of the London and Eastern Banking Corporation, 11*th of April and* 11*th of July* 1857.

LIABILITIES.

	11th of April.			*11th of July.*		
	£.	s.	d.	£.	s.	d.
To creditors on drawing accounts	8,469	19	8	1,629	10	8
„ ditto on Deposit	49,641	19	10	35,796	0	0
„ ditto Bills payable	167,233	10	6	164,497	9	2
	225,345	10	0	201,922	19	10
Bombay Branch	43,120	16	9	....		
Calcutta Branch	28,581	9	11	....		
United Service Branch	2,732	5	8	515	8	4
Delhi Bank	11,843	0	3	19,755	17	9
Agra Savings' Bank	240	7	4	....		
Oriental	28,377	12	3	60,475	14	0
Liabilities ...	340,240	2	2	282,669	19	11

ASSETS.

	11th April, Estimated Value.	11th July.			Estimated Value.		
	£	£	s.	d.	£	s.	d.
By Cash Balance	2,740	87	10	3	87	10	3
„ Bills received	58,950	64,305	11	6	64,305	11	6
„ Bills discounted	29,820	....			....		
Drs. on Advances and Drawing Accounts ...	115,000	102,066	19	9	53,000	0	0
Past-due Bills and Past-due Loans	12,500	31,427	0	7	20,000	0	0
Banking-houses and Furniture	15,000	15,000	0	0	15,000	0	0
Calcutta Branch	......	42,791	1	2	17,500	0	0
Simla Bank	......	103	5	2	103	5	2
Assets ...	234,010	255,781	8	4	169,996	6	11
Colonel Waugh	100,000	100,000	0	0	100,000	0	0
	334,010	355,781	8	4	269,996	6	11

September.—A petition was presented to Vice-Chancellor Wood, on behalf of Mr. Abel Stuart, of South-bank, Regent's-park, and Mr. George Duplex, of Torrington-square, praying that an order absolute may be granted for the dissolution of the London and Eastern Banking Corporation, and that its affairs may be wound up under the provisions of the Joint Stock Companies Winding-up Acts. The petitioners cited, among other reasons for the said winding up, the following :—That the Bank was formed in 1854; that a deed of settlement was prepared on the 1st of September 1854, setting forth that Mr. Joseph Harris, of Frederick-place, London, Mr. James Gray William Curtis, of Thornhill Bray, Ireland, and Mr. Thomas Chadwick, of 26, Porchester-terrace, London, agreed with others to form the Joint-Stock Bank in question, and that its captial should be £500,000, in shares of £100 each, with power to augment the same; and that each shareholder has paid up £50 on each said share. That the first officers of the Company were the Hon. J. C. Erskine, Mr. R. J. Lattey, Mr. J. C. Morris, Colonel Thomas Chadwick, Mr. Robert Griffith, and Mr. John Edward Stephens, Directors; and Mr. James E. Coleman and Mr. George Edward Lyons, Auditors of the Company. Having referred to the conditions on which the Bank was proposed to be formed, the following are cited:—

"The books relating to the general affairs of the Company shall be balanced thirty days at least before each ordinary general meeting, and forthwith on the books being so balanced an exact report and balance-sheet shall be made up, which shall exhibit a true statement of the capital, stock, credits, and property of every description belonging to the Company, and the debts due by the Company at the date of making such balance-sheet, and a distinct view of the profit or loss which shall have been arisen on the transactions of the Company in the course of the preceding year; and previously to each ordinary general meeting, such report and balance-sheet shall be examined by the Directors, or any three of their number, and shall be signed by the Chairman of the Directors, and shall thereupon be recorded in the books of the Company.

Whenever a loss of at least twenty-five per centum on the capital for the time being paid up has been sustained, it shall be incumbent on the Directors to summon an extraordinary general meeting, to consider the propriety of dissolving the Company, and any meeting so summoned may come to a resolution to dissolve the Company, and the same shall thereupon be dissolved in all respects as is provided by the next clause.

Whenever a loss of at least seventy-five per centum on the subscribed capital for the time being of the Company has been sustained, it shall be incumbent on the Directors, and in their default for twenty-one days after notice given to them so to do, it shall be lawful for any one shareholder to summon an extraordinary general meeting, for the dissolution of the Company; and the dissolution of the Company by such meeting, or by any meeting at which it shall appear that a loss of seventy-five per centum on the subscribed capital shall have been incurred, shall be valid and effectual, without the confirmation of any second or other general meeting; and although the number of shareholders required by any regulation of the Company, either for the resolving on a dissolution or as the quorum of a general meeting, shall not have been present.

That numerous persons applied for shares in the said Company, to whom the same were allotted, and in respect whereof they executed the said deed of settlement, and paid the first instalment of £50 per share thereon, to the amount in the aggregate of £250,000.

That a sufficient amount of the capital of the said Company for that purpose having been subscribed, the said Association or Company applied for and obtained a Charter of Incorporation, but such charter contains no limitation of the liability of the shareholders in the said Company to the proportion of capital subscribed for by them respectively.

That the said Company commenced business in or about the year 1854, and established a Head Office at No. 27, Cannon-street, in the city of London, and Branch Offices at the following places:—An Eastern Branch at No. 44, Mark-lane, London; a Hyde Park Branch at No. 136; Western Branch at No. 20, Pall Mall, St. James'-street; a Calcutta Branch at Council House-street, Calcutta; and a Bombay Branch at Church-street, Bombay.

The Directors of the said Company were: the Hon. Cadwallader Erskine, Chairman; John Carnac Morris, Deputy Chairman; Colonel Chadwick, Mr. Henry Fendall, Mr. John Edward Stephens, and Colonel William Petre Waugh.

That the said John Edward Stephens was also the Manager.

That very shortly after the said Company had commenced business, the Directors commenced making advances, out of the paid-up capital of the said Company, to each other, on insufficient, or without any security other than personal, and at a rate of interest considerably lower than would and ought to have been obtained for such advances, had the same been made to persons unconnected with the said Directors and in the ordinary and proper conduct of the business of the said Bank, and, among others, the said John Carnac Morris, John Edward Stephens, and Colonel Waugh.

The Directors advanced and lent to Colonel Waugh the sum of £237,000 upon security of a nature and value wholly insufficient to warrant such an advance, even if made *bonâ fide* to a stranger, and upon the realisation of such security a loss to the amount of £100,000 and upwards, or some other very considerable loss, will in all probability arise.

That the said Colonel Waugh has, since the stoppage of the business of the said Banking Company, become bankrupt.

That the mode in which such advances had been made and the capital of the Company dealt with by the Directors was wholly concealed by them from the shareholders, until after the failure of the said Company, and, although they continued to hold meetings of the shareholders, no mention whatever was made in any of their accounts or statements that the Company was in any other than a flourishing condition; and that its paid-up capital was invested in good and sufficient security.

That the first annual meeting of shareholders in the said Company was held on the 31st of July 1856, when a report was presented by the Directors, with the account of assets and liabilities; but neither in the statement of assets nor in the said report is there any mention made of the advances made to the said Directors. At this meeting Colonel Chadwick and Mr. John Edward Stephens retired from the Direction, and Colonel E. R. W. Wingfield Yates and Robert John Lattey, who was one of the Auditors of the said Company, were appointed Directors in their stead.

That the Directors, according to the provisions of the said statute, published in the *London Gazette* a monthly statement of assets and liabilities, and the last monthly statement which they published of the assets and liabilities of the said Company, on the 27th of February 1857, dated from the Head Office in Cannon-street, was signed by the said John Edward Stephens, Manager, and among the assets is the following item:—'East India and Government Securities, Bills of Exchange, Treasury and Agency Draughts, Credits, Discounts, and cash in hand, £989,925. 14*s* 4*d*.'

That such item was delusive and untrue, inasmuch as therein was included the advances made to the said Colonel Waugh, then amounting to £237,000, which absorbed nearly the whole of the paid-up capital of the Company, and which security the Directors then well knew was not only insufficient, but not immediately available even to the extent of its sufficiency, and it included also the advances made to the said John Carnac Morris and the said John Edward Stephens, the Manager.

That in less than a month after the publication of the said statement the business of the Company as bankers stopped, and a meeting of the shareholders was called and held on the 25th of March 1857, at which meeting the shareholders were, for the first time, made aware of the alarming position of their affairs, and that the liabilities of the said Company over and above the assets expected to be realised exceeded £240,000, and that, not only was the capital paid up of £50 on each share lost, but that it would require at least the remaining £50 per share to be paid up by the shareholders, who were all individually responsible for the full amount of the total liabilities of the said Company.

That a proposition was made and assented to by some of the shareholders that promissory notes should be given for the remaining £50 per share, payable at twelve months' date, and that arrangements should be made with the Oriental Bank for a transfer of the Indian assets and liabilities of the said Company, guaranteed by the personal security of shareholders, to be approved by the said Oriental Bank.

That your petitioners are duly registered shareholders in the said Company and contributors thereof, and upon the discovery of this conduct upon the part of the Directors, ceased to have any confidence in them or their management, and declined to give any such promissory notes, although your petitioners have heard that some of the shareholders so did.

That in consequence of such refusal on the part of the dissentient shareholders to give such promissory notes, the Directors, although the said Company had virtually ceased to exist, and assuming to act under the power of the said deed of settlement, made a call in the month of April 1857, of £15 per share, and on the 10th of April issued and sent to your petitioners the following circular letter announcing such call:—

London, April 9, 1857.

SIR,—I hereby give you notice that the Directors of the London and Eastern Banking Corporation have made a call of £15 on the shares of £100, into which the capital of the Company is divided, and that such call has been made payable on the 24th day of April instant, at the office of the Oriental Banking Corporation, Threadneedle-street, in the city of London, and I hereby give you notice that if the amount of the said call on the two shares held by you is not paid at the time and place aforesaid, interest at the rate of five per cent per annum will be charged thereon from the day aforesaid until payment.

I am, Sir,
Your obedient servant,
Charles J. F. Stuart,
Interim Manager.

To Abel Stuart, Esq., M. D.

N. B.—The Directors intimate, for the convenience of the shareholders, that further calls will be made at the periods provided by the deed of settlement to realise the capital of the Company.

That your petitioners, for the reasons aforesaid, declined to pay such call, or make any payment of money to be administered by the said Directors.

That the Directors proceeded in the month of July 1857 to make another call of £15 per share, and on the 16th of July 1857, your petitioners received the following circular letter, announcing such call:—

London, July 16, 1857.

Sir,—I hereby give you notice that the Directors of the London and Eastern Banking Corporation have made a call of £15 on the shares of £100, into which the capital of this Company is divided, and that such call has been made payable on the 1st day of August next, at the office of the Oriental Bank Corporation, Threadneedle-street, in the city of London; and I hereby give you notice that if the amount of the said call on the two shares held by you is not paid at the time and place aforesaid, interest at the rate of five per cent per annum will be charged thereon from the day aforesaid until payment.

I am, Sir,
Your obedient servant,
Charles J. F. Stuart,
Interim Manager.

To Abel Stuart, Esq., M. D.

N. B.—The Directors intimate, for the convenience of the shareholders, that further calls will be made at the periods provided by the deed of settlement to realise the capital of the Company.

That your petitioners still declining to make any payment to the said Directors, your petitioner, Abel Stuart, received, on or about the 8th day of August 1857, the following letter from Messrs. Oliverson, Lavie, and Peachey, the Solicitors of the said Corporation :—

SIR,—We beg to refer you to a letter we addressed you under date of the 13th of May last, on behalf of the London and Eastern Banking Corporation, as one of the few shareholders who had not yet given their promissory notes. That notice not having been attended to, we beg to inform you that the Corporation have instructed us to take the necessary proceedings to enforce the payment of the calls in arrear against the parties who have not given their promissory notes. We beg to hear from you before Wednesday next, whether or not the promissory note will be given by you. You have already had the form, or, if not, it will be supplied to you without delay.

We are, your obedient servants,
OLIVERSON, LAVIE, AND PEACHEY.

Frederick's-place, E. C.,
August 7.

DR. ABEL STUART, M.D.

That your petitioners believe it is the intention of the said Directors to proceed to enforce payment of the said calls against them, and to make and enforce other calls.

That your petitioners, even if willing to make such payments, have no means of obtaining a release from liability except by the dissolution of the said Company, and the final winding up of its affairs by and under the direction of this Honorable Court.

That your petitioners believe that the Directors in the conduct of the affairs of the said Company have committed great irregularities, and that if the accounts of the Company were properly taken by this Honorable Court, great benefit would result to the shareholders.

That your petitioners are advised and believe that the assets of the said Company can only be fairly and properly realised, the accounts of the company taken, and proper contributions obtained from the shareholders under the provisions of the Joint-Stock Companies Winding-up Acts, 1848 and 1849.

That under the circumstances aforesaid the Directors are not proper parties to have any control over or interference in the taking the accounts and winding up the affairs of the said Company, and ought not to be at liberty to put in force any of the powers or authorities of the said deed of settlement or charter.

That your petitioners believe that the said Company has not been formally dissolved under the provisions of the said deed of settlement and charter.

That various questions will arise in the winding up the affairs of the said Company, which can only be settled under the provisions of the said Joint-Stock Companies Winding-up Acts, and that it will be for the interest of the shareholders that the same should be so wound up.

Your petitioners therefore humbly pray your Lordship that an order absolute may be made for the dissolution of the said London and Eastern Banking Corporation, and that the affairs thereof may be wound up under the provisions of the Joint-Stock Companies Winding-up Acts, 1848 and 1849, and that proper directions may be given for that purpose, or that your Lordship will be pleased to make such further or other order as the circumstances of the case may require, and to your Lordship may seem meet.

And your petitioners will ever pray, &c."

September 28.—The Vice-Chancellor dismissed the petition to make absolute an order for the dissolution of the Corporation.

November 25.—Vice-Chancellor Sir W. P. Wood made an order upon the petition of Major Corfield, a shareholder, for the winding up of this concern, and appointed Mr. Stuart Interim Manager. On December 12 the question as to the appointment of official Managers was argued before the Vice-Chancellor's chief clerk, who nominated Messrs. Ball and Harding. With this appointment some of the shareholders were dissatisfied, and the case was on the 21st argued in open court, when the Vice-Chancellor ultimately appointed Messrs. Stuart and Ball to be the Managers. As soon as it was determined that the Bank should be wound up, Mr. James Edward Stephens, the late Manager, retired to Scotland, and declared himself, in the Bankruptcy Court at Edinburgh, a bankrupt, and his name forthwith appeared in the *Official Gazette.* His examination took place before Mr. Sheriff Substitute Hallard, when he underwent a most severe examination, which extended over four entire days, during which he was compelled to make some very extraordinary disclosures with respect to the general conduct of the Bank, his own share therein, and also that of some of the Directors. At the end of the fourth day his examination was adjourned till the following Monday, but on that day he did not appear. He, however, sent a letter, excusing himself on the ground of ill-health, and the necessity he found himself under of investigating certain books and accounts before he made any further revelations. This excuse was deemed unsatisfactory, and a warrant, on the application of the opposing creditors, was immediately issued for his apprehension; but when he was sought for he was *non est,* and from that time to the present it is understood that nothing whatever has been heard of him. So the matter rests. Although, not in person, Mr. Stephens was again brought before public notice on the 18th December, when an action was brought against him in the Court of Exchequer by the Directors of the Oriental Bank (who took up the business of the Eastern Bank) to recover the amount of a bond which he had given to the latter establishment for money advanced, &c., and the jury, without hesitation, returned a verdict for the plaintiff, for £6,011 6*s.* 5*d.*

1858, April 22.—An important meeting in the matter of winding up this unfortunate undertaking was held at the Chambers of Vice-Chancellor Wood, before

Mr. Leman, his chief clerk, to proceed to make a call on all the shareholders in Class A, being the holders of shares at the date of the winding-up order, and also on those included in Class C, being shareholders who had transferred their shares within three years prior to the date of such order, the amount of call proposed to be made being at the rate of £50 per share.

The financial statement of Messrs. Stuart and Ball, the Official Managers engaged in investigating and in winding up the affairs of the Bank, set forth that the liabilities of the Corporation on the 6th of April last amounted to £193,512, which amount was made up as follows:—drawing accounts, £200; deposit accounts, ex-interest, £7,042; bills payable, £107,700; Delhi Bank, £2,000; Uncovenanted Service Bank, £570; Indian claim, £13,000; Oriental Bank, £63,000—total, £193,512. The actual and estimated assets of the Corporation amounted to £102,750, made up as follows:—Cash in hand, £1,100; Bank houses in Pall-mall (leasehold), and King William-street (leasehold), £1,900; bills receivable current, £4,500; past due bills, say, £35,250; sundry debtors, say £10,000; Branksea Island and other assets, £50,000; total, £102,750. The Official Managers believed that the above estimate of the assets and liabilities was fair and reasonable, but the assets were insufficient to meet the liabilities by the sum of £90,762, or thereabouts. To meet this deficiency, it would be necessary to make a call on the shareholders of £50 per share, but inasmuch as on a call being made prior to the winding-up order, *viz.*, on the 9th of April last, of £15 per share, and a similar call on the 14th of July last, many of the shareholders have made payments in respect of the same, such shareholders will have credit for the amount so paid. In arriving at the necessity of a call being made of £50 per share, the Official Managers had used the following estimate of the result of the said calls, and which they believed to be fair and reasonable:—uncollected arrears of call of the 9th of April 1857 (which was to produce nominally £75,000), £40,000, of which available amount is £10,000; call the 14th of July 1857, of which the available amount is £45,000; a further call of £20 per share, to produce nominally £100,000, of which the estimated available amount would be £60,000—total, £155,000. If a call of £50 per share were made, the Official Managers believed that, after giving credit for sums paid on account of the calls of April 9 and July 14, it would not produce more than the above estimated amount of £115,000; and that the margin of £24,238, which it was estimated that the call of £50 per share would produce in excess of the estimated deficiency of £90,762, was a fair and reasonable margin to insure the discharge of the liabilities of the Bank, and to cover contingencies arising from interest, costs, and charges, and other sources which could not now be specifically estimated.

Considerable discussion—in which Lieutenant-Colonel Tucker, Colonel Bevan, Colonel Yates, and others connected with the East India Company's service, through their solicitors, took part—ensued on this proposition, for a call of £50 per share on shareholders in Class A.

Messrs. Burchell, Solicitors to the Official Managers, stated that although it had been proposed to make the call on Class C, still from the present uncertain state of the law in regard to the transfer of shares, the call on them would not be pressed at the present moment, and it was probable it would not be necessary to call on shareholders in Class C for payment.

Messrs. Tatham, Upton and Johnstone, Messrs. Smith and Nelson, solicitors for sundry shareholders in this category, applied that the call in respect of Class C should be discharged. The chief clerk ordered a discharge, but refused payment of costs.

Lieutenant-Colonel Tucker said he was a large shareholder, and, that, without his consent, his name was published in the Company's prospectus as a Director, and sent out to India. He regretted to find that Major-General Corfield and General Brooke and others, who had taken an active part in the affairs of the Bank and held shares largely, now sought to obtain exemption from their liability, while numbers of military officers in the East India Company's service, and ladies and civilians, connected with India, who had embarked the hard earned savings of years in this Bank, were sought to be held liable, to their loss and ruin. He should strongly object to their names, and those of Mr. G. H. Smith and Mr. Stephens and others being erased from the list of those to be held liable. It was a point of honor with him to protect the absent shareholders. He (Lieutenant-Colonel Tucker) had already contributed £8,000, and was about to pay £4,000 more, although he had been grossly deceived by the misrepresentations of the Managers of this Bank, and he hoped that other Directors and shareholders would be compelled to pay their just quota. On the ground of moral and commercial principle* he felt it to be his duty

* *This is the reason why these articles, recording frauds, are entered at such length.*

to call the attention of the public and of the Attorney-General to the gross mismanagement, and to the transactions that had taken place in this Bank between four of its Directors—Colonel Waugh, Mr. Stephens, Mr. G. H. Smith, and Mr. Griffith—among whom a very gross breach of trust had been committed, by which the unfortunate shareholders were saddled with the total loss of all the money they had vested in the Corporation, together with the £50 per share they were now called on to pay. If the Official Managers, Messrs. Stuart and Ball, did their duty on behalf of the shareholders, which he hoped they would do, they would work this matter out and carry it into a public court. Were he (Lieutenant-Colonel Tucker) not now a ruined man, through the transactions of the Directors of this Bank, he would himself retain the first men at the bar for the purpose; but he now called on the Official Managers to protect the interests of the shareholders, believing that they were well and handsomely paid by the Court of Chancery to do it. During the last few months he had written to them continually, and had pointed their attention to several matters that appeared to have escaped their observation, and he felt convinced that if this affair was properly sifted, Mr. G. H. Smith would be found liable for £19,000, and the other Directors in proportionate amounts, and justice would be done to all parties. He (Lieutenant-Colonel Tucker) was induced to go into the Bank on the representations of Smith that it was a flourishing concern, and that he (Smith) held 400 shares, which 400 shares, however, he sold in three weeks after; that Colonel Waugh was a leading man in London: that he had married a lady worth £25,000 a-year, had introduced an immense business to the Bank; that his personal property was very great, and his real property £70,000 a-year; and, although in March 1857, the affairs of the Bank and the delinquencies of Stephens were not fully known, there was quite enough to damn him. It would be highly desirable to have these gentlemen examined on their oaths and honor. In consequence of their conduct he (Colonel Tucker) had to sell his house and furniture to meet this call.

After some further discussion, the call was made, and declared payable on the 31st of May.

In the Court of Bankruptcy, on the 29th April, Mr. Commissioner Evans gave judgment, on an application to supersede a petition in bankruptcy which had been filed against the Corporation.

His Honor said :—This is an application to supersede the petition in bankruptcy in this case.' I do not find that there is any distinction between this and the case of the British Bank, except that in that case the dissolution of the Company was by the act of the Company itself, and in this case the dissolution was by the Court of Chancery. In both cases the dissolution appears to me to be equally conclusive as to future acts, but not to interfere with what the Company had already done. If a person when in trade contracts debts he continues a trader till those debts are discharged. It is argued that all the property is vested in the Official Manager: if so, he cannot suffer any injury from the bankruptcy, and the whole cost must fall on the petitioning creditor. I consider the case of the British Bank a decisive authority for refusing the application.

The adjudication was accordingly confirmed.

By subsequent proceedings the Court of Chancery

have decreed that the Bank be made bankrupt, and it was accordingly declared bankrupt through the *London Gazette.*

THE CAWNPORE BANK.

This Bank was established at Cawnpore in 1845, with a capital of five lacs of rupees, divided into five hundred shares of one thousand rupees each. The parties who were instrumental in its formation were James Manson, Esq., a Major in the Bengal Infantry; George Gilbert Brown, Doctor of Medicine, of the Bengal Medical Establishment; John Kirk, Esq., of Cawnpore, Merchant; Peter Lawrie Pew, Esq., a Lieutenant-Colonel in the Bengal Artillery; and Richard Wilcox, Esq., a Lieutenant-Colonel in the Bengal Army; the Trustees being Colonel Pew and Colonel Wilcox, two of the Directors: the former the Officer who was so unpleasantly mixed up with the discreditable failure of the Benares Bank.

"The deed of co-partnership recited:—

That the present partnership shall be, and continue, for and during the term of ten years, from the date of this deed, but may be enlarged at the will of the existing shareholders.

That in case the Company shall, at any time, previous to that period, sustain a loss of one-third of its capital, the affairs of the Company shall be wound up and closed.

That the business of the said Company shall consist in issuing Promissory Notes; in the purchase, sale, and negotiation of Bills of Exchange; in discounting Bills and Notes; in lending money on the security of individuals and of personal or real property, for such periods, and on such terms of interest, as may be determined by the Directors; in granting Cash Credits; in the purchase and sale of coin and bullion, and Government Securities; in the receipt of cash at interest; in money agency; and any other branches of business commonly carried on by bankers, subject always to such rules and restrictions, as the proprietors at any general meeting may from time to time direct."

The figured statement in the following page is referred to for useful information.

STATEMENT.

STATE

Date of Primary Establishment of the Bank and dates of Increase to Capital.		Number of Shares first subscribed for, and afterwards increased.		PROFITS REALISED AND			
		Number of Shares.	Amount.	Dates when dividends have been declared.		Amounts of Dividends.	Amount carried to Reserve Fund.
1845.				1845.			
May ..	1	500	5,00,000	Dec. ..	23	Nil ..	4,480 12 3 Equal to a dividend of 8 per cent per annum.
Nov. ..	15	500	5,00,000	1846.			
Dec. ..	22	500	5,00,000	June ..	20	25,000 A dividend at 10 per cent on original stock.	1,709 15 6
1846.							
Oct. ..	15	500	5,00,000	1847.			
				Feb. ..	10	60,000 A dividend declared at 8 per cent per annum.	20,030 and 1,288 7 8 to Profit & Loss.
Total ..	..	2,000	20,00,000				
				Aug. ..	11	60,000 A dividend declared at 8 per cent per annum.	19,414 3 9
				1848.			
				Feb. ..	16	50,000 A dividend at 5 per cent per annum.	57,367 2 4
				Aug. ..	10	60,000 A dividend of 6 per cent per annum.	22,017 3 4

MENT.

How appropriated.		Present Capital of the Bank.	Whether the Bank has a Charter, and if so, when granted.	Number of Shareholders.	Bonus to Shareholders, being part of premium realised on sale of Stock.
Premium realised on sale of Stock.	Total profits realised.				
..	4,180 12 3				
..	26,709 15 6				
.. 29,105 Carried to Reserve Fund.	81,288 7 8	20,00,000	The Bank has no Charter.	One hundred.	12,175
..	79,414 3 9				
..	1,07,367 2 4				
..	82,017 3 4				

The late commercial crisis reduced the value of stock from five per cent *premium* to *par*.

1847.—The Bank established branches at Patna and Tirhoot. Paid-up capital Rupees 10,50,000. No circulation.

1848.—The Bank sustained considerable losses during the heavy mercantile disasters, both in England and Calcutta. An extraordinary meeting of shareholders is called to consider certain questions affecting the welfare of the institution. In order to render the Bank as useful as possible to the class of proprietors, the following notice was published :—

THE CAWNPORE BANK draws Bills on its Agents in London, on the National Bank of Scotland, and its under-mentioned Branches :—

Aberdeen,	Inverary,
Airdrie,	Islay,
Anstruther,	Jedburgh,
Banff,	Kelso,
Bathgate,	Kirkaldy,
Castle-Douglas,	Kirkwall,
Dalkeith,	Langholm,
Dingwall,	Leith,
Dumfries,	Montrose,
Dundee,	Nairn,
Falkirk,	Oban,
Forres,	Perth,
Fort William,	Portree,
Galashiels,	Stirling,
Glasgow,	Stornoway,
Grantown,	Stromness,
Inverness,	Burntisland.

Bills at sight and ten days' sight (and at any longer term that may be required) on Calcutta and Bombay, on the Agra, North-Western, Delhi, Simla, and Benares Banks, on Mussoorie, Umballa, and Madras, can be granted at all times by the Cawnpore Bank. For remittances to places where the Bank has no Agent, it will procure hoondies, and guarantee them by its endorsement, on a commission of ($\frac{1}{2}$) a half per cent.

1849, September 11.—A special meeting of the proprietors resolves :—

"*1st.*—That the Calcutta Agency be closed.

2nd.—That the present capital of Rupees 19,83,000 be reduced to Rupees 9,91,500, and that the surplus portion be returned to the proprietors.

3rd.—That the shares of the Cawnpore Bank be reduced in value to that of other Mofussil Banks, *viz.*, from Rupees 1,000 to Rupees 500, so that when the surplus portion of capital above Rupees 9,91,500 has been returned to the proprietors, the capital may consist of 1,983 shares of Rupees 500 each.

4th.—That the second special general meeting for the confirmation of proposition 3rd, which involves an alteration of the trust deed, be held at the Bank House, at noon, on Tuesday, the 9th October next."

1851.—Mr. Berresford having resigned the Secretaryship to proceed to Delhi to take charge of the Delhi Bank, was succeeded by Mr. F. H. Cavanagh. This year the Bank ceased to exist.

THE AGRA SAVINGS' FUND.

This Fund was established in January 1842, as the Savings' Fund. Its business, as well as that of the Uncovenanted Service Bank, was chiefly among the members of the Uncovenanted Service, who both borrow, as well as deposit; though the former preponderate. Institutions of this character are calculated to do a vast amount of good, by encouraging habits of frugality; but, unless most carefully and cautiously worked, are liable to injure themselves as well as others.

This Fund commenced with a capital of Rupees 1,500 in 30 shares of Rupees 50 each. From the period of its being launched, it continued to prosper, from year to year increasing its capital with its deposits and loans far beyond the conception of its originators. In fact, the fund grew in their hands, and they could not *curb* its growth without destroying it.

1842, July 1.—There were but four interest depositors, aggregating Rupees 164-12-0, and on the 1st January last, eight, amounting to Rupees 510-7-1; but the report of the 30th June exhibits a total of Rupees 1,902-10-11 among eighteen depositors, being an increase of Rupees 1,392-3-10 during the past half-year; this of itself will suffice to show how rapidly the Fund has increased; while it also evinces the confidence that depositors feel in the durability and solidity of the Institution. Looking to the continued calls for loans, the sudden increase of deposits, the very great demand for shares, and the safety of money invested in the Savings' Fund stock, the shareholders increased the capital of the Fund in the further sum of 1,000 rupees, thus making the capital of the Fund Rupees 4,000.

1843.—The following are the particulars and staff of the Fund:—

Capital Stock	Rs.	4,000
Number of Shares		80
Par value of a Share	Rs.	50
Premium..................................		26 per cent.
Or per Share............................	Rs.	13

DIRECTORS.

J. PARSICK.	A. D. JOHNSON.
A. CARLOW.	J. JAHANS.
J. McCONNELL.	

Secretary ... J. C. PARRY.
Assistant Secretary ... W. KELLY.
Treasurers ... AGRA AND UNITED SERVICE BANK.

Premium on shares rises from ten to twenty-six per cent. Dividend declared twenty per cent or five rupees per share.

1814, January 1.—Capital stock increased to Rupees 5,000. Dividend declared twenty per cent.

1845, January 14.—Dividend twenty per cent per annum. Premium on shares forty per cent. July.—Reserve Fund, Rs. 750-15-7. General meeting presents the Secretary, Mr. J. C. Parry, with a gold watch, in testimony of their approbation of his services.

1846, January 8.—Dividend sixteen per cent. General meeting increases the capital of the Fund by creating 100 new shares of Rupees 50 each. Owing to the existence, in Calcutta, of an Institution under the same style and denomination, resolved that the institution at Agra be thenceforth denominated THE AGRA SAVINGS' FUND. The gold watch subscribed for by the shareholders was presented to Mr. J. C. Parry, with the following inscription:—

"Presented by the Proprietors of the SAVINGS' FUND, to MR. JOSEPH CHATWINE PARRY, for the unwearied zeal, judgment, and ability he has displayed in discharging the duties of Secretary to the Institution."

The following are the particulars of Fund and staff:—

Capital Stock	Rs.	10,000
Reserve Fund	,,	2,000
Number of Shares		200

Premium	40 per cent.
Cost per Share,.........................	Rs. 70
Average Dividend	16 per cent.

TRUSTEES.

B. Griff. | J. W. Urquhart.

DIRECTORS.

J. Parsick.
John Jahans.
J F. McConnell.
J. E. Jahans.
Peetumber Dutt.

Auditor ... John Parsick.
Secretary ... Joseph C. Parry.
Treasurers ... Agra and United Service Bank.

1847, January 14.—Dividend sixteen per cent. Directors establish an Agency at Meerut. Reserve Fund, Rupees 2,000, equal to one-fifth of the capital. November.—Closed the Meerut Agency.

1848, January.—Dividend sixteen per cent. Directors announce the transfer of the Calcutta Agency of the Fund to the Oriental Bank. The Board, in order to increase the usefulness of the Institution, have deemed it advisable to extend the period for re-payment of loans from six to nine and even twelve months, on obtaining from the borrower, in addition to two or more personal securities, an Insurance Policy on his life in the New Oriental Life Insurance Company, with whom they have entered into arrangements, which will not fail to prove beneficial to proprietors. In all cases where a Life Insurance is given, no other charge than that of interest at twelve per cent will be made.

Following is the state of the Fund and staff :—

Capital Stock	Rs.	10,000
Reserve and Bonus Funds	„	3,000

Number of Shares	200
Par value of a Share	Rs. 50
Premium and Share in the Reserve Fund	40 per cent.
Cost per Share	Rs. 70
Lowest Dividend	16 per cent.

Exclusive of a bonus of ten per cent on the par value of shares in January 1846.

TRUSTEES.

B. GRIFF. | J. W. URQUHART.

DIRECTORS.

J. PARSICK.
JOHN JAHANS.
W. BERWICK.
J. E. JAHANS.
F. F. DECRUZE.

Auditor ...	JOHN PARSICK.
Secretary ...	JOSEPH C. PARRY.
Treasurers ...	AGRA AND UNITED SERVICE BANK.

July.—Dividend sixteen per cent. General meeting increases the capital by Rupees 5,000, for which purpose 100 new shares of Rupees 50 each are created. Directors authorise these shares to be sold at a premium of Rupees 40 each. The Directors, owing to the prevailing distrust in Joint Stock Banks, have thought it advisable that the books and half-yearly accounts of the Institution should undergo a strict examination.

1849, January.—The Directors report that, with the exception of 14 shares, which were subscribed for by three parties, who have since died, *all* the new stock has been taken up at forty per cent premium, and nearly all paid for. The premium received by the sale of the new stock, amounting to 2,000 rupees, has been disposed of as directed at the last meeting, *viz.*, Rupees 1,000 to the

Reserve Fund, and the other 1,000 as a *bonus* ratably to proprietors of 5 rupees per share, for which parties have accordingly received credit in their respective accounts on 31st December. To complete the Reserve Fund to the proportion of one-fourth the capital, the sum of Rupees 250 has been taken for that purpose from the Bonus Fund.

Following is the state of the fund and staff:—

Capital Stock	Rs. 15,000
Reserve and Bonus Funds	„ 4,500
Number of Shares	300
Par value of a Share	Rs. 50
Premium and Share in the Reserve Fund	40 per cent.
Cost per Share	Rs. 70
Lowest Dividend	16 per cent.

TRUSTEES.

B. GRIFF. | J. W. URQUHART.

DIRECTORS.

J. PARSICK.
JOHN JAHANS.
W. BERWICK.
J. MCCONNELL.
F. F. DECRUZE.

Auditor ... JOHN PARSICK.
Secretary ... JOSEPH C. PARRY.
Treasurers ... AGRA AND UNITED SERVICE BANK.

UNCOVENANTED SERVICE BANK LIMITED.

This Institution, originally opened as the Uncovenanted Bank, was set on foot at Agra, on the 17th March 1846, for the purpose of encouraging deposits on the part of the Uncovenanted Service, and of placing within their reach an establishment with advantages, which the smallness of the means of the majority would enable them to avail themselves of.

1847—Dividend twelve per cent. The Directors explain to the proprietors that all the shares in the new stock would ere this have been disposed of, were it not for Rule 33, which restricts their sale to Uncovenanted Servants only; and they were necessitated, under the Rule in question, to refuse certain applicants; the Directors would therefore recommend that one-fourth of the total number of shares be thrown open to the public without reference to parties being in the Uncovenanted Service. The reasons for this measure are:

1*st.*—That it would do away, to some extent, with the purchases made in trust for persons out of the Uncovenanted Service.

2*nd.*—That no difficulty may be experienced by the present shareholders in disposing of their shares; as, under the existing Rule, they cannot sell to any but those in the Uncovenanted Service. The shareholders present Mr. J. McKenzie, their Secretary, with a gold watch, valued at £25, with a suitable inscription, to be paid out of the profits for the present half year.

1848, January.—Dividend twelve per cent, or three rupees per share. An attempt to change the designation of the Bank, and throw it open to all classes, was met by a resolution to the effect—

"That the Uncovenanted Bank be restricted, as nearly as conformity with its present constitution will allow, to the Uncovenanted Service. That existing shareholders not in the Uncovenanted Service be left in undisturbed possession of their present shares; that no increase of shares be permitted to them; and that in all respects, except as regards the said shareholders, resolution 2nd of the last general meeting be annulled. It being understood that parties of all classes are free to take shares to any extent by appointing uncovenanted men their representatives as voters under the designation of Trustees."

Following is the state and staff of the Bank :—

Capital Stock	Rs. 10,000
Number of Shares	200
Premium	10 per cent.
Cost per Share	Rs. 55

DIRECTORS.

W. Johnson.	E. G. Fraser.
James Eede.	W. H. Coxon.
R. H. Smith.	

Secretary ...	J. McKenzie.
Assistant Secretary ...	J. MacLeod.
Treasurers ...	Agra and United Service Bank.

July.—General meeting double the stock, making it Rupees 20,000, and add the premium realised from it to the Reserve Fund. Dividend sixteen per cent. Directors intimate that in conformity with an understood Rule, one of their number withdrew, on having occasion to apply for a loan from this Bank.

1849, January.—Dividend twelve per cent. General meeting passed a resolution—

"That this Bank having been originated for the benefit of a proprietorship composed exclusively of members of the Uncovenanted Service; and, others than members of that body having subsequently been allowed to obtain shares, on condition of such shares being held by Uncovenanted Servants as trustees for the owners, it is judged that, with the existing amount of influence over the affairs of the Bank already secured by the Uncovenanted Service, the time has arrived for further concession to the public at large, *viz.*, that in future any person be at liberty to purchase and hold shares without the intervention of any uncovenanted trustee, and to vote at general meetings personally or by proxy; but (to guard the distinctive character of the Bank and to retain as much as possible the advantages of its original constitution) that no one shall be eligible to act as Director or Secretary who is not an Uncovenanted Servant.

Also that this restriction shall be held irrevocable, unless rescinded by three-fourths of the votes of the proprietary."

This resolution compelled the Directors partly to cancel a Resolution of a previous half-year, as they could not sell their stock to those in the Uncovenanted Service. But, still, the restriction about acting as a Director effectually prevented others, not servants of Government, from joining, for they could not buy while excluded from supervising their own affairs.

State of the Bank and staff:—

Capital Stock	Rs. 30,000
Number of Shares	600
Premium	10 per cent.
Cost per Share	Rs. 55

DIRECTORS.

W. Johnson	G. R. Gardner.
James Eede.	E. G. Fraser.
Francis Frost	R. H. Smith.
Jas. MacLeod.	

Secretary ... Mr. J. McKenzie.

Treasurers ... Agra and United Service Bank.

THE COMMERCIAL BANK OF INDIA.

Registered under Act XIX. of 1857 *of the Legislative Council of India.*

This Bank was established at Bombay, in 1845, for the purpose of affording encouragement and aid to the *local* trade, which, it was considered, was not sufficiently given by the other Banks. The number of shares subscribed for was 8,772, which were taken up almost in a day, by a large body of residents. The parties principally concerned in getting up the Bank were John Smith, Esq., of Bombay, merchant; William Graham, Esq., of

Bombay, merchant; William Seton Brown, Esq., of Bombay, merchant; David McCulloch, Esq.; Bomanjee Hormusjee, of Bombay, merchant; Jejeebhoy Dadabhoy, of Bombay, Parsee merchant; Manockjee Limjee, of Bombay, Parsee merchant, and Acton Smee Ayrton, Esq., of Bombay, Solicitor; Cursetjee Cawasjee and Cawasjee Nanabhoy, respectively of Bombay, Parsee merchants. The Bank has no charter, and does not issue notes.

The deed of settlement recites as follows:—

"The capital of the said Company shall be ten millions of rupees, divided into ten thousand shares, of one thousand rupees each; but may be increased in such manner as is hereinafter expressed.

The management of the business and affairs of the Company shall be, and is hereby vested, in such a number of Directors as the shareholders shall, for the time being, deem expedient, so only that such number be not less than seven.

The business of the Company shall be carried on at Bombay, and in such other places and countries as the Directors shall, in pursuance of the power hereinafter vested in them, in that behalf, direct, and such business shall commence in Bombay, on or before the first day of March, and in any other places as aforesaid at such time or times as the Directors shall think fit, although the capital of the Company is not nor shall be wholly subscribed, nor the said entire number of ten thousand shares allotted or taken up.

The business of the said Company shall be exclusively confined to that of Banking, as mentioned and particularised in the rules next following, and shall be carried on, and conducted pursuant thereto, that is to say,—

The Company may receive deposits and keep the accounts of customers, and issue notes payable on demand or at any other period, and at such rate of interest and in such manner as the Directors shall think fit.

The Company may act as Agents and transact any business for any person for commission, or profit, or otherwise, as the Directors may think fit.

The Company may purchase and sell bullion and Government Bills, Securities, or obligations, and Shares in the Chartered Banks of India, as the Directors shall think fit.

The Directors may purchase, discount, or make advances on Bills of Exchange drawn from one place on another, not having a longer period to run than the usance of exchange, and all other Bills and Notes not having a longer period to run than four months.

All Bills of Exchange and Notes, except those of Government and of Joint Stock Banks, to be purchased, discounted, or advanced upon by the Company, shall bear the several responsibilities of at least two sufficient persons or firms unconnected with each other in general partnership, or shall be accompanied by the guarantee of another party of sufficient credit, or by such collateral securities as the Directors may take.

The Directors may grant Cash Credits to a party on his entering into a bond either with two sufficient securities unconnected with him in general partnership, or with the addition of such collateral security as the Directors may take, to repay all advances; but such Cash Credits shall be withdrawn from the party, unless the amount of his debt shall be turned over as often as the Directors may appoint in that behalf.

The Directors may accept the following collateral securities from any person dealing with the Bank, that is to say, bullion, Government Securities, Shares in Banks (always excepting the shares in this Company) and other public Companies, in which the amount advanced by the Company shall not be more than that actually paid up. Goods not of a perishable nature, Bills of Lading, with Policies of Insurance for Goods, and Policies of Insurance which have been adjusted and accepted by public Companies.

The Directors may also accept ships registered at Bombay and landed property in Bombay as collateral security for Cash Credits only.

Any Agents of the Bank, not being Bankers or salaried Agents, shall not be entrusted with the funds of the Bank, except for some special purpose under specific instructions from the Directors of the Bank.

The Directors shall not re-discount or sell any Notes or Bills of Exchange with the responsibility of the Company thereon or thereto, except Bills of Exchange or Notes made by the Company, or Bills or Notes of Joint Stock Banks, and short Bankers' Bills.

The amount of cash, bullion, and Government Securities in possession of the Bank and immediately available, shall always be equal to at least one-fourth of all the claims against the Bank outstanding for the time being, and payable on demand."

1846, December 31.—Paid-up capital of the Bank, Rupees 34,28,800. Reserve Fund, Rupees 42,085-5-6.

1848, December 30.—Capital of the Bank, *one crore*, of which there has been paid up Rupees 500 per share, or Rupees 37,43,000. This sum was reduced from Rupees 43,86,000—1,286 shares having been purchased by the Directors on account of the Bank. The discount arising from this purchase was carried to the credit of Reserve Fund, which stands at Rupees 1,32,456-10-1. During the commercial panic, the shares were subjected to considerable depression, in a proportionate ratio to those of all other Joint Stock Companies in Bombay. Some properties, upon which the Bank had made advances in Ceylon, are reported as not likely to make a sufficient return to cover the balance of account. Auditors report the assets as more than equal to the amount of the paid-up capital.

1849, June 30.—Paid-up capital, Rupees 36,78,000. Reserve Fund, Rupees 77,684-15-6. Dividend six per cent for the half year, after writing off some bad debts. July—Some alterations were made in the deed of settlement. Some losses are announced by sale of Oriental Bank Shares, which had been formerly taken in pledge.

1850, January.—Directors report the establishment of an Agency in China, entirely confined to exchanges, and under strict regulations. They report likewise having discontinued to make advances on the security of shares of other unchartered Banks. Dividend declared for the half year, eight per cent per annum. Some losses are anticipated from the failure of a Parsee firm, which had received a loan from the Bank on security of landed property.

1851.—A pressure on the market manifests itself at Bombay, as well as at Madras. Directors limit the accommodation for any individual or firm to *two lacs*, and resolve that the future dividend of shares in the Bank, held by parties non-resident in India, be remitted to them in Bills on London, payable on demand, at 2*s*. or at six months' sight at their purchasing rate. A recommendation is made that landed property be realised as soon as possible. A difficulty arises regarding the settlement of part of a claim of Rupees 1,71,000 against the Union Bank of Calcutta. Directors report the Ceylon estate ordered to be sold off, but that there is much difficulty in finding a purchaser.

1852.—Dividend seven per cent per annum for the first half year.

1853, February 17.—Some alterations and additions are made in the deed of settlement. June 30.—Bank writes off a sum of Rupees 18,562-11-9, claim against the Union Bank of Calcutta. General meeting places the limit for the Reserve Fund at twenty per cent on the capital.

1854, February.—Some alterations and additions made in the deed of settlement. Directors report that the Bank holds large quantities of forest land in Ceylon. They open a Branch at Calcutta. General meeting increases the capital to about forty-five lacs by an issue of new shares. Dividend nine per cent per annum. Mr. Anderson, Manager of the Bank, resigns, and is succeeded by Mr. Edgar Corrie.

1858.—Mr. E. Corrie resigns the Managership and is succeeded by Mr. R. Angus.

1859.—Directors report realisation of some of the Ceylon properties.

1862, April 5.—Some alterations and additions are made to the deed of settlement. A serious loss occurs in China, which affects the dividend. This year Mr. W. S. FitzWilliam resigns the Calcutta Agency to become Agent of the Chartered Mercantile Bank of India, London and China; Mr. Alex. Fielding, Sub-agent and Accountant, retaining charge.

The following dividends have been declared :—

1847	...	22 January	...	6	per cent.
"	...	15 July	...	9	"
1848	...	17 January	...	8	"
"	...	12 July	...	8	"
1849	...	January	...		"
"	...	July	..	6	"
1850	..	January	..	8	"
"	...	July	...	7	"
1851	...	January	...	7	"
"	...	July	...	7	"
1852	...	January	...	7	"
"	...	July	...	7	"
1853	...	January	...	7	"
"	...	July	...	7	"
1854	...	January	...	9	"
"	...	July	...		"
1855	...	January	...		"
"	...	July	...		"
1856	...	January	...		"
"	...	July	...		"
1857	...	January	...		"
"	...	July	...		"
1858	...	January	...		"

1858	...	July	...	6 per cent.
1859	...	January	...	8 „
„	...	July	..	7 „
1860	...	January	...	7 „
„	...	July	...	„
1861	...	January	...	„
„	...	July	...	„
1862	...	January	...	„
„	...	July	...	„
1863	...	January	...	4 „

A Branch has been recently opened at *Foochow,* in China, and the Bank is about to obtain a charter and remove the Head Office from Bombay to London.

Paid up Capital, Rupees 50,00,000, in 10,000 Shares of Rupees 500 each.

BOARD OF DIRECTORS.

Chairman ... William Trevor Roper.

John Pares Bickersteth.
Limjee Manockjee.
Munguldass Nathoobhoy.
Byramjee Jejeebhoy.

The Manager, *ex-officio.*

TRUSTEES.

Byramjee Jejeebhoy. | Sorabjee Framjee.

AUDITORS.

George Hamilton. | Sorabjee Pestonjee Framjee.

Head Office, Bombay.

Manager ... Robert Angus.
Accountant ... Michael R. De Quadros.
Secretary ... Patrick Rose Harper.
Deputy Secretary ... Alex. Thos. Angus.

Branch Banks.

Inspector of Branches ... Patrick Rose Harper.

CALCUTTA.

Agent ... DAVID BEDDINE CLINKER.
Sub-Agent and Acctt. ... GEORGE ASHWELL KNEEBONE.

HONG-KONG.

Interim Agent ... PATRICK ROSE HARPER.
Sub-Agent and Acctt. ... CHARLES F. BEART.

SHANGHAI.

Agent ... HENRY HOWE WIGGINS.
Accountant ... JOHN ALEX. HANDY.

FOOCHOW.

Agent ... RICHARD NEWBY.

HANKOW.

Sub-Agent ... CHARLES S. S. LYNELL.

LONDON.

Agent ... DAVID ALLARDICE.
Accountant ... W. J. YOUELL.

LONDON BANKERS.

THE LONDON JOINT STOCK BANK.

GOVERNMENT SAVINGS' BANK.

This Bank was established on the 1st November 1833, not very long after the disastrous failure of all the large Commercial Houses. Its object was to afford to all classes, British and Native, a means of investing their savings, free from all the uncertain influences of commerce. The following notification from the Financial Department, with the office rules of the Bank, are all that it is necessary to insert here:—

FINANCIAL DEPARTMENT.

Resolution of the Supreme Government in the Financial Department, dated 7th October 1833.

The Right Hon'ble the Governor-General in Council directs that the following Rules of a Savings' Bank established in Calcutta under the guarantee, and responsibility of Government, be published for general information.

1. The Bank to be denominated the Government Savings' Bank.

2. All classes, British and Native, may invest their savings in the Government Savings' Bank.

3. The return of the exact sum deposited, together with the interest due thereon at the undermentioned rate, is secured to the depositor under guarantee of the Supreme Government.

4. The general direction and control of the Bank shall be vested in a Committee of Management, consisting of Covenanted Civil and Military Officers of the Government, and other persons to be nominated by the Governor-General in Council. The Committee shall meet at such stated periods as may be necessary for the due and efficient control of the proceedings of the Bank.

5. The Government Agents are charged with the immediate superintendence and execution of all details connected with the Bank. They will also be *ex-officio* members of the Committee of Management. The third Government Agent will be *ex-officio* Secretary to the Bank.

6. A register of deposits will be kept, and generally such other accounts as may be determined on, and approved of by the Managing Committee.

7. Any sum not less than one rupee will be received in deposit.

8. Whenever any sum deposited by any one individual shall amount to Rupees 1,500, the same, or so much thereof as may be necessary, will be transferred from the Bank to the Government Agent, subject to the Rules which obtain in his department for the purchase of a Government note in the Four per Cent or any other Loan, which may be preferred and pointed out by the depositor, a delay of one month being allowed in all cases where the depositor may intimate intention to withdraw the whole or any portion of the funds within one month from the date it has reached that amount, when, should no withdrawal have been made, a transfer will be effected as if no such notice had been given.*

9. Interest at three per cent per annum will be allowed on deposits until further notice.†

* † No. 23.

Read a despatch from the Hon'ble the Court of Directors, No. 14, of 1854, dated 22nd March.

Notification.—In obedience to the orders of the Hon'ble the Court of Directors, conveyed in their despatch above-mentioned, the Most Noble the

10. Interest will be calculated on a deposit from the first day of the month succeeding that in which it shall be received and up to the last day of the month preceding that in which it shall be withdrawn. No interest will be allowed for broken periods of a month, nor calculated on fractional parts of a Rupee.*

11. The Government reserves to itself the power of lowering or raising the rate of interest; such alteration not to affect deposits above Rupees 500, previously invested in Public Securities, and due notice to be given in the *Calcutta Gazette* of the intention of Government six months before the alteration shall take effect.

12. All deposits will be regularly entered in a book at the time they are made. The depositor of the deposit made at the Presidency, will be furnished with a small book having a duplicate of the entry. This book is to be brought to the Bank whenever any sum is to be deposited or withdrawn. The account thus kept, will be closed on the 30th April of every year, and the balance of interest due at that period will be paid to the depositor, or carried to account, thenceforward to accumulate at compound yearly interest, until it shall amount to Rupees 1,500, when the same will be transferred from the accounts of the Bank books, and subscribed on account of the depositor to the Government Four per Cent Loan as per Rule 8, unless notice of withdrawal be given within one month as above, or unless the rate of interest be altered as provided for in Rule 11.

13. No person or persons to deposit money for the benefit of

Governor-General of India in Council is pleased to resolve that, after six months from the date of the publication of this Notification, the rate of interest on civil deposits in the Government Savings' Bank be reduced from four to three per cent per annum; that the limit of deposits in regard to depositors of all classes be extended from Rupees 500 to Rupees 1,500, and that the interest of four per cent per annum on the deposits of the Soldiery be reduced to three and three-quarter per cent, the rate authorised by the Royal Warrant relating to Regimental Savings' Banks.

Published by order of the Most Noble the Governor-General of India in Council.

FINANCIAL DEPARTMENT, 31st May 1854. (Signed) C. H. LUSHINGTON, *Offg. Secy., Government of India.*

* Orders of Government conveyed in Mr. Secretary Dorin's letter, No. 824, of the 18th August 1843, authorise payment of a full month's interest on deposits made within the first four working days of a month.

any other person or persons, except parents on behalf of, and on account of their children being minors.* If such deposits are made in the children's names, they cannot be withdrawn during the minority of the children, nor without an authority from them after they have come of age; no trust will be allowed to appear on any deposit: provided, however, that this Rule shall not be construed to prohibit individuals resident out of Calcutta, or females who, according to the manners and customs of the country, do not usually make their appearance in public, from making their deposit in their own names by the hands of other persons as agents in their behalf.

14. No sum deposited to be transferrable excepting on the personal application of the depositor, supported by written sanction. When peculiar circumstances render a deviation from this Rule necessary, the case shall be submitted to the Committee of Management for their sanction.

15. No person will be allowed to deposit any money without making known his or her name, together with his or her profession, business, occupation, calling, and residence, a duplicate of this description will be entered in each depositor's book, to be produced whenever any sum is afterwards deposited or withdrawn.

16. Depositors will be at liberty at any time to withdraw any sums or portions of sums deposited by them, receiving interest calculated up to the end of the month preceding that in which the withdrawal is made.

17. As a general rule, deposits, with the interest due thereon, will be repaid to the depositors personally in all practicable cases. In the case of individuals unable to attend in person, the Secretary will exercise his discretion in regard to re-payment of deposits to responsible persons, duly authorised by such absentees to receive the same.

18. Military Officers and Soldiers, European and Native, will be allowed to invest their savings in the Government Savings' Bank through the Pay Masters of Corps or Divisions, and Pay Masters are hereby authorised to receive subscriptions to the Bank, or deduct monthly from their abstracts such sums as the parties within their circle of payment may be desirous of depositing, not being less than one rupee, nor more than 1,500 rupees.

19. The deposits referred to in the preceding Rule, are to be

* *Vide* decisions of the Committee of Management, F. page 15.

brought to the credit of subscribers on the last day of the month in which the payment or deduction is made; and Rules 16 and 17, respecting the withdrawal of deposits by parties subscribing through Pay Masters, will be carried into effect under instructions which will be furnished to the Pay Masters, by the Accountant to the Military Department.

20. In case of the death of a Depositor, the sum at his credit will be paid to his or her executors or assigns; or in case of no Will, according to the law on this head, or the Regulations of the Service, if the deceased be Military.

21. In case of any difference between the Secretary of the Bank and any depositor, it shall be referred for the decision of the Committee of Management.

22. A General Statement of the Funds of the Bank shall be annually made out to the 30th April after the 1st May. The same to be submitted for the information of Government, and published in the *Calcutta Gazette.*

23. The Bank to be opened daily, Sundays and Holidays excepted, and all balance above Rupees 1,500 to be paid over at the close of each day's proceedings by the Secretary into the General Treasury, where an account with the Bank will be opened and kept.

N. B.—Besides the modifications introduced by Government Notification, dated 31*st May* 1854, (*ante p.* 337) *Rules* 8 *and* 13 *as they now stand are modifications of the original Rules.*

On the abolition of the Government Agency, in conformity with Government Notification, dated 26*th January* 1855, *the duties performed by the Agent on behalf of the Bank will be performed by the Bank itself.**

---

* FROM THE SECRETARY TO THE GOVERNMENT OF INDIA, FINANCIAL DEPARTMENT.

No. 281, *dated the* 18*th January* 1856.

No. 28.

TO THE SECRETARY TO THE GOVERNMENT SAVINGS' BANK,

Fort William.

SIR,

I AM directed to acknowledge the receipt of your letter No. 1039, dated the 31st ultimo, enquiring whether, as it is in contemplation to abolish the Government Agency at this Presidency, the work hitherto performed by the Agency of purchasing and keeping Government promissory notes on

Office Rules of the Government Savings' Bank.

1. The Actuary is authorised to certify by his signature in brief all deposits or (on his own responsibility) to nominate the Deputy Actuary to that duty.

2. The Bank opens for the transaction of business at 10 A. M. and closes at 2½ P. M. every day, Sundays and Holidays excepted.

3. Every depositor or withdrawer is expected to transact business in person.

4. No money will be received and kept except in the name of the actual proprietor, nor can it be withdrawn unless on the application of the said proprietor.

5. No sum less than one rupee can be credited.

6. All copper coin will be rejected, and only the Bengal Bank notes are allowed to be received.

7. Whenever the individual desires to deposit or withdraw any sum of money, the Bank account book must be produced, in order that the necessary entry of the transaction be made.

8. Promissory notes to be claimed by proprietors residing in Calcutta or its neighborhood in person at the Bank within three months of investment, after which period promissory notes unclaimed will be transferred to the custody of the Government Agent, subject to the Rules of that department.*

---

account of Savings' Bank depositors will hereafter, on the abolition of the Agency in January 1857, be transacted by the Bank of Bengal, or whether it is to devolve on the Savings' Bank itself.

In reply I am desired to inform you that the Most Noble the Governor-General in Council has been pleased to resolve that the work in question shall be performed by the Secretaries to the Government Savings' Banks at the several Presidencies.

With reference to an enquiry from the Government Agent at this Presidency as to arrangements for the safe custody of Soldiers' treasury notes on the final abolition of the Agency, His Lordship in Council further resolves that the Secretaries to the Government Savings' Banks at the several Presidencies shall be charged with the custody of these notes also.

I have, &c.,

(Signed) C. H. Lushington,
Secy. to the Government of India.

Council Chamber,
The 18th January 1856.

* *Vide* note * ante page 340.

9. No trust accounts allowed as per advertisement, *Government Gazette*, 15th January 1843.

10. Interest at three per cent per annum will be allowed on Presidency deposits until further notice."

BANK OF ASIA.

This Bank was projected in London, in February 1841, principally through the exertions of Mr. Robert Montgomery Martin, who was appointed Secretary.

The project met with the most unequivocal reception at Bombay and India, and, generally, the establishment of the Institution was hailed with great satisfaction. The qualification for each Director was stated to be 20 shares, but by a minute of 5th March 1841, 50 were allotted to each Director, of which he was at liberty to dispose of 30 to his friends. The total number of responsible shares subscribed for in the United Kingdom amounted to 1,627, *viz.*, 1,007 among seventy-nine proprietors, and 620 shares among thirteen Directors. There were allotted to Bombay, 1,000 shares; to Calcutta, 1,500 shares; to Madras, 1,000; and to China, Ceylon, &c., 500 shares. In Bombay alone the amount of shares applied for was about 4,000, although the number of shares allotted to Bombay was only 1,000. The shares were principally taken by native gentlemen, and they were at *a premium of twelve per cent* on the scrip being issued. At Calcutta, about 1,482 shares were granted by the Agents. Some difficulty was experienced in regard to a charter for the Bank. Earl Auckland and the Government of India approved the terms of a charter, but the Directors of the East India Company finally quashed it. The Agents appointed in India were Messrs. Grey and Russell, in *Bombay;* Messrs. Cantor and Co., in *Calcutta;* Messrs.

Line and Co., in *Madras;* Messrs. Jardine Matheson and Co., in *China.*

In 1841, Mr. Martin, on some misunderstanding with Mr. Jardine, one of the Directors of the Provisional Board, whose private interests were said to be adverse to the Bank, resigned his post of Secretary, on which occasion the following entry was made in the records of the Bank:—

"*Bank of Asia,* 17*th April* 1841.

Resolved—that Mr. Robert Montgomery Martin *having resigned the office of Secretary, there be appropriated to him, in consideration of his past services, twenty shares in the capital stock of the Company,* such shares to be held by him or his assigns, exempt from liability to any payment in respect of deposits or calls thereon, to the extent of 100*l.* on each share, but to entitle him or them to all the rights to which other shareholders are entitled, and in all respects to be subject to the laws, rules, and regulations of the Company, *other than those requiring the contribution of capital.*

Resolved also—that a sum of five hundred pounds be forthwith paid to Mr. Martin, as a further compensation for his past services, which, with the twenty shares in the capital stock of the Company, appropriated to him by the preceding resolution, are to be received by him in full discharge of all claims and demands of any kind soever upon the Company.

W. Jardine, *Chairman.*"

Later in the year, Mr. Martin addressed the following letter to Mr. Jardine:—

"To William Jardine, Esq., M. P.,

Chairman of the Provisional Direction of the Bank of Asia.

Sir,—I am in receipt of your letter of this date. You must be aware that no resolution passed by any or all of the Provisional Directors can alter the *facts* of the case.

You determined six months ago to get the *Bank of Asia* into your hands: the object of such procedure, and the means adopted for the purpose, I will not now advert to; although they are generally talked of and understood. It is sufficient for the question at issue to state that you agreed to give what I considered and what you stated to be equivalent to £2,000 in the *Bank of Asia*, in consideration of my past services, being the amount proposed by Mr. Cayley, one of the Directors: your words to me as Chairman were—'The full £100 on each share will soon be required.' With this understanding I accepted it, although unaccompanied by a seat in the Direction, which was proposed by Mr. Cayley, agreed to by Mr. Brooking, and urgently pressed by myself; but which you, Sir, for obvious motives, strenuously refused.

Nothing but your repeated assurances, that if I would give the *Bank of Asia* into your hands, it would be immediately and effectively brought into operation,—would have induced, or *could* have justified me in the resignation of my responsibility to the shareholders and to the public into your charge. My anxiety for the well-being of the Bank made me patiently endure the most unmerited calumnies, and the most insulting treatment; but there must be an end to a quiescence which has not been appreciated, and which, it is now quite evident, will not benefit the Institution.

It is not merely £2,000 that I have at stake; my character, as the founder of the Bank, and my reputation for the successful progress of the Company are also involved; and my faith is pledged to those who have invested their capital in the association on my recommendation: for, I need scarcely, I hope, point out to you, Sir, that there are other essential requisites for the establishment or conduct of a Bank than the mere reputation of wealth.

There are three courses on which I have to request your prompt decision:—

1*st.*—Convene a public meeting of the shareholders (giving me due notice of time and place) and let the whole of the past proceedings be submitted to their adjudication; or,

2*ndly.*—Permit me to resume actively my duties as Secretary, that my energies and influence may be used for bringing out the Bank; or,

3*rdly.*—Resign the Bank entirely into my hands, that I may procure immediately another Board of Direction, who will indemnify you personally and furnish a guarantee for the payment of the past expenses.

If you decline to adopt either of these courses, I shall hold you responsible to me for the payment of the £2,000 stock guaranteed to me by your resolution of the 17th April 1841 (for which I have performed my part of the contract); and I must take immediate measures for its realisation.

It will also be my duty to make the shareholders and the public acquainted with the whole transaction.

I remain, Sir,
Your obedient servant,
R. Montgomery Martin.

131, *Piccadilly*,
20*th September* 1841."

1842, February.—Mr. Anderson handed the Chairman a despatch, from the Board of Trade, dated 16th February 1842, stating the unwillingness of the Court of Directors of the East India Company to grant a charter in India to the *Bank of Asia*, and, that the Board would not feel justified, unless upon the strongest ground of public advantage and necessity, to recommend the grant of a charter by the Crown in England, which might lead to general and legal difficulties. Under these circumstances the Committee resolved to leave the question of a charter out of consideration, and to recommend to the Directors the establishment of the Bank under a deed of settlement, and an application for an Act of Parliament to empower the Bank to sue and be sued in the name of an individual Director or Secretary. March 7.—A general meeting of shareholders was convened at the Bank of Asia Offices, 34, Great Winchester Street, Old Broad Street.

Present: Mr. Jardine, in the Chair—Sir J. Campbell—Mr. Goldsworthy—Mr. Brooking—Mr. Anderson—Mr. Walkinshaw—Mr. Maynard, Solicitor—and about twelve proprietors. There were no minutes of the previous general meeting read.

Mr. Jardine requested Mr. Clay (who was Chairman on the second day of the Committee of twelve proprietors,) to read the report of the Committee, which was to the effect that 1,392 shares were taken in the United Kingdom; that " 5,283 shares was subscribed for in various parts of India; but that from the great difficulties which they had to encounter in their efforts to obtain a charter, and the unavoidable delay in arriving at a satisfactory conclusion, alarm was created in the minds of the subscribers in India, and their subscriptions were returned." The expenses of the Bank here were stated, £2,071-11-8; and the liabilities at about £700. The money received, £7,725, and £650 still due on shares allotted.

Mr. Jardine said, the shareholders in India took their shares on the expectation that a charter was already or would soon be granted; and as that was not ultimately the case, they were entitled to have their money back.

The dissensions in the Committee were, from the first, fatal to the existence of this Bank. Mr. Martin wanted a Scotch Banker, named Dunlop, to be sent to India, while Mr. Goldsworthy, a Director and quondam attorney in Calcutta, wanted to go himself on a salary of £2,000 per annum. On Mr. Martin resigning the Secretaryship, Mr. Goldsworthy acted temporarily as Secretary. But the most effectual steps had been taken to weary and disgust the shareholders, and the consequence was—the Bank was broken up.

THE EAST INDIA BANK.

Capital £250,000, in 5,000 Shares of £50 each.

(SUBECT TO INCREASE.)

N. B.—Never started.

This Bank was projected under better auspices, and with far greater pretensions than the Bank of Asia. *One* of its latent objects was the suppression, or rather the absorption, of the Bank of Bengal; and, so great was the interest which was created, that the Court of Directors of the East India Company actually sent out a despatch to the Bengal Government to communicate with the Directors of the Bank of Bengal, and to learn what they had to say on the subject. The project was never very favorably received in the Bank of Bengal parlour, and this was the first spoke in the wheel of the East India Bank, which prevented its onward progress.

The explanatory Prospectus which was put forth in 1842, was well calculated to encourage the most liberal subscriptions, and to inspire confidence. India, at the time of the project, was greatly destitute of local banks. The banking *mania* had not then set in. In the whole British India there were but five public Banks, *viz.*, two at Calcutta, one at Bombay, one at Madras, and one at Agra; the available capital of these Banks was about two million sterling, and their business was restricted chiefly to the limited population of the Presidencies in which they were placed. There was no Joint Stock Bank for the valuable trade of several millions sterling which was carried on with the "Straits;" in fact, no part of the globe labored under such a defective banking accommodation as the Eastern Hemisphere.

India was the only portion of the British dominions which had no Bank in London for conducting its exchange operations; although this country evidently required such an establishment more than any other part of the Empire. The annual remittances (in favor of England) from India to Great Britain were made either in specie, or by consignment of merchandize, or in bills negociated through private individuals engaged in various transactions; who thus injuriously combined the distinct operations of trading in produce and banking in money, instead of the banker being the intermediate agent between the buyer and seller of commodities. The East India Company had ceased making advances on goods in India for consignment to England from want of funds; and the Court of Directors in London had raised the exchange on India to 2*s.* 1*d.* the rupee for the same reason, and with a view of preventing application for Bills on India. The legitimate trader was therefore at the mercy of those who possessed capital, or he was compelled to entrust his goods, on doubtful security, to those who were his rivals in mercantile enterprise; while the retiring civil and military servants returning to England with the accumulated savings of years of toil, sickness, and anxiety, were, in many instances, entirely impoverished by the failures of those to whom they had entrusted their property.

The losses sustained by the East India community, in consequence of the failures of the conjoint private bankers and merchants in India, had been very grievous. The defalcation on six houses alone at Calcutta were as follows:—

Palmer and Co.	£2,600,000
Alexander and Co.	3,440,000
Mackintosh and Co.	2,470,000
Ferguson and Co.	3,260,000
Colvin and Co.	1,210,000
Cruttenden and Co.	1,350,000
	£14,330,000

Fortified, therefore, by the experience of the safe and profitable working of all the Colonial and Metropolitan Banks, and encouraged by the acknowledged want of such an Institution for British India, then brought within thirty days' post of London, the *East India Bank* was established on a small scale, but capable of extension as prudence and circumstances might afterwards demand. The East India Company had declared by letter (30th April 1840) that "they are sensible of the advantages to be derived from Banking establishments formed and conducted upon sound principles," and, in another letter (16th September 1840), stated that "they are anxious to afford every facility for extending to India all the benefits to be derived from an accession of capital." Similar opinions had been expressed by Her Majesty's Government.

The development of the numerous resources of India is essentially dependent on the establishment of a sound and extensive monetary system. No country, whatever be its form of government,—whatever be the industry and skill of its people, or the vegetable and mineral riches of its soil—can thrive while the interest of money is at twenty, thirty, forty, and fifty per cent per annum. This astounding fact was substantiated by Sir Charles Edward Trevelyan, the present Financial Minister of India—once one of the Secretaries to Government in Bengal, afterwards one of the Secretaries of Her Majesty's Treasury in London, and more recently Governor of Madras; who visited almost every part of India preparatory to an invaluable report which he published on the transit duties. Sir Charles Trevelyan stated that he found in some places money borrowed at short intervals and for small sums, at the enormous rate of *fifty to seventy-five per cent per annum!* "The lowest rate of interest is twenty-four per cent, the ordinary rate will hardly be believed in England, it is an *anna* a month per Rupee—about seventy-five per cent per annum. I would mention twenty-four per cent as the lowest rate of interest." The Right Honorable Holt Mackenzie, Financial Secretary to Government in 1826, states in his evidence before both Houses of Parliament, that the *lowest* rate of interest paid by cultivators in the Bengal part of India is two per cent per month. Mr. Gordon says, "that the native bankers, in small dealings, charge as high as five per cent per month=sixty per cent per annum!"

The benefits derivable from conducting monetary operations arising out of trade transactions by means of sound public banking institutions are indeed now fully recognised. By means of the Metropolitan Banks for Australasia, the West Indies, British North America, the Ionian Islands, Ceylon, &c., important advantages accrue to the Colonies and to the Parent State, which are thus united by the permanent tie of mutual interest. The necessity of exporting specie to or from the Colonies for the payment of obligations is avoided; scarcity of capital in one place is immediately remedied by its transmission through those Banks from wherever it is abundant;—the interest of money lowered—the rates of exchange steadied and equalised,—trade augmented,—confidence established,—profitable investment provided for funds, which might otherwise be sunk or utterly lost in foreign loans or South American mining speculations;—and, by separating the functions of banker and merchant, the latter is induced to direct all his skill, energy, and means, to the advancement of the Dependency with which he is connected; while England becomes the centre of a vast monetary circle, and is enabled to extend her commerce over distant regions and to enrich every portion of her great and powerful Empire.

The following advertisement appeared in connexion with the Prospectus, but the whole affair gave way before any action could be taken, and the EAST INDIA BANK never existed in anything but in name :—

" The *East India Bank* was established for conducting exchange operations, including the safe remittance of money between England and India; and for transacting the profitable banking business arising from our extensive and increasing intercourse with the Eastern Hemisphere. It was not intended that the Bank should issue notes payable on demand :—Its operations to be restricted to the remitting of funds between India and England, from which an ample profit may be derived;—to the receipt of deposits in India at the current rate of interest; to granting letters of credit for funds lodged with the Bank;—and to the transaction of general banking business as practised by the other Colonial Banks in London.

" II. The operations of the Bank will be commenced on an economical and moderate scale, conducive to the permanent advantage and stability of the Company, yet capable of extension as circumstances and experience may render advisable.

" III. A proportion of the first and of any future issues of shares will be allotted to India;—and the dividends will be payable in India or in England at the option of the shareholders.

" IV. A deposit of £1 per share must be paid on application for shares;—future calls will not exceed £5 per share;—and not less than thirty days' notice will be given previously to any call.

" V. The management of the *East India Bank* will be vested in a Court of Directors, resident in London, whose interests will be identified with those of the proprietors.

Branch Banks will be established at Calcutta, Bombay, and Madras, under the supervision of local Boards of Directors,—aided by Managers deputed from England of practical banking experience.

"VI. The business of the Bank will, in the first instance, be conducted under the provisions of a carefully arranged deed of settlement.—Letters Patent or an Act of Parliament enabling the Bank to sue and be sued in a corporate capacity will be obtained.

"VII. A general meeting of the Company will be convened annually in London, at which a full report of the affairs of the Bank will be submitted for the consideration of the shareholders."

CHARTERED BANK OF ASIA.

This Bank was projected and set on foot in 1852. Its capital was £1,000,000, in 40,000 shares of £25 each, of which £200,000, or £5 per share were paid up immediately.

1853.—Obtained a charter, equal in its advantages to that of the Oriental Bank.

1854, July 21.—A meeting of shareholders held in London, when it was notified that negotiations were pending for an amalgamation with the Mercantile Bank of India, London and China. Directors attach great importance to the association with them in the Bank, of an influential local proprietary in India.

1855, February 23.—A meeting of proprietors was held, when a report was presented respecting the proposed amalgamation of the Chartered Bank of Asia with the Mercantile Bank of India, London and China, which was merely delayed in consequence of it being found necessary to refer to the Directors of the latter Bank, at

Bombay, some questions arising out of a doubt which had been started of a legal and technical description. June 30.—The first ordinary general meeting of shareholders was held. Directors reported that the negotiations which had been pending for an amalgamation with the Mercantile Bank of India, London and China, had, for the present, terminated unfavorably. The question of dissolving the Bank, and relinquishing the charter were then fully discussed. In the course of the discussion, it was explained, that the reason why the negotiation for the amalgamation with the Mercantile Bank of India had failed, was a doubt which had arisen whether the clause in the charter, which empowered the Bank of Asia to do, in India, business of exchange, deposit, and remittance, empowered them to receive money on deposit, and use it, by lending, or otherwise dealing with it. Sir R. Bethell, by whom the charter had been drawn, on being appealed to, gave it as his opinion, that it empowered the Bank to use money received on deposit for all proper banking purposes. This, however, was not satisfactory to the Mercantile Bank of India, and, then, it became necessary to obtain an indorsement on the charter, by the Board of Trade, explanatory of the clause. This, however, might have occasioned a delay of eight, ten, or twelve months, which the shareholders would probably have objected to. The Directors, under these circumstances, submitted to the shareholders, by circular, in May last, three alternatives—1*st*, to proceed with the calls and to organise the Bank; 2*nd*, to keep the funds in abeyance and wait for a more favorable opportunity for commencing operations; and the 3*rd*, to wind up the Company. Had there been anything like the required majority of two-thirds in favor of winding up, the Directors would have waived their own opinions, and submitted a proposition for that purpose; but, out of 16,000 shareholders 8,100 only were in favor of that course. The dissentient shareholders, consequently, had to choose between holding their shares and selling them in the market. At this juncture the proposition of buying up, at par, the shares of such of the shareholders as wished to retire from the concern was made by the parties who represented the Mercantile Bank. By this arrangement, which was most beneficial to all parties, and especially so to dissentient shareholders, the Mercantile Bank would take no portion of the existing surplus, they having stipulated only that all outstanding liabilities should be discharged, and that arrangements should be made for representing their interest at the Board, to comply with which latter requirement four seats in the Direction would be placed at their disposal.

1856, March 25.—Directors report that, after much discussion, they succeeded in obtaining a communication from the Lords of the Treasury, which removes all further difficulty, and which is also deemed satisfactory by the Mercantile Bank. Since the receipt of this communication, the Board have been occupied in discussing, with the Mercantile Bank, the manner in which the complete amalgamation of the capital of the two Banks can be most satisfactorily effected. Each share of the Mercantile Bank represents a capital of £25, with £20 paid thereon, while a share in the Bank of Asia represents the same amount of capital (£25), but with only £5 paid; and it was determined that the first steps towards the amalgamation must be the perfect assimilation of the shares in each Bank respectively. The most satisfactory mode of accomplishing this object, and which the Board recommend the shareholders to adopt, is to convert at once every four of the present shares of the Bank of Asia, with £5 paid, into one share of £20 fully paid up, and thus place the shares of the Banks on an equal footing. The Directors have accordingly concluded an arrangement to this effect with the Mercantile Bank, in conformity with the plan already submitted to the general meeting of the 23rd of February 1855. The Directors believe that it will entirely meet the convenience and approval of the shareholders; but, in order to provide for the case of any proprietor who may not accept the proposed conversion, the Board recommend that an immediate call of £15 be paid on any such shares, so that every share in the Bank of Asia shall be raised forthwith to £20 paid. In carrying out this plan, the Directors propose to offer to such proprietors, the number of whose shares may not be divisible by four without a practical remainder, the option either of subscribing at par for such an additional amount of stock as will render their shares exactly divisible by four, or of surrendering at par for such amount of their present stock as will be necessary to admit of a division of the remainder by four. Acting under the opinion of counsel, and also in accordance with the resolutions formerly passed by the proprietors of the Mercantile Bank in contemplation of this amalgamation, it has been deemed advisable, on behalf of both Institutions, to apply jointly to Government for a substituted charter, which, without interference with the favorable terms of the present charter, shall contain provisions for the amalgamation of the two Banks, the union of their respective capital, and generally for carrying into full effect the objects contemplated by the joint association.

June 30.—The second ordinary general meeting of proprietors held. November 3.—An extraordinary general meeting of proprietors held, when the Directors communicated the result of the application made to Her Majesty's Government on the part of this Bank, and of the Mercantile Bank of India, London and China, for a substituted charter in favor of the amalgamated Bank, and to determine on the course to be adopted. On applying for the substituted charter, certain alterations in the terms of the original charter were required by the Mercantile Bank, to which the Directors acceded with some reluctance. They regret to find, from the communication recently received from the Lords of the Treasury, and referred to in their circular of the 22nd October last, that their lordships have declined to grant a substituted charter on the terms proposed. The Directors entertain the same confident opinion they have always expressed, as to the profitable field which exists for their operations, and much as they regret the position in which the Bank is placed by this decision on the part of her Majesty's Government, they consider, after the delay which has already taken place, and the confidence with which they have been treated by the proprietors, that they have no alternative but to place the matter fairly before the shareholders, and leave them to decide whether the Bank shall at once be dissolved, and the affairs thereof wound up, or whether any other course shall be adopted with a view to keep alive the charter. In order to leave the shareholders perfectly at liberty to adopt whatever course they may consider most expedient, the Directors passed a formal resolution, in accordance with the provisions of the deed of settlement, recommending the dissolution of the Bank, so that if a resolution to that effect be adopted by two-thirds in value of the shareholders present at the approaching meeting, no technical difficulties may interpose in carrying out the views of the shareholders, and no further meeting will be necessary to determine upon the course of proceeding. At the conclusion of the report, a resolution was passed for the dissolution and winding up of the Company.

CHARTERED MERCANTILE BANK OF INDIA, LONDON AND CHINA.

This Bank, established at Bombay on the 30th November 1853, was principally projected by William Howard, Edwin Heycock, Thomas Stenhouse, Juggonath Sunkersett, Cowasjee Jehanghier Heerjee, Henry Green, Munguldass Nathoobhoy, Cowasjee Nanabhoy, and several other persons, and was called The Mercantile Bank of India, London and China, with a capital of 50,00,000 of rupees, divided into 20,000 shares, of 250 rupees each, to carry on business at Bombay, Ceylon, China, and London. Previously to its commencing business the whole of the subscribed capital was paid up.

1854, January 3.—Bank opened for business with a paid-up capital of Rupees 6,10,650. Early in the year the attention of the Direction was turned to Ceylon as a favorable field for operations, and Branches were accordingly opened in Colombo and Kandy. Its first attempts to do business, on this new field, were met with opposition, which eventually subsided, and left the Bank to act in concert with the other local institutions. September 13.—A special general meeting of shareholders, held at Bombay to take into consideration proposals made to the Directors by the Chartered Bank of Asia, for an amalgamation of the capital and shareholders of the two institutions. The chief suggestions for an amalgamation, put forward on behalf of the Chartered Bank of Asia, were :—

1. The capital of the Mercantile Bank to be incorporated with the capital of the Bank of Asia by the allotment of shares in the Bank of Asia to the extent of the paid-up capital of the Mercantile Bank. The remainder of shares in the Bank of Asia to be held by the present subscribers.

2. No further call to be made upon the shares acquired by the Mercantile Bank, until an equal amount shall have been called up on all the other shares of the Bank of Asia. In like manner, as the present holders of shares in the Bank of Asia will have reduced the number of their shares, in order to admit the Mercantile Bank, the Directors shall be authorised to allot to the present holders of Asia Bank shares, out of the first issue of new shares, so many new shares of a like denomination as will equalise the number of their shares with the number to be acquired by the Mercantile Bank.

3. The business of an amalgamated Company in India, to be conducted by a local Board at Bombay, to be appointed in conformity with the charter.

A second general meeting confirmed the amalgamation approved of by the previous meeting.

1855, February 28.—First half yearly general meeting of shareholders held at Bombay. Directors had called up a total of Rupees 32,88,266-10-8, which, being found insufficient, they resolved to issue to the proprietors new shares in the proportion of one to every three old shares. Agencies were established at Colombo, Canton, London, Kandy, Shanghai, and Calcutta. A proposition to pay the Directors by fee was overruled. The true mode of giving strength to the Bank was to make the management, not the Directors, strong. If money were to be set aside as a remuneration for the Direction, instead of dividing it in small sums amongst that body, it would be better to pay the whole amount to one Director, versed in the Indian exchanges, and experienced in the business of the place, who should be a sort of consulting Director, bound to look in the Bank every day, and to assist the Manager with his advice, and this, of course, no one would do who was not well remunerated. A better course, however, than this, would be, to have another paid officer of the Bank, by the name of the "Secretary," and who would always be at the Bank an assistant and counsellor to the Manager, and ready to take charge of the head quarters in case of accidents; and, as the correspondence with so many Branches was now becoming very voluminous, it would be necessary ere long to consider, if the amalgamation should not be carried out, in what way could effective and permanent assistance best be given to the chief executive officer. In the meantime the Directors did not ask for nor wish remuneration. December 28.—The Governor of Ceylon announced that the privilege of issuing notes was formally relinquished, by command of the Secretary of State for the Colonies, and that the promissory notes payable on demand of any Chartered Bank in the Island would be recognised under certain conditions. These conditions required that the Bank of issue should maintain, at its Head Office in Colombo, a reserve of cash amounting at least to one-third of its average weekly circulation, to be verified by the Colonial Treasurer; and also provided for the periodical exchange of silver for the notes accumulated at the different cutcherries of the Island. This liberal concession on the part of England was at once accepted by the Oriental Bank Corporation—then the only Chartered Bank in Ceylon—and would have been accepted by this Bank had its notes been recognised by the Government.

1856, March 13.—Annual meeting of proprietors held at Bombay. Reference was made to the contemplated amalgamation with the Chartered Bank of Asia. At present things stood thus: the capital subscribed by the shareholders of the Bank of Asia amounted to £100,000. Of this sum the Mercantile Bank held shares amounting to £60,000 in the names of Mr. Flower and Mr. Meeke, who had been admitted into the Direction of the Bank of Asia as Trustees for the Mercantile Bank. £20,000 more of the above capital was held by the Directors of the Bank of Asia, and the remaining £20,000 by parties believed to be favorable to the transfer. The Mercantile Bank, therefore, had the charter of the Bank of Asia at its command. It was mentioned that the Solicitors of the two Banks were employed in arranging the manner in which the charter of the Bank of Asia should be made available for the Mercantile Bank. In answer to a question, whether the shareholders of the Bank of Asia would come in at par, or whether they would contribute a proportionate sum as a Reserve Fund, the Chairman said that the Reserve Fund of the Mercantile Bank now amounted to four per cent on the capital, and that of course that sum could not be made a present to shareholders of the Bank of Asia. Capital, Rupees

50,00,000; Reserve Fund, Rupees 2,87,218-4-8; Dividend eight per cent per annum.

1857, February 19.—Reserve Fund, Rs. 4,02,197-11-6. April 6.—Annual general meeting held at Bombay. November 26.—A deed for winding up THE MERCANTILE BANK OF INDIA, LONDON AND CHINA was signed and executed by the parties connected with the Institution, on which occasion a new deed was executed by the shareholders of the Bank of Asia and the Mercantile, for the establishment of a new incorporated Company, to be called THE CHARTERED MERCANTILE BANK OF INDIA, LONDON AND CHINA.

1858, July 15.—The Directors furnish all their officers with a copy of the charter, of the deed of settlement, and of the rules framed by the Board for the conduct of the business of the Bank. The Directors enjoin system and order; and deprecate loose habits of business, particularly trifling with the rules of the Bank, which is the prolific source of all mal-administration.

1859, December 31.—Dividend ten per cent.

1860, May 22.—A general meeting of shareholders. Directors report having opened a Branch at Mauritius. Dividend for the whole year ten per cent.

1861, May 21.—Annual meeting. Directors announce having opened a Sub-Agency at Penang, as a feeder to the Agency at Singapore. The consent of the Lords Commissioners of Her Majesty's Treasury had been obtained for the issue of notes by the Singapore Branch. Capital paid up, £500,000; Reserve Fund, £46,858-16-4. The Bank had written off £21,000 for bad debts against £3,000 of previous year. There had also been a great deal of sickness among the officers, particularly in China, which had led to extra charges. Dividend for the whole year ten per cent.

1862, May 20.—Annual general meeting. Reserve Fund, £60,000, invested in Government Securities. October 8.—An extraordinary general meeting of proprietors.

The following is the state and staff of the Bank:—

Paid-up Capital, £500,000—Reserve Fund, £60,000.

COURT OF DIRECTORS, 1861-62.

G. G. Nicol, *Chairman.*
D. Larnach (*Director of the Bank of New South Wales and London Joint-Stock Bank*).
George Palmer Robinson (*late Manager in Bombay*).
George May, (*of May, Pickford & Co., Calcutta*).
Thomas Stenhouse (*of Bates, Stenhouse & Co., Liverpool*).
Sir F. J. Halliday, K. C. B. (*late Lieutenant-Governor of Bengal*),
David Trail Robertson, *Manager, Ex-Officio.*

LONDON BANKERS.

Bank of England and London Joint-Stock Bank.

SOLICITORS.

Clarke and Morice, *Coleman Street.*

AUDITORS.

Coleman, Turquand, Youngs & Co. (*Public Accountants*).
J. Smith (*of W. Nicol & Co., Bombay*).
J. A. Russell (*late of Bombay*).

Branches.

BOMBAY.
Agent, Harry John.

CALCUTTA.
Acting Agent, Robert Campbell.

MADRAS.
Agent, R. C. Walker.

SINGAPORE.
Manager, James Davidson.

COLOMBO.
Acting Manager, F. W. Lemarchant.

HONG-KONG.
Manager, Walter Ormiston.

SHANGHAI.
Manager, William Jackson.

KANDY.
Acting Agent, J. G. Buchanan.

MAURITIUS.
Manager, R. G. Lancaster.

PENANG.
Manager, Septimus Short.

THE BANK OF CEYLON.

The Bank of Ceylon was established at Colombo in 1841, with a nominal capital of £125,000, subscribed chiefly by London Firms connected with Ceylon, for the avowed purpose of fostering the cultivation of coffee, then recently commenced, as well as to carry on other ordinary banking business. It had a Branch in Kandy and Agencies at the Presidency Towns of India. The rules of this Institution prohibited advances to Planters, except *upon crops*, but, in spite of these and the presence of a local Board of Directors, some of the Managers lent large sums of money to several individuals on what is known as *block* debts, and in one instance they were actually so far gulled as to lend on a defective title deed. In 1847, which was a most disastrous year for Ceylon, for the price of coffee fell so low in the London market, that the article could have been purchased in Kandy at 12 shillings the cwt., when Merchants and Planters were ruined, and estates sold for *a song*, nearly the whole of the Bank's paid-up capital was locked up, and £60,000 ultimately lost, £28,000 being by one individual alone. In 1849, as stated at page 144, under the head of the Oriental Bank Corporation, this Institution, which had been established in the Island for some years, stepped forward and took over the business and liabilities of the Bank of Ceylon, and advanced a sum of money to its shareholders in lieu of its outstanding securities, which it undertook to realise. Unlike the Bank of Ceylon, which was purely a local establishment, the Oriental Bank, in Ceylon, was one of the numerous Branches of an Exchange Bank that was originally formed in Bombay under the style of the Western Bank of India, and from its foreign connections, offered greater facilities to its customers than the other. One of the reasons that induced the Oriental Bank to take over the business of the failing Bank, was, as we have stated elsewhere, to obtain the Royal Charter possessed by the latter. The Bank of Ceylon issued notes payable on demand; but, up to the end of 1855, only the notes of the Government of Ceylon were officially recognised and received from the public, in payment of duties and other taxes. The average circulation of the Bank of Ceylon, seldom if ever exceeded £30,000.

Prior to the establishment of this Bank, there appears to be no authentic information as to the manner in which the merchants of Colombo procured their supplies of money. It appears that the *Chetty* (Hindoo) traders, agents of large Native Houses from Madras and other towns of Southern India, acted as bankers in those days, and supplied the British Merchant with cash for his Bills of Exchange on Madras, Bombay and Calcutta, which they remitted in payment for grain and other goods they imported. The merchants were, therefore, obliged to have agents at the Presidencies on whom they drew, sending them at the same time Bills on London drawn against credits or Produce shipped from this, for negotiation. Judging from the fact that the entire grain trade was in the hands of the *Chetties*, and that coffee planting was then but in its infancy,—the exports consisting principally of cinnamon, cocoanut oil and coir,—we may conclude that they met all the requirements of the merchants, and that importations of specie were but rarely needed.

The rate of Exchange on London thirty years ago, must have been comparatively moderate, for the export trade from India had not then assumed its present gigantic proportions; besides which, the East India Company drew largely from London on the Presidencies, at rates exceedingly favorable to remitters of money to India. To those who required to make remittances from Ceylon, Missionary Bills, drawn on the Parent Societies in London, were available *at par*, as also Government drafts on H. M. Treasury, but the latter could not be obtained except at a high premium. In fact, we find in the Chamber of Commerce Report of 1840, a correspondence between that body and the Government relative to Treasury Bills for £10,000, which had been forwarded to Bombay, and there sold at one shilling and eleven pence per Rupee, or about four per cent premium, while the Merchants here were willing to buy them *at par*, the net result to Government after deducting interest for loss of time and freight, insurance, and other charges on the rupees obtained in return from Bombay. The Governor, however, replied that his instructions from the Secretary of State precluded him from selling them under three per cent premium in Ceylon. The merchants' business in those days was extremely simple. There were neither Telegraphs nor Steamers; sailing vessels, by means of which all the correspondence was carried on, usually took five or six months to perform a voyage between Europe and India, now reduced to three by the longest route. Hence the Colonial trade was regulated by certain fixed principles, and not the speculative basis upon which it is now founded. There could be neither orders nor counter-orders upon every fluctuation of the markets, which now so seriously complicate the merchants' calling; and to use a common phrase, they had "an easy time of it." No cares lurked behind their desks, or spoilt their appetite, under the guise of the "latest bulletins," or special telegrams from Europe. Their path was smooth, and their digestion unimpaired.

1849.—An arrangement was made with the Oriental Bank to take over the business of this Bank.

CHARTERED BANK OF INDIA, AUSTRALIA AND CHINA.

The establishment of this Bank is of as recent date as 1853, and may be traced to the desire of the capitalists of London to share in the extended sphere of Australian and Indian adventure. Some difficulties were, in the outset, thrown in the way of their obtaining a charter of the Corporation, and the circular which was addressed to this Bank, conjointly with some others, on 1st April 1853, would show the desire of the Lords of the Treasury, and of the Commissioners for the affairs of India, to use great caution. In Sydney, the proposal was not favorably received: on the contrary; violent opposition was shown, through the Press, to the introduction of new Anglo-Australian Banks. A report having gained currency that it was proposed, by these charters, to give a liability to the shareholders, limited only to the amount of their shares, the Liverpool Chamber of Commerce, moved by the recollection of undue encouragement given to speculation in our colonies in times past, were prepared to remonstrate against such a course, and sought the aid of other bodies constituted like itself for the protection of commerce. The Manchester Commercial Association, however, thinking it desirable to know how far the report was correct before they took action, addressed the Board of Trade on the subject, and received an explanation in the following letter:—

" *Office of the Committee of Privy Council for Trade, Whitehall.*

SIR,—I am directed by the Lords of the Committee of Privy Council for Trade to acknowledge the receipt of your letter of the 4th instant, in which you state that the Directors of the Manchester Commercial Association have learnt that the promoters of a Joint Stock Company, proposing to establish Banks in India, China, and Australia, are seeking to obtain from Her Majesty's Government a charter limiting the liability of the shareholders to the amount of their respective subscriptions; and you desire to be furnished with a copy of the charter so applied for.

In reply, I am to state to you, for the information of the Directors of the Manchester Commercial Association, that two draft charters—the one for the Chartered Bank of India, Australia and China, and the other for the Bank of India—for which application has been made, have been referred by Her Majesty in Council to this department for their report. These drafts have been submitted by my Lords to the Commissioners for the Affairs of India and the Lords of the Treasury, and are now under the consideration of those departments.

With reference to your question, whether similar privileges as to limitation of liability have been granted by Her Majesty's Government to like establishments, either in India or in any other dependency of Great Britain, I am to inform you, that no charters for the establishment of Banks in India have been granted by Her Majesty's Government, and that no charters by which the liability is restricted to the amount of the subscriptions of the shareholders have, of late years at least, been granted for establishing Banks in any other dependencies of Great Britain. According to the rules established by Her Majesty's Government in 1846, with respect to charters to be granted for the incorporation of Banking Companies in the colonies, it is the practice to insert in charters of incorporation granted to Banking Companies in the colonies a provision under which the shareholders are responsible for the engagements of the Company to the extent of twice the amount of their subscribed shares; that is, for the amount subscribed, and for a further additional amount equal thereto.

I am to add, that my Lords regret that they cannot comply with your request to be furnished with copies of the charters applied for.

I am, SIR, your obedient servant,

JAMES BOOTH.

HUGH FLEMING, ESQ."

A question was subsequently raised between the Directors and a large number of scripholders of the Chartered Bank of India, Australia and China, as to the desirableness of proceeding with the foundation of that establishment. The altered aspect of the money market—the competition in banking, not only in Australia but also in India—were the reasons specially adduced by the dissentients for not concurring in the views propounded by the Directors; an endeavor was therefore made to resist the payment of calls, and to organise a movement for finally "winding up." The Board taking an entirely opposite course, expressed their determination to carry out the undertaking, relying upon the valuable privileges of the charter, and the ascertained field for profitable operations in the Indian Presidencies, China and Australia. At a meeting of scripholders, held on the 16th of March, the position assumed by both parties was freely discussed, not unaccompanied by serious allegations against retired Directors, who were said to have sold their shares at a high premium before they left the Board. The character of the existing Directors was too high to warrant the assumption that they were actuated by any doubtful motives in the plans they were pursuing, and the elaborate statement which they circulated, describes what they conceived to be the prospects of success :—

"1*st*.—That during the intermediate period, the progress of steam communication has greatly increased, and the trade with Australasia, both direct and circuitous, has been rapidly developing itself. 2*nd*.—

That the test of experience, as to the expansion of this vast commerce, confirms the importance attached by the prospectus to the extended operations which the charter permits to this Company, and leaves no reasonable doubt that the expansion will continue; it being a peculiar feature of this Bank, as already pointed out, that it follows the natural course of commerce round the world, whilst it possesses all the advantages of the dircet communication with the mother-country. *3rd.*—That it is well understood that the government has no intention of granting any more banking charters. *4th.*—That many important banking projects which were competitors in 1852, are now permanently withdrawn. *5th.*—That this Bank will commence its operations at a period when the important trade with Australia will have been established on a sound basis, and the risks incidental to the development of a new trade will have been avoided. The Court are not insensible to the pressure which at present exists in the money market. They, however, felt it a duty, on receiving the charter from government, to make a first call. It was necessary to do so, in order that the true state of the proprietary should be ascertained, and that the deed of settlement should be executed; and those who take an interest in the future prospect of the Bank must bear in mind that it cannot begin its effective business until half its capital is paid up; and it is therefore the duty of the Directors, and the interest of the shareholders, that there should be no delay in the calls beyond what is necessary to prevent an undue pressure during a period of scarcity of money. But, in making further calls, the Directors will not be indifferent to the state of the money market, and other circumstances, and they will continue to exercise the same caution and economy as hitherto in conducting the affairs; but they are under the conviction, that if they were to delay the present call, as some parties have requested, or if they hesitated to declare their intention to carry out, gradually and cautiously, an undertaking so important to the public, and so full of promise to the interests of all concerned in it, they would be virtually sacrificing a most valuable property, and abandoning a most imperative duty."

The dissentient scripholders at length applied for an injunction against the Directors to restrain them from enforcing the call of £2 per share due the 20th of April, and from forfeiting the shares upon which the amount may not be paid. The contest between the litigant parties came fully before the public, who were enabled to judge of the real merits of the question at issue. It was alleged that the dissentients numbered 19,000 of the 32,000 shares appropriated; and, being a strong majority, they contended that the Board should listen to their representations. The Directors, on the contrary, appeared to view them as a band of speculators; many of whom, having obtained shares at low prices, were anxious to dissolve the establishment and divide the remaining deposits. Upon this the former, determined to bring the point to a conclusion, and, to test the power of the Board, entered into a subscription not exceeding 2*s.* per share. With the funds so raised, were commenced proceedings, the result of which was awaited with anxiety by all interested. It is to be regretted that some mutual understanding could not have been come to before an appeal to Chancery for arranging this dispute, the position of the principal Directors and that of a great number of the dissentients not permitting it to be supposed that other causes than a difference of opinion influenced them in adopting so unpleasant an alternative.

1854, March.—Directors publish a statement explanatory of the origin of the Bank, and the difficulty in obtaining its charter, arising from the necessity of conciliating the Government and the East India Company as to its extension in India. November.—The Bank, with respect to the question which was lately agitated as to the power of the Directors to enforce calls, issued dividend warrants at the rate of five per cent upon the amount of the call made in March last, and to which only about a third of the shareholders responded. These warrants were to be signed in the presence of a witness, and against the word "Proprietor;" and, as this mode was an uncommon one, it was suggested that its scope might be equivalent to that of signing the deed, and thus give the Directors, in those instances where it was complied with, the power, in case of any non-payment of future calls, of forfeiting the shares. The Directors are too respectable for any suspicion to be entertained of a stratagem on their part.

1855, February 28.—First ordinary general meeting held. Capital paid-up, £97,700. The delay in granting the charter, and difficulties which had sprung up induce the Directors to make proposal for an amalgamation with one of the Banks in India.

1856, February 29.—Second general meeting. Directors report that 3,116 shares have been allotted in India to a highly respectable constituency. Capital paid-up, £104,700.

1857, February 13.—Annual general meeting. Directors report that their endeavors to obtain from Her Majesty's Government a supplemental charter had proved unsuccessful, but that arrangements were in view which promised to bring the Bank into existence immediately under its original charter. Capital paid-up, £145,820. Directors report their expectation of being able to begin business with India and China by end of the summer, but do not think it adviseable, for the present, to establish Branches in Australia.

1858, July 25.—Ordinary general meeting. Directors report commencement of business at the close of last year, since which they have opened a Branch at Shanghai, and concluded arrangements for an Agency at Singapore. The Bombay and Calcutta Agencies stated to be working successfully. It was their intention to confine themselves to Agencies in India and China, and adjacent parts of the world. September 23.—An extraordinary general meeting.

1860, September 27.—An extraordinary general meeting. Dividend seven per cent per annum.

1861, March 28.—Ordinary general meeting. Dividend, six per cent per annum. Directors report their intention to apply to the Lords Commissioners of the Treasury for the privilege of issuing bank-notes at Singapore, which is a privilege they could not enjoy in the territories formerly under the Government of the East India Company. Capital paid-up, £644,000. Reserve Fund, £5,000. April 18.—Extraordinary general meeting to move a resolution—

"That the Court of Directors be authorised to apply for and accept her Majesty's supplemental royal charter, authorising the Bank to establish a Branch Bank at Singapore, in lieu of the existing agency, for the purpose of carrying on general banking business there; and also to issue and circulate in the island of Singapore, and the adjoining British settlements, notes payable to bearer on demand, and to re-issue the same, subject to such restrictions and conditions as Her Majesty should deem fit to impose."

October 30.—An extraordinary general meeting. Dividend six per cent per annum. Directors report appointment of an Agent at Bombay, who however had not fulfilled the expectations entertained of him, and had involved the Bank in a liability of £20,000.

1862, April 30.—Ordinary general meeting. Reserve Fund, £10,000. Dividend, five per cent per annum. This falling off was attributable to the unfavorable state of the Exchange in China, which had also pressed on other Banks.

1863, January 1.—Mr. R. L. Eglinton resigns the Calcutta Agency to join a mercantile establishment.

April.—Mr. A. F. Hewett, Accountant to the Calcutta Branch of the Chartered Mercantile Bank of India, London and China, is appointed to the Agency.

The following is the present state and staff of the Bank:—

Paid-up Capital, £644,000.

COURT OF DIRECTORS, 1861-62.

THOMAS ALEXANDER MITCHELL, M. P., (*Sampson, Mitchell and Co.,*) *Chairman.*
PETER BELL (*Scott, Bell & Co.*)
JAMES FRASER (*Maclaine, Fraser and Co., Singapore*).
JOHN GLADSTONE (*Jno. Gladstone & Co.*)
CAPTAIN C. W. GORDON, M. P. (*Fyvie Castle, Aberdeenshire.*)
JOHN JONES (*Hyde and Jones*).
THOMAS LANCASTER (*late of Bombay*).
WILLIAM MACNAUGHTEN (*late of Mincing Lane*).
WILLIAM SCHAW LINDSAY, M. P. (*W. S. Lindsay and Co.*)
JOSEPH R. MORRISON (*late of Messrs. J. Morrison & Co.*)

Manager ... G. U. ADAM.
Secretary ... J. C. STEWART.

Agencies.

CALCUTTA.	BOMBAY.
Agent, A. F. HEWETT.	*Agent*, ANTHONY MORRISON.

RANGOON.
Agent, G. A. WHITE.

Branches.

SINGAPORE.	HONG-KONG.
Manager, C. S. SHERWOOD.	*Acting Manager*, A. H. ANDERSON.

SHANGHAI.
Acting Manager, C. IGGULDEN.

March.—Bank declared a dividend of only five per cent, in consequence of the loss of about £50,000, or five lacs of rupees, sustained in China by the great opium swindle, from which other Banks, conjointly, likewise suffered to the extent of ten lacs of Rupees, or £100,000 sterling.

LONDON BANK OF AUSTRALIA AND INDIA.

This Bank was projected in 1852-53, for the purpose of engaging in banking and exchange operations both in Australia and India. Its capital was represented by £500,000, in 25,000 shares of £20 each, of which £2 per share in £50,000 was paid up Difficulties, however, having been started by the Colonial Office in the granting of a charter, the Directors returned the deposit paid by the scripholders, less 1*s.* 2*d.* for preliminary expenses. The numerous applications made for charters for Banks starting in connection with India and Australia, made the Colonial Office adverse to any active interference on the question, without first consulting the local authorities. The Bank was therefore never brought into active operation.

PUNJAB BANK LIMITED.

This Institution is principally local, and is of recent formation. Its Head Office is at Rawul Pindee, with Branches at Peshawur, Mooltan, and Poona. The following is the present state and staff of the Bank :—

Capital, Rupees 5,00,000, *in* 5,000 *Shares of Rupees* 100 *each.*

Manager at Rawul Pindee ... E. Herbert.
Agent in Poona ... W. F. Hunter.
Agent in Mooltan ... H. S. Spencer.
Agent in Peshawur ... W. R. Lewsey.

SCINDE, PUNJAB, AND DELHI BANK CORPORATION LIMITED.

This Institution, just starting into life, has been announced under encouraging auspices. The proposed capital is £1,000,000 sterling, in 50,000 shares of £20 each, the first issue to be 25,000 shares; but it seems it is not proposed to call up more than £10 per share. The Union Bank of London are the bankers in London, and the Oriental Bank Corporation will be the bankers in Calcutta, Madras and Bombay, and the organisation of the undertaking being in connection with the Scinde, Punjab, and Delhi Railways, a large nucleus of business is already secured. Legitimate banking facilities in the improving provinces of the country alluded to, it is stated, are positively required, and application has been made for the privilege of circulating the notes of the Government, and of participating in the other advantages conceded to Banks in India. The trade of these localities is assuming a position of importance, and while the chief office will be in London, Branches and Agencies will, in the first instance, be opened at Kurrachee, Lahore, Umritsur, and Delhi, and ultimately at Mooltan, Shikarpore, and Hyderabad. One great feature is that the preliminary charges will be confined to the necessary expenses, no remuneration whatever being allowed for originating the Bank.

Mr. Neale Porter, the Managing Director in India of the Scinde, Punjab, and Delhi Bank Corporation, left on the 3rd of March, to proceed to India *viâ* the overland route, with the view of establishing the Bank in Scinde and the Punjab; and Mr. H. I. Lee, late acting Secretary and Treasurer of the Bank of Bengal in Calcutta, was to follow in a few days, as the Sub-manager and Chief Accountant of the Bank at Kurrachee.

CENTRAL BANK OF WESTERN INDIA.

This Bank was formed at Bombay, and started into existence in November 1860, with a capital of fifty lacs of rupees, divided into 20,000 shares of 250 rupees each. Provision is however made for an increase to one crore of rupees should it be found necessary. With very few exceptions the proprietary body are natives. The first Directors were Vurjeevundass Madhowdass, Elliaoo David Sassoon, Byramjee Jejeebhoy, Cursetjee Nusserwanjee Cama, Venayeckrow Jugonnathjee, Dhurumsey Poonjabhoy, Sorabjee Pestonjee Framjee, Khanbhoy Hubbibhoy, and Fazel Goolam Hussein. The Head Office is at Bombay. Agencies have been established at Calcutta, Hong-Kong, Shanghai, and London.

1861, June 30.—Proprietors' capital paid up, Rupees 28,58,050. Dividend was declared upon 19,405 registered shares, upon Rupees 150 paid up, at 2½ per cent. December 31.—Capital paid up, Rupees 33,71,550. No dividend was declared, but the profits for the half year, added to the balance of profits of the preceding half year, amounting altogether to Rupees 50,000, were transferred to form the nucleus of the Reserve Fund.

1862, June 30.—Paid-up capital, Rupees 48,18,600. Reserve Fund, Rupees 50,000. Profits for the half year, Rupees 2,36,222-12-8. These, added to the balance of the preceding half-year, Rupees 15,343-14-5, increased the amount to Rupees 2,51,566-11-1, which, however, were not divided, being retained to meet a loss of Rupees4, 64,086-2-8, sustained from fraud and failures in Hong-Kong.

1863, April.—It is stated that negotiations are in progress to amalgamate this Bank with the newly started Bank of Hindustan, China, and Japan, and that the Head Office will continue at Bombay. The junction of the two establishments will give to the Central Bank a capital of Rupees 75,00,000, which will, of course, give greater stability to the shares which are already at a premium of six and seven per cent.

The following are the present staff of the Bank:—

BOMBAY.

Manager	...	EDWIN HEYCOCK.
Accountant	...	J. GORDON.

CALCUTTA BRANCH,
Office, No. 26, Tank-Square.

Manager	...	M. MACIVER.
Accountant	...	HARRY JAMES.

BANK OF HINDUSTAN, CHINA, AND JAPAN LIMITED.

This Bank was announced under very satisfactory auspices in 1862, and boasts of a proprietary of the very highest character. Its capital has been fixed at £1,000,000, in 10,000 shares of £100 each, of which £250,000 or £25 per share have alone been called up. The fields for operation embrace China, Japan, and India. With prudence in management, it doubtless holds out the promise of success. Branches have been established at Bombay, Hong-Kong, and Shanghai, and, as the sphere for its transactions is sufficiently large to prevent interference with the previously existing establishments, it is to be presumed that it will go on smoothly. It is believed that negotiations are in progress to amalgamate this Bank with the Central Bank of Western India, the head establishment of which is in Bombay, with Branches in other parts of India and in China. The paid-up capital of the latter is £500,000, in shares of £25 each, or 250 rupees, the last price in Bombay being six to seven per cent premium. The capital of the Bank of Hindustan is £1,000,000, in shares of £100, £25 of which is the total to be called up, so that the united paid-up capital would be £750,000. The amount of £15 is already paid on the

Bank of Hindustan shares, and their quotation is two to one and three-quarters discount.

The following is the present staff of the Bank:—

Head Office, London.

No. 18, *Cornhill.*

General Manager	...	John Ouseley.
Secretary	...	R. S. Tomlin.

CALCUTTA BRANCH,

No. 4, *Hastings' Street.*

Manager	...	W. H. Fuller.
Accountant	...	David Hean.

BANK OF ROHILKUND (RAMPORE).

This is quite an infant Institution, having only been in operation since December 1862. No information can yet be given of its proprietary body, nor other particulars, but, it would seem, that sufficient success has been met with to enable the Bank to declare a dividend of six per cent per annum for the first quarter of its existence. The establishment of the Bank appears to have met with great opposition from the native money-lenders in the neighborhood, but the Nawab of Rampore gave it his support, and very materially assisted in establishing it on a firm basis. We shall watch its progress.

PEOPLE'S BANK OF INDIA LIMITED.

This Bank was projected in 1860 by its present Manager to meet a want in Calcutta in banking matters, *viz.*, an Institution which would not despise small business.

The following is an extract from the prospectus:—

"None of the older Banks will cash a cheque for less than Rupees

20. and cheques, which in England are used almost instead of bank-notes, are in Calcutta useless, except for large transactions. No one ever walks into a shop, buys a book or a coat, and pays for it by a cheque. The weight of the currency disinclines Europeans to carry a purse. Notes, for some not very explicable reason, are rarely carried, and small cheques offer the quickest and easiest inducement to payments in ready money. The abuse of credit, particularly for small sums, is perhaps the greatest grievance of Calcutta tradesmen, and a Bank, which would render cash payments easy, as cash payments are now desired to be the order of the day, deserves, on that account alone, the support of the community; for, in advertisements, it has become quite an usual thing to see the cash and credit prices both stated, side by side—the difference between the two being in every instance equal to a very heavy percentage—the best possible proof of the value set upon cash transactions by the trading community."

Private individuals and small capitalists requiring a loan on a Government promissory note for Rupees 500, found it practically impossible to obtain it, that amount being much below the minimum granted by the Bank of Bengal. The other Banks, whose business is chiefly with exchange operations, if they cared to grant such small loans, confine the term to the shortest possible period, *viz.*, three days, whereas the borrower may require it for 3, 6, 9 or 12 months, or even more (subject to renewal intermediately). An inducement to save money is held out by the small sum which is receivable, at one time, in fixed deposits for 3, 6, 9 and 12 months certain, *viz.*, Rupees 10, a sum within the power of any one to accumulate monthly, and which others can increase according to their means.

In one matter connected with the People's Bank, it is stated, that some people labor under a great mistake in imagining, because the Bank undertakes to cash small cheques (down to Rupees 5), that it cannot, or does not undertake, or seek other than small accounts. The small accounts being the unprofitable ones, it is assumed to be hardly fair on the part of those, who *really* bank elsewhere, to give their *unprofitable* business to this establishment, unless on the understanding that a commission be levied by the Bank to remunerate it for its trouble, there being no chance of its obtaining any in the usual course, *i. e.*, from any balance always at credit of the constituent. The management argue, that if people lack confidence in the Bank, it is better to keep away from it altogether, as the Bank itself is better without such accounts, which certainly entail "more plague than profit." This is scarcely a right view to take of the case. The only chance of success a Bank of this kind has, is to open itself out to small operations, because the other numerous larger Institutions are, in every respect, better able to carry on a large business. Small transactions insensibly lead to larger, and the question of confidence is clearly one of time alone. It would be a pity were anything to mar the utility of this really useful little institution, which is much needed in a city like this, and the value of which, there is little doubt, will be appreciated with the increase of the population.

The accommodation afforded by this Institution is such as probably could not be afforded elsewhere. Some individuals who want to "save a little by degrees," from time to time, can manage to *pay off* by instalments, but cannot *save up* by instalments: these individuals manage as follows, and to such, it is undeniable, the People's Bank is a very beneficial Institution. According to the party's wishes an investment is made in some description of security, on which a loan is given. This loan is repaid by instalments, and, when fully discharged, the borrower becomes the owner of the security, for purchase of which he would probably *never* have *saved* the funds, though, in the above way, he gains the end in view.

The first Board of Directors were :—

DIRECTORS.

Chairman ... A. BOYLE.

A. B. GOODALL.	JOHN SMITH.
W. R. LACKERSTEEN.	HORREE MOHUN SEN.

NILMONEY MUTTY LALL.

The following statement of the sums which passed through the Bank, under the various heads, (inclusive of the balances from the previous half-year,) for the half-year ending 31st December 1862, will enable a judgment to be made of the Bank's business to that date.

The total sum advanced on loans on Personal Securities was	Rs.	65,913	0	0
And on deposit of Securities	„	3,17,678	0	0
The total amount of Bills discounted	„	2,14,038	0	0
The total sum received on account of Floating Deposit (or current accounts) was	„	10,45,316	0	0
And the total paid on ditto	„	9,29,502	0	0
The total sum received on account of the four classes of *Fixed* Deposits was	„	56,501	0	0
And the total paid on ditto	„	15,458	0	0

1862.—This year the Bank sustained some trifling losses, by means of forgeries and advances upon goods of a perishable nature and insufficiently covered.

The following is the present state and staff of the Bank:—

Capital, Rupees 5,00,000, in 5,000 Shares of Rupees 100 each.

OFFICE, *No. 3, Hare Street.*

DIRECTORS.

JOHN SMITH, *firm of Smith and Stanistreet.*
WILLIAM BONNAUD, *Consulting Accountant and Auditor.*
M. C. JOAKIM, *firm of M. C. Joakim and Co.*
HOREE MOHUN SEN, *Banian.*
NILMONEY MUTTY LALL, *Zemindar.*

Manager ... R. E. K. WILKINSON.
Accountant ... C. SARKIES.

THE COMPTOIR D'ESCOMPTE OF PARIS.

Incorporated by National Decrees of 7th and 8th March 1848, *and by Imperial Decree of 25th July* 1854.

Paid-up Capital ...... Francs 40,000,000 (£1,600,000)
Reserve Fund .... „ 8,350,000 (£334,000)

The establishments located at Calcutta, Bombay, Bourbon (Réunion), and Shanghai, are merely Branches of the great parent institution—the National Discount Bank of Paris. As the National Discount Banks are subject to the same operations as the ordinary banking establishments, there would have been no occasion to allude specially to them were not the circumstances connected with their formation, and the importance acquired by that of Paris, in respect of its extensive system of loans on security, such as to invest these institutions with a public and independent character above all similar ones.

The political revolution that occurred during the last period of the commercial crisis, which commenced in 1847, had most seriously affected credit. Towards the close of February 1848, the bankers of Paris had intimated to their correspondents, that it was their intention to put themselves into liquidation, and to stop all ordinary business, even the recovery of outstandings. This determination overturned all calculations and most seriously affected trade. The panic was most extensive, and general attention was directed towards the Government. The Bank of France and the Treasury alone remained firm and solvent, though the panic was so wide spread as to affect even these; for there was a simultaneous rush upon the Savings' Banks under the control of Government, and upon the Bank itself, for coin in exchange for notes. Four houses alone, whose entire worth was estimated at 50 millions of francs, suspended payment, with numerous others, of inferior standing, largely connected with railways. Such was the magnitude of the gap, the filling up of which was in question. The only way of relief was through the Government, and they came forward on the occasion. On the 7th March the Government, conceiving it to be one of the first duties of the State to interpose, when the public themselves feel the need of combination for the creation of a species of mutual assurance, issued the following decree :—

"*Art.* 1.—In all manufacturing and commercial towns, a National Bank of Discount shall be established.

Art. 2.—The capital shall be raised in the following proportions :—1*st.*—One-third in silver by the subscribing partners. 2*nd.*—One-third in bonds by the towns. 3*rd.*—One-third in treasury orders by the State."

The following day another decree fixed the basis of the Bank of Paris, established with a guaranteed capital of 20 millions, of which one-third alone, divided into shares of 500 francs, contribnted in cash by the suscribers. The decree stated :—

"*Art.* 3.—The profits of the Comptoir d'Escompte shall be exclusively appropriated to the shareholders: neither the State, nor the town desiring to derive any benefit from their intervention.

Art. 4.—The capital, to be furnished by the State and the City of Paris, will guarantee to the amount of the losses which may arise from the operations of the Bank."

There was something unusual in this association of the State, of the inhabitants of a town, and of trades-people to establish a Bank; the State and the towns burthening themselves, beforehand, with all losses, and surrendering to the shareholders all profits. On the 18th March, the Comptoir began its operations with a capital of 2,587,021 francs, of which *one million* was lent by the State. By the 31st August following, the capital had augmented to 4,051,804 francs. The 7th and 8th articles of the statutes define the operations of the establishment:—

"*Art.* 7.—The business of the Bank consists in discounting mercantile bills, payable at Paris or in the districts. All other transactions are forbidden.

Art. 8.—The Bank will only discount bills bearing at least two names, and the currency of which shall not exceed *one hundred and five days* for paper payable in Paris, and *sixty days* for paper payable in the districts. For bills on the districts, the due date may be extended to *ninety days*, but only in cases of bills payable at places where there shall be a local Bank, or a Branch of the Bank of France. No bill shall be discounted having a shorter currency than *five days*."

At first the Bank only discounted paper on Paris, and the towns where the Bank had Branches; but afterwards paper on the principal towns of France, having thirty days to run, was discounted.

On 31st August 1848, the Bank had discounted 80,378,326 francs of bills, and 6,924,266 francs of receipts for goods. It had been employed to realise 15,904,956 francs in the districts, and had passed through its books more than 88 millions. It had re-discounted the contents of its bill case, at the Bank of France, to the amount of 59,389,215 francs.

Such was the beginning of the National Discount Bank of Paris. The following table, prepared from the annual reports at the meeting of shareholders, will give some idea of the extent of its operations :—

JUNE 30.	ACTIVE CAPITAL	ENCASH-MENTS.	DISCOUNTS.	RECEIPTS OF THE AGENCIES.	CURRENT ACCOUNTS.	BALANCE OF DOUBTFUL BILLS.
1848	6,051,804	15,904,956	78,350,789	14,774,796	2,988,086	1,389,757
1849	7,143,063	14,977,529	73,781,534	24,492,753	3,656,937	747,954
1850	7,330,579	17,664,181	92,504,248	35,462,143	8,269,133	539,575
1851	7,223,991	20,039,441	142,791,386	52,365,074	14,911,403	1,444,378
1852	9,666,500	25,200,342	177,693,660	70,579,898	15,148,449	403,545
1853	22,008,769	33,358,113	353,935,560	148,734,874	29,320,357	474,691
1854	22,499,271	44,836,485	555,679,282	128,016,024	20,160,690	64,217
1855	22,782,851	53,631,766	492,567,093	127,744,945	25,611,768	Worthless.
1856	23,157,368	55,123,534	462,642,635	187,180,147	17,560,419	99,433

Since 1853, the constitution of the Bank has been considerably modified. The capital has been raised to 20 millions, exclusive of the Reserve; and it has been decided that, if deemed necessary, new stock shall be created for a like amount.

On 31st December 1854, the guarantee given by the State and the city of Paris to the Comptoir d'Escompte ceased to operate, without its having been once enforced. At the same time that the Bank took a firmer stand, it modified its statutes and prolonged the existence of the society for thirty years from the 18th March 1857. Thus, from this expedient or shift, intended only to last till 1851, but afterwards extended and enlarged in 1857, has arisen a powerful Bank, the constitution whereof is but little removed from the common right. The nomination of the first and second Directors is submitted for the approval of the Minister of Finance.

The operations of the Bank have been extended by new statutes, and defined in the following articles:—

" *Art.* 9.—The operations of the Bank consist :—

1st.—In discounting Mercantile Bills, payable in Paris, in the districts, and abroad; Bills to order of the Bank, accompanied by deposit receipts for goods in the general ware-houses approved of by the State; and, generally, all sorts of pledges to order and at fixed usance arising out of commercial or manufacturing transactions.

2nd.—To make advances on French stock, shares or obligations of manufacturing undertakings, or of credit placed in French Joint Stock Companies, but only to the extent of two-thirds of the market value of the stocks or shares, and on condition that these advances shall only be for ninety days, and shall at no time exceed the fifth part of the paid-up capital, and half of the amount of the Reserve Fund.

3rd.—To undertake all payments and realisations at Paris, in the districts, and abroad; to grant and accept all Orders, Drafts, and Bills of Exchange for which security shall have been previously given, either in goods deposited in the general ware-houses, in specie, or in paper approved of by the discounting board; to collect all arrears of stocks, interests or dividends on shares, either for purchase or sale on account of third parties, on condition of charging a stipulated Commission, and all kinds of public funds, or manufacturing paper.

4th.—To open subscriptions for public or other loans, and for the realisation of all Joint Stock Companies, but always on account of third parties, and on the understanding of a settled commission, with this reservation, that no tenders for Foreign Funds, or for the realisation of Joint Stock Companies shall take place without the sanction of the Minister of Finances.

5th.—To receive in deposit on current account and to the extent of one and a half of the amount of the paid-up capital the sums which shall be deposited, at a rate of interest fixed by the Board of Directors, the balance at credit of these current accounts never being allowed to exceed the fixed limit.

6th.—In fact, to receive in deposit all descriptions of paper, or other valuables, on condition of a fee being charged.

All other transactions are forbidden.

Art. 10.—The Bank shall only discount Mercantile Bills bearing at least two names, and the currency of which shall not exceed one hundred and five days for paper payable in Paris, and seventy-five days for paper payable in the districts. For Bills payable in the districts the currency may be extended to ninety days, but only in the cases of Bills payable in places where there shall be an Agency of the Bank of France.

No Bills with a currency of less than five days will be discounted."

1860, October 2.—An extraordinary general meeting was held at Paris, when the Directors referred to the rejection of their proposal, in 1856, to raise the capital from twenty to forty millions of francs. On this occasion, they renew their recommendation, basing it on the commercial treaty concluded with England, which had rendered more indispensable and urgent the settlement of French credit in producing countries. On their application, the Minister of Finance had, by a special order, authorised the Bank to establish Agencies at Shanghai, Calcutta, Madras, Bombay, and Pondicherry, subject to the approval of the shareholders. Acting on this permission, the Directors had already effected the establishment of the China Agency, and reported that the staff for Calcutta were ready to embark. The meeting agree to raise the capital to the forty millions authorised to be called up, by the decree establishing the Bank.

1861, July 31.—The operations this year represent a sum of 1,034,736,753 francs, against 732,488,820 francs of the previous year, being an increase of 302,247,933 francs. Discounts alone had increased in the sum of 230,353,514 francs. Bank shares number 80,000. The Agencies at Shanghai and Calcutta are reported to be in full operation, the former under the direction of Mr. Cordier, the latter under that of Mr. Pietsch, both men of experience. Although sufficient time had not elapsed to appreciate the success of these recently established Agencies, the Directors report that they already hold an important place in the relations of the International Commerce of France with India and China, and that they look to future satisfactory results. The Agencies of Réunion, Madras, Bombay, and Pondicherry had only been provisionally organised. Dividend 8-4-5 per cent, with 4,85,000 francs carried to the Reserve.

1862, July 31.—Operations show an increase over the preceding year of 20,430,059 francs. Reserve attained 8,351,343 francs. Maximum fixed at 10,000,000 francs. Dividend for the year 7-4-5 per cent per annum on shares of 500 francs each. Directors report that the Calcutta Agency is in regular working order, and that, under the skilful and firm hand of the gentleman who directs it, it has realised, during the experiment of one year, all the expectations that could be legitimately anticipated. With respect to the Shanghai Agency, the civil war, which desolates the provinces in the north-east of China, and the embarrassments caused to the silk trade by the events in America, had retarded its growth. Government had availed themselves of the services of the latter Agency to realise the war indemnity due by the Chinese Government to France. The establishment of the Réunion (Bourbon) Agency is announced under the direction of Mr. Carré, Senior, formerly Cashier of the Colonial Bank. The value of money, in those countries where Agencies are established, being generally very high, the outturn of the operations of those establishments will compensate for the low rate of interest in Europe.

The following comparative statement will show the operations for four consecutive years:—

1858-59.		1859-60.		1860-61.		1861-62.	
Bills.	Amount.	Bills.	Amount.	Bills.	Amount.	Bills.	Amount.
999,755	703,757,423 92	1,099,064	732,488,820 47	1,199,336	1,034,736,753 64	1,202,912	1,055,166,812 77

The difference on the profit and loss account is shown by the following table:—

	1858-59.	1859-60.	1860-61.	1861-62.
Amount of Discounts and different commissions	4,099,140 33	4,168,356 10	7,104,151 39	7,751,366 98
Amount of re-discounts and different losses	2,238,098 81	2,307,916 43	3,797,566 32	4,121,736 05
Balance	1,861,041 52	1,860,439 67	3,306,585 07	3,629,630 93
Amount of dividend per share	33 0	36 0	44 0	39 0

The following is the present staff of the respective Agencies in India, China, and Bourbon:—

CALCUTTA,

Office, No. 2, Mangoe Lane.

Manager	... G. PIETSCH.
Accountant	... C. FOURNEL.
Cashier	... S. BRUSSEL.
Assistant	... E. LE TOURNEUX.
Ditto	... F. JARRIAT.
Ditto	... E. NEECHOLASS.

BOMBAY,

Office, No. 23, Rampart Row.

Manager	... T. R. R. DAVISON.
Accountant	... M. TALLADA.
Cashier	... E. HAHN.

SHANGHAI.

Manager	... E. CORDIER.
Accountant	... PHILIPPÉ.
Cashier	... A. DALOR.
Assistant	... BOUSSENOT.

BOURBON (REUNION).

Manager	... CARRE, SENIOR.
Assistant	... CARRE, JUNIOR.
Cashier and Accountant	... WALLICH.

BENGAL BANK.

So far back as the year 1790, a Bank, under the above designation, was in existence in Calcutta, though the records thereof are not sufficiently perfect to enable the details to be given. The Bank had a limited circulation. The following is a copy of one of the notes in circulation :—

বেঙ্গাল ব্যাঙ্ক

No. $\frac{2}{2749}$. BENGAL BANK,

CALCUTTA,

15th *November* 1791.

এক শত

টাকা সিক্কা

১০০ সিক্কা

I promise to pay Ramcaunt Dutt or Bearer on demand One Hundred Sicca Rupees.

For the Bengal Bank.

One Hundred. BENJAMIN MEE.

Exd.

It cannot be stated when the Bank ceased to exist, but it was long previous to the year 1800. This Bank was in no wise connected with the Bank of Bengal, and ought not to be confounded in any way with that Institution.

BANK OF INDIA.

This Bank was projected in 1828 by Rajkissore Dutt, the man whose forgeries, well planned and carried out, are alluded to at page 102 of this work. Prawnkissen Holdar, once the wealthy proprietor of the splendid mansion on the bank of the Hooghly, at Chinsurah, now used as the College of Mahomed Mohsin, was led to connect himself with Rajkissore's schemes, and, as a consequence, suffered loss of property and transportation. The Bank of India had a note circulation, which was received by the natives.

GENERAL BANK OF INDIA.

A Bank under the title of the General Bank was in existence in Calcutta in 1790, and though not at present in possession of full particulars respecting it, it is probable that it was started, like the Bank of Hindustan, by some mercantile firm of the period. Mr. J. Pollard was the Secretary.

1791, January—It was in contemplation to make the Bank more generally useful, and to change its name from that of the GENERAL BANK to that of the GENERAL BANK OF INDIA. The great scarcity of cash, however, temporarily interfered with the project. May.—The alteration was effected this month, and the first meeting of proprietors was held on the 1st of June 1791.

THE CARNATIC BANK.

This is the name of a Bank which was in existence at the Madras Presidency, in 1791. At present we are without knowledge of the proprietary body, and other particulars.

APPENDICES.

***STATEMENT** showing the Total Amount Outstanding*
Interest in

	LOANS.					
	1824-25, 4 per cent.	1828-29, 4 per cent.	1832-33, 4 per cent.	1835-36, 4 per cent.	1842-43, 4 per cent.	1854-55, 4 per cent.
Amount on which Interest was paid in London up to 31st August 1860	21,000	3,300	10,44,400	18,82,300	59,55,100	35,94,400
Ditto up to 30th Nov. 1860	21,000	3,300	10,68,900	19,39,200	59,33,100	37,41,300
Ditto up to 28th Feby. 1861	21,000	4,300	12,07,400	19,66,000	61,20,000	37,82,600
Ditto up to 31st May 1861	21,000	4,300	12,12,105	18,86,000	65,50,900	37,19,900
Ditto up to 31st Aug. 1861	21,000	4,300	12,21,089	18,61,100	63,31,000	39,32,600
Ditto up to 30th Nov. 1861	21,000	4,300	14,40,240	19,06,400	65,75,000	44;29,900
Ditto up to 28th Feby. 1862	27,000	4,300	15,42,143	19,34,600	65,79,400	48,30,000
Ditto up to 31st May 1862	21,000	4,300	19,17,338	20,11,400	81,04,400	53,43,600
Ditto up to 31st Aug. 1862	21,000	4,300	20,74,300	21,02,800	84,34,500	58,32,800
Ditto up to 30th Nov. 1862	21,000	4,300	20,67,400	21,45,800	86,35,400	60,43,000
Ditto up to 28th Feby. 1863	21,000	4,300	21,65,600	22,68,900	87,74,800	62,45,900

1st.—Enfacement Notice, dated 12th November 1858, took effect from 1st December 1858.

of Government Promissory Notes enfaced for payment of London.

LOANS.

1856-57, 4½ per cent.	1853-54, 3½ per cent.	1854-55, 5 per cent. P. W.	1856-57, 5 per cent.	1859-60, 5½ per cent.	Total Amount.	Increase.	Decrease.
1,000	11,500	21,08,100	3,96,77,900	2,66,47,100	8,09,46,100	......	
1,000	11,500	22,58,600	4,04,69,200	2,56,99,700	8,11,46,800	2,00,700	
1,000	11,500	22,46,700	4,02,72,300	2,55,67,100	8,11,99,900	53,100	
1,000	12,500	24,66,800	4,16,42,600	2,60,31,400	8,35,48,005	23,48,105	
6,000	12,500	25,05,700	4,45,44,600	2,55,32,300	8,59,72,189	24,24,184	
6,000	12,500	26,48,500	4,51,45,500	2,65,04,200	8,86,91,543	27,19,354	
6,000	12,500	27,76,700	4,61,19,500	2,80,65,200	9,18,91,343	31,99,800	
6,000	17,600	30,43,100	4,86,51,400	2,92,77,000	9,83,97,138	65,05,795	
6,000	17,600	30,70,900	4,86,16,600	2,81,25,700	9,83,06,500	......	90,638
6,000	17,600	31,01,100	4,81,93,700	2,69,28,400	9,71,63,700	......	11,42,800
6,500	18,600	31,75,300	4,87,95,100	2,64,93,400	9,79,69,400	8,05,700	

2*nd.*—Income Tax took effect from 1st August 1860.

***STATEMENT** showing the Highest and Lowest Value of Company's Four per Cent Paper, commencing from 1853 to 1862 inclusive.*

1853.

	Highest Premium and Discount.	Lowest Premium and Discount.	Average.	Rate of Interest in Bank of Bengal.
January ...	6 0 d.	1 8 d.	4 8 d.	4 pt.
February ...	1 8 "	0 2 "	0 8 "	"
March ...	0 4 "	0 2 "	0 2-8 "	"
April ...	0 4 "	0 2 "	0 2-3 "	"
May ...	0 2 "	0 2 "	0 2-0 "	"
June ...	par	0 4 "	0 1-9 "	"
July ...	"	0 6 "	0 3-10 "	"
August ...	"	0 4 "	0 2 "	"
September ...	3 12 p.	0 2 "	1 9 p.	"
October ...	4 12 "	3 2 p.	3 9 "	"
November ...	4 8 "	1 8 "	2 14 "	"
December ...	1 8 "	0 8 "	1 2 "	"

1854.

	Highest Premium and Discount.	Lowest Premium and Discount.	Average.	Rate of Interest in Bank of Bengal.
January ...	1 0 p.	0 8 d.	0 7 p.	4 @ 5
February ...	0 8 "	1 0 "	0 10 d.	5 " 6
March ...	par.	2 4 "	1 6 "	6
April ...	"	2 4 "	1 8 "	"
May ...	1 4 d.	0 6 "	0 14 "	5 @ 6
June ...	1 8 "	0 12 "	1 4 "	5 p.
July ...	4 0 "	2 1 "	2 14 "	"
August ...	3 0 "	1 8 "	2 6 "	"
September ...	1 12 "	1 4 "	1 7 "	"
October ...	1 9 "	0 12 "	1 3 "	"
November ...	2 8 "	1 8 "	1 13 "	"
December ...	3 4 "	2 4 "	2 9 "	"

1855.

	Highest Premium and Discount.	Lowest Premium and Discount.	Average.	Rate of Interest in Bank of Bengal.
January ...	6 4	2 8	4 4	8 @ 10
February ...	6 8	4 8	5 4	10 0
March ...	17 0	4 8	11 12	10 @ 11
April ...	13 12	10 0	11 11	10 " 11
May ...	12 12	9 8	11 5	9 " 10
June ...	11 4	7 0	9 15	9 0
July ...	9 12	7 0	8 7	9 0
August ...	14 8	9 8	11 10	9 @ 10
September ...	12 8	11 4	11 12	12 0
October ...	13 8	11 4	12 12	12 0
November ...	14 8	13 4	13 15	12 0
December ...	17 8	14 4	16 2	12 0

STATEMENT showing the Highest and Lowest Value of Company's Four per Cent Paper, commencing from 1853 to 1862 inclusive.—(Continued.)

1856.

	Highest Discount.	Lowest Discount.	Average.	Rate of Interest in Bank of Bengal.
January ...	17 8	14 8	16 8	12 0
February ...	16 8	14 0	15 8	„
March ...	15 8	12 8	14 8	„
April ...	16 4	15 0	15 7	„
May ...	16 4	10 12	13 2	9 @ 12
June ...	13 8	11 8	12 12	8 @ 9
July ...	12 8	11 0	11 11	5 @ 8
August ...	11 8	10 8	10 15	4 @ 5
September ...	13 4	11 12	12 13	4 0
October ...	13 8	13 4	13 5	„
November ...	16 0	13 8	14 12	4 @ 5
December ...	16 12	16 0	16 6	5 @ 6

1857.

	Highest Discount.	Lowest Discount.	Average.	Rate of Interest in Bank of Bengal.
January ...	19 8	16 0	17 6	6 @ 11
February ...	20 12	17 8	19 8	11 @ 13
March ...	17 8	15 8	16 7	9 @ 11
April ...	15 8	13 8	15 1	7 @ 8
May ...	14 8	12 4	13 3	6 @ 7
June ...	20 4	14 0	16 12	7 @ 8
July ...	19 0	16 4	17 8	8 @ 10
August ...	24 0	18 0	21 2	10 0
September ...	31 0	24 8	27 12	10 0
October ...	26 0	25 8	24 10	10 @ 11
November ...	24 8	21 8	22 3	11 0
December ...	25 8	20 8	25 6	11 0

1858.

	Highest Discount.	Lowest Discount.	Average.	Rate of Interest in Bank of Bengal.
January ...	25 8	17 8	22 7	9 @ 10
February ...	19 8	17 8	18 6	9 0
March ...	20 8	17 8	18 12	8 @ 9
April ...	19 0	17 12	18 10	8 0
May ...	20 0	17 8	18 12	8 0
June ...	20 8	18 0	19 10	8 0
July ...	19 0	16 4	18 1	7 @ 8
August ...	16 4	13 8	15 0	6 @ 7
September ...	16 0	13 8	15 1	6 0
October ...	14 0	12 8	12 12	6 0
November ...	13 0	11 4	12 4	6 0
December ...	15 8	12 8	13 5	6 @ 7

***STATEMENT** showing the Highest and Lowest Value of Company's Four per Cent Paper, commencing from* 1853 *to* 1862 *inclusive.—(Continued.)*

1859.

	Highest Discount.		Lowest Discount.		Average.		Rate of Interest in Bank of Bengal.		
January ...	20	4	14	4	15	0	7	@	8
February ...	29	0	20	4	23	2	8		0
March ...	24	4	20	4	22	5	8		0
April ...	25	8	20	0	22	8	8		0
May ...	28	8	25	8	26	14	8		0
June ...	27	0	24	8	25	11	7	@	8
July ...	25	0	22	4	23	4	6	@	7
August ...	24	0	22	8	23	2	6		0
September ...	25	0	23	8	24	7	6		0
October ...	24	8	24	0	24	1	6		0
November ...	24	0	23	0	23	10	6		0
December ...	23	8	21	8	22	12	6		0

1860.

January ...	23	0	22	0	22	4	6	@	8
February ...	23	0	17	12	20	0	8	@	9
March ...	18	8	17	4	18	0	10		0
April ...	17	4	15	8	16	3	7	@	10
May ...	17	8	16	0	16	10	6	@	7
June ...	17	8	16	0	16	7	5	@	6
July ...	17	4	16	8	16	14	5		0
August ...	18	0	17	0	17	4	5		0
September ...	19	8	17	8	18	1	5		0
October ...	19	0	17	12	18	10	5		0
November ...	20	0	18	0	18	11	5		0
December ...	20	12	19	8	19	15	5		0

1861.

January ...	19	12	19	0	19	7	5	@	6
February ...	20	0	19	8	19	12	6		0
March ...	20	4	19	8	19	15	6		0
April ...	21	8	20	0	20	15	6	@	7
May ...	20	8	19	4	19	8	7		0
June ...	20	4	19	4	19	14	7		0
July ...	20	12	19	0	19	14	7		0
August ...	19	0	18	0	18	9	6		0
September ...	18	8	16	4	17	12	6		0
October ...	16	4	15	4	15	9	4½	@	6
November ...	16	8	15	0	15	14	4½		0
December ...	15	4	12	4	13	14	4½		0

STATEMENT showing the Highest and Lowest Value of Company's Four per Cent Paper, commencing from 1853 *to* 1862 *inclusive.—(Continued.)*

1862.

	Highest Discount.		Lowest Discount.		Average.		Rate of Interest in Bank of Bengal.	
January ...	16	0	11	4	13	15	4½	0
February ...	12	12	10	4	11	11	5 @	7
March ..	12	4	11	0	11	12	5 @	7
April ...	11	0	6	8	8	10	7	0
May ...	8	4	6	0	6	13	6 @	7
June ...	7	0	6	4	6	8	6	0
July ...	7	4	6	8	6	13	6	0
August ...	6	12	4	12	6	3	5	0
September ...	5	12	4	12	5	5	5 @	6
October ...	6	4	5	12	6	0	6	0
November ...	5	12	4	8	5	3	6	0
December ...	5	12	4	8	5	0	6	0

3½ Loan opened 28th October 1853, closed 30th August 1856.

4 Sicca ditto 7th June 1831, closed 16th September 1835.

4 Of 1835-36 ditto 16th September 1835, closed 15th May 1841.

4 Of 1842-43 ditto 4th January 1843, closed 16th September 1853.

4½ Loan opened 30th August 1856, closed 16th January 1857.

5 Public Works Loan opened 12th March 1855, closed 19th October 1855, guaranteed until 31st March 1870.

4 Of 1842-43 from the 23rd April 1853, was a conversion of Sicca 5 per Cent, closed 13th September 1853.

4 Of 1854-55 opened 28th October 1853, by transfer of Sicca 5 per Cent into this Loan.

5 Of 1856-57 opened 16th January 1857, closed 30th April 1859, guaranteed until 16th January 1872.

5½ Opened 21st February 1859 by transfer of 5 per cent, closed 14th February 1860, guaranteed until 1st May 1879.

Government Loans up to August 1860.

4 Per Cent Sicca and Company's	30,17,31,781
3½ Company's	8,68,200
Public Works Loan, 5 per Cent	2,36,13,700
4½	37,30,300
5 1856-57	15,73,58,325
5½	10,65,01,100
Stock Receipts	2,61,25,375
	61,99,28,781

Act No. VII. of 1860.

AN ACT TO ENABLE JOINT STOCK BANKING COMPANIES TO BE FORMED ON THE PRINCIPLE OF LIMITED LIABILITY.

Preamble.

WHEREAS it is expedient to enable Joint Stock Banking Companies to be formed on the principle of Limited Liability: It is enacted as follows:—

Laws repealed.

I. So much of Section I. of Act XIX. of 1857 *(for the incorporation and regulation of Joint Stock Companies and other Associations, either with or without Limited Liability of the Members thereof)* as provides that nothing in that Act shall authorise any persons to form themselves into a Joint Stock Company or Association with Limited Liability for the purpose of Banking; and so much of Section XCIX. of the said Act as provides that no Company established for the purpose of Banking shall be registered under that Act as a Limited Company, are hereby repealed, subject to the following proviso, that no Banking Company, claiming to issue notes in India, shall be entitled to Limited Liability in respect of such issue, but shall continue subject to unlimited Liability in respect thereof, and that, if necessary, the assets shall be marshalled for the benefit of the general creditors, and the shareholders shall be liable for the whole amount of the issue in addition to the sum for which they would be liable as shareholders of a Limited Company.

Existing Company before obtaining registration under this Act, to give notice to Customers.

II. Every existing Banking Company which shall register itself as a Limited Banking Company, shall at least thirty days previously to obtaining a certificate of Registration with Limited Liability, give notice that it is intended so to register the same to every person and partnership firm who shall have a Banking Account with the Company, and such notice shall be given either by delivering the same to such person or firm, or leaving the same or putting the same into the post in a registered letter addressed to him or them at such address as shall have been last communicated or otherwise become known as his or their address to or by the Company; and in case the Company shall omit to give any such notice as is hereinbefore required to be given, then as between the Company and the person or persons only who are for the time being interested in the account in respect of which such notice ought to have been given, and so far as respects such account and all variations thereof down to the time at which such notice shall be given, but not further or otherwise, the certificate of registration with Limited Liability shall have no operation.

Limited Banking Company to furnish a statement.

III. Every Limited Joint Stock Banking Company shall, before it commences business, or if a Banking Company at the time carrying on business with unlimited Liability, before it avails itself of the provisions of this Act, and also on the 1st day of February and 1st day of August in every year during which it carries on business, make a statement in the form contained in the Schedule hereto annexed, or as near thereto as circumstances will admit; such statement shall be in addition to the balance sheet required by the said Act to be made out and filed with the Registrar of Joint Stock Companies; a copy of such statement shall be put up in a conspicuous place in the registered office of the company, and in every Branch Office or place where the Banking business of the Company is carried on; and if default is made in due compliance with the provisions of this section, each Director shall be liable to a penalty not exceeding fifty rupees for every day during which such default continues, and such penalties shall be recovered in a summary manner.

Trust property.

IV. All such estate or interest in moveable and immoveable property, and all such deeds, bonds, obligations, and rights, as may belong to, or be vested in, any person or persons in trust for any Banking Company at the date of its registration under this Act, or in trust for any other Company at the date of its registration under the said Act XIX. of 1857, shall immediately on registration vest in such Banking or other Company, but no merger shall take place of any estates by reason of their uniting in the Company under this section, without the express consent of the Company, certified by some instrument under their common seal.

Existing Banking Companies may register under this Act.

V. Any Banking Company consisting of seven or more persons, having a capital of fixed amount and divided into shares also of fixed amount, legally carrying on the business of Banking previously to the passing of this Act, may at any time hereafter, with the assent of a majority of such of its shareholders as may have been present in person, or in cases where proxies are allowed by the regulations of the Company by proxy at some general meeting summoned for the purpose, register itself as a Company under this Act, and when so registered, all such provisions contained in any Letters Patent or Deed of Settlement constituting or regulating the Company as are inconsistent with the said Act XIX. of 1857, or with this Act, shall no longer apply to the Company so registered, but such Registration shall not take away or affect any powers previously enjoyed by such Company of Banking, issuing notes payable on demand, or of doing any other thing.

Registration under this Act not to affect obligations incurred previously to registration.

VI. The registration under this Act of any Banking Company existing at the time of the passing of this Act, and hereby authorised to be registered, shall not affect or prejudice the liability of such Company to have enforced against it or its right to enforce any debt or obligation incurred, or any contract entered into, by, to, with, or on account of such Company, previously to such Registration, and all such debts, obligations, and contracts shall be binding on the Company when so registered, and the other parties thereto, to the same extent as if such registration had not taken place.

Saving of liabilities of persons holding shares before registration under Act.

VII. Every person who at or previously to the date of the registration under this Act of any Banking Company hereby authorised to be registered, may have held shares in such Company, shall, in the event of the same being wound up by the Court or voluntarily, be liable to contribute to the assets of the Company the same amount that he would, if this Act had not been passed, have been liable to pay to the Company, for, or on account of any debt of the Company in pursuance of any action, suit, judgment, or other legal proceeding that might, if this Act had not been passed, have been instituted or enforced against himself or the Company.

Continuation of existing actions and suits.

VIII. All such actions, suits, and other legal proceedings as may at the time of the registration under this Act of any Company hereby authorised to be registered have been commenced by or against such Company or the Public Officer thereof, may be continued in the same manner as if such registration had not taken place; nevertheless execution shall not issue against the effects of any individual shareholder in, or member of, such Company, upon any judgment, decree, or order obtained against such Company in any action, suit, or proceeding so commenced as aforesaid; but in the event of the property and effects of the Company being insufficient to satisfy such judgment, decree, or order, an order may be obtained for winding up the Company in manner directed by the said Act XIX. of 1857.

Winding-up.

IX. All Companies registered under this Act shall be wound up in the manner directed by the said Act XIX. of 1857.

Act not to apply to Banks of Bengal, Madras, or Bombay.

X. Nothing in this Act shall affect Act VI. of 1839 *(relating to the Bank of Bengal)*, Act III. of 1840 *(for the incorporation of a Bank at Bombay)*, or Act IX. of 1843 *(for the incorporation of a Bank of Madras)*, or shall be deemed to apply to the several Banks of Bengal, Madras, and Bombay incorporated by the said Acts respectively.

Construction of Act.

XI. This Act shall be deemed to be incorporated with and to form part of the said Act XIX. of 1857.

SCHEDULE.

Form of Statement to be published by a Limited Joint Stock Banking Company.

The Liability of the shareholders is limited.

The capital of the Company is divided into shares of rupees each.

The number of shares issued is

Calls to the amount of per share have been made, under which the sum of Rupees has been received.

The liabilities of the Company on the first day of January (or July) were—

	Rs. As. P.
Notes issued	
Deposits not bearing Interest	
Deposits bearing Interest	
Seven Day and other Bills	
Total ...	

The assets of the Company on that day were—

	Rs. As. P.
Government Securities..	
Bills of Exchange..	
Loans on Mortgage	
Other Loans	
Bank Premises	
Other Securities, exclusive of unpaid Calls on Shares	
Total ...	

Dated the first day of or one thousand eight hundred and

Act No. XIX. of 1861.

AN ACT TO PROVIDE FOR A GOVERNMENT PAPER CURRENCY.

Preamble.

WHEREAS it is expedient to provide for the issue by the Government of India of Promissory Notes payable to bearer on demand, and to regulate the mode of issuing and securing payment of the same; and whereas due notice has been given by the Governor-General of India in Council to the Banks of Bengal, Bombay, and Madras respectively, as required by Acts VI. of 1839, III. of 1840, and IX. of 1843, that the said Banks are to be modified by the power of the said Banks to issue Promissory Notes payable on demand ceasing from and after the day hereinafter provided; It is enacted as follows :—

Laws repealed.

I. Section XXXI. of the said Act VI. of 1839, Section XXXI. of the said Act III. of 1840, and Section XXXIII. of the said Act IX. of 1843, so far as the said Sections authorise the Banks of Bengal, Bombay, and Madras respectively to issue Promissory Notes payable on demand, are repealed from and after the first day of March 1862.

No Body Corporate or person to issue Notes, &c., payable to bearer on demand.

II. After the passing of this Act, no Body Corporate, person or persons whatsoever in British India, (except the Banks of Bengal, Madras, and Bombay, up to the said 1st day of March 1862 and except as hereinafter provided,) shall draw, accept, make, or issue any Bill of Exchange or Promissory Note, or engagement for the payment of money payable to bearer on demand, or borrow, owe, or take up any sum or sums of money on the Bills or Notes payable to bearer on demand of any such Body Corporate, or of any such person or persons.

Exception in favor of Cheques.

Provided that Cheques or Drafts payable to bearer on demand or otherwise may be drawn on Bankers, Shroffs, or Agents by the customers or constituents of such Bankers, Shroffs, or Agents, in respect of deposits of money in the hands of such Bankers, Shroffs, or Agents, and held by them at the credit and disposal of the persons drawing such Cheques or Drafts.

Department of Issue to be established.

III. There shall be established by the Governor-General of India in Council a department of the Public Service, to be called the Department of Issue, either in connection with the Mints or otherwise, and from and after the passing of this Act there may be issued from the said Department, as hereinafter provided, Promissory Notes of the Government of India payable to bearer on demand, for such sums, not being less than ten Rupees, as the Governor-General of India in Council shall from time to time direct.

Head Commissioner and Commissioners to be appointed.

IV. The Governor-General in Council, after the passing of this Act, shall appoint some person, who may be the Master of the Mint at Calcutta, to be called the Head Commissioner of the Department of Issue, and two other persons, who may be the Master of the Mint at Madras, and the Master of the Mint at Bombay, who shall be called respectively the Commissioners of the Department of Issue at Madras and Bombay, and it shall be lawful for the Governor-General of India in Council, from time to time, by Rules to be published in the Gazettes of Calcutta, Madras, and Bombay, to make such arrangements through any Officers of Government, or with any persons, Banks, or Bodies Corporate, either at Calcutta, Madras, and Bombay, or elsewhere, as may be required to regulate and facilitate the issue and payment, under the provisions of this Act, of Promissory Notes of the Government of India, of such denominations as shall be prescribed under the last foregoing Section, not being for any less sum than ten Rupees.

V. It shall be lawful for the Governor-General of India in Council from time to time, by order to be published in the Gazettes of Calcutta, Madras, and Bombay, to establish in British India, Districts, to be called "Circles of Issue," three of which Circles shall include the Towns of Calcutta, Madras, and Bombay, respectively, and in each Circle to appoint some one city or town to be the place of Issue of Notes, as hereinafter provided. It shall be lawful for the Governor-General of India in Council, by an order to be published as aforesaid, from time to time, to alter or extend the limits of the said Circles or any of them. Promissory Notes of the Government of India may be issued in the several Circles of Issue as hereinafter provided.

Power to Governor-General in Council to establish Circles of Issue.

VI. For each Circle of Issue other than those which include the Towns of Calcutta, Madras and Bombay, there shall be appointed by the Governor-General in Council, an Officer of the Government or other person to be called the Deputy Commissioner of Issue. In any Circle of Issue there may be also established an Agency or Agencies of Issue in connection with a Bank or otherwise.

Deputy Commissioners to be appointed.

VII. For the purposes of this Act, the Commissioners at Madras and Bombay shall be subordinate to the Head Commissioner; the Deputy Commissioners and Agents in the Presidency of Fort William in Bengal shall be subordinate to the Head Commissioner; and the Deputy Commissioners and Agents in the Presidencies of Fort Saint George and Bombay shall be subordinate to the Commissioners of Madras and Bombay respectively.

Commissioners to be subordinate to Head Commissioner, Deputy Commissioners to Commissioner.

VIII. The Head Commissioner of Issue for the time being shall provide, on paper to be specially manufactured for the purpose, Promissory Notes of the Government of India payable to bearer on demand, of the denominations which shall be from time to time prescribed under Section III. of this Act; and shall supply or cause to be supplied to the Commissioners at Madras and Bombay, and to the several Deputy Commissioners and Agents, such Notes as they shall require for the purposes of this Act, and all Notes shall bear upon them the name of the city or town from which they are

Notes to be prepared by Head Commissioner and distributed by him.

severally issued, and shall be payable only at the Office or Offices or Agencies of Issue of such city or town and at the Presidency Town of the Presidency within which such city or town is situated.

Where payable.

IX. The Head Commissioner, the Commissioners, and the Deputy Commissioners and Agents shall, in their respective "Circles of Issue," on the demand of any person, issue from such Office or Offices or Agencies of Issue as shall be established in the appointed city or town in their respective Circles, Promissory Notes of such denominations as shall be prescribed under Section III., not being for any less sum than ten Rupees, on the terms following:—

When such Notes may be issued.

First.—In exchange for the amount thereof in current silver coin of the Government of India;

Or, *secondly.*—In exchange for the amount thereof in standard silver bullion or foreign silver coin computed according to such standard, at the rate of 979 Rupees per 1,000 tolahs of standard silver fit for coinage.

Provided that the said Head Commissioner, Commissioners, Deputy Commissioners, and Agents shall, in all cases, be entitled to require such silver bullion and foreign coin to be melted and assayed at the expense of the person tendering the same, and provided also that in all places where there is no Mint of the Government of India, it shall be optional for any such Head Commissioner, Commissioner, Deputy Commissioner, and Agents, to issue Notes in exchange for silver or foreign coin under this Section;

Proviso.

Or, *thirdly.*—In exchange for other Notes of the Government of India payable to bearer on demand of other amounts issued within the same Circle.

Provided also, that it shall be lawful for the Governor-General in Council from time to time to direct, by order to be published in the Gazettes of Calcutta, Madras, and Bombay, that Notes to an extent to be specified in the order, not exceeding one-fourth of the total amount of issues represented by coin and bullion as herein provided shall be issued at such Offices or Agencies of Issue as may be named in the order, in exchange for gold coin of full weight of the Government of India, or for foreign gold coin or gold bullion computed at such rates and according to such rules and conditions as shall be fixed by such order, and which rates, rules, and conditions shall not be altered without six months' previous notice. Whenever such order shall be issued, the Head Commissioner, Commissioners, Deputy Commissioners, and Agents, at the Offices or Agencies specified in the order, shall be bound to issue Notes on demand in conformity with such order.

The whole amount of bullion and coin received for Notes to be kept as a reserve to pay such Notes excepting an amount not exceeding 4 crores of Rupees to be fixed as the minimum limit of circulation.

X. The whole amount of the bullion and coin so received for Notes shall be retained and secured as a reserve to pay such Notes, with the exception of such an amount, not exceeding four crores of Rupees, as the Governor-General in Council, with the consent of the Secretary of State for India, shall from time to time fix. The amount so fixed shall be published in the Gazettes of Calcutta, Madras, and Bombay, and shall be invested in Government Securities, and the said coin, bullion, and securities shall be appropriated and set apart to provide for the satisfaction and discharge of the said Notes; and the said Notes shall be deemed to have been issued on the security of the coin, bullion, and securities so appropriated and set apart, as well as on the general credit of the Government. Provided that any gold coin or bullion which may be received under this Act, may be sold or exchanged for silver coin or bullion to be so appropriated and set apart, instead of the gold coin or bullion.

In what names the Government Securities to stand.

XI. The Government Securities purchased under this Act in the Presidency of Fort William in Bengal shall stand in the name of the Head Commissioner and the Master of the Mint at Calcutta; the Government Securities purchased under this Act in the Presidency of Fort Saint George shall stand in the name of the Commissioner at Madras and the Master of the Mint at Madras; and the Government Securities purchased under this Act in the Presidency of Bombay shall stand in the name of the Commissioner at Bombay and the Master of the Mint at Bombay. Provided that if the Head Commissioner or Commissioner in any case be the Master of the Mint, the Governor-General in Council shall appoint another Trustee or Trustees in addition to the Master of the Mint.

XII. The Head Commissioner from time to time shall frame Rules to be approved by the Governor-General of India in Council, for keeping the accounts of the said Department of Issue, and for the auditing of such accounts, and for otherwise regulating the business of the Department; provided that such Rules shall be in no wise inconsistent with the provisions of this Act.

Rules to be framed for keeping and auditing the Accounts.

XIII. An abstract of the accounts of the Department, showing the whole amount of Notes in circulation, the amount of coin and bullion reserved, distinguishing gold from silver, and the amount of the Government Securities held by the said Department, shall be made up monthly in Calcutta, and published as soon as may be in the Gazettes of Calcutta, Madras, and Bombay.

Abstract of Accounts to be published.

XIV. It shall be lawful for the Head Commissioner in respect of the Presidency of Fort William in Bengal, and for the Commissioners at Madras and Bombay in respect of the Presidencies of Madras and Bombay respectively, at any time when they shall be ordered so to do by the Governor-General of India in Council, to sell and dispose of any portion of the above-mentioned limited amount of Government Securities standing in their names respectively, and in the names of the Masters of the Mint or Trustees as aforesaid; and for the purpose of effecting such sales, the said Masters of the Mint or Trustees respectively shall, on a request in writing from the said Head Commissioner or Commissioners in their respective Presidencies, at all times sign and endorse such Government Securities as shall stand in their names respectively; and it shall be lawful for the said Head Commissioner or Commissioners, if directed by the Governor-General of India in Council, to purchase Government Securities to replace their sales.

Securities to be disposed of when necessary.

XV. The interest accruing due on the Government Securities purchased and held under this Act shall be entered in a separate account, to be annually rendered by the Head Commissioner to the Governor-General of India in Council; and the amount of such interest shall, from time to time, as it becomes due, be paid by the Accountants General in the several Presidencies of India, into the revenues of the Government of India, under the head of "Profits

Interest of Securities to be paid to the credit of Government.

D 2

of Note circulation," and an account showing the amount of profits of the Note circulation and of the charges and expenses incidental thereto, shall be made up and published annually in the Gazettes of Calcutta, Madras, and Bombay.

Notes where legal tender.

XVI. Within any of the "Circles of Issue," as hereinbefore provided, a tender of a Note or Notes issued under this Act from any Office or Agency of Issue of such "Circle of Issue," shall be a legal tender to the amount expressed in such Note or Notes, and shall be taken to be valid as a tender to such amount in payment of any revenue or other claim to the amount of ten Rupees and upwards due to the Government of India, and in payment of any sum of ten Rupees and upwards due by the Government of India, or by any Body Corporate, or by any person or persons in British India, on all occasions whatsoever on which any tender of money can be legally made. Provided that no such Note or Notes shall be deemed to be a legal tender of payment by the Government of India at any Office or at the Issue Department of any Agency of Issue.

Name of Head Commissioner, &c., may be impressed with machinery.

XVII. The name of the Head Commissioner, of either of the Commissioners, of any Deputy Commissioner or of any other person authorised by the said Head Commissioner, or by either of the said Commissioners, to sign Notes issued under this Act, may be impressed or affixed by machinery provided for that purpose by the Government of India, and such printed names shall be taken to be good and valid signatures to all intents and purposes, as if such Notes had been subscribed in the proper hand-writing of any one of the persons aforesaid whose signatures the said printing purports to represent.

Notes may be described as Promissory Notes.

XVIII. All Notes issued under this Act shall be deemed and taken to be Promissory Notes of the Government of India, and may and shall be described as Promissory Notes of the Government of India in all indictments, aud in criminal and civil proceedings, any law or usage to the contrary notwithstanding.

Penalty for issuing such Notes contrary to provisions of this Act.

XIX. If any Body Corporate or person, after the passing of this Act, shall, contrary to the provisions of this Act, draw, accept, make, or issue any Bill of Exchange, Promissory Note, or engagement for the payment of money payable to bearer on demand, or borrow owe, or take up any sum or sums of money on the Bills or Note or engagements for the payment of money payable to bearer on demand of any such Body Corporate or person, such Body Corporate or person shall be liable to a penalty to the amount of every such Bill of Exchange, Promissory Note, or engagement for the payment of money, to be recovered on the prosecution of the Head Commissioner, Commissioner, or Deputy Commissioner, as the case may be, of the "Circle of Issue," in which such Bill of Exchange, Promissory Note, or engagement for the payment for money is issued before any Police Magistrate or Magistrate within such "Circle of Issue," and in case of conviction, and default of payment of such penalty, the Police Magistrate or Magistrate who shall try the case shall issue his warrant to levy the amount thereof, together with the reasonable costs of the prosecution, by distress and sale of goods and chattels of the Body Corporate or person so convicted.

Definition of "British India."

XX. The words "British India" in this Act shall denote the Territories that are or may be vested in Her Majesty by the Statute 21 and 22 Vic., c. 106, entitled "An Act for the better Government of India," except the Settlement of Prince of Wales' Island, Singapore, and Malacca.

Act No. XXIV. of 1861.

AN ACT TO ENABLE THE BANKS OF BENGAL, MADRAS, AND BOMBAY TO ENTER INTO ARRANGEMENTS WITH THE GOVERNMENT FOR MANAGING THE ISSUE, PAYMENT, AND EXCHANGE OF GOVERNMENT CURRENCY NOTES AND CERTAIN BUSINESS HITHERTO TRANSACTED BY THE GOVERNMENT TREASURIES.

Preamble.

WHEREAS it is expedient to authorise the Banks of Bengal, Madras, and Bombay to enter into the agreements hereinafter mentioned; It is enacted as follows:—

Banks may enter into certain arrangements with Government.

I. It shall be lawful for any of the said Banks, by agreements under their corporate seal, to enter into agreements or arrangements with the Secretary of State for India in Council through the Governor-General of India in Council, the Governor of Madras in Council, and the Governor of Bombay in Council respectively, for superintending, managing, and becoming agents, for the issue, payment, and exchange of Promissory Notes of the Government of India payable on demand under Act XIX. of 1861 *(to provide for a Government Paper Currency)* or any Act which may hereafter be passed in relation to the Paper Currency of the Government of India; for the carrying on the business of an Agency of issue under the said Act XIX. of 1861 in any circle of issue in which any of the said Banks shall have established a Branch Bank under Act VI. of 1839 *(relating to the Bank of Bengal)* or any other Act; and for transacting any part of the business of, or hitherto generally transacted by or at the General Treasuries of the Governments at the several Presidencies of Fort William, Madras, and Bombay respectively.

Banks may transact the business incident to such arrangements.

II. It shall be lawful for the said Banks of Bengal, Madras, and Bombay, in addition to the modes of business in which they may now by law be respectively engaged, to transact, in accordance with the provisions of the said agreements or arrangements entered into under Section I. of this Act, all or any of the business appertaining to the superintendence, management, or agency for the issuing, payment, or exchange in the first Section mentioned, and the business of an Agency of issue under the said Act XIX. of 1861 in any such circle of issue as aforesaid, or all or any of the business of, or hitherto generally transacted by, the General Treasuries in that Section mentioned.

Act No. XIII. of 1862.

AN ACT TO PROVIDE FOR A NEW SILVER AND A NEW COPPER COINAGE.

Preamble.

WHEREAS it is expedient to provide for a new Silver and a new Copper Coinage; It is enacted as follows:—

Repeal of Acts.

I. From the 1st day of November 1862 so much of the 1st and 2nd Sections of Act XVII. of 1835 *(relating to Gold and Silver Coinage)* as provides that only the Silver Coins therein mentioned shall be coined at the Mints within the territories of the East India Company, and that such Coins shall bear on the reverse the words "The East India Company;" also Act XXXI. of 1837 *(relating to Coinage)*; Act XXI. of 1838 *(relating to the Silver Coin)*; Act XXI. of 1835; Act XXII. of 1844, and Act XI. of 1854 *(relating to the Copper Coin)*, shall be repealed, except as to any act already done or Coin already coined or issued under the same.

Description of Coins.

II. From the 1st day of November 1862, except as provided by Act VI. of 1847 *(for establishing a Copper Currency in the Settlements of Penang, Singapore, and Malacca)* in respect of Cents, Half Cents, and Quarter Cents, no Silver or Copper Coins, except those mentioned below, shall be coined at the Mints in British India:—

Silver Coin.

A Rupee, to be called the Government Rupee.

A Half Rupee.

A Quarter Rupee or Four-Anna Piece.

An Eighth of a Rupee or Two-Anna Piece.

Copper Coin.

A Double Pice or Half Anna.

A Pice or Quarter Anna.

A Half Pice or one-eighth of an Anna.

A Pie, being one-third of a Pice, or one-twelfth of an Anna.

Weight and Standard of Silver Coin.

III. The Rupee so coined shall be of the same weight and standard as those provided for the Company's Rupees by the said Act XVII. of 1835, that is to say, the weight shall be 180 grains Troy, and the standard as follows:—$\frac{11}{12}$th or 165 grains of pure Silver; $\frac{1}{12}$th or 15 grains of alloy. The other Silver Coins shall be of proportionate weight and of the same standard.

Weight of Copper Coins.

IV. The Copper Coins so coined shall be of the weight prescribed for Coins of the same denominations respectively by Acts XXI. of 1835 and XI. of 1854, that is to say:

The Double Pice shall weigh 200 grains Troy.

The Pice ...	 100	„
The Half Pice	 50	„
The Pie ...	... ... 33⅓	„

Inscriptions on Coins.

V. Until the Governor-General in Council shall otherwise order under the power hereinafter reserved, the Silver and Copper Coins so coined shall bear on the obverse the likeness and the name of Her Majesty Queen Victoria, and the inscription "Victoria Queen," and on the reverse the designation of the Coins in English filled by the word "India" with such date and embellishments on each Coin as the Governor-General in Council shall from time to time direct.

Governor-General in Council may order other devices, &c.

VI. It shall be lawful for the Governor-General in Council, from time to time, to direct the coining and issuing of all Coins authorised by this Act, and to prescribe in lieu of the likeness and inscription as heretofore prescribed, such other devices and inscriptions and embelishments for all or any of the Coins hereby authorised as, by an order in Council to be published in the Official *Gazette*, he may direct.

VII. The said Rupee and Half Rupee shall be a legal tender in payment or on account of all engagements whatever, provided the Coin shall not have lost more than two per cent in weight, and provided it shall not have been clipped or filed, or have been defaced or diminished otherwise than by use.

Rupee and Half-Rupee to be legal tender.

VIII. The Quarter Rupee and Eighth of a Rupee shall be legal tender only for the fractions of a Rupee, subject to the same provisions as in the last preceding Section mentioned.

Quarter and Eighth Rupee how to be legal tender.

IX. The Double Pice shall be a legal tender for a thirty-second part of a Rupee or for half an Anna.

Copper Coin how to be legal tender.

The Pice for a sixty-fourth part of a Rupee, or for one-fourth of an Anna.

The Half Pice for a hundred-and-twenty-eighth part of a Rupee, or for one-eighth of an Anna; and the Pie, one-third of a Pice, for a hundred-and-ninety-second part of a Rupee, or the twelfth of an Anna.

Provided that none of the said Copper Coins shall be legal tender, except for the fractions of a Rupee, and except in the Settlement of Prince of Wales' Island, Singapore, and Malacca for the fractions of a Dollar at the rate fixed by Act XVII. of 1855, *viz.*:—The Pice for a hundred-and-fortieth part of a Dollar; the Double Pice for a seventieth part of a Dollar; the Pie for a four-hundred-and twentieth part of a Dollar; and the Half Pice for a two-hundred-and-eightieth part of a Dollar.

X. All Silver Coin of the weight and standard specified in the said Acts XVII. of 1835, and XXI. of 1838, issued since the passing of those Acts respectively and before the first day of November 1862 and declared by those Acts respectively to be a legal tender, and all Copper Coins of the weight specified in the said Acts XXI. of 1835, XXII. of 1844, and XVII. of 1855 issued since the passing of those Acts respectively and before the first day of November 1862, and declared by those Acts respectively to be a legal tender, shall continue to be a legal tender for the amounts thereof respectively, subject to the same conditions and provisions as under those Acts respectively anything in this Act contained notwithstanding.

Coin coined under former Acts still to be legal tender.

XI. All Acts and Laws in force in British India at the time of the passing of this Act respecting the Queen's Coin, or the Silver or Copper Coin current in British India, and not repugnant to the provisions of this Act, shall be and continue in full force and effect, and shall be applied to the Silver and Copper Coin to be coined in pursuance of this Act.

Existing Acts to continue in force.

XII. The words "British India" in this Act denote the territories which are or may become vested in Her Majesty by the Statute 21 and 22 Vic., c. 106, entitled "An Act for the better Government of India."

Definition of "British India."

INDEX.

A

B

E 2

C

D

E

F

O

P

R

S